# Google™ Apps
## FOR
# DUMMIES®

## by Ryan Teeter and Karl Barksdale

WILEY

Wiley Publishing, Inc.

**Google™ Apps For Dummies®**

Published by
**Wiley Publishing, Inc.**
111 River Street
Hoboken, NJ 07030-5774

www.wiley.com

WILEY

# About the Authors

**Ryan Teeter** is an accomplished writer and technology trainer. He has worked closely with business teachers throughout the country and consulted with the National Business Education Association, businesses, and school districts on Google Apps implementation. Ryan spent time working at Google in Mountain View, California, as an External Training Specialist, developing curriculum used for training Fortune 500 companies.

When he's not conducting training workshops or writing, Ryan's pursuing his passion for teaching as a doctoral student at Rutgers University, where he's completing a PhD in accounting information systems. (www.ryanteeter.com, www.technonerd.info)

**Karl Barksdale** was a former Development Manager for the Training and Certification team at WordPerfect Corporation and a Marketing Manager in the Consumer Products division. He was also the External Training Manager for Google's Online Sales and Operations division. He's best known for authoring and co-authoring 59 business and computer education textbooks. Albeit, the job he enjoys most is teaching at the Utah County Academy of Sciences, an early college high school on the Utah Valley University campus. (www.karlbarksdale.com)

# Dedication

**Ryan Teeter**

This book is dedicated to my parents and my friends, for whom this book was originally intended.

**Karl Barksdale**

For Hilary, Cory, and Mari, who make it all worthwhile.

# Authors' Acknowledgments

This book wouldn't have happened without the inspiration and guidance of Esther Wojcicki of Palo Alto High School and Jeremy Milo, the Google Apps Product Marketing Manager at Google. Nor could we have accomplished so much without the External Training Team at Google, of which we were so fortunate to be a part. Here's to Lance Cotton, Erik Gottlieb, Lauren Frandsen, Kristina Cutura, Charbel Semaan, Tyrona Heath, Mary Hekl, Brian Schreier, and Jared Smith. You guys rock!

We'd also like to give special recognition to our outstanding team at Wiley Publishing, including Greg Croy, executive editor; Jean Nelson, project editor; Laura K. Miller, copy editor; James Kelly, technical editor; and the other incredibly talented and amazing people who made working on this project a real treat.

Along those lines, we'd also like to acknowledge our friends and colleagues at the Rutgers Business School and the Utah County Academy of Science for their support.

Finally, we acknowledge you, the reader, for trusting us to help you make the most out of this amazing and incredibly useful technology.

## Publisher's Acknowledgments

We're proud of this book; please send us your comments through our online registration form located at www.dummies.com/register/.

Some of the people who helped bring this book to market include the following:

*Acquisitions and Editorial*

**Project Editor:** Jean Nelson

**Executive Editor:** Greg Croy

**Copy Editor:** Laura K. Miller

**Technical Editor:** James Kelly

**Editorial Manager:** Kevin Kirschner

**Editorial Assistant:** Amanda Foxworth

**Sr. Editorial Assistant:** Cherie Case

**Cartoons:** Rich Tennant
(www.the5thwave.com)

*Composition Services*

**Project Coordinator:** Katherine Key

**Layout and Graphics:** Claudia Bell, Carl Byers, Reuben W. Davis, Melissa K. Jester, Ronald Terry, Christine Williams

**Proofreaders:** Laura Bowman, John Greenough, Dwight Ramsey

**Indexer:** Slivoskey Indexing Services

**Publishing and Editorial for Technology Dummies**

**Richard Swadley,** Vice President and Executive Group Publisher

**Andy Cummings,** Vice President and Publisher

**Mary Bednarek,** Executive Acquisitions Director

**Mary C. Corder,** Editorial Director

**Publishing for Consumer Dummies**

**Diane Graves Steele,** Vice President and Publisher

**Joyce Pepple,** Acquisitions Director

**Composition Services**

**Gerry Fahey,** Vice President of Production Services

**Debbie Stailey,** Director of Composition Services

# Contents at a Glance

# Table of Contents

# Introduction

*W*hen most people hear *Google,* they think of the powerful search tool with its squeaky-clean search box, colorful logo, and reliable search results. A few may know about its advertising tools, AdWords and AdSense, which generate Google's astounding profits quarter after quarter. Google recently became even more indispensable to teams and useful to organizations when it released *Google Apps,* a suite of online applications that enables you to create, share, and publish documents, spreadsheets, presentations, and more from any computer with an Internet connection.

If you think it may be time for your team, business, school, or organization to move out of costly, time-consuming information technology boondoggles and start using these powerful online Google applications, then *Google Apps For Dummies* is for you. If you're on the fence, turn to Chapter 1, where we discuss all the advantages and disadvantages of complementing your work or academic life with Google Apps. We hope that Google Apps has piqued your interest, even if it's only because you can save a lot of money and reduce your computing hassles.

If you want to use Google Apps for just yourself (not as part of a business or school), you can. Go to www.google.com and click the iGoogle link in the upper-right corner of the screen. You are given a customizable Start Page that will work like a springboard to the Internet and your Google Apps. From this page, you can set up your gadgets and create a user experience similar to what Google Apps users enjoy. Look for the tips throughout this book directed to iGoogle users.

## *About This Book*

We realize that before you can make any software solution effective within an organization, you have to meet the needs of two audiences, so we address each audience in specific parts of this book to keep your training neat and tidy:

- ✔ **General users:** Chapters 3 through 13 show you how to use the parts of Google Apps you'll want to use the most: The Start Page, Gmail, Chat (or Talk), Calendar, Docs, Spreadsheets, and Presentations. If you're using the apps with a normal Google account, the information in Chapters 3 through 13 will work for you, too.

> ✔ **Information technology (IT) administrators:** Chapter 2 shows you how to set up Google Apps, and Part IV is your step-by-step guide to administering Google Apps. (Of course, you're free to read the rest of the book to make sure you can help users with any of the apps.)

This book is an enterprise-wide training solution for users at every level, but it can also help small businesses, groups, families, and even individual users. We guide the IT team while they set up Google Apps. We bring users up to speed and show them tips and tricks to get the most out of Google Apps. Why? Because we know how frustrating IT administrators can find setting up a new software system and then having staffers or students fail to make good use of the new tools.

# How This Book 1s Organized

We divided this book into parts and chapters, organizing the chapters into five parts (which we describe in the following sections).

## Part 1: Up and Going with Google Apps

Part I is the obvious place to start if you're brand new to Google Apps. Chapter 1 provides a general overview; we kept it short because we realize that if you have the great wisdom to pick up this book in the first place, you're probably anxious to get started. For Team Edition users and administrators, Chapter 2 runs through the process of setting up Google Apps for your team, business, school, agency, or nonprofit organization. For general users, Chapter 3 introduces your organization's personalized Start Page and shows you how easily you can access all your Google Apps from one place.

## Part 11: Keeping in Touch and on Time: Gmail, Talk, and Calendar

Chapters 4 through 6 take you through the Gmail and Contacts List so that you can become proficient with Google's communications tools. Chapter 7 takes you into Gmail Chat and Google Talk to satisfy your instant-messaging needs. Chapters 8 and 9 show you how to set up and use your Google Calendars personal calendar to keep track of your own activities and how to share that information with other people quickly.

## Part III: Getting to Work: Documents, Spreadsheets, and Presentations

Chapter 10 introduces you to the Google Docs Home and discusses how to create and organize your documents, spreadsheets, and presentations. Chapter 11 covers documents, and it has you creating and formatting documents by using Google Docs, as well as accessing documents in Google Docs that you created by using a different word processor. Chapter 12 introduces Google Spreadsheets and has you calculating, writing formulas, creating imaginative charts, and sharing your spreadsheets in the blink of an eye. Chapter 13 takes you through Google Presentations and helps you create professional Web presentations — you can even show off a bit by using Google's highly visual and shareable Presentations app.

## Part IV: Popping the Hood: Google Apps Administration

The chapters in this part are aimed at administrators. Chapter 14 delves into the Dashboard and helps you set up users and adjust basic domain settings. Chapter 15 walks you, step by step, through the process of setting up the Start Page — customizing it to your business, school, or organization, complete with your own logo, domain name, and look and feel. In Chapter 16, we show you the Page Creator and go through the basics of creating a simple, professional-looking Web page. Finally, Chapter 17 helps you tweak your apps even more and add controls for your users.

## Part V: The Part of Tens

This part begins by giving you ten solutions to common problems in Chapter 18. Chapter 19 suggests more Google Apps and services that you may want to explore. (This final chapter is one of our favorites.)

# Conventions Used in This Book

To make using this book as easy and convenient as possible, we've set up a few conventions:

- ✓ When we throw a new term at you, we place it in *italics* and define it.
- ✓ We place text that you actually type in **bold**.

- Web site addresses and file names appear in a monospace font, like this: `www.dummies.com`. When part of a file name or Web site address varies (depending on what your own Web site address is), we use italics to indicate a placeholder. For example, when you see `http://start.your domain.com`, you type the address with your own domain name in place of *yourdomain.com*.

- When you need to use a menu to select a command, we use the command arrow (➪). For example, File➪Rename simply means that you should click the File menu and then select the Rename command.

- When we show keyboard shortcuts, we place the plus sign (+) between keys. For example, to use the Cut command, press Ctrl+X. This means to press the Ctrl key and the X key at the same time.

# Icons Used in This Book

Everyone gets distracted, starts to daydream, gets a little hungry, and quits paying attention to the lovely prose that they're reading. In an attempt to regain your attention from that long-overdue Snickers bar, we place icons throughout this book. Each has its own sleep-preventative powers.

We mark paragraphs that we think you'll find very useful with this icon. Tips show you shortcuts, time-savers, or something that's otherwise worth noting. So, wake up and pay attention!

When you see this icon, beware. From experience, we know when you can easily make a mistake that may cause irreparable harm or damage to the Internet or national security. Well, maybe the Warning icon doesn't point out something that dire, but you should still pay attention or risk losing data, time, and possibly hair (because you're pulling it out in frustration).

Rather than repeat ourselves (because maybe you didn't pay attention the first time), we pop this icon in place. Commit the information to memory, and it can help you later.

Okay, we don't use this icon unless we have to. When you see this icon, we're flagging some information that's more technical and nerdy than the rest of the text. You might find the information really cool and very interesting, despite being technical, so read it at your discretion.

When you see this icon, we show you how to use Google's powerful search features to help you find e-mail messages, calendar events, and so on by using the Search text box at the top of each Google Apps window.

# *Where to Go from Here*

Hey, users! If you're somewhat timid with software or your computer skills, start with Chapter 3 and read through Chapter 13 to get up to speed with each app. Don't be afraid to challenge yourself and try some of the advanced instructions, as well. Trust us — you'll find any time spent in those chapters well worth it.

We don't want to insult your intelligence and go over basic computing skills, such as highlighting text or using a drop-down list. Instead, we focus on showing you how to use the apps to do your work.

Hey, administrators! Looking for the technical step-by-step details of setting up and running Google Apps for your organization? A little concerned about leaving your old tried-and-traditional software solutions and jumping into Web 2.0? Start by looking over Part I, then immediately jump to the technical stuff in Part IV. General users want to avoid this information like a self-replicating malevolent32 virus. You, on the other hand, should find it as comfortable as a walk along the beach — which is where you can vacation by using the bonus you receive because everyone's so pleased with how well Google Apps is working.

One final thought: All you IT administrators may want to scan quickly through Parts II and III of this book. A quick skim can let you know exactly where you can send staffers, employees, or students when they have questions that you may not have time to answer on the spot.

# Part I
# Up and Going with Google Apps

The 5th Wave    By Rich Tennant

"The funny thing is he's spent 9 hours organizing his Start Page."

# In this part . . .

Take a moment to get to know Google Apps, the perfect complement to your business, group, family, or organization. In this part, we take you on a quick tour of the Google Apps editions, and then we help you register a new domain or point your existing one to Google's awesome services.

If your group or organization is using Google Apps already, or if you're a casual Gmail user, we recommend that you skip ahead and start with Chapter 3.

# Chapter 1

# Introducing Google Apps

*T*he Internet has evolved, and Google is leading the way. Google began as a small Internet search engine experiment, but when the folks at Google found they had a hit on their hands, they didn't stop there. Today, you can keep track of everything, from e-mail to stock portfolios to photos, by using free services created by the ingenious *Googlers* (the bright engineers at Google who work behind the scenes to make the Internet cool and easy for everyone). Google is pushing forward into new territory with the innovative Google Apps and taking key functions, such as calendaring and word processing, into the Internet realm.

This chapter gives you a better understanding of how Google Apps works and helps you choose the version that's best for your organization. You can also find out more about Google Apps by visiting www.google.com/a. If you're interested in Google Apps for school or work teams, go to www.google.com/apps instead.

## Meeting the Google Apps

With little fanfare, the Mountain View, California, behemoth known as Google has been building, buying, and beta-testing scores of online applications. And Google has been releasing them in a flurry, one right after another, to an unsuspecting world. The first 30 or 40 apps seemed random. It appeared that any cool idea any Googler could think of was turned into an app and tossed onto the Internet just for the fun of it. It was a blur. If you blinked, you missed something. It didn't seem to have a pattern or a purpose.

With the creation of the Google Apps initiative, the strategy behind the software releases came into sharp focus: Google is building a radically different way of working that can shatter the primacy of the current methods and reduce the need for all the tired, old office productivity software on your hard drive. Oh, and Google provides most of the apps for free or at a fraction of the cost of traditional software.

*Google Apps* is a powerful set of tools that Google has bundled together to meet the needs of businesses, schools, government agencies, and other organizations of any size. You can use Google Apps as a powerful digital communications infrastructure for your business or school that Google maintains for you. (Very sweet.) The key Google Apps are

- ✔ **Gmail:** An e-mail app based on Google's popular Gmail platform. This version lets you use your organization's domain, such as `user@ yourdomain.com`.

- ✔ **Calendar:** A calendar and scheduling app that allows easy collaboration.

- ✔ **Talk:** Instant messaging, available directly from within Gmail or as a standalone software application. Talk also allows voice calls, voice mail, and file sharing.

- ✔ **Docs:** A simple, yet powerful, set of word processing, spreadsheet, and presentation apps.

- ✔ **The Start Page:** An app that you can personalize by adding gadgets to access any or all of the other Google Apps, as well as news, weather reports, entertainment information, and more from one place.

In addition to the apps themselves, Google provides some powerful tools for administrators in the Google Apps Dashboard. Features for administrators include

- ✔ Web page creation tools

- ✔ Domain settings

- ✔ Advanced tools, including administrative support and migration tools

- ✔ Individual apps settings

- ✔ Custom Web addresses for your Google Apps

- ✔ Phone-based support tools

# *Welcome to the New Internet*

Google believes that you want to spend more time doing things with your organization, family, group, or school in an online environment.

Called *cloud computing,* the premise is that users can create, edit, and store massive amounts of information through the Internet (or "cloud") with any device that has a Web browser (such as a computer or cellphone) and Internet access. The Web applications (or apps, for short), as well as the files themselves, are stored securely on powerful servers in data centers throughout the world, as illustrated in Figure 1-1.

Users can share their information with others, including friends and co-workers, and collaborate in real time on important projects. Because the files are already online, a user simply sends a message to his or her friends that contains a link to a file, and those friends can click the link to see and contribute to the sender's great work. Using Google Apps, you don't need to send attachments back and forth or keep track of different file versions.

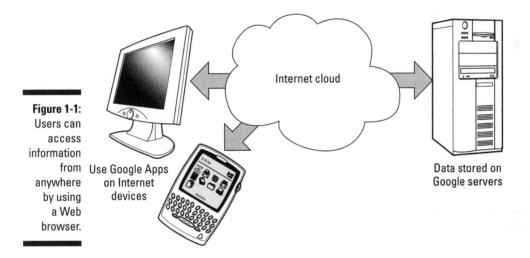

**Figure 1-1:** Users can access information from anywhere by using a Web browser.

Internet cloud

Use Google Apps on Internet devices

Data stored on Google servers

Google Apps brings cloud computing to the masses. And it helps alleviate some of the issues of traditional computing:

- ✔ **Cost:** Computer hardware and software is expensive. For schools and businesses alike, buying PCs and servers, and all the software that goes with them, is making less and less financial sense — especially when it all becomes obsolete before anyone figures out how to use the new stuff. These organizations want solutions that can provide a better return on investment.

- ✔ **Maintenance:** Maintaining all those PCs and the network software is a pain. Information technology costs even more money and uses a lot of resources — especially when organizations grow and someone needs to maintain all those new users.

✔ **Hassle:** People are tired of installing new software, downloading and installing updates, backing up files, scanning for viruses, maintaining firewalls — it's all a bit much. Most people just want to get their work done, and most companies want to focus on their real business, not on information technology. (Unless, of course, their business *is* information technology. Those companies love all the hassle.)

So, why not go with Google and leave all the tedious technical stuff to the people not savvy enough to jump on the Google bandwagon? If you keep your information in their Internet cloud, you don't need to buy any servers, load any software, scan for any viruses, or back anything up. No more rebooting the server or your PC when the system crashes, again. Everything just works with a lot less cost, maintenance, and hassle because it's coming to you directly from Google.

To put it all into perspective, here's an analogy for you: Would you rather hide your life savings under your mattress and risk it being stolen or lost in a fire, or store it in a bank where you have access to it anytime, anywhere, from an ATM machine?

In this new, Web-enabled world, your Web browser becomes your ATM, and Google becomes your bank. You can use your own domain name, company logo, and all that branded identity stuff to personalize your Google Apps. You can preserve your corporate, school, or organizational identity and slash your costs in a dramatic way.

# Choosing the Right Google Apps Edition

As we mention in the "Meeting the Google Apps" section, earlier in this chapter, Google Apps consists of four main programs: Gmail, Calendar, Docs, and Talk. Anyone can use these services without signing up for Google Apps, but to help organizations replace or complement their existing systems, Google has some powerful administrative and collaborative tools for those ready to take the plunge.

You can choose from four Google Apps editions: Team, Standard, Premier, and Education. Each edition has been customized to meet the needs of different types of organizations, large and small:

✔ **Team Edition:** This is the easiest way to start using the collaborative tools available with Google Apps with your school or work team. You don't have to change your e-mail address or worry about any administration tools. Sign up for free with your existing e-mail address (see Chapter 2 on how to do this) and you can start connecting with other people in your domain right away. Gmail is not included in this edition.

✔ **Standard Edition:** Use this edition if you're a family, group, or small business. Register or transfer your domain to access Gmail, Calendar, Talk, Docs, and the Start Page. This version is free (meaning ad-sponsored) and supported by online help. You can always upgrade to Premier Edition later, if you want to.

✔ **Premier Edition:** Medium to large organizations should generally use this edition. At the time of this publication, it costs $50 per user per year, but you likely currently spend more than that on maintenance of your existing setup. Because this is a paid edition, you can choose to turn Gmail ads off. This edition also has additional administration tools and security settings. Your users receive significantly more storage space than with the Standard Edition.

✔ **Education Edition:** Built for — you guessed it — schools, colleges, and universities. Nonprofit organizations can also use this version. This version is free (although not supported by ads), and it includes many of the features from the Premier Edition (albeit a little less storage space). If you're interested in the Education Edition, Google requires you to provide proof of accredited not-for-profit status.

The best program is the one that best meets the needs of your organization. See Chapter 2 to find out how to sign up.

Table 1-1 shows which features are available in each edition of Google Apps.

| Table 1-1 | Features in the Google Apps Editions | | | |
|---|---|---|---|---|
| *Feature* | *Team* | *Standard* | *Premier* | *Education* |
| Gmail, Calendar, Docs, Talk, Page Creator, and Start Page | Calendar, Docs, Talk, and Start Page | Yes | Yes | Yes |
| E-mail storage | No | 6+ GB per user | 25+ GB per user | 6+ GB per user |
| Conference room and resources scheduling | No | No | Yes | Yes |
| IMAP for Gmail | No | Yes | Yes | Yes |
| Mobile access | Yes | Yes | Yes | Yes |
| Administrator control panel (Dashboard) | No | Yes | Yes | Yes |

*(continued)*

**Table 1-1** *(continued)*

| Feature | Team | Standard | Premier | Education |
|---|---|---|---|---|
| Policy management | No | No | Yes | No |
| APIs to integrate with existing structure | No | No | Yes | Yes |
| E-mail migration and routing | No | No | Yes | Yes |
| Online support | Yes | Yes | Yes | Yes |
| Live/phone support | No | No | Yes | Yes |

# What's in It for My Organization?

As part of the Google Apps program, Google hosts your e-mail, documents, spreadsheets, presentations, calendars, and more at little or no cost. A team, business, school, or organization of any size can have Google Apps up and running quickly. When you use Google Apps, your IT resources aren't so drained because Google takes care of the technical details. Oh, yeah — and they keep your information safe and secure.

Here are a few additional features of Google Apps that may grab the attention of decision makers and your IT department:

- ✔ You don't have to purchase or set up any hardware.

- ✔ Because Google Apps are Web-based applications, you don't need to download, install, update, or pay for software again when new versions are released. (Except for a Web browser, of course, and at least you don't have to pay for that.)

- ✔ Your organization can use its own domain name for e-mail addresses and Web pages when you use Google Apps.

- ✔ Google boasts a 99.9% reliability rate, which means that the service rarely, if ever, goes down.

- ✔ Google takes care of all the data backup and support operations.

- ✔ Google provides online support resources for free and gives 24/7 support — including phone-based support — for Premier Edition and Education Edition users.

✔ You can set up users quickly by using the Dashboard.

✔ A single sign-on adds convenience for Premier Edition users. Users can sign in once and access all their Google Apps in addition to other corporate intranet or school resources.

✔ Gmail can support an existing e-mail gateway.

✔ Administrators can access e-mail migration tools for Premier Edition and Education Edition customers.

✔ Gmail protects users by constantly updating and running very effective and efficient spam-blocking, virus-protection, and filtering software.

Don't forget one of the biggest advantages of using Google Apps: Whether you're at the office, traveling, working from home, or sipping a latte in a café that has a wireless hotspot, as long as you have a live Internet connection, you can log into your Google Apps account. Also, you can check your e-mail and do other tasks from your mobile device.

# Can There Possibly Be a Downside?

If using Google Apps has any disadvantages, they mostly revolve around your personal relationship with your Internet connection. Assuming you do have a decent connection (something high-speed in nature is best), you're good to go. If you don't have an Internet connection, we recommend you put this book down, buy another book — we recommend *Writing on Stone Tablets For Dummies* — and take up activities that don't require the use of electricity.

You must be online to use Google Apps. Checking your e-mail, updating your calendar, and collaborating on a document require online interactivity. Google Apps doesn't work without an Internet connection. Internet connection speed is important, too: Google Apps does work over dial-up connections, but it's soooo slow. (Nevertheless, you can always connect with dial-up when you're away from your high-speed connection.)

When deciding whether to use Google Apps, remember that all these services are in *perpetual beta,* meaning that unlike traditional software that gets a new, big update every year or so, Google is constantly updating its services and adding new features. Although the most common features are fully implemented, you should check to make sure that the features your organization needs are available. (Along those lines, you may occasionally notice a slight difference between what you see on your screen and what you see in the figures in this book if Google made an update after this book was published.)

The upside, of course, to the perpetual beta model is that by the time the features of the new version have been rolled out, Google Apps users are already familiar with the changes, so you have to deal with only a minimal learning curve. When you and your fellow users get up to speed, you just need to keep using the products to stay up to date. And keeping ahead of the curve is an advantage, all by itself.

# Chapter 2

# Signing Up for Google Apps

● ● ● ● ● ● ● ● ● ● ● ● ● ● ● ● ● ● ● ● ● ● ● ● ● ● ● ● ● ● ● ● ● ● ● ● ● ● ● ● ● ● ● ● ● ● ●

## *In This Chapter*

▶ Getting online with Team Edition

▶ Starting with Standard Edition

▶ Upgrading to Premier Edition

▶ Using Education Edition for your school or nonprofit organization

▶ Proving that you own your domain

● ● ● ● ● ● ● ● ● ● ● ● ● ● ● ● ● ● ● ● ● ● ● ● ● ● ● ● ● ● ● ● ● ● ● ● ● ● ● ● ● ● ● ● ● ● ●

*W*ouldn't you know it, your good fortune has led you to the most exciting chapter in the book! You're either dipping in your big toe to test the water, or you're ready to make the cannonball that gets the pool party started. Either way, we take you through the steps of setting up Google Apps for your team or organization and show you how simple the setup process is. (Okay, you can find a couple not-so-simple sets of steps at the end of this chapter, but we guide you through those steps in a breeze, too.)

Because no two organizations are the same, this chapter helps you register for the edition of Google Apps that best fits your organization's needs. Each edition has its own unique registration requirements that we discuss in each edition's section in this chapter.

Chapter 1 provides a detailed breakdown of features available in each edition of Google Apps. Here's our quick advice about choosing among the different editions of Google Apps:

✔ Use Google Apps Team Edition to get your school team or work group collaborating online in a snap, without having to register a domain name. All you need to sign up is a school or work e-mail address. The very next section of this chapter will take you through the setup.

✔ If you own a small business or plan to use Google Apps for your family or group, you probably want to use Google Apps Standard Edition. You likely won't need the advanced features and support (and cost) of Premier Edition. Also, if you don't already have a domain name, sign up for Standard Edition first. You can then upgrade to Premier or Education Edition later. Follow the instructions in the "Signing Up for Standard Edition," later in this chapter.

> ✔ If you're the IT administrator or decision maker for a medium to large business or enterprise, we recommend that you skip ahead to the section "Signing Up for Premier Edition," later in this chapter. Premier Edition has the added migration and security tools, APIs, and support that your larger organization needs. You will need to have an existing domain name to register for Premier Edition.
>
> ✔ If you're the techie for your school, school district, or nonprofit organization, you get most of the benefits of Premier Edition for free with the Education Editions. You will need to have an existing EDUCAUSE or other domain name to sign up for Education Edition. Otherwise, you should start with Standard Edition. Flip to the "Signing Up for Education Edition" section, near the end of this chapter. We wrote it for you.

Although everything in this chapter was accurate when this book went to press, Google is constantly updating. By the time you register for your chosen edition of Google Apps, you may notice slight differences between what you see on your screen and the steps and figures in this chapter.

# Signing Up for Team Edition

Are you ready to bring your team up to speed? Follow the steps in this section to set up your own Google Apps account and then invite your fellow team members to join in on the fun:

1. **Open your Web browser and navigate to `www.google.com/apps` for work teams or `www.google.com/apps/edu` for students.**

   You see a screen similar to Figure 2-1.

2. **In the Email text box, enter your work or school e-mail address and click the Get Started button.**

   A sign-up screen appears.

3. **Fill in all the text boxes (they're all required) and click the I Accept. Continue to Google Apps button at the bottom of the screen.**

   The Email Verification screen appears, telling you to verify that you own your e-mail account.

If you already have a Google account associated with your work or school e-mail address, all new calendar and document invitations will go to your Google Apps account. You're given the option to migrate your existing calendar events and documents into your new account when you log into these services for the first time.

4. **Log into your work or school e-mail account and open the message titled Google Apps: Sign-up Verification.**

   The e-mail message looks similar to Figure 2-2.

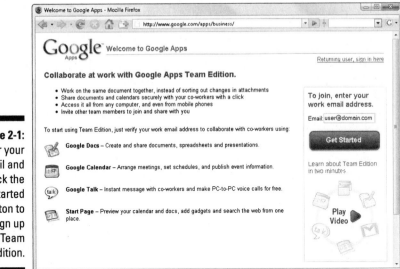

**Figure 2-1:**
Enter your
e-mail and
click the
Get Started
button to
sign up
for Team
Edition.

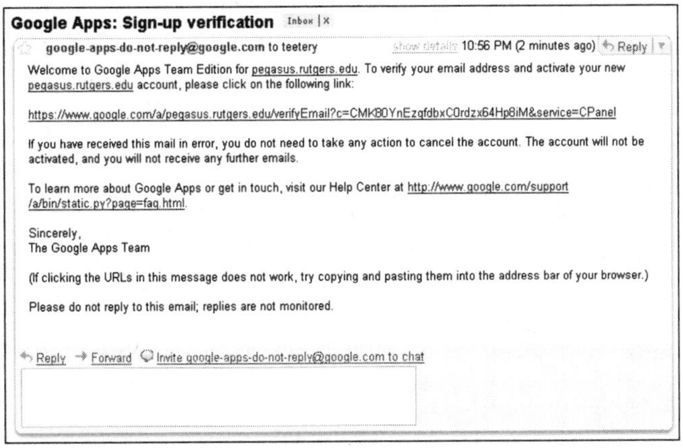

**Figure 2-2:**
Click the
verification
link to
activate
your Google
Apps
account.

5. **Click the verification link in the e-mail message to activate your Google Apps account.**

   A new window opens, indicating that your e-mail address has been verified.

6. **Click the Click Here to Continue link to go to your Google Apps sign-in screen. Enter your new username and password in the text boxes on the left and click the Sign In button.**

   You are taken to your Google Apps Dashboard, shown in Figure 2-3. Here you can click the links located on the right side of the screen to access your apps, such as Docs and Calendar. To view other users from your office or school, click the *X* Users link on the left side of the screen.

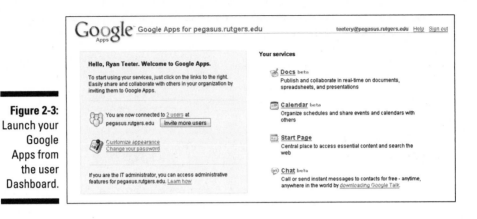

**Figure 2-3:**
Launch your
Google
Apps from
the user
Dashboard.

7. **Invite other team members by clicking the Invite More Users button, located on the left side of the screen.**

8. **On the screen that appears, type your co-workers' or fellow students' e-mail addresses, separated by commas, into the first text box. Write a short invitation message in the second text box and then click the Invite Users button.**

   When you are finished, you will be taken to the User Accounts screen where you can see all the other users who have joined from your company or school.

9. **Click the Back to Home link in the top-left corner of the screen to return to your Dashboard.**

To add a custom logo to your Google Apps, click the Customize Appearance link on the left side of the screen. There you can upload your company or school logo and change the color of the sign-in box. See the section about customizing your domain's appearance in Chapter 14 for more details.

Table 2-1 has all the quick links you need to get back into your apps. Just replace *yourdomain.com* with your actual work or school domain. If you forget these, look for a Welcome e-mail message from Google that contains these links.

| Table 2-1 | Team Edition Quick Links |
|---|---|
| *Google App* | *Quick Link* |
| Dashboard | www.google.com/a/*yourdomain.com* |
| Docs | http://docs.google.com/a/*yourdomain.com* |
| Calendar | http://calendar.google.com/a/*yourdomain.com* |

| Google App | Quick Link |
|---|---|
| Start Page | `http://partnerpage.google.com/`*yourdomain.com* |
| Talk | `http://google.com/talk` |

# Signing Up for Standard Edition

If you're a small business owner or decision maker who's taking the initiative, this section is for you.

The easiest way to start using Google Apps is to start from scratch and register a shiny new domain name. A *domain* is the address for your Web site or the part of an e-mail address that follows the @ sign (such as `www.`*yourdomain.com* or `jdoe@`*yourdomain.net*). If you want to register a new domain name for your organization, head to the following section. If your organization already has a Web address, skip ahead to the section "Signing up and migrating an existing domain," later in this chapter.

After you register your domain name with Google and create an administrator account, you can begin using Google Apps. In Part IV of this book, we go more in depth into setting up users, creating your own Web pages, and customizing your organization's personalized Start Page.

## Signing up and registering a new domain

So, you have a business or group but don't have a Web address yet. You're not alone. Organizations may not have a Web site because setting one up and maintaining it was very difficult in the past. First, you had to register a domain and find a place to host it (which either cost a lot of money or forced you to display annoying banner advertisements). After that, you had to use complicated software to create your site, and you could only hope that your software would connect with your host. And that's not even getting into setting up other programs for features such as e-mail and calendars.

Google Apps changes all that. With Google, you can register a new domain in three steps: choose a domain, sign up for Google Apps, and create an administrator account.

You pay ten dollars per year to register a domain name with one of Google's domain registration partners. You need a credit card to sign up for Google Apps with a new domain.

The toughest part of signing up for Google Apps is finding the right domain name. A lot of other people have already registered many of the more common names, so don't be surprised if someone has already taken the first name that you think of. You might have to be a little creative if someone has already taken your first choice for a domain name.

Follow these steps to register a new domain name and sign up for Google Apps Standard Edition:

1. **Go to `www.google.com/a` and click the Businesses and Employees button or the Organizations and Members button on the right side of the page. Then, on the next screen, click the blue Compare Editions and Sign Up button in the top-right corner.**

2. **In the Standard Edition column, click the blue Sign Up button.**

   The Google Apps Sign Up screen appears. You can enter an existing domain name (if you already have one) by clicking the I Want to Use an Existing Domain Name tab or register for a new domain name by clicking the I Want to Buy a Domain Name tab, as shown in Figure 2-4.

3. **Click the I Want to Buy a Domain Name tab (on the right side of the screen), enter the domain name that you want in the text box, and select a top-level domain (for example, `.com` or `.net`) from the drop-down list.**

Figure 2-4:
Choose a
domain
name on
the Google
Apps sign
up page.

A *top-level domain* (TLD) is the last part of a domain name. The most common TLD, `.com`, is primarily used for commercial businesses. Many businesses are also using `.biz` now. Depending on what your organization does, you can choose other TLDs, also. Use `.net` or `.info` for an information-only site, such as a blog or group site. The TLD `.org` is generally used by nonprofit organizations.

4. **Click the Check Availability button.**

   If someone has already taken the domain name that you want, Google suggests other related names that are available, as shown in Figure 2-5. Repeat Steps 3 and 4, trying different words or names until you find an available one that works for you.

5. **When you find an available domain name that works for you, click the Continue to Registration button.**

   Have your personal information and credit card ready.

6. **In the form, click in the text boxes and enter your personal information.**

   Make sure you select the Automatically Renew My Registration Every Year check box to ensure that your domain name doesn't expire and leave you without your e-mail and other services. Google automatically bills your credit card on the same day that you originally registered your domain name. You can always cancel the service later.

**Figure 2-5:**
Google
suggests
other
available
domain
names if
someone
has already
taken the
one you
enter.

Google™ Welcome to Google Apps
Apps

| 1. Choose a domain name | 2. Sign up | 3. Set up |

**Choose a domain name** (step 1 of 3)

You need a domain name to use Google Apps. A domain name is a unique name that will be assigned to your Google services. For example, if you choose example.com, you can create an email address for john.smith@example.com and web pages at buy.example.com. You can also sign up with a subdomain, such as sales.example.com, to create an email address for jane.doe@sales.example.com.

✖  **books.com is already registered**

   **Similar available names**
   These domain names are available for registration. Learn more

   ○ studiesbooks.com    ○ housebooks.net    ○ housebooks.org
   ○ pressbooks.net      ○ housebooks.biz    ○ studiesbooks.net
   ○ streetbooks.net     ○ pressbooks.org    ○ treebooks.net
   ○ roombooks.com       ○ studiesbooks.org  ○ worldbooks.biz
   ○ booksmusic.net      ○ streetbooks.org   ○ hillbooks.net

   ● Find another domain name  ardsleybooks        .com ▾

   [ Continue ]    powered by GoDaddy.com Learn more

   © 2007 Google - Terms of Service - Privacy policy

7. **After you enter all the registration information, click the I Accept. Proceed to Google Checkout button.**

   The Google Checkout page appears, as shown in Figure 2-6.

**Figure 2-6:**
Use Google
Checkout
to pay for
your new
domain.

8. **If you already use a Google account, click in the Email and Password text boxes on the right of the screen and enter your e-mail address and password, respectively, then click the Sign In and Continue button on the right. Otherwise, click in the text boxes below Create a Google Account to Complete This Purchase and enter the appropriate information, and then click the Agree and Continue button at the bottom of the screen.**

   Google Checkout allows you to store your credit card information in one place. If you haven't used Google Checkout with your Google account before, Google gives you the option to save your billing information for future Internet purchases. You can find out more about Google Checkout at http://google.com/checkout.

9. **Review your order, then click Place Your Order Now — $10.00.**

   Google sends you a receipt by e-mail, along with instructions to access your account.

10. **On the next screen click the Click Here to Retrieve Your Purchase link. You can also log into your e-mail account later and click the link in the message from Google to access the Dashboard.**

    The last thing that you need to do to register for Google Apps is to create an administrator account. You need an administrator account to access the Google Apps Dashboard and create additional users.

If you don't have time to create an administrator account now, don't worry. Remember that e-mail Google sent you? It tells you how to get back to this page later.

11. **Enter a username and password for yourself (if you're going to be the administrator) or for the person whom you want to administer your account.**

12. **Click the Continue with Set Up button to open your Dashboard.**

    If you're ready to explore the Dashboard, skip ahead to Chapter 14.

Congratulations! You've successfully signed up for Google Apps. Because you registered your domain name through Google, your Gmail and Calendar should be ready for you to use in a few moments, although it may take up to 24 hours for all the services to activate.

## Signing up and migrating an existing domain

Like so many other organizations out there, you have a Web site, and you're ready to trade your old set of e-mail and Web services for the power and ease of Google Apps. Just follow these three steps to register your domain with Google Apps: Enter your existing domain name, sign up and create an administrator account (both of which we cover in this section), and verify your domain ownership (described in the "Verifying Domain Ownership" section, later in this chapter). Have your original domain registration information (either your Web site's FTP address and login, or your domain registrar's address and login) handy for that third part.

Follow these steps to sign up for Google Apps Standard Edition by using your existing domain name:

1. **Go to www.google.com/a and click the Businesses and Employees button or the Organizations and Members button on the right side of the page. Then, on the next screen, click the blue Compare Editions and Sign Up button in the top-right corner.**

2. **In the Standard Edition column, click the blue Sign Up button.**

    The Google Apps Sign Up screen appears. You can enter an existing domain name (if you already have one) by clicking the I Want to Use an Existing Domain Name tab or register for a new domain name by clicking the I Want to Buy a Domain Name tab, as shown in Figure 2-7.

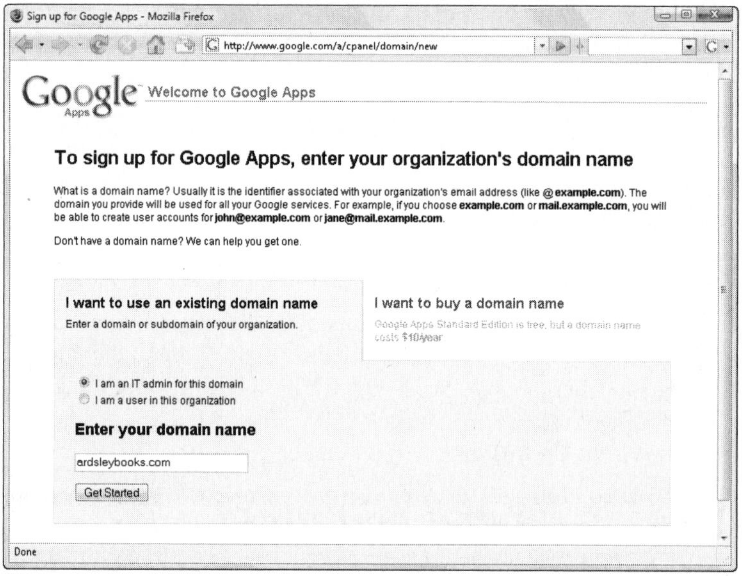

Figure 2-7:
Enter your
domain
name in
the Google
Apps Sign
Up page.

3. **In the I Want to Use an Existing Domain Name section, select the I Am an IT Admin for This Domain radio button, click in the text box below and enter your existing domain name, and finally click the Get Started button.**

   The Google Apps Information screen appears.

4. **Click in the text boxes and fill in the organization information associated with your domain, then click Continue.**

   The Domain Setup screen appears. You create an administrator account on this screen.

5. **Enter a username and password for yourself (if you're going to be the administrator), and then click the I Accept. Continue with Set Up button.**

   The Dashboard appears.

Now, you're registered for Google Apps! Grab your domain registration information and head to the "Verifying Domain Ownership" section, later in this chapter.

# Signing Up for Premier Edition

So, your enterprise wants to add Google Apps to its arsenal. Fortunately for you, Google has some robust tools to help make the transition as smooth as possible.

If you don't have a domain already, follow the instructions in the "Signing up and registering a new domain" section, earlier in this chapter. After you register, you can upgrade to Premier Edition from the Dashboard.

You need to follow three steps to register your domain for Premier Edition: Sign up for Google Apps, purchase the subscription service, and set up your administrator account. You then have to verify your domain by following the instructions in the "Verifying Your Domain" section, later in this chapter.

Ready to sign up for Google Apps Premier Edition? Grab your company credit card and follow these steps:

1. **Go to www.google.com/a and click the Businesses and Employees button or the Organizations and Members button on the right side of the page. Then, on the next screen, click the blue Compare Editions and Sign Up button in the top-right corner.**

2. **Click the blue Sign Up button in the Premier Edition column. Select the Administrators: I Own or Control This Domain radio button, enter your domain name in the text box below, and click the Get Started button.**

3. **On the Sign Up page that appears. click in the text boxes and fill in your organization information, as shown in Figure 2-8.**

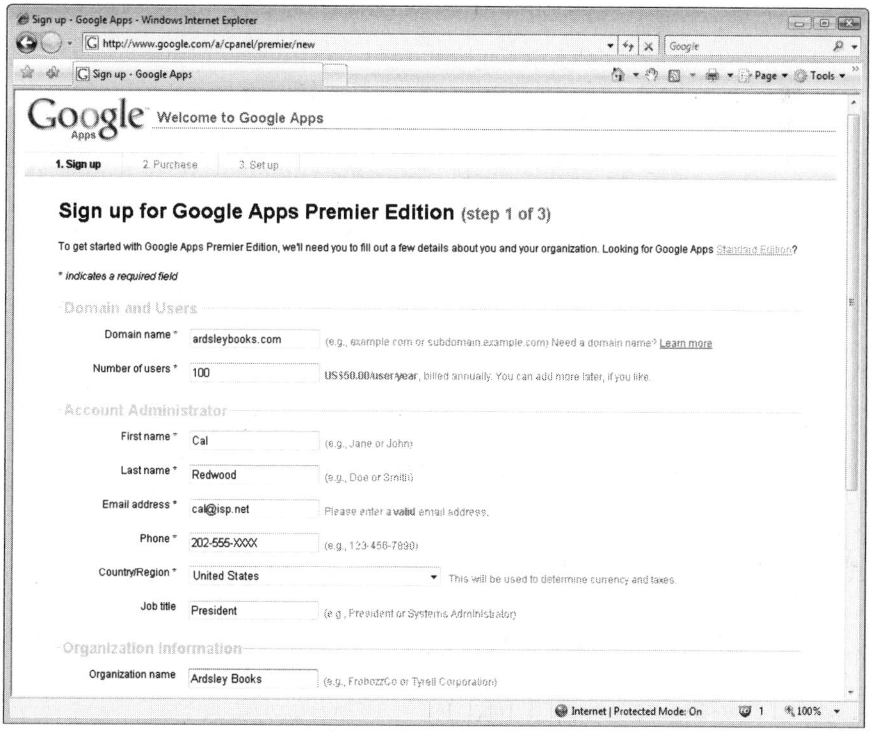

**Figure 2-8:** Fill in your organization information on the Sign Up page.

4. **Click Continue to Go to Google Checkout.**

   A page with your purchase options appears, as shown in Figure 2-9.

5. **Review and/or adjust your purchase options, and then click the I Accept. Proceed to Google Checkout button.**

   You see a page that displays a summary of your order. Google Checkout requires you to use a credit card to make purchases. If you need to use an alternate form of payment, click the Contact Us link near the top of the page and fill out the form that appears on the next page.

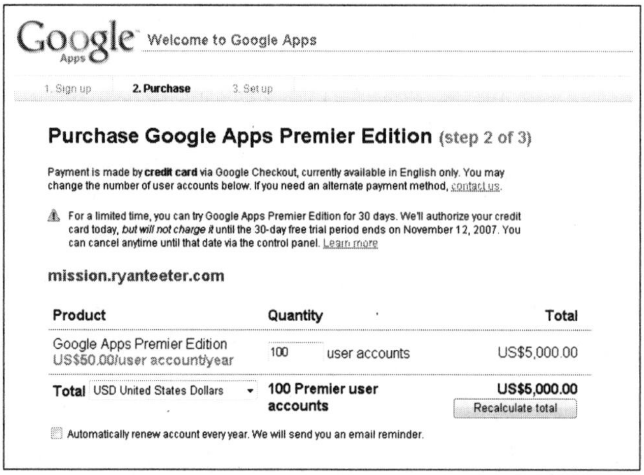

**Figure 2-9:**
Decide how
many users
you want to
add to your
Google Apps
account.

6. **If you already use a Google account, click in the Email and Password text boxes and enter your e-mail and password, then click the Sign In and Continue button on the right side of the screen. Otherwise, click in the text boxes on the left and enter your billing information, and then click the Agree and Continue button.**

   You will see an order confirmation screen. Google Checkout allows you to store your credit card information in one place. If you haven't used Google Checkout with your Google account before, Google gives you the option to save your billing information for future Internet purchases. You can find out more about Google Checkout at `http://google.com/checkout`.

7. **Review your order and click Place Your Order Now — $*XX*00.00.**

   Google sends a receipt to you by e-mail, along with instructions to access your account.

8. **On the next page, click the Click Here to Retrieve Your Purchase link. You can also open your e-mail program later and access the Dashboard by clicking the link in the e-mail from Google.**

You need an administrator account to access the Google Apps Dashboard and Google's migration tools that help you transition your existing users.

If you don't have time to set up an administrator account now, don't worry. Remember that e-mail Google sent you? It tells you how to get back to this page later.

9. **Enter a username and password for yourself (if you're going to be the administrator) or for the person whom you want to administer your account.**

10. **Click the Continue with Set Up button to open your Dashboard.**

Done! Now grab your domain registration information and head to the "Verifying Domain Ownership" section, later in this chapter.

# Signing Up for Education Edition

We're so glad that your school or nonprofit organization is making the move to Google Apps. Google Apps can make life easier for teachers, students, and volunteers alike with its powerful tools.

You need to follow only two steps to register your domain for Education Edition: Sign up for Google Apps and set up an administrator account. Google contacts you by e-mail to verify your eligibility. In the meantime, you can verify that you own your domain name by following the instructions in the "Verifying Your Domain" section, later in this chapter.

Make sure that you're an administrator for your school or organization. If you can't access your domain information to verify ownership, you (or your administrator) will find signing up for Google Apps impossible.

Signing up for Education Edition is a breeze! Just follow these steps:

1. **Go to www.google.com/a and click the Schools and Students button on the right side of the page. Then, on the next screen, click the blue Compare Editions and Sign Up button in the top-right corner.**

2. **In the Education Edition column, click the blue Sign Up button. On the next screen, select the Administrators: I Own or Control This Domain radio button, enter your domain name in the text box below, and then click the Get Started button.**

   A screen similar to Figure 2-10 appears, asking you to fill out your organization information.

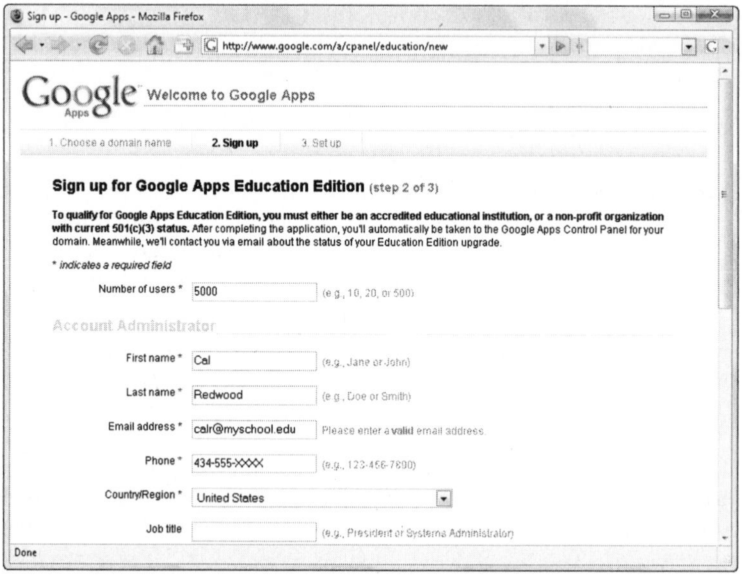

**Figure 2-10:**
Fill in your
school or
nonprofit
organization
information.

3. **Click in the text boxes and enter your school's information, then click the Continue button.**

   You need to create an administrator account to access the Google Apps Dashboard and Google's migration tools to help you transition your existing users.

4. **Enter a username and password for yourself (if you're going to be the administrator) or for the person whom you want to administer your account.**

5. **Click the I Accept. Continue with Set Up button to open your Dashboard.**

Piece of cake! Now, grab your domain registration information and continue to the following section.

# Verifying Domain Ownership

To prevent abuse, Google requires you to verify that you actually own the domain you register within 30 days of signing up for Google Apps. You can't use any of the services until you verify ownership, so we recommend that you do it immediately after you register for your chosen edition of Google Apps.

If you don't verify domain ownership within 30 days, Google removes your domain from its system and you will have to sign up for Google Apps all over again.

You have two ways to verify your domain ownership:

✔ **The easy way:** Verify your domain ownership by uploading an HTML file to your existing Web server. You need the FTP (file transfer protocol) address for your Web server, as well as your login name and password. If you don't have access to your Web server, use the next method.

✔ **The not-so-easy way:** Verify your domain ownership by making changes to your DNS (domain name server) entries using your current registrar. You need your domain registrar's address (such as www.godaddy.com or www.networksolutions.com), your login name, and your password.

If you don't have access to this information, you need to find the person who does. Otherwise, you may want to rummage through your desk drawers or e-mail folders to locate your account information. If changing these settings makes you nervous, you may want to bring in your IT administrator or computer guru.

You need to change your DNS settings when you set up your Gmail service later (we cover this in Chapter 17). If you lost your registrar login information, contact your registrar's support center. You can find your domain's registrar by going to www.who.is and searching for your domain name.

## Uploading an HTML file

You can easily verify your domain by uploading an HTML file. Google gives you a special key, and if you can upload it to your server as a specific HTML file, Google can see that you're really the owner of the domain. Be sure to have your FTP login information handy and follow these steps:

1. **Sign into your Google Apps Dashboard, if you aren't there already.**

   If you just registered, you should be at the Dashboard. If you're coming back to it, go to http://google.com/a/*yourdomain.com* (replace *yourdomain.com* with your actual domain name), click in the Username and Password text boxes on the left side of the screen and enter your username and password, respectively, then click the Sign In button. Your screen should look like Figure 2-11.

2. **Click the Verify Domain Ownership link at the top of the screen.**

3. **Select Upload an HTML File from the drop-down list in the Verify Your Domain Ownership section.**

   Your screen should look like Figure 2-12.

**Figure 2-11:**
Sign into
the Google
Apps
Dashboard.

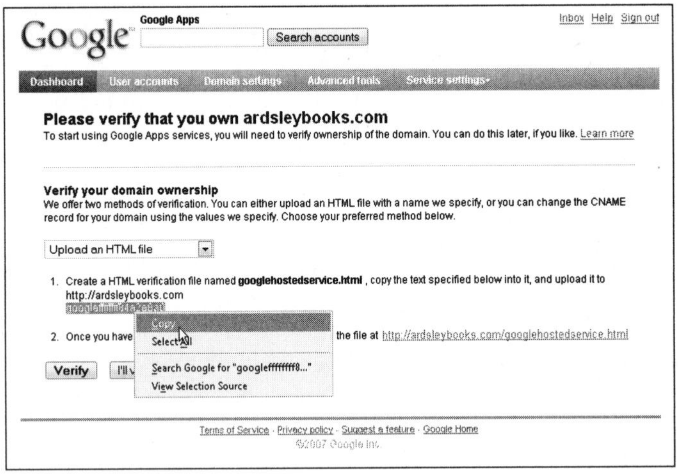

**Figure 2-12:**
Copy this
code and
then paste
it into an
HTML file.

4. **Highlight the text located in the page's Step 1, right-click, and select
   Copy from the contextual menu that appears.**

5. **Open Notepad (Windows) or TextEdit (Mac) and paste the code into a
   new, blank document.**

6. **Choose File⇨Save.**

7. **In the Save As dialog box that appears, click in the File Name text box and type** googlehostedservice.html, **navigate to your desktop (or some other easy-to-find location on your computer), and click the Save button.**

Make sure the HTML file is named googlehostedservice.html. Otherwise, Google can't verify it.

8. **Log into your Web server by using your FTP address and open your Web folder as follows:**

   • In Windows Explorer, type the address in the address bar, like this: **ftp://*username*@ftp.*yourdomain.com*** (replacing the italic words with your username and domain name). Press Enter. A login window appears. Enter your username and password in the corresponding text boxes and click the Log On button.

   • On a Mac, open an FTP client, such as Fetch (www.fetchsoft works.com). Click the New Connection button, and then enter your hostname (ftp://ftp.yourdomain.com), your username, and your password in the corresponding text boxes. Click the Connect button.

   It is important that you upload your .html file to the Web folder, otherwise verification won't work. The Web folder usually contains an index.htm or default.html file, as shown in Figure 2-13. If you don't see either of these files in the Web server when you log on, look for the Web folder. It is sometimes called www, pub, or public_html.

9. **Find the** googlehostedservice.html **file on your computer and drag it to your Web server, as shown in Figure 2-13.**

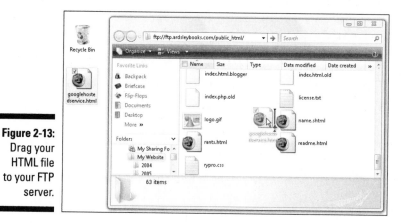

**Figure 2-13:**
Drag your
HTML file
to your FTP
server.

10. **Go back to your Web browser and click the www.yourdomain. com/googlehostedservice.html link in the Verify Your Domain Ownership page's Step 2 (refer to Figure 2-12).**

    The code that you copy in Step 4 of this list should appear in the top-left corner of the screen. If you don't see it, repeat Steps 3 through 9 and make sure you name the googlehostedservice.html file correctly and place it in the correct Web folder.

11. **If the text you copy in Step 4 appears on the page, return to the Verify Your Domain Ownership page and click the Verify button.**

Hooray! You've successfully completed your domain verification and you should return to your Dashboard. Now, you just need to wait for Google to verify your domain. (Google usually verifies your domain in a few minutes, but it can take up to 48 hours.) After Google verifies your domain, a message appears along the top of your Dashboard, and you can then activate all your apps.

Take a quick coffee break — you deserve it! When you come back, flip to Chapter 14, where we help you find your way around the Dashboard and show you how to create additional users. You don't really want to keep this goodness all to yourself, do you?

## Changing your CNAME record

Well, you're a brave soul. This process takes you through connecting your domain to Google Apps using your registrar's control panel. On the bright side, you can use this opportunity to adjust all your other domain settings if you like. While you're on your registrar's site, you might want to complete the steps in the section about creating custom apps addresses in Chapter 17. Ready? Here we go:

1. **Sign into your Google Apps Dashboard, if you haven't already.**

   If you just registered, you should be at the Dashboard. If you're coming back to it, go to http://google.com/a/yourdomain.com (replace yourdomain.com with your actual domain name), click in the Username and Password text boxes and enter your username and password, respectively, and then click the Sign In button. The Dashboard opens. (Refer to Figure 2-11.)

2. **Click the Verify Domain Ownership link at the top of the screen.**

3. **Select Change Your CNAME Record from the drop-down list in the Verify Your Domain Ownership section.**

   Your screen should look like Figure 2-14.

4. **Highlight the unique string located in the Verify Your Domain Ownership page's Step 2, right-click, and select Copy from the contextual menu that appears.**

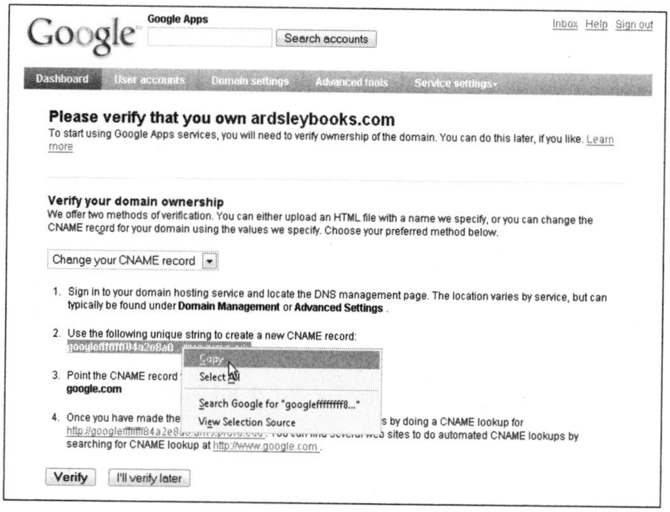

**Figure 2-14:**
Copy this
unique
string and
paste it into
your DNS
manage-
ment page.

5. **In a new browser tab or window, log into your domain registrar's Web site and look for a page that is titled either DNS Management or DNS Control Panel.**

    This page displays a list of your CNAME entries, like the page shown in Figure 2-15.

    If you have trouble finding the DNS management page, contact your registrar's support center. They can tell you exactly where you need to go.

6. **In either the CNAME or Alias section (whichever appears on your DNS page), click the link or button to add or create a new CNAME (the name of the link or button varies, depending on your registrar).**

7. **In the Alias Name text box, paste the unique string that you copied in Step 4.** *Remember:* **Remove any extra spaces that may be in the unique string.**

8. **Click in either the Host Name or Points To text box and type** google.com.

9. **If there is a text box or drop-down list for TTL, enter the default value (usually 1 Hour) and click OK.**

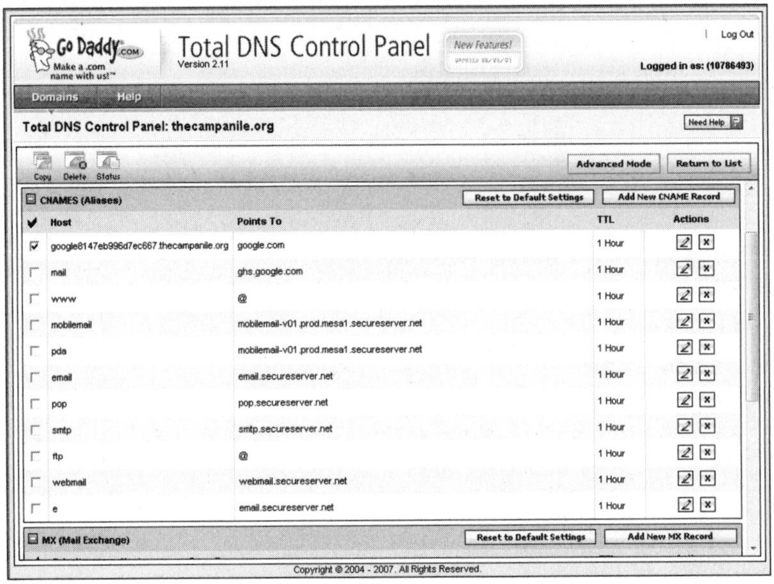

**Figure 2-15:**
The DNS
control
panel for
GoDaddy.
com.

**10. Return to the Google Apps Dashboard and click the first link in the Verify Your Domain Ownership page's Step 4.**

If you configured the correct CNAME record with your registrar, the link loads Google's main search page. If the Google search page doesn't appear, your CNAME record isn't correct. Try repeating Steps 3 through 10.

**11. If clicking the link correctly loads www.google.com, click the Verify button.**

That's it! You've successfully registered for Google Apps *and* completed your domain verification. Google may take up to 48 hours to verify your domain. A message appears along the top of your Dashboard after Google has officially verified you, and you can then activate all your apps.

# Chapter 3

---

# The Start Page

*Y*ou can find a lot of information out there on the Internet. Wouldn't it be nice to bring your e-mail, news headlines, and games all together in one place? Well, you can with one of the most important Google Apps — the Start Page.

The Start Page is based on the popular iGoogle personalized page (`www.google.com/ig`) offered to normal Google users. If you've used iGoogle before, you'll be right at home with the Start Page. In fact, a lot of what we cover in this chapter can be helpful to anyone who wants to make the most of iGoogle, as well.

With the Start Page, you can display all the information that's useful to you in a single location. Little Web programs called gadgets make this setup possible. *Gadgets* are essentially mini Web pages created to show specific information, such as news or weather. The Start Page is fully customizable, so you can choose which gadgets you see and interact with. You don't have a limit to the number of gadgets you can add to your Start Page.

To help you out, Google maintains a whole directory of gadgets that let you see and interact with your e-mail, calendar, documents, chat contacts, weather, sports, news headlines, snippets from your favorite Web sites, mini-games, comic strips, YouTube videos, and a plethora of other useful or fun stuff. After you add gadgets to your page, you can move them around to create the perfect launch pad for all your Google Apps and beyond.

In this chapter, we show you how to access your Start Page, help you authenticate your Google Apps account when you log in for the first time, add and remove gadgets to your Start Page, and help you resolve some basic Start Page issues.

If you are an administrator and want to customize the Start Page template for your group or organization, check out Chapter 15.

# Meeting the Start Page

When your organization makes the switch to Google Apps, you should receive your username and password from your administrator. Sometimes, this information comes in an e-mail message to your old e-mail account, or you may receive a printout directly from your administrator in the mail. The instructions include your username, a temporary password, your e-mail address, and the Start Page address for any new Google Apps account, as shown in Figure 3-1.

You can always check with your administrator if you haven't received your login information or have forgotten your password.

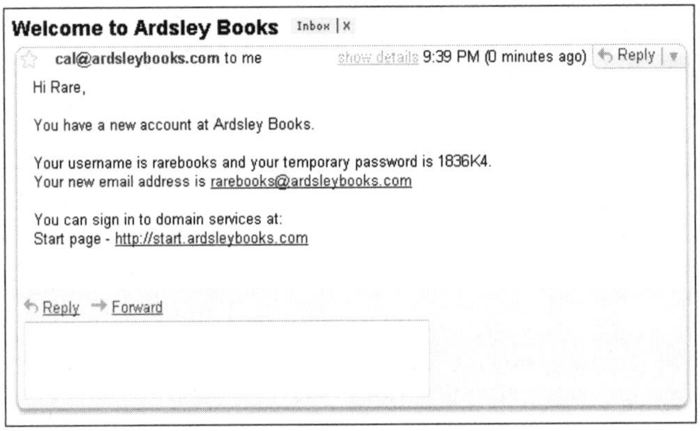

**Figure 3-1:**
Your system administrat-or gives you a username and temporary password.

> **Welcome to Ardsley Books**  Inbox | X
>
> ☆  cal@ardsleybooks.com to me        show details 9:39 PM (0 minutes ago)  ↩ Reply | ▾
>
> Hi Rare,
>
> You have a new account at Ardsley Books.
>
> Your username is rarebooks and your temporary password is 1836K4.
> Your new email address is rarebooks@ardsleybooks.com
>
> You can sign in to domain services at:
> Start page - http://start.ardsleybooks.com
>
> ↩ Reply  → Forward

If you haven't received your login information, you can still follow along with the setup process outlined in this chapter, but you have to make all your changes again after you log in.

Open your Web browser and navigate to your organization's Start Page. The default address will look something like `http://start.yourdomain.com`. You can also access your page at `http://partnerpage.google.com/yourdomain.com` (replace `yourdomain.com` with your organization's domain name).

Your administrator has likely already set up a custom Start Page template for your organization. A typical Start Page has a search box and three customizable columns, as shown in Figure 3-2. Your administrator has the option to lock the left column (for example, if that column contains links to company procedures or announcements) so that you can't edit it. If the gadgets in the left column are a different color than the rest of the gadgets or they won't move when you try to change them, that column is locked. You can't close gadgets in a locked column either because they don't have an X button.

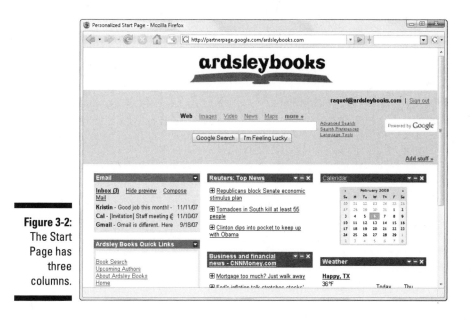

**Figure 3-2:**
The Start
Page has
three
columns.

Take a moment to familiarize yourself with your Start Page. When you're ready to start customizing it, click the Sign In link in the top-right corner. On the next screen, enter your username and password in the Username and Password text boxes, respectively, and click the Sign In button.

# Authenticating Your Account

Before you begin using any of the Google Apps for the first time, you may need to authenticate your account. Authentication tells the system that you're a real user. It also lets your administrator know that you're able to log into your Google Apps account. If you've successfully logged in before, feel free to jump ahead to the following section.

To authenticate your account, follow these steps:

1. **Open your Web browser and navigate to your organization's Start Page (for example, `http://start.ardsleybooks.com`).**

2. **Click the Sign In link in the top-right corner.**

3. **Enter your username and temporary password in the Username and Password text boxes, respectively, and then click the Sign In button.**

   The authentication screen appears, as shown in Figure 3-3.

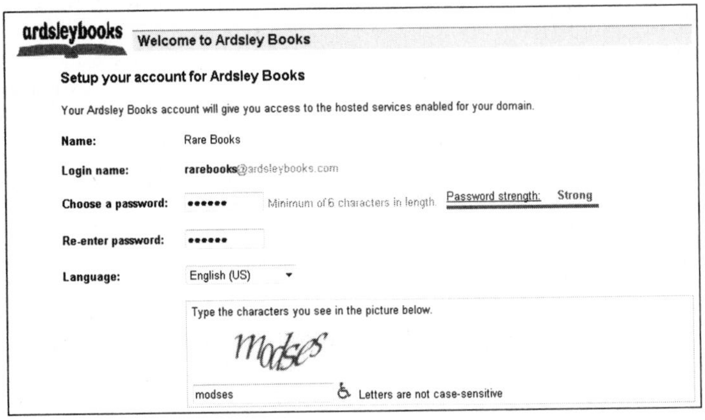

**Figure 3-3:**
Create a
password
and
authenticate
your new
Google Apps
account.

**Figure 3-3:** Create a password and authenticate your new Google Apps account.

4. **Enter a new password in the Choose a Password text box and then enter it again in the Re-enter Password text box.**

   Choose a password that people can't easily guess or figure out. Because you need at least six characters, we recommend you use a mix of upper- and lowercase letters, numbers, and symbols to make your password harder to guess or crack. The password strength bar on the authentication screen helps you see how strong and secure your password is. Green is good!

5. **Select your language from the Language drop-down list.**

6. **Click in the text box below the jumbled letters and enter the letters that you see.**

   If you have difficulty interpreting the letters, don't worry — they confuse a lot of other people too. You may have to try it once or twice before you get it just right. The wheelchair icon to the right of the text box will help users with visual impairment by playing an audio version of the jumbled letters.

7. **Scroll down to the bottom of the screen, read the Terms of Use policy (it's the fine print inside the box), and click the I Accept. Create My Account button.**

If authentication works correctly, you're taken back to your own, shiny new Start Page. If the authentication doesn't work, try repeating the steps in the preceding list a few times, correcting the fields that are highlighted in red.

## Gadgets demystified

Google Gadgets are made up of little pieces of code (such as HTML, JavaScript, Flash, and XML) and are designed to accomplish specific tasks, such as display a clock, calculator, or game. The idea behind gadgets isn't new. The original Macs had little computer applications called *desk accessories,* such as Calculator, Note Pad, and Puzzle. PDAs, such as the Palm Treo, also use these mini apps. As computers have become more interactive and Internet-enabled, computer operating systems and mobile devices have incorporated gadgets. Macs now use Dashboard widgets. Windows Vista has gadgets. Yahoo! Widgets and Google Desktop both allow users to add gadgets to their computers. Even your iPhone uses gadgets. With iGoogle and the Google Start Page, anyone can choose the gadgets they want and access them from any Web browser. What do you want to make your gadgets do?

After you've been thoroughly frustrated by those pesky jumbled letters, ask your administrator for help if authentication still doesn't work. Be sure to let your administrator know which step is giving you issues.

# *Adding Google Gadgets*

Adding Google Gadgets is a snap. Google maintains a directory of hundreds of gadgets that companies and users have created. Those gadgets put the information that's useful to you at your fingertips. In the following sections, we introduce you to the Google gadget directory, help you customize your Start Page, and show you how to use the gadgets for key Google Apps.

Before you start playing around with your Start Page gadgets, be sure that you're logged in. If you aren't, you have to make the changes all over again the next time you come to the Start Page.

You can easily set your Start Page as your home page. In Firefox, load your Start Page and then choose Tools⇨Options; in the Options dialog box that appears, select the Main tab, click the Use Current Page button, and click OK. In Internet Explorer, load your Start Page and then choose Tools⇨Internet Options; in the Internet Options dialog box that appears, select the General tab, click the Use Current button, and click OK.

## Checking out the gadget directory

To access the gadget directory, click the Add Stuff link near the top of the Start Page. The directory looks similar to Figure 3-4 (the items that appear vary because Google adds new gadgets all the time). When you find a gadget you like, click the Add It Now button just below the gadget to place it on your Start Page (you can always remove it later).

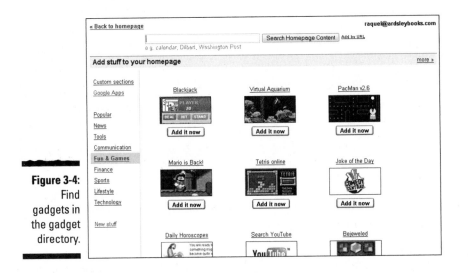

**Figure 3-4:**
Find gadgets in the gadget directory.

The main gadget categories, which you can access by clicking a category name in the left column, are as follows:

- ✔ **Custom Sections:** If your administrator has added custom gadgets, such as organization links, company calendars, and so on, you can find them here.

- ✔ **Google Apps:** Add gadgets for Gmail, Google Docs, Google Talk, and Google Calendar to give yourself one-click access from your Start Page. (Later in this section, we show you how to use and customize these gadgets.)

- ✔ **Popular:** Find gadgets that other people use a lot, such as weather and photo albums.

- ✔ **News:** Keep track of the latest headlines from your favorite news service, such as CNN or BBC News.

- ✔ **Tools:** Need to find information? Here, you can add dictionaries, Wikipedia, to-do lists, and more.

- **Communications:** Add your other e-mail services, instant messaging clients, and more to keep in touch with the important people in your life.

- **Fun & Games:** Time wasters? Mind sharpeners? You decide — just be sure to hide your Solitaire game when your boss shows up.

- **Finance:** Follow your stock portfolio or the market, in general. From news to market summaries, you can find a gadget for it here.

- **Sports:** Know how your favorite teams are doing without having to check the Sports page. Add ESPN or search the directory for your favorite team.

- **Lifestyle:** Horoscopes, recipes, lyrics, date ideas, and pop culture — they have gadgets for all that, too.

- **Technology:** Release your inner geek with tech news and trends.

- **New Stuff:** Don't forget that Google and other Web developers are releasing new gadgets all the time. Check here for the latest and greatest Start Page tools.

In addition to browsing these categories, you can enter a search term at the top of the gadget directory and click the Search Homepage Content button at the top of the page to find a specific gadget. If you're interested in making your own gadget for your Start Page, search Google for *make your own gadget* or visit www.google.com/ig/gmchoices.

After you add the gadgets that you want — and we bet you probably add more than you thought you would — click the Back to Homepage link at the top of the page to return to your Start Page.

Back on the Start Page, you can use the small buttons on the gadget title bar to customize your gadgets, as shown in Figure 3-5. Here's what the buttons do:

- **Down-arrow:** Click the down-arrow in the title bar of the gadget to show a list of options. Click Edit Settings from the list to make basic gadget adjustments, if they're available. After you make your changes, click Save. You can also use this list to find similar gadgets or find out more about the gadget's creator.

- **Hide/Show:** Clicking the minus button minimizes your gadget and shows only the title bar. Click the plus button to make your gadget reappear. Sorry, you can't minimize gadgets that show up in the locked column.

- **Close:** Click the X button to remove the gadget from your Start Page. Go back to the gadget directory if you want to add that gadget again later. When you click this button, a yellow bar appears below the main search box that lets you undo the removal if you clicked the button by accident.

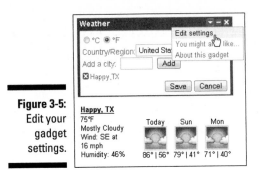

**Figure 3-5:**
Edit your
gadget
settings.

# Creating your perfect layout

After you add the gadgets that will (hopefully) help you be more productive (see the preceding section for how to add gadgets), you can practice your organizational skills and move the gadgets where you want them.

To move a gadget, simply click and drag the gadget's title bar to the location you want, as shown in Figure 3-6. When you move the gadget, a dashed box will follow your gadget around the page and move the other gadgets out of your way so you know exactly what your new arrangement will look like. Find the location that you want and release the mouse button. That's it!

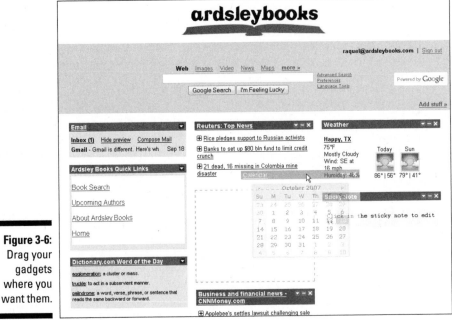

**Figure 3-6:**
Drag your
gadgets
where you
want them.

You can't move gadgets to or from a locked column. Your administrator wants you to have that information for a reason. Hang loose — you can still go crazy with the other two columns!

## *Previewing your Inbox*

The Gmail/Email gadget (see Figure 3-7) almost always shows up by default on your Start Page and shows you your most recent messages. This gadget features the following useful links:

- ✔ **Inbox (#):** See how many new messages you have and go directly to your e-mail inbox.

- ✔ **Hide/Show Preview:** View your most recent messages in the e-mail gadget. Or not.

- ✔ **Compose Mail:** Click this link to skip the mailbox and start writing a new message in a new window.

If you don't see the Gmail gadget, click the Add Stuff link, click the Google Apps link, and finally, click the Add It Now button below the Gmail gadget. (You can find out more about Gmail in Chapters 4 through 6.)

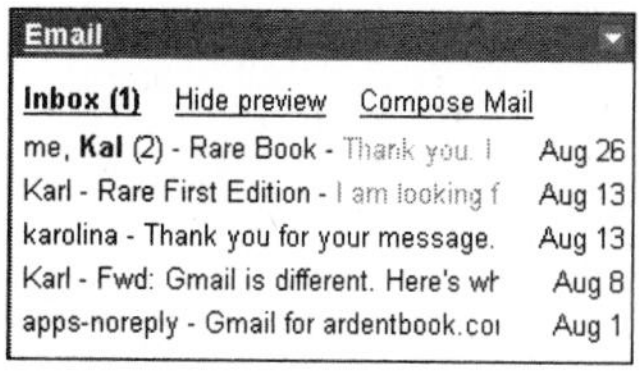

**Figure 3-7:**
**Keep on**
**top of your**
**e-mail.**

| Email | | |
|---|---|---|
| **Inbox (1)** Hide preview Compose Mail | | |
| me, **Kal** (2) - Rare Book - Thank you. | | Aug 26 |
| Karl - Rare First Edition - I am looking f | | Aug 13 |
| karolina - Thank you for your message. | | Aug 13 |
| Karl - Fwd: Gmail is different. Here's wh | | Aug 8 |
| apps-noreply - Gmail for ardentbook.cor | | Aug 1 |

## *Seeing what's happening on your Calendar*

Use the Google Calendar gadget, shown in Figure 3-8, to keep on top of what's going on. Click the Google Calendar title to go directly to your calendar. If you access your Start Page after you log into your calendar, you see the following additional features:

- ✔ **Create Event:** Opens a new window and lets you add a new appointment directly to your calendar.

- ✔ **Show/Hide Agenda:** View your upcoming events in the gadget. You can also click a day on the mini-calendar to see events for that day. Click Hide Agenda if you don't want to see your events here.

**Google Calendar**

| « | | October 2007 | | | | » |
|---|---|---|---|---|---|---|
| S | M | T | W | T | F | S |
| 23 | 24 | 25 | 26 | 27 | 28 | 29 |
| 30 | 1 | 2 | 3 | 4 | 5 | 6 |
| 7 | 8 | 9 | 10 | 11 | 12 | 13 |
| 14 | 15 | 16 | 17 | 18 | 19 | 20 |
| 21 | 22 | 23 | 24 | 25 | 26 | 27 |
| 28 | 29 | 30 | 31 | 1 | 2 | 3 |
| 4 | 5 | 6 | 7 | 8 | 9 | 10 |

Create Event  Hide Agenda

*Today*                                   **Sat 10/13**
              *No events on October 13*
*Next Week*                               **Mon 10/15**
12:00pm  Author meeting
                                          **Wed 10/17**
9:00am  Editor review
                                          **Thu 10/18**
6:30pm  Book launch party
*In 2 weeks*                              **Mon 10/22**
12:00pm  Author meeting

**Figure 3-8:**
Jump
quickly
to your
Calendar.

If you don't see the Google Calendar gadget on your Start Page, click the Add Stuff link, click the Google Apps link, and finally, click the Add It Now button below the Google Calendar gadget. Turn to Chapters 8 and 9 to discover more about Google Calendar.

You can customize your Calendar settings to edit your date and time format, as well as show and hide the mini-calendar.

## Viewing your latest Docs

The Google Docs gadget displays your most recent documents, spreadsheets, and presentations, as Figure 3-9 shows. This gadget may ask you to sign into Google Docs before it shows your current list. Click the Sign In link to go to your docs. When you return to the Start Page (simply re-enter your Start Page address in your browser again), your list will show your recent Docs. Here are the key Docs links:

- ✔ **New:** Click this menu to create a new document, presentation, or spread-sheet directly from the gadget.
- ✔ **View All Items:** Go directly to your Docs Home and view all your documents.

**Figure 3-9:**
Open your
most recent
Docs.

| **Google Docs** | |
|---|---|
| Author Schedule | 7:20 pm |
| Author Presentation | 7:19 pm |
| Fall Book Sales Figures | Oct 8 |
| New Book Flyer | Aug 11 |
| New ▾   View all items | |

If you don't see the Google Docs gadget, click the Add Stuff link, click the Google Apps link, and finally, click the Add It Now button below the Google Docs gadget. Part III of this book covers Google Docs in depth.

The Google Docs gadget shows five documents by default. You can edit the gadget settings to preview more or less, and to hide or show the last edit date.

## Chatting with your contacts

Use the Google Talk gadget to see whether your contacts are online and begin chatting with them. The Google Talk gadget, shown in Figure 3-10, gets a whole section in Chapter 7, so we don't go into details about how to use it here.

If you don't see the Google Talk gadget on your Start Page, click the Add Stuff link, click the Google Apps link, and finally, click the Add It Now button below the Google Talk gadget.

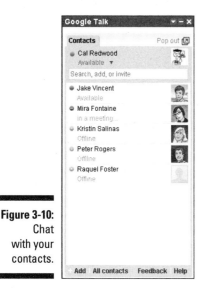

**Figure 3-10:**
Chat
with your
contacts.

# What to Do When the Start Page Misbehaves

Once in a great while, your Start Page may not load correctly or a gadget may not function properly. If this happens, don't panic! You can fix the problem pretty simply. Try each of the following troubleshooting options to restore your Start Page to a peaceful state:

- ✔ **Restart your Web browser.** Close all your browser windows, wait a moment, and then open your browser again. Return to your Start Page.

- ✔ **Remove the troublesome gadget and add it again from the gadget directory.** Gadgets are updated from time to time, so if you find a bug, replacing the gadget usually fixes it.

- ✔ **Clear your browser's cache.** Sometimes, the files in your browser cache become corrupted. In Firefox, choose Tools⇨Clear Private Data; in the Clear Private Data dialog box that appears, select the Cache check box, and then click the Clear Private Data Now button. Restart Firefox. In Internet Explorer, choose Tools⇨Internet Options; on the General tab in the Internet Options dialog box that appears, click the Delete button in the Browsing History section. In the Delete Browsing History dialog box that appears, click the Delete Files button. Restart Internet Explorer.

- ✔ **Search the Google Apps Help Center.** Go to the bottom of your Start Page and click the Help link or visit `www.google.com/support/a/users`.

# Part II
# Keeping in Touch and on Time: Gmail, Talk, and Calendar

The 5th Wave          By Rich Tennant

"He saw your laptop and wants to know if he can check his Gmail."

# *In this part . . .*

In this part of the book, we cover the Google Apps that you're most likely to use every day. Sliced bread wishes it was as cool as Gmail. That's why we dedicate three chapters to it, which include a discussion of the Google Apps Contact List. We also cover Talk, Google's integrated chat technology. We show you the ins and outs of Talk — before you know it, you'll be communicating like a pro!

Don't forget about Google Calendar. We didn't! In the two Calendar-focused chapters in this part, we take you through Calendar in a jiffy, and pretty soon, everyone will be asking you what's happening. For those of you who love your Outlook, or other popular e-mail and calendar software, we help you make sure you don't miss a beat.

# Chapter 4

# Connecting with Gmail

*H*ave you ever felt besieged by e-mail as you go through the daily ritual of purging your Inbox? Messages appear unrelentingly. Many are trivial, others are inane, and then you have *spam* — unsolicited ads for products too bizarre to mention. You have to deal with the time-consuming tasks of sifting through your Inbox for important messages and filing away old messages so you can find them later. You also have to decide what messages to delete so you don't exceed your mailbox size limit.

Responding to e-mail can eat into your day, taking valuable time away from more important tasks, such as enjoying a leisurely lunch. For businesses, schools, and agencies, e-mail has become a necessary evil. It's costly to maintain, and the service level, software quality, and reliability often suffer from a potential lack of resources.

Gmail is Google's answer to the daily e-mail onslaught. It's Google's interpretation of how e-mail should work. Gmail can help you battle back and get control of your Inbox, eliminating many of the frustrations associated with the spam-clogged, virus-ridden e-mail systems of the past.

In this chapter, we get you up and running quickly with Gmail. We start by explaining some of the innovations that make Gmail unique, and then we run you through the basics. In Chapter 5, you can find out about Gmail's advanced searching, sorting, archiving, and filtering solutions. Chapters 6 and 7 build your expertise with Gmail's Contacts list, built-in chat tool, and the related Google Talk App.

 Sorry, Team Edition users, you're stuck with your old e-mail system — for now. If you like Gmail, talk to the decision makers at your school or workplace about how cool it would be if everyone used Gmail, and maybe they'll make the switch to Google Apps!

# Setting Up E-mail

An *e-mail* is a message sent electronically over the Internet. Messages can go from one person to another or from one person to a group. Electronic mail finds its way through the Internet by following an address. Every e-mail address has three parts, as shown in Figure 4-1:

✔ The username, nickname, buddy name, or handle of the account owner.

✔ The characteristic @ sign (pronounced "at").

✔ The name of the domain or Web site that hosts the e-mail service.

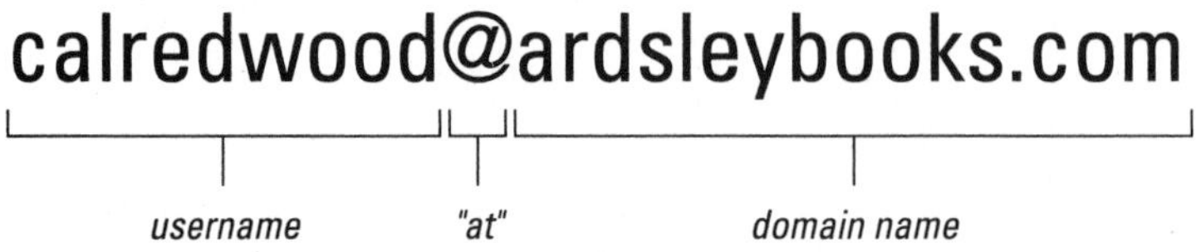

**Figure 4-1:**
An e-mail address has three parts.

calredwood@ardsleybooks.com

*username*          *"at"*          *domain name*

If your organization has Google Apps running, you probably already have your username and password, which means you can start using Gmail immediately. (Check with your administrator if you don't have this information.) Even though Google's servers save all your incoming and outgoing messages, your e-mail address probably carries the name of your company, school, or organization. Normally, your username serves as the prefix for your e-mail address, followed by @ and your organization's domain name, as shown in Figure 4-1. If your system is set up differently, talk to your system administrator to find out the specifics about your Google Apps implementation.

## Gmail: Safe and sound

Every business and organization in every corner of the globe needs reliable e-mail. Google servers are running 99.99 percent of the time — which is great by any standard. Gmail is not stored on someone's computer or on a local server, so if your computer gets lost with your luggage at Denver International Airport or the battery blows up and torches your laptop, no worries! You just need any computer with an Internet connection, and you're right back in business.

To keep the mail safe and working trouble-free, Google stores and maintains Gmail in its immense data centers. Even if your local servers crash, again, no worries! Google redundantly backs up all Gmail as a precaution on other Google servers dotted around the world, so it's highly unlikely that Gmail will ever lose your e-mail.

## Blame Ray!

If you want to blame someone for your daily deluge of Inbox-clogging e-mail, Ray Tomlinson is as good a candidate as anyone. He single-handedly created e-mail long before the World Wide Web was even a glimmer in Tim Berners-Lee's eye. In fact, e-mail is one of the oldest Internet applications still in widespread use.

Back in 1971, Ray Tomlinson successfully tested the first use of e-mail while working on the Department of Defense's ARPANET project. The early supercomputers used a program called SNDMSG (short for SeND MeSsaGe). Technicians, such as Tomlinson, used that program to leave messages for their colleagues working on the same supercomputer. Thompson figured out a way to make SNDMSG work between super-computers over the supercomputing network.

Tomlinson calculated that a network username could serve as a prefix, such as `calredwood`, and the network domain name counted as a suffix, such as `ardsleybooks.com`. He separated the two names by an @, creating the very effective user e-mail addressing system that we use today; for example, `calredwood@ardsleybooks.com`.

Tomlinson's colleagues liked his idea and started using the innovation, thus piloting one of the most revolutionary technologies in history. Tomlinson, however, remained low-key about his impact on history, probably because he didn't want to get blamed for all the spam that soon followed. For the record, Tomlinson didn't invent spam. But we know who did.

Before you begin using Gmail for the first time, you may need to authenticate your account. Flip back to Chapter 3 to discover how to do this authentication.

# Starting Gmail

You can get to your Gmail account in a couple of ways. The most convenient method is to use the Email gadget on your organization's Start Page (we describe the Email gadget in Chapter 3). With the Email gadget, you can view recent messages and access some common Gmail tools directly from your Start Page. You can also load Gmail by clicking the Inbox link or the Email gadget title. If you don't want to use your Start Page, you can load your organization's Gmail address directly in your browser, as described in the "Starting Gmail directly" section.

## Opening Gmail from a Start Page gadget

Open your browser and navigate to your Start Page. After you come to your Start Page, look for the Email gadget, shown in Figure 4-2. As we describe in Chapter 3, you may find this gadget very useful. It allows you to monitor incoming e-mail messages without actually having to open Gmail itself. If you see a message that you want to reply to quickly, just click it, and you can send an instant reply. However, if you decide you need to do more than send a few quick replies, click the Inbox link, and the fully featured version of Gmail opens.

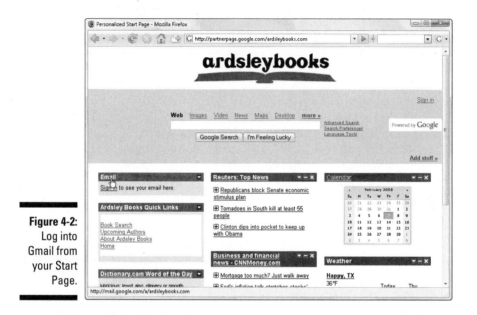

**Figure 4-2:**
Log into
Gmail from
your Start
Page.

If you want to view your personal (as in, nonwork) Google Apps and gadgets in a personalized Start Page with your own Gmail address, you can set one up by taking advantage of iGoogle (www.google.com/ig). Check out Chapter 3 to find out more about setting up a Start Page for your own personal Google Apps.

## *Starting Gmail directly*

If, for some reason, you don't want to use your organization's Start Page, you can access your e-mail directly by typing **mail** and the domain name of your organization in the address bar and pressing Enter; for example, an employee of Ardsley Books types the address **mail.ardsleybooks.com**. This address takes you to your Gmail login page, as shown in Figure 4-3. On this page, you can log into your e-mail account directly.

You need to log in with your username and password every time you begin a new session of Gmail unless you select the Remember Me on This Computer check box.

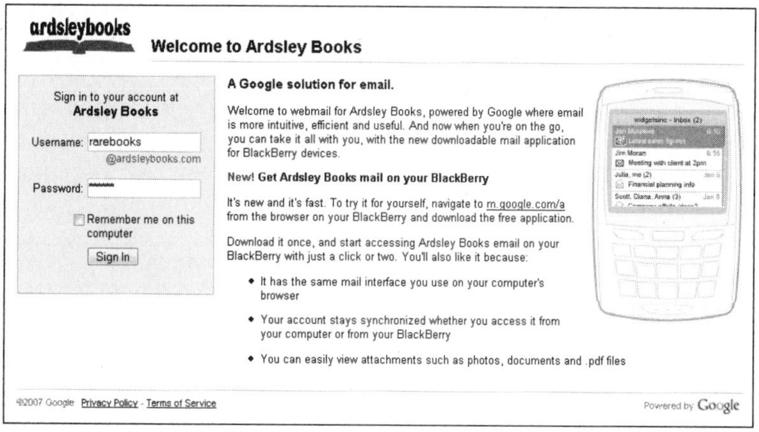

**ardsleybooks**

**Welcome to Ardsley Books**

Sign in to your account at
**Ardsley Books**

Username: rarebooks
@ardsleybooks.com

Password: ▪▪▪▪▪▪

☐ Remember me on this
computer

[Sign In]

**A Google solution for email.**

Welcome to webmail for Ardsley Books, powered by Google where email is more intuitive, efficient and useful. And now when you're on the go, you can take it all with you, with the new downloadable mail application for BlackBerry devices.

**New! Get Ardsley Books mail on your BlackBerry**

It's new and it's fast. To try it for yourself, navigate to m.google.com/a from the browser on your BlackBerry and download the free application.

Download it once, and start accessing Ardsley Books email on your BlackBerry with just a click or two. You'll also like it because:

* It has the same mail interface you use on your computer's browser

* Your account stays synchronized whether you access it from your computer or from your BlackBerry

* You can easily view attachments such as photos, documents and .pdf files

©2007 Google  Privacy Policy · Terms of Service

Powered by Google

**Figure 4-3:**
Go directly
to your
e-mail's
login page.

# *Getting to Know the Inbox*

When you open Gmail, you go directly to your Inbox. Any message coming to you first arrives in your Inbox. From your Inbox, you can access any feature within Gmail by using the navigation panel on the left side of the screen and the other links all around the page. Here are the key parts, as shown in Figure 4-4:

✔ **Links to other Google Apps:** Quickly jump to your Start Page, Calendar, Documents, and more by clicking the links at the top-left corner of the screen.

✔ **Your e-mail address:** In case you forget, Gmail gives you a friendly reminder up at the top.

If you have more than one Gmail account, you can always tell which account you're currently using by looking at your e-mail address at the top of the Gmail window.

✔ **Search Mail and Search the Web:** Enter a term in the text box and click the Search Mail button to search your messages for the term; click the Search the Web button to do a normal Google search.

✔ **Compose Mail:** Click this link to open a message window in which to write a new e-mail message.

✔ **Inbox, Starred, Chats, Sent Mail, Drafts, All Mail, Spam, Trash:** These links take you to the standard folders that hold your messages.

✔ **Incoming messages:** Your messages appear in the center of the screen, and any new messages appear in bold. Messages that you've already read have a shaded background.

✔ **Labels:** The equivalent of folders for Sent Mail, Drafts, Trash, and so on. If you have created your own folders to organize your e-mail, these folders appear under the Labels heading.

**Figure 4-4:**
Find
everything
in Gmail's
Inbox.

The basic parts of the Inbox, described in the preceding list, are pretty standard fare for e-mail applications. What makes Gmail different (and better) than other e-mail applications is that it gives more than 6GB (gigabytes) of storage to all Standard and Education Edition users, and 25GB of storage for Premier Edition participants. Having such large personal storage capacity, and applying the power of the Google search engine to your e-mail, allows for a few changes in how you handle your e-mail:

✔ **Don't trash your messages.** Gmail encourages users to archive old messages, not trash them. With so much storage available, you don't need to delete messages that may have any possible importance later.

✔ **Start a conversation.** Gmail organizes e-mail into conversations by keeping track of whom you send e-mail to, what they say in response, and what you say to their replies. Gmail's conversation tracking is so unique that we dedicate the section "Following the Conversation" to it, later in this chapter.

✓ **Search instead of playing hide and seek.** With so many messages piling up day after day, you may have trouble finding a specific message in your incessantly swelling Inbox. No longer. Gmail takes advantage of Google's search technologies. If Google can find exactly what you need from the billions of pages on the Internet, imagine what it can do when searching a relatively tiny Inbox.

# Composing Mail

When you're ready to send an e-mail, click the Compose Mail link in the left column of your Inbox. One of the oldest, time-tested forms of online communication still in existence appears. Very little has changed in the way an e-mail form looks and works since its earliest days. E-mail stole its original format from the interoffice memo. The memo's classic organization gave us a few terms that don't actually apply to electronic messages, such as *Cc* (carbon copy).

E-mail forms are organized into fields. A few fields are required; others are optional. We discuss each of these fields in detail in the following sections. As you can see in Figure 4-5, here are the main parts of the mail form:

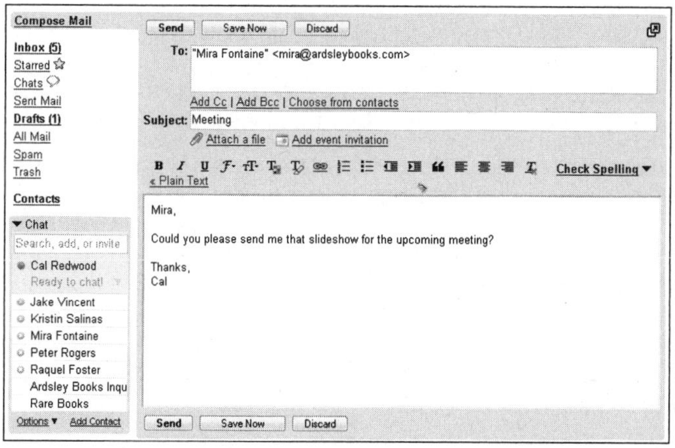

**Figure 4-5:**
The
Compose
Mail form.

✓ **Header:** In the header section, you indicate key message information, such as whom the message is going to and what it's about. The header section includes the To, Cc, Bcc, and Subject text boxes. (See the following sections for everything you need to know about these text boxes.) It also includes the Attach a File link, as well as the Send, Save Now, and Discard buttons. (See the "Attaching files" and "Sending, saving, or discarding" sections, later in this chapter, for details.)

✔ **Body:** The meat of the message goes in the body section. This section also includes the Formatting toolbar and Spell Check tools. (Check out the "Composing your message" section, later in this chapter, for more information.)

To send an e-mail message, follow these basic steps:

1. **Click in the To text box and enter the addresses to which you want to send the message.**

   Optionally, click the Add Cc button to see the Cc and Bcc text boxes. You can then enter more addresses in the Cc and Bcc text boxes.

2. **Click in the Subject text box and enter a subject.**

3. **Click in the message field and type what you want to say.**

4. **Click the Send button.**

In the following sections, we talk more in depth about each of the steps in the preceding list.

## Entering addresses

Before you can send a message, you first need to address it to a recipient (or several recipients). To add a recipient for your message, follow these steps:

1. **If you're not already at the Compose Message screen, click the Compose Mail link in the left column of your Gmail screen.**

2. **Click in the To text box and type the e-mail address of the person to whom you want to send the message.**

   For example, in Figure 4-6, we typed **cal@ardsleybooks.com** for the first e-mail address.

   You place the e-mail address of the primary recipient or recipients in the To text box. This is a required field. If you don't put at least one e-mail address in this text box, you get a plea from Gmail saying, "Please specify at least one recipient."

3. **(Optional) Type a comma and then enter another e-mail address.**

   You can add as many e-mail addresses as you want.

4. **(Optional) If you have a long list of people to whom you're sending the message, click the Add Cc link, click in the Cc text box that appears, and type more addresses.**

5. **(Optional) If you want to send the same message to several people, but you don't want them all knowing to whom the message went, click the Add Bcc link, click in the Bcc text box that appears, and enter their addresses in the Bcc text box.**

Gmail automatically adds the e-mail address of anyone whom you e-mail, or who e-mails you, to your Contacts list. When you begin entering a few letters in the To or Cc text box, Gmail anticipates the address you're typing and displays recipient names containing those letters, as shown in Figure 4-6. Arrow down to the correct e-mail address. When it appears highlighted, press Enter or just choose it from the list. (You can find out much more about your Contacts list in Chapter 6.)

Gmail automatically enters the open (<) and close (>) angle brackets that appear before and after e-mail addresses. You don't need to enter them.

**Figure 4-6:**
Select
recipient
e-mail
addresses
from the list
that appears
after you
enter just a
few letters.

```
Send   Save Now   Discard                                          

To:  "Cal Redwood" <cal@ardsleybooks.com>, "Rare Books" <rarebooks@ardsleybooks.com>,

Cc:  mira@ardsleybooks.com

Bcc: ra

          "Raquel Foster" <raquel@ardsleybooks.com>
Subject:  "Rare Books" <rarebooks@ardsleybooks.com>
          Attach a file    Add event invitation
```

## Getting to the subject

In the Subject text box, you enter a few descriptive words to let your reader know what the e-mail message is about.

Many readers make a snap decision about the contents of the message just by reading the subject line, so get into the habit of writing snappy, interesting descriptions of your messages in the Subject text box. For business correspondence, keep your subject lines short and to the point.

## Composing your message

You compose all your great one-liners, tell your jokes, speak your mind, and set things straight in the message (or body) field. Simply click in the body text box and start typing away.

TIP

You can use the formatting buttons just above the body text box to apply bold, italics, colors, highlighting, and other formatting to your text, just like you do with a document in Google Docs or any rich-text editor. To apply text formatting, simply highlight the text that you want to format and click the appropriate formatting button.

## Attaching files

Quite often, you want to send a file along with an e-mail message. You can attach any file to an e-mail: a word processing document, a spreadsheet, a picture of your dog Charlie, or that video of your recent fishing trip. To attach a file to your message, follow these steps:

1. **Click the Attach a File link that appears below the Subject text box.**

2. **Browse to the particular file that you need, select it, and then click the Open button.**

   See Figure 4-7 for an example.

**Figure 4-7:** Browse to a file that you want to attach to your e-mail message.

The name of the attached file appears just below the subject line in your e-mail form. If you want to add another file, click the Attach Another File link that appears below the name of the file you already attached, as shown in Figure 4-8. You can attach files as large as 20MB (megabytes) to a Gmail message, which should be plenty unless you're planning to attach the collected works of Shakespeare or the 20 years' worth of family videos you converted to Quicktime files.

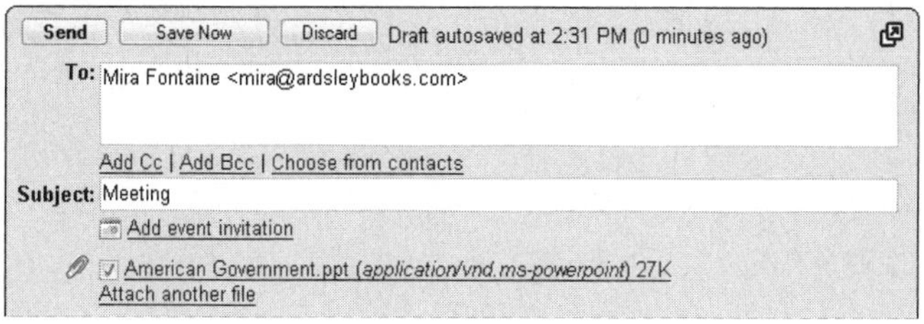

Figure 4-8:
See the
name of the
file you
attached
to your
message
and attach
another file.

| Send | Save Now | Discard | Draft autosaved at 2:31 PM (0 minutes ago) | |
|---|---|---|---|---|

To: Mira Fontaine <mira@ardsleybooks.com>

Add Cc | Add Bcc | Choose from contacts

Subject: Meeting

Add event invitation

☑ American Government.ppt *(application/vnd.ms-powerpoint)* 27K
Attach another file

## Sending, saving, or discarding

After you finish composing your message and adding any attachments you want (which we talk about in the preceding sections), you have three options:

- ✔ **Send:** Simply click the Send button, and your message whisks across the Internet at the speed of light, touching all the recipients anywhere in the world.

- ✔ **Save Now:** If you're having second thoughts about sending a particular e-mail message, or if you simply haven't finished it yet, you can save it and work on it later. To save your message, simply click the Save Now button.

- ✔ **Discard:** Many messages simply shouldn't be sent at all. Okay, you vented — or you exaggerated, or you suddenly realized that you don't know what the heck you're talking about. No harm done. Just click the Discard button and forget the whole thing.

Any e-mail message that you send can be forwarded to anyone else or subpoenaed by a court. Publicly traded companies must keep a record of all their e-mail. An e-mail message can come back to haunt you. And, it can exist forever in a recipient's private Inbox, where you can't delete it. Want to run for political office? You may want to think twice about sending that message flip-flopping on major issues or wildly exaggerating your role in single-handedly deterring global warming. Don't believe for a second that any e-mail conversation is private. E-mail has a habit of returning at the most inopportune moment.

## Following the Conversation

Gmail has a unique way of tracking your messages and all the related replies. In Google parlance, this tracking of related messages is called a *conversation.*

Think of a conversation among people. One person starts talking, a second person replies, another person chimes in, and so on. Gmail keeps track of the messages, just like the back-and-forth of a conversation, to maintain context and relevancy.

## Stack it up!

Gmail groups conversations by subject, making each group of messages into a *conversation stack*. Gmail stacks replies, one on top of another, in the order they're sent. The most recent replies appear at the top of the stack.

Think of a stack as a pile of cards, each containing the next part of a conversation. You can tell how many reply cards are in the stack by the number that appears in parentheses after the senders' names, as shown in Figure 4-9.

**Figure 4-9:**
You can view conversations in your Inbox.

| Start Page | **Mail** | Calendar | Documents | more » | | cal@ardsleybooks.com | Settings | Help | Sign out |

**ardsleybooks**

[ _____ ] [ Search Mail ] [ Search the Web ]  Show search options
Create a filter

**Compose Mail**

CNN.com Recently Published/Updated - Djokovic cruises to Vienna   Web Clip  < >  Customize

**Inbox (4)**   [ Archive ] [ Report Spam ] [ Delete ] [ More actions... ▾ ] Refresh          1 - 6 of 6
Starred ☆
Chats ◯   Select: All, None, Read, Unread, Starred, Unstarred
Sent Mail     ☐ ☆  me, Kal (2)         **Rare Book** - Thank you, I will buy it! Or   **Aug 26**
Drafts        ☐ ☆  **Karl Barksdale**   **Rare First Edition** - I am looking for a r  **Aug 13**
All Mail      ☐ ☆  karolina tonono     **Thank you for your message. Re: W** **Aug 13**
Spam          ☐ ☆  **Karl Barksdale**   **Fwd: Gmail is different. Here's what**  **Aug 8**
Trash         ☐ ☆  apps-noreply        Gmail for ardentbook.com - Bulk accoun  **Aug 1**
**Contacts**  ☐ ☆  Gmail Team          Gmail is different. Here's what you need  **Aug 1**

▾ Quick Contacts
Search, add, or invite   [ Archive ] [ Report Spam ] [ Delete ] [ More actions... ▾ ]         1 - 6 of 6
● Cal Redwood

Conversations are automatically brought to the top of your Inbox when someone replies to one of your messages. This list also displays each message's subject line, followed by a snippet of the message. These bits of information give you clues as to what the conversation is about. (Writing a clear subject line really helps you figure out a conversation's topic.) You can also see the date a message was sent at the end of the snippet. To view any conversation in the stack, pick it from the list by either clicking on the sender's name, subject line, or date. Click in any of these places and you can open that portion of the conversation. The conversation appears as a stack of messages, as shown in Figure 4-10.

Not only does the conversational approach remind you of the context of a new message, but you can also reply to any single part of a conversation. For example, say you have a conversation going with two recipients, and one recipient replies directly to you and not to the other person. Replying just to the sender doesn't impact the rest of the recipients in the stack.

**Figure 4-10:**
Reply
quickly to a
conver-
sation.

Stack headers give you a lot of information. First of all, you can tell exactly when the reply was sent by looking at the extra information provided in the top-right corner of the message in the stack. Also, you can send out related e-mails from each stack in the conversation:

- ✔ **Reply:** Reply only to the sender. You can find a Reply link at both the top and the bottom of the message.

- ✔ **Reply to All:** Click Reply to All to send a reply to everyone involved in the conversation. (Find Reply to All by clicking the down arrow next to the Reply button or jump to the bottom of the message window.)

- ✔ **Forward:** Send a copy of the e-mail message to anyone you want: the news media, your boss, the Federal Trade Commission, Homeland Security. . . . (Find Forward by clicking the down arrow next to the Reply button or jump to the bottom of the message window.)

Very few people enjoy sifting through replies that don't apply to them. The Reply to All command has annoyed millions of unhappy cubicle inhabitants in offices all over the world, so click it thoughtfully. If you're sending a reply intended for a single recipient, don't send it to everyone listed in the header. You really need to remember this bit of e-mail etiquette if you're replying to a message that was sent to the entire company.

## Collapsing and expanding conversation stacks

After you open a conversation stack, it appears in a collapsed view with the most recent reply open at the bottom. (Refer to Figure 4-10.) To expand the stack so that you can view all the conversations, click the Expand All link (it's to the right of the conversation stack). To collapse the conversations, click the Collapse All link. (See Figure 4-11.) To read just one reply or part of the conversation, click the snippet or header at the top of the particular message.

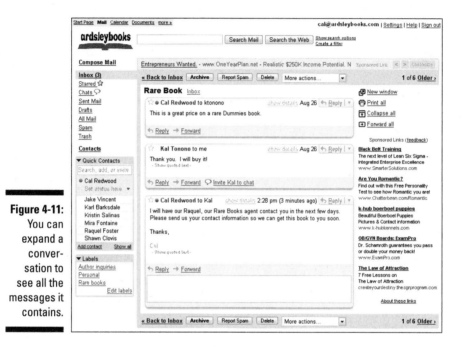

**Figure 4-11:**
You can
expand a
conver-
sation to
see all the
messages it
contains.

In the Collapse All mode, Gmail displays a snippet of the conversation at the top of each message.

## Marking important messages

Gmail gives you a simple way to highlight important messages. Whether you're in the Inbox or viewing a conversation, simply click the Star icon on the left side of the message header, and a bright, shiny star appears in the icon's place. (See Figure 4-12.) You can remove a star by clicking the Star icon again.

# Google Apps Gmail vs. public, ad-supported Gmail

Anyone can go online and get a Gmail account free from Google. If your organization isn't part of a Google Apps program, or if you want the convenience of Gmail at home, you can use Gmail by setting up your own personal account. Just go to http://mail.google.com and follow the setup instructions. Nearly everything we talk about in this book applies to public and Google Apps versions of Gmail.

Google Apps provides some extra features for businesses and organizations, allowing them to customize Gmail to fit their own specific business or organizational needs. An organization can customize the Google Apps version of Gmail with that organization's logo and domain address. Even though Google hosts the service, it stays out of sight. Google slips into the background and provides ways for an organization to promote its own brand and organizational identity. (The rest of this book provides a more comprehensive overview of how Google Apps integrates with the IT infrastructure of a business, school, or organization.)

Google pays for the free, public Gmail system with the ad revenue from the AdWords ads shown in the right panel of your e-mail messages. The ads themselves stay out of the way. Allowing AdWords advertising can bring certain advantages. Say you receive an e-mail from a friend telling you about the latest Toshiba laptops or Apple iPhone gadgets — you see ads relevant to the conversation. The ads give you a chance to look up information about a product that you're genuinely interested in.

However, businesses and schools can prohibit ads. Google provides alternatives by allowing businesses to pay a small fee for the service, eliminating the need for an ad-supported system.

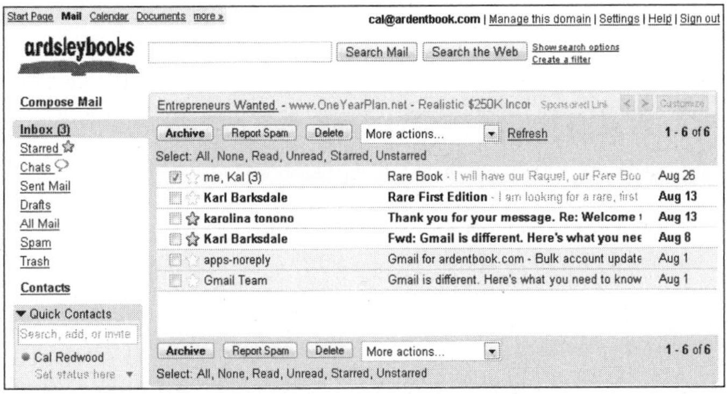

**Figure 4-12:** Mark the important messages with stars.

If you receive a lot of e-mail messages, you may end up with some of the important starred conversations pushed way to the bottom of your Inbox. You may have trouble finding some of your starred messages. To view all the messages that you've starred, click the Starred link in the left column.

Clicking this link hides your normal messages and shows only messages that have a yellow star on the left side of their headers. (Clicking the Inbox link shows you all your current messages.)

In the Inbox, the check boxes to the left of the stars (or Star icons) allow you to select many messages at the same time. After you select the check boxes to the left of messages, you can perform the following actions to all the selected messages (on a single viewable page of the Inbox):

✔ **Archive:** Archiving conversations places selected messages in storage and removes them from your Inbox. You may want to archive messages that you've already read. Archiving is a great way to save your messages, but get them out of your Inbox so you don't have to deal with the clutter.

✔ **Report Spam:** If you receive spam, select that message's check box and let Gmail know about it by clicking the Report Spam button. Reporting spam helps Gmail do a better job of stopping it in the future.

✔ **Delete:** Clicking the Delete button removes conversations from your Gmail account. Because you have so much storage capacity, you don't need to delete messages very often. Deleting a message only places the message in the Trash label. To get rid of the message permanently, you must go into the Trash label and delete it again from that screen.

When you archive or delete conversations, all the messages in that conversation move, not just the selected messages. If you archive a conversation, you can always search for it later. After you delete a conversation and empty the Trash label, you can't retrieve your message again.

## Searching Your Messages

You can use the same powerful tools that allow you to find exactly what you need on the Internet to find any lost e-mail messages in your Inbox. The search features can also search your archived messages.

To search your e-mail account for a particular message, follow these steps:

1. **Click in the Search text box that appears at the top of every Gmail account page and enter a search term.**

   For example, say you remember only a snippet of an e-mail sent to you, such as *Uncle Jake is having a birthday*. Enter the keywords *jake birthday*. You can search for e-mail addresses, subjects, or even text within a message. And the same rules that apply to a Google search on the Internet apply to your e-mail searches, as well:

- Statistics point out that a phrase of two to five words is better than a single keyword in narrowing down a search.

- If you put words in quotation marks (" "), Google searches for that exact phrase.

- You don't need to use capitalization.

2. **Click the Search Mail button.**

   As shown in Figure 4-13, Gmail returns a list of messages that contain the term(s) you enter in the Search text box in Step 1.

**Figure 4-13:**
Search your conversations by using the Search Mail feature.

# Chapter 5

# Discovering Advanced Gmail Tools

*I*n Chapter 4, we introduce you to the world of Gmail and give you a chance to dig in and get dirty with the basics. However, if you suffer from *infomania* (the tendency to get distracted by information overload from incoming e-mail) or have more than a healthy portion of *bacn* (mailing lists and newsletters that you subscribe to but may not want to read right away), we have some solutions for you in this chapter.

Besides helping you slim down your Inbox, this chapter helps you do other nifty stuff, such as enable vacation reminders, add signatures, and access your e-mail from Outlook or a cellphone. But first, we show you how well Gmail plays with file attachments.

## Opening Attachments

E-mail attachments are an important part of everyday life, and Google understands that. Every time you receive documents, spreadsheets, or presentations as attachments, you have three ways you can open them directly from Gmail: View as HTML, Open as a Google Document or Spreadsheet or View as Slideshow, or Download, as shown in Figure 5-1.

**Upcoming Event** Inbox | X

⭐ ● **Mira Fontain** show details         (0 minutes ago) 📎 ↩ Reply | ▼

Hi Cal,

Here are the files we discussed earlier today. Please take a look at the Press Release and Sales Figures documents and work on the presentation draft I have attached here.

Thanks,

Mira

_____

**3 attachments** — Download all attachments

📄 **Press Release.doc**
   50K   View as HTML   Open as a Google document   Download

📄 **Sales Figures.xls**
   21K   View as HTML   Open as a Google spreadsheet   Download

📄 **Business Preso.ppt**
   58K   View as HTML   View as slideshow   Download

↩ Reply   → Forward   ● Reply by chat to Mira

**Figure 5-1:**
Select an
option to
view your
attach-
ments.

# View as HTML

The first option is to view the attachment as a Web page right in your browser, as shown in Figure 5-2. You don't need any special plug-ins or software to view an attachment as HTML because Google uses special tools to extract the text and graphics so that you can preview the document right away. This method is also the fastest way to get to your important proposal or budget report. It works for PDF attachments, too.

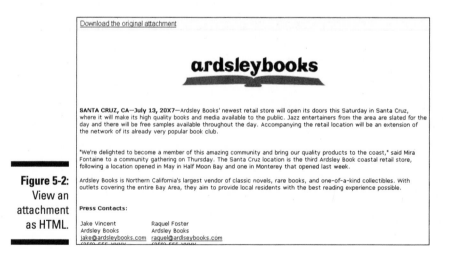

Download the original attachment

## ardsleybooks

SANTA CRUZ, CA—July 13, 20X7—Ardsley Books' newest retail store will open its doors this Saturday in Santa Cruz, where it will make its high quality books and media available to the public. Jazz entertainers from the area are slated for the day and there will be free samples available throughout the day. Accompanying the retail location will be an extension of the network of its already very popular book club.

"We're delighted to become a member of this amazing community and bring our quality products to the coast," said Mira Fontaine to a community gathering on Thursday. The Santa Cruz location is the third Ardsley Book coastal retail store, following a location opened in May in Half Moon Bay and one in Monterey that opened last week.

Ardsley Books is Northern California's largest vendor of classic novels, rare books, and one-of-a-kind collectibles. With outlets covering the entire Bay Area, they aim to provide local residents with the best reading experience possible.

**Press Contacts:**

Jake Vincent        Raquel Foster
Ardsley Books       Ardsley Books
jake@ardsleybooks.com   raquel@ardsleybooks.com

**Figure 5-2:**
View an
attachment
as HTML.

Although the HTML option does its best to show you the information quickly, documents that contain a lot of page layout and advanced formatting may not appear completely accurately.

## Open as a Google document

Rather than save the document to your computer, you can simply choose to open the attachment as a Google document or spreadsheet, or view a presentation as a slideshow, directly in your browser.

When you open an attachment in Google Docs, you can view and edit the document right away. In fact, Gmail copies the document into your Docs Home, and you can access that document any time you log into Google Docs. For more information on using Google Docs, check out Part III.

## Download

For documents that have advanced formatting, or don't open easily as HTML or a Google document, you still have the traditional download file method. Click the Download link to the right of the attachment, and the File Download dialog box appears, asking whether you want to open or save the file. If you would like to find the file on your computer later, we recommend that you click the Save button to save the file. The Save As dialog box will appear, giving you the option to navigate to the folder on your computer where you want to save the file. Finally, click the Save button to save the file.

Mail messages that contain multiple attachments also give you the option to download all your files at the same time in a Zipped archive. Click the Download All Attachments link to start saving yourself a lot of time by down-loading one smaller file. After you click the Download All Attachments link, the File Download dialog box appears. To make it easy for you to locate your files later, we recommend that you click the Save button to save the Zip file to your computer. The Save As dialog box appears, which will let you navigate to the folder where you want to save the file on your computer. Click the Save button to save the Zip file.

Don't forget, Google automatically scans your attachments for viruses. To keep you extra safe, Gmail never accepts attachments that contain exe-cutable files (files that end in .exe) or archives that contain executables. If you need to send or receive those types of files, you'll have to resort to another method of transporting the files, such as using FTP or a file transfer site (such as www.yousendit.com), burning them to a CD, or copying them to a flash thumb drive.

# Creating Signatures and Vacation Responses

Your communication reflects a lot about who you are and what you represent. If you're in touch with a lot of important people, we think it's a good idea to let them know how they can contact you in a way other than an e-mail address. You can most easily give this information by adding a signature that contains your contact information. You can set Gmail to automatically add a signature to new messages, which can save you more than a few keystrokes. Additionally, vacation responses help people know when you're decidedly unavailable. Whether you're on a trip to Hawaii or spending a quiet weekend at home, we can think of a ton of situations in which you may find Gmail's vacation responder handy.

In the following sections, we show you how to use both the Gmail signature and vacation responder — they're both incredibly simple to use.

## Adding a signature

To add a signature, log into your Gmail Inbox and click the Settings link in the top-right corner. Halfway down the Settings page, look for the Signature box, as shown in Figure 5-3.

**Figure 5-3:**
Add a
signature on
the Settings
page.

| Signature: | ○ No signature |
| (appended at the end of all outgoing messages) | ● Cal Redwood |
| | President, Ardsley Books |
| | 303-867-XXXX |
| | cal@ardsleybooks.com |

You can type whatever you want in the Signature box, but most people include their name, a phone number, perhaps a Web site URL, and a random quote (such as a Buddhist saying that only makes sense to another Buddhist). Make sure that the radio button to the left of the signature box is selected and click the Save Changes button at the bottom of the Settings page to make your signature active.

After you activate your signature, whenever you compose a new e-mail message, your signature appears in the message body automatically, as Figure 5-4 illustrates. Cool, huh?

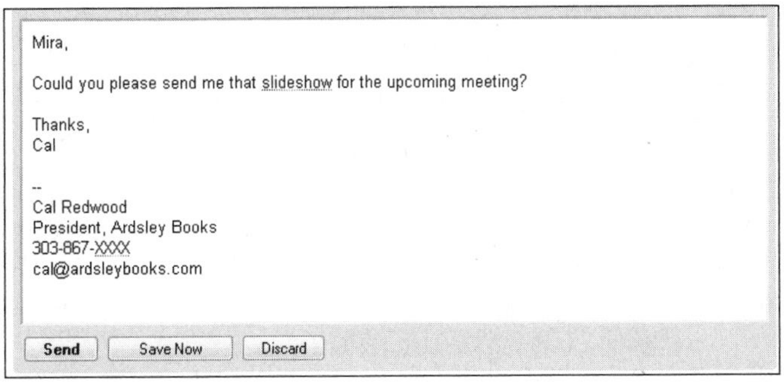

Figure 5-4:
New
messages
add the
signature
auto-
matically.

Mira,

Could you please send me that slideshow for the upcoming meeting?

Thanks,
Cal

--
Cal Redwood
President, Ardsley Books
303-867-XXXX
cal@ardsleybooks.com

Send    Save Now    Discard

## Turning the vacation responder on and off

When you're ready for your break from the everyday onslaught of e-mail, flip the switch to turn on your vacation responder. A *vacation responder* lets people who send you e-mails know that you're on vacation, out of the office, or otherwise can't get back to them right away. When someone e-mails you, Gmail will automatically send a message of your choosing informing the sender that you are unavailable at the moment. To turn your vacation responder on, follow these steps:

1. **Log into Gmail.**

2. **Click the Settings link in the top-right corner of the screen.**

   Near the bottom of the page, you can see the Vacation Responder section, as Figure 5-5 shows.

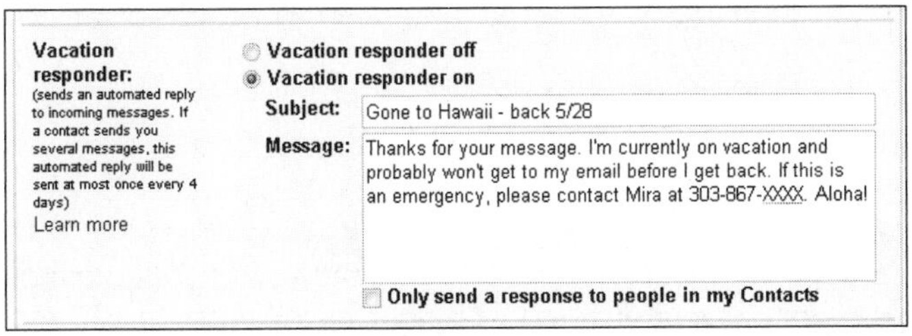

Figure 5-5:
Add a
vacation
responder
on the
Settings
page.

Vacation responder:
(sends an automated reply to incoming messages. If a contact sends you several messages, this automated reply will be sent at most once every 4 days)
Learn more

○ Vacation responder off
◉ Vacation responder on
  Subject: Gone to Hawaii - back 5/28
  Message: Thanks for your message. I'm currently on vacation and probably won't get to my email before I get back. If this is an emergency, please contact Mira at 303-867-XXXX. Aloha!

☐ Only send a response to people in my Contacts

3. **Select the Vacation Responder On radio button.**

4. **Click in the Subject and Message text boxes and enter a subject and message that let people who e-mail you know that you're on vacation (or otherwise unavailable).**

> If you use your Gmail for business, give contact information for someone who can cover for you while you're unavailable.

5. **(Optional) If you don't want everyone to know that you've snuck off on a weekend getaway to Rome, select the Only Send a Response to People in My Contacts check box.**

   When you select this check box, only people you know can receive the message from your vacation responder.

6. **Click the Save Changes button.**

   Now, Gmail notifies people who e-mail you that you've headed off to Fiji.

Vacation responders send only one e-mail per address every four days, and you can have only one vacation responder active at a time. Hopefully, your friends and associates catch the drift the first time.

When you activate your vacation responder, a peach bar appears along the top of your Gmail page, as shown in Figure 5-6. To turn off your responder, click the End Now link on the right side of the bar (or select the Vacation Responder Off radio button in Step 3). If you want to make changes or update your e-mail response, click the Vacation Settings link to the right of the End Now link.

**Figure 5-6:**
Turn off the
vacation
responder
by clicking
the End Now
link on the
peach bar.

| Google **Mail** Calendar Documents more » | cal@ardsleybooks.com | Manage this domain | Settings | Older version | Help | Sign out |
|---|---|
| Gone to Hawaii - back 5/28 | **End now  Vacation Settings** |

Search Mail    Search the Web    Show search options / Create a filter

# Using Labels and Filters to Take Control of Your Inbox

You can whip your Inbox into shape by using labels and filters. *Labels* are like folders, only better — they sort and organize your messages so that you can easily find a particular message later. *Filters* are sets of rules that every new e-mail message is checked against; if the message matches a rule, then Gmail performs an action with the message, such as starring or deleting it.

How can labels and filters help you? Imagine sending all your incoming work-related messages to one folder and your travel plans to another. Filters let you tell Gmail exactly where the messages should go, and labels help you organize messages that you've already received.

## Labeling your messages

Labels are one of the best ways to organize your messages. If you've used other e-mail programs before, you're probably used to creating folders and storing your messages in them. The problem with folders is that, many times, your messages fit in more than one folder, which means you have to remember in which folder you put those messages, often causing a lot of confusion and frustration when you need to find those messages later. Labels alleviate this problem by allowing you to tag messages and view all your similarly tagged messages in a list, much like a folder. Unlike folders, however, you don't have to move any messages around, and you can easily tag a message with multiple labels.

Think of it this way: You can find all the mail messages you've sent and received by clicking the All Mail link (it's in the list on the left, below the Drafts link). New messages are tagged with the Inbox label, so they appear in the Inbox. When you archive a message, the Inbox label is removed, and the message no longer appears in the Inbox list.

You can create your own set of labels and tag your messages so that similar messages appear together in a list without any folder confusion. Even though a message has a label, you can still find it by clicking the All Mail link or by using Gmail Search.

Click the Edit Labels link in the green labels box in the bottom-left corner of any Gmail screen. You can also click the Settings link at the top of the screen and then click the Labels tab, as shown in Figure 5-7. In the Labels tab, you can do the following:

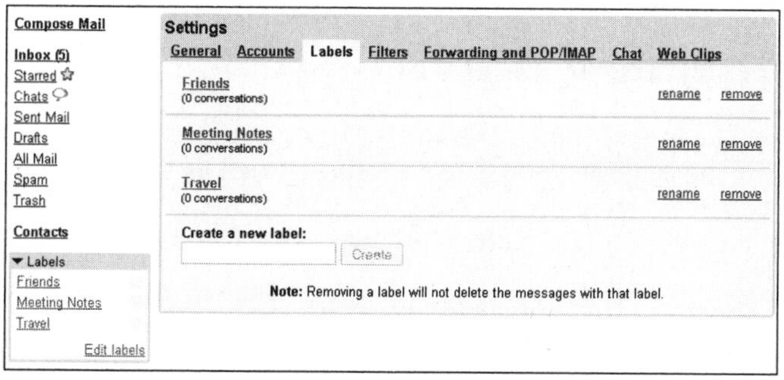

**Figure 5-7:** Click the Edit Labels link to add, rename, and remove labels on the Settings screen.

✔ **Add a new label:** Click in the Create a New Label text box and enter the new label's name, then click the Create button.

✔ **Rename a label:** Click the Rename link to the right of the label that you want to change. A blue box appears, allowing you to change the label name or enter a new label name. Click OK when you're done to return to the Labels Settings screen.

✔ **Delete a label:** Click the Remove link to the right of the label name. A dialog box appears, asking whether you really want to remove the label. Click OK, and the label disappears. When you delete a label, messages with that label stay in the Inbox (or the All Mail label if you have archived it previously).

When you're ready to tag a message or two, return to the Inbox. Select the check box for the message(s) that you want to tag, and then choose a label from the More Actions list at the top of the screen. The label that you choose now appears to the left of your message's subject, and your message appears when you click the corresponding label link on the left side of the screen. If the label you want doesn't exist, choose New Label from the More Actions list and then enter a name for your new label in the dialog box that appears.

You can also customize your labels by adding colors. Click the color square to the right of a label in the Labels list and choose the color that you want, as shown in Figure 5-8. Dark and bold colors can really make more important messages stand out.

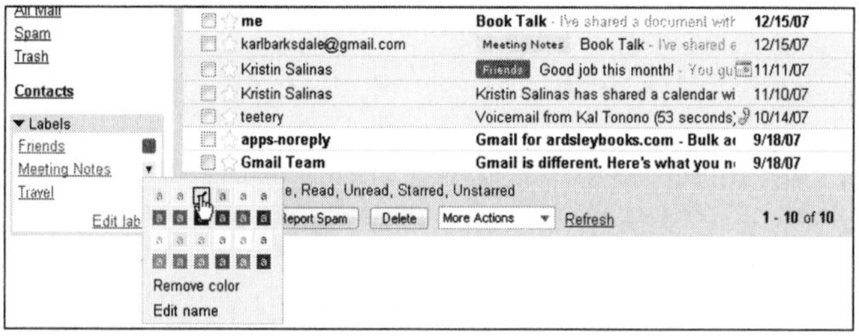

**Figure 5-8:** Labels work just like folders, only cooler!

# Creating new filters

Filters help keep your Inbox free of clutter by automatically performing an action on a message as soon as it's received, such as deleting any message from a certain e-mail address. You can create as many filters as you want; you can best keep your Inbox clutter-free by creating a good number of filters.

Creating effective filters involves two steps. First, choose the type of messages that you want to filter; second, choose an action that you want Gmail to perform on those messages. The following sections describe these steps in detail.

To create a new filter, follow these steps:

1. **Log into your Google Apps Gmail (if you haven't already).**

2. **Click the Settings link at the top of the screen.**

3. **Click the Filters tab.**

   A screen that looks like Figure 5-9 appears.

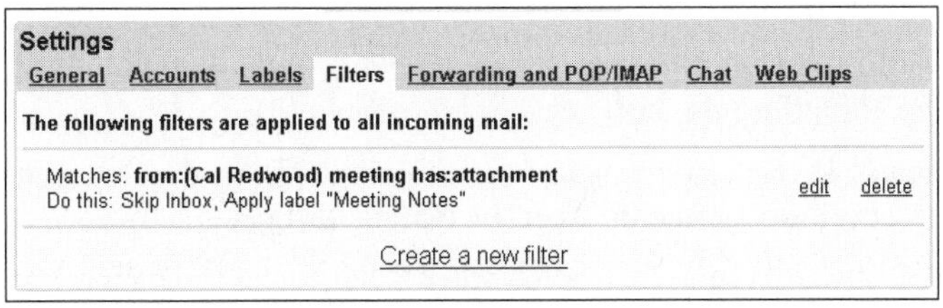

**Figure 5-9:**
Create a
new filter on
the Settings
page.

**Settings**
General   Accounts   **Labels   Filters**   Forwarding and POP/IMAP   Chat   Web Clips

**The following filters are applied to all incoming mail:**

Matches: **from:(Cal Redwood) meeting has:attachment**                    edit       delete
Do this: Skip Inbox, Apply label "Meeting Notes"

Create a new filter

4. **Click the Create a New Filter link.**

   Your screen will show you some search boxes and look similar to the upcoming Figure 5-10.

5. **Describe what messages you want the filter to catch by filling in the text boxes in the Choose Search Criteria screen.**

   See the following section for details on choosing your filter criteria.

6. **Click the Next Step button, and then select the appropriate check boxes in the Choose Action screen that appears.**

   See the "Choose an action" section, later in this chapter, for details.

7. **Click the Create Filter button to create your filter.**

## Choose your search criteria

To create an effective filter, you need to identify the types of messages that you want to filter. You can specify what messages you want to filter in the Choose Search Criteria screen, shown in Figure 5-10 (refer to the step list in the preceding section to find out how to get to this screen). You have six different ways to filter the messages, described below, and you can use any combination to help you narrow your list of filtered messages further.

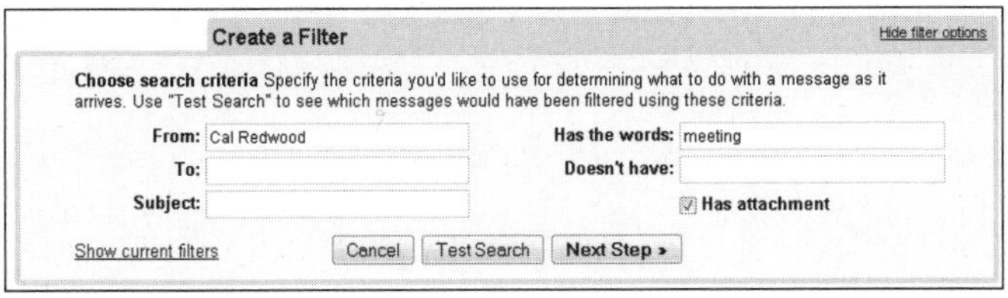

**Figure 5-10:**
Choose your
filter's
search
criteria.

**Create a Filter**                                                    Hide filter options

**Choose search criteria** Specify the criteria you'd like to use for determining what to do with a message as it
arrives. Use "Test Search" to see which messages would have been filtered using these criteria.

From: Cal Redwood                    Has the words: meeting

To:                                  Doesn't have:

Subject:                             ☑ Has attachment

Show current filters        Cancel    Test Search    Next Step »

The following list describes what to enter in the Choose Search Criteria screen:

✔ **From:** Enter an e-mail address or the name of a person or company that you want to filter, such as **cal@ardsleybooks.com** or **Cal**.

✔ **To:** Use this text box to find messages that were sent to another person, in addition to you. You can use this option to find messages that were sent to a mailing list.

✔ **Subject:** Enter keywords that appear in the message's subject line.

✔ **Has the Words:** Enter keywords that may appear anywhere in the message, including the subject and address fields.

✔ **Doesn't Have:** Enter keywords in this text box to show messages that don't contain a specific word or e-mail address.

The keywords in all the fields work together to limit your search results. For example, enter **wall** in the Has the Words text box and enter **facebook** in the Doesn't Have text box to find messages from the *Wall Street Journal,* but not messages notifying you that someone wrote on your Facebook Wall.

✔ **Has Attachment:** Select this check box to filter messages that contain attachments. This setting is also useful in conjunction with keywords in other fields.

The filter looks for messages that have something from all the fields into which you enter text. If you want to use the same action for messages that have many different fields, type **OR** or a comma between the keywords, such as **delta OR united OR american airlines OR continental** for travel-related messages and **facebook, myspace, linkedin** for messages from social networking sites.

After you enter the keywords that you like, click the Test Search button to see how well the filter works on your existing messages. A list will appear just below your filter box, showing you all the messages that match your search criteria.

As an example, if you enter **Cal Redwood** in the From text box, enter **meeting** in the Has the Words text box, and select the Has Attachment check box, the filter finds only messages that include any kind of file attachments that Cal sent about a meeting.

When you narrow the messages as far as you want, click the Next Step button. The following section gives you details on the Choose Action screen that appears.

## *Choose an action*

In the Choose Action screen, you need to decide what to do with your newly filtered messages. You can choose from six different options, and you can select more than one action to perform, as shown in Figure 5-11.

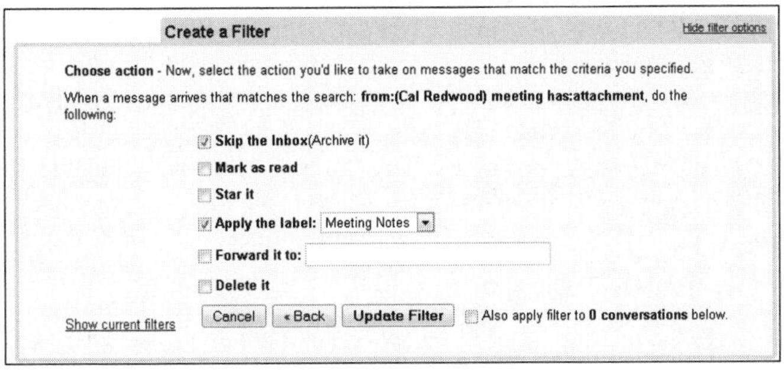

**Figure 5-11:**
Add an
action or
two to your
filtered
messages.

> **Create a Filter**      Hide filter options
>
> **Choose action** - Now, select the action you'd like to take on messages that match the criteria you specified.
>
> When a message arrives that matches the search: **from:(Cal Redwood) meeting has:attachment**, do the following:
>
> ☑ **Skip the Inbox**(Archive it)
> ☐ **Mark as read**
> ☐ **Star it**
> ☑ **Apply the label:** Meeting Notes ▾
> ☐ **Forward it to:**
> ☐ **Delete it**
>
> Show current filters    [ Cancel ] [ « Back ] [ **Update Filter** ]   ☐ Also apply filter to **0 conversations** below.

You can choose one or more of the following actions:

- ✔ **Skip the Inbox (Archive It):** Select this option to have the message automatically sent to the All Mail label.

- ✔ **Mark as Read:** Choose this action, and filtered messages no longer appear bold and therefore don't show up as new messages.

- ✔ **Star It:** Check this option to highlight important messages and have them appear in the Starred label.

- ✔ **Apply the Label:** Select this check box, and then choose a label from the drop-down list to send your messages to that label.

  If you select both the Apply the Label check box and the Skip the Inbox option, new messages appear in the selected label, but you don't have to deal with them in the Inbox.

- ✔ **Forward It To:** Select this check box, click in the text box to the right of Forward It To, and enter the address to which you want the message forwarded. A copy of the filtered messages goes to the other mailbox or person that you specify.

- ✔ **Delete It:** Select this check box to create your own spam filter — you never even have to see the message.

You can return to the previous screen by clicking the Back button. When you're ready to activate your filter, click the Create Filter button, and you're done. Be sure to check the Also Apply Filter to Conversations Below check box if you want to filter your old messages, not just messages you receive going forward.

## Do you smell bacn?

*Bacn* is a fairly new term. It refers to the messages that you subscribe to from various Web sites, whether news, social networking, or travel. Unlike spam, these messages are useful and somewhat important, otherwise you wouldn't have subscribed to them. But sometimes you get so many of them that they interfere with your really important e-mail conversations and can make your e-mail seem overwhelming. Nobody deserves that.

Rather than let bacn accumulate and ruin an otherwise pleasant day, use filters in Gmail to shuffle them away so that you can give them attention when you really have time. Here's what we do: For promotional e-mails from various airlines, such as Delta and American Airlines, we create a filter, entering the words *Delta, American Airlines, United, Travel, Flight,* or *Fare* in the Has the Words text box. Then we select the Skip the Inbox check box, select the Apply the Label check box, and select the Travel label from the Apply the Label drop-down list. By using this filter, these messages never clutter the Inbox, but the Travel label on the left of the screen tells us right away how many new travel messages, whether offers or reservations, we have. When we have time at the end of the day, we can click the Travel label and begin planning where we want to take our next vacation.

## *Adjusting filters later*

After you set up a filter, you may find that it doesn't run quite the way you want it to. Maybe the filter's catching too many messages, or maybe you decide that you want to have the filtered messages sent to another label.

To adjust a filter that you've already created, follow these steps:

1. **Log into Gmail (if you haven't already).**

2. **Click the Settings link at the top of the screen.**

3. **In the Settings screen that appears, click the Filters tab.**

   The Filters tab lists all the filters that you've already created.

4. **Click the Edit link to the right of the filter that you want to change.**

   The Choose Search Criteria screen appears, showing what you had previously entered for the filter.

5. **Change the options in the Choose Search Criteria screen as desired (refer to the "Choose your search criteria" section, earlier in this chapter, for details), and then click the Next Step button.**

   The Choose Action screen appears, showing the options that you selected when you first created the filter.

6. **Change the options in the Choose Action screen as desired (refer to the preceding section for details), and then click the Update Filter button.**

If you don't like the filter after all, click the Delete link to the right of the filter, and that filter disappears forever.

# Alternative Access: Forwarding, POP/IMAP, and Mobile

Just because Gmail is one of the most simple, intuitive, and powerful Web-mail services available, that doesn't mean you have to stick with the same Web site day after day. You can access your important messages in many ways, such as downloading them to your computer or getting them on your mobile phone. Fortunately, no matter where you check your mail, you can still always return to the friendly Gmail Web page from any computer with an Internet connection.

In the following sections, we go over how to enable forwarding so that you can send your e-mail somewhere other than your Gmail Inbox (if your administrator allows you to), how to sync Outlook with your Gmail mailbox using POP or IMAP, and even how to check your messages when you're on the go from your Web-enabled mobile phone.

## Turning forwarding on and off

E-mail forwarding is one of the best ways to consolidate e-mail from multiple addresses. If your Google Apps Gmail account isn't your primary account, you can turn forwarding on in two clicks and pass your Gmail messages on to your primary account.

If you have a personal Gmail account, you can also use this option to forward your personal e-mail to your Google Apps account. Then you have to look in only one place for all your messages.

To set up forwarding for your Google Apps e-mail, log into Gmail and click the Settings link in the top-right corner of the screen. Click the Forwarding and POP/IMAP tab, as shown in Figure 5-12.

**Figure 5-12:**
Decide
what you
want to
do with
forwarded
messages.

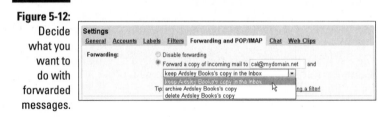

Here's a brief description of what you can do in the Forwarding and POP/IMAP tab:

- ✔ **Disable Forwarding:** Select this radio button if you don't want your messages going anywhere.

- ✔ **Forward a Copy of Incoming Mail:** Select this radio button to send a copy of all incoming messages to another address. Enter the address that you want your messages to go to in the text box, and then select one of the following options from the Forward a Copy of Incoming Mail drop-down list:

  - *Keep Gmail's Copy in the Inbox:* Everything happens invisibly. Your messages get forwarded, and Gmail never knows.

  - *Archive Gmail's Copy:* New messages don't appear in the Inbox, but you still can read them from your Gmail account by clicking the All Mail link.

  - *Delete Gmail's Copy:* Gmail deletes forwarded messages from your Gmail account.

If you want to forward only certain messages, create a filter (flip back to the section "Creating new filters," earlier in this chapter) and check the Forward It To check box in the Choose Action screen. Enter an address in the Forward It To text box, and Gmail passes on only those select messages to the address you specify.

## Sending mail as someone else

It's always fun to pretend to be somebody else. Gmail gives you that option — as long as that someone else is also you. When you have several e-mail addresses to manage, such as your personal one, one for work, and one for your soccer league, Gmail makes it easy to send and receive all your messages in one place, from up to five different accounts.

To add an account, follow these steps:

1. **Click the Settings link in the top-right corner of the Gmail main page.**

   The Gmail Settings screen will appear with tabs along the top.

2. **In the Settings screen, click the Accounts tab, which you can see in Figure 5-13.**

| Settings | |
|---|---|
| <u>General</u>  **Accounts**  <u>Labels</u>  <u>Filters</u>  <u>Forwarding and POP/IMAP</u>  <u>Chat</u>  <u>Web Clips</u> | |

| **Send mail as:** (Use Ardsley Books to send from your other email addresses) Learn more | Cal Redwood <cal@ardsleybooks.com>                                  <u>edit info</u> |
| | Cal Redwood <dixoncal@gmail.com>          unverified  <u>verify</u>        <u>delete</u> |
| | <u>Add another email address</u> |
| | **When I receive a message sent to one of my addresses:** |
| | ○ Reply from the same address the message was sent to |
| | ◉ Always reply from my default address (currently cal@ardsleybooks.com) |
| | (Note: You can change the address at the time of your reply. Learn more) |
| **Get mail from other accounts:** (Download mail using POP3) Learn more | <u>Add another mail account</u> |
| **Change Password:** | Follow this link Change Password to reset your password. |

3. **In the Send Mail As section, click the Add Another Email Address link.**

   A new window opens, asking you for the name and address that you want to add.

4. **Fill in the information and click the Next Step button.**

   The screen that appears asks you to verify that you are, in fact, the owner of the address you enter in this step.

5. **Click the Send Verification button.**

   The next screen asks you to enter a verification code. When you clicked the Send Verification button, the Gmail team sent a message to your other e-mail account. Because the message contains a link that will automatically verify your account, you can skip entering the verification code at this time and simply close the verification window. This takes you back to your Gmail screen.

6. **In a new browser window, log into the e-mail account that you enter in Step 4 and look for the new message from the Gmail team.**

7. **Open the message and click the very long, cryptic-looking link to verify your address.**

   If you leave the window open in Step 5, you can alternatively copy and paste the verification code from the message into that window and click the Verify button.

Congratulations! Now your other e-mail address is verified. The next time you compose a new message in Gmail, the From field will change into a drop-down list from which you can select your Google Apps e-mail address or your other e-mail account, as shown in Figure 5-14.

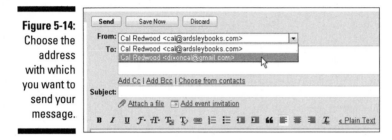

**Figure 5-14:** Choose the address with which you want to send your message.

If your other e-mail account allows POP access, find out what those POP set-tings are (you may have to call your service provider) and then return to the Gmail Accounts tab (click the Settings link at the top of the screen, and then click the Accounts tab). Click the Add Another Mail Account link near the bottom of the page and follow the instructions that appear on the screen. Unless you choose otherwise, new messages are automatically labeled with your other address when they arrive so that you can tell which messages came to which e-mail address.

## Activating POP or IMAP

POP (Post Office Protocol) and IMAP (Internet Message Access Protocol) both provide you access to your Gmail messages from other e-mail programs, such as Microsoft Outlook, Apple Mail, and Mozilla Thunderbird. We think that IMAP is by far the best way to access your messages because it automat-ically syncs your Gmail every time you make changes to your messages. For example, if you're using IMAP and read a message in Outlook, the next time you visit Gmail, the message is already marked as read.

POP, on the other hand, allows you to download a copy of your messages to your computer, but it doesn't sync back up with Gmail. You may find this lack of syncing a bit problematic if you're using more than one computer to down-load your messages because new messages download only to the last com-puter that asked. IMAP syncs each of your devices with Gmail so each one has the same messages making it the obvious better choice.

These services aren't turned on by default, so you have to make changes to your Gmail settings. To activate POP or IMAP, follow these steps:

1. **Log into Gmail and click the Settings link at the top of the Gmail page.**

2. **Click the Forwarding and POP/IMAP tab.**

   Your screen should now look similar to Figure 5-15.

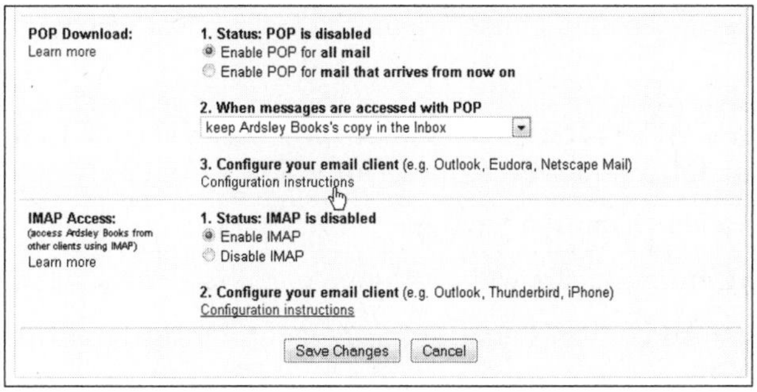

**Figure 5-15:**
Enable POP
or IMAP
from the
Settings
screen.

3. **To turn IMAP on, select the Enable IMAP radio button.**

4. **(Optional) To turn on POP, select the Enable POP for All Mail radio button or the Enable POP for Mail That Arrives from Now On radio button.**

   Unless you're really passionate about POP or you're using a very old e-mail program, you should ignore the POP Download section altogether. However, if you really, really want to use POP for your Gmail account, here is a description of the two choices in the POP Download section:

   • You can select the Enable POP for All Mail radio button, which downloads to your computer every message that you've ever received since you began using your Gmail account.

   • You can select the Enable POP for Mail That Arrives from Now On radio button, which downloads only new messages that you receive. You can then choose in Step 2 of the POP Download section whether you want Gmail to keep messages in the Inbox, archive them, or delete your accessed messages.

5. **Click the Save Changes button.**

   You will be taken back to your Inbox. Continue to the following section to find instructions for how to set up Outlook.

## Configuring Outlook to work with Gmail

Many users are already familiar with Microsoft Outlook, so we put together some step-by-step instructions to get your Gmail account up and running in Outlook using IMAP.

Google has put together some useful configuration instructions online to help you configure many other e-mail software programs for IMAP or POP. To access these instructions, log into your Gmail account, click the Settings link at the top of the screen, click the Forwarding and POP/IMAP tab, and click the appropriate Configuration Instructions link.

Follow these steps to configure Outlook so that you can use it to access your Gmail:

1. **Make sure IMAP is enabled (see the preceding section to find out how to enable IMAP), and then open Outlook.**

2. **Choose Tools⇨E-mail Accounts.**

   A new window appears with Outlook's e-mail accounts setup screen.

3. **Select the Add a New E-mail Account radio button, and then click the Next button.**

4. **On the Server Type screen that appears, select the IMAP radio button, and then click the Next button.**

5. **In the Internet E-mail Settings screen that appears, fill in all necessary text boxes with the following information (as we've done in Figure 5-16):**

---

**Add New E-mail Account**

**Internet E-mail Settings**
Each of these settings are required to get your e-mail account working.

**User Information**

Your Name: `Cal Redwood`

E-mail Address: `cal@ardsleybooks.com`

**Server Information**

Account Type: `IMAP`

Incoming mail server: `imap.gmail.com`

Outgoing mail server (SMTP): `smtp.gmail.com`

**Logon Information**

User Name: `cal@ardsleybooks.com`

Password: `******`

☑ Remember password

☐ Require logon using Secure Password Authentication (SPA)

**Test Account Settings**

After filling out the information on this screen, we recommend you test your account by clicking the button below. (Requires network connection)

[ Test Account Settings ... ]

[ More Settings ... ]

[ < Back ]  [ Next > ]  [ Cancel ]

**Figure 5-16:** Enter your account settings in Outlook.

---

• *User Information:* Enter your name in the Your Name text box in the way that you want others to see it when they receive mail from you. In the E-mail Address text box, enter the full Google Apps e-mail address (***user@yourdomain.com***).

- *Server Information:* In the Incoming Mail Server text box, type **imap.gmail.com**. In the Outgoing Mail Server (SMTP) text box, enter **smtp.gmail.com**.

- *Logon Information:* Type your full Google Apps e-mail address (*user@yourdomain.com*) in the User Name text box and enter your password in the Password text box.

6. **Click the More Settings button, and then click the Outgoing Server tab in the Internet E-mail Settings window that appears.**

7. **Select the My Outgoing Server (SMTP) Requires Authentication check box, and then select the Use Same Settings as My Incoming Mail Server check box.**

8. **Click the Advanced tab, as shown in Figure 5-17.**

9. **Below Incoming Server (IMAP), select SSL from the Use the Following Type of Encrypted Connection drop-down list, and then enter 993 in the Incoming Server (IMAP) text box.**

10. **Below Outgoing Server (SMTP), select SSL from the Use the Following Type of Encrypted Connection drop-down list, and then enter 465 in the Outgoing Server (SMTP) text box.**

11. **When your screen looks like Figure 5-17, click OK.**

**Figure 5-17:**
Make sure
your server
port
numbers
match these
ones.

Internet E-mail Settings

General | Folders | Outgoing Server | Connection | Advanced

Server Port Numbers

Incoming server (IMAP): 993 | Use Defaults

Use the following type of encrypted connection: SSL

Outgoing server (SMTP): 465

Use the following type of encrypted connection: SSL

Server Timeouts

Short — Long 1 minute

Folders

Root folder path:

OK | Cancel

12. **Click the Test Account Settings button to make sure everything works correctly.**

You should receive a message that says "Congratulations! All tests completed successfully." If you get an error message, repeat the steps in this section.

13. **Click the Close button to close the Congratulations dialog box.**

14. **On the Internet E-mail Settings screen, click the Next button, and then click the Finish button.**

The Internet is always changing and so is the software. That's why you should download the latest updates for Outlook so that you don't run into any problems. You can download them at `http://update.microsoft.com`.

## Accessing Gmail from your mobile device

We're not sure whether you're the type of person who sits on the edge of your seat waiting for your next e-mail to arrive and responding to those messages as fast as they come, or whether you're the casual type who checks your e-mail once in a while and is content with just that. No matter what your level of e-mail anxiety, Gmail makes it easy to check your messages, even when you're away from a computer.

If you're a BlackBerry debutant, open your mobile browser and go to `http://m.google.com/a` to download a special Gmail client. This application gives you many of the same features as the normal Gmail interface. Simply log in, using your Google Apps account username and password, and you're good to go.

iPhone fanatics can use the iPhone's built-in Mail client to access Gmail, as well. Be sure to set up a custom IMAP account (see the section "Activating POP or IMAP," earlier in this chapter, to find out how to set up an IMAP account) if you want your messages to sync back to the main program. You can find detailed instructions for setting up Gmail on your iPhone by logging into Gmail, clicking the Settings link at the top of the screen, clicking the Forwarding and POP/IMAP tab on the Settings page, and finally, clicking the Configuration Instructions link.

If you have a simple Web-enabled phone, open your phone's Web browser application and navigate to `http://mail.yourdomain.com`. Enter your Google Apps account username and password in the login page that appears, then press the Sign In button. Links to your messages and your labels appear in a very simple, easy-to-use format.

Beyond everything we cover in this chapter, you can find more Gmail tips and new features back on your computer. From the Gmail Inbox screen in your browser, look for the tips banner along the bottom of your screen or click the New Features link at the top of the screen.

# Chapter 6

# Keeping in Touch with the Contacts List

*In This Chapter*

▶ Getting to know your Contacts list

▶ Sorting and changing your Quick Contacts list

▶ Creating, editing, and using groups

*Y*ou need to keep track of the people that you communicate with, and Google helps you with that task by giving you the *Contacts list* (a database of contact information). This chapter is all about creating, adding to, and using your Contacts list with Gmail. Chapter 7 covers using your Contacts list with Gmail Chat and Google Talk. Your Contacts list also fuels your Google Calendar app (which we talk about in Chapters 8 and 9). You can even migrate Contacts lists to your smart phone. Without contacts, digital communication grinds to a screeching halt.

Everything in this chapter applies to anyone who uses Gmail, Gmail Chat, and Google Talk, whether or not they use Google Apps. iGoogle users, rejoice!

# Creating a Contacts List

Gmail automatically adds a contact to your address database when you reply to a message from someone who isn't already in your Contacts list. The Contacts list also accumulates addresses and information when you're using the Google Chat and Talk apps.

You can use your Contacts list a little or a lot, depending on your needs. For instance

✔ In Google Talk and Chat, your contacts are monitored to see who's online and who's available.

✔ In Gmail, the Contacts list allows you to enter just part of a name and have the most likely choices appear so you don't have to type the entire e-mail address in the To text box.

✔ In Google Calendar, you can use your Contacts list to facilitate the scheduling of attendees, rooms, and resources for meetings and events.

If all you need from the Contacts list is a little help addressing your e-mail, that's valuable enough. But if you want to get the most out of this potent tool, take a few minutes and browse through the following sections. We go under the hood and look at all the Contacts list's powerful features.

## *Viewing your contacts*

Want to find your Contacts list? Okay, pay attention. If you blink, you may miss this. Just follow these steps:

1. **Open Gmail.**

2. **Click the Contacts link in the left-hand panel.**

If your Google Apps administrator has set everything up according to Hoyle, you should see a list of the people in your organization — that is, all the colleagues in your domain listing. For example, all the employees at Ardsley Books were automatically added into the Contacts list shown in Figure 6-1. Groups that the organization created are also included in the Contacts list. We discuss groups in more detail in the "Sorting Contacts into Groups" section, later in this chapter.

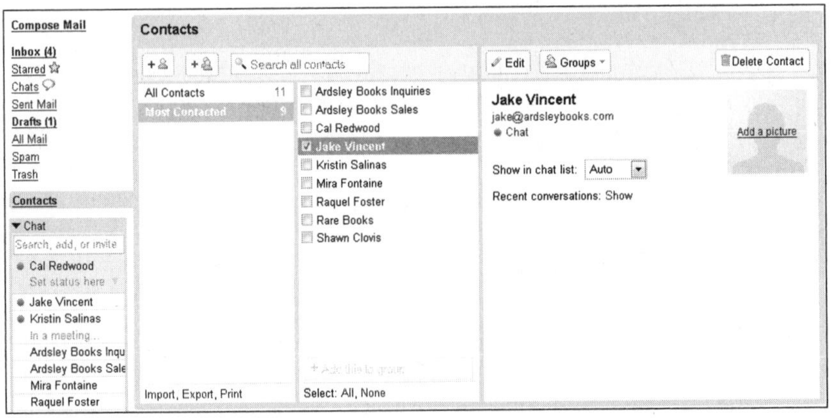

**Figure 6-1:** View your Contacts list by clicking the Contacts link.

And it doesn't stop there. Gmail keeps track of anyone you've e-mailed, replied to, or showed the slightest interest in and adds them to the Contacts list.

Gmail automatically groups your contacts, as shown in Figure 6-1, by these three categories:

- ✔ **Frequently Mailed:** An abbreviated list of the most frequently used contacts in your Contacts list.

- ✔ **All Contacts:** A list of everybody in your Contacts list. (Think of the proverbial kitchen sink.)

- ✔ **Groups:** A list of groups that either you or your organization creates. Groups facilitate e-mailing large numbers of people. Instead of entering multiple e-mail addresses individually, a group will e-mail dozens, even hundreds, of people with a single common e-mail address. We show you how that works in the later section, "Sorting Contacts into Groups."

## *Rolling through your Contacts list*

Take a second to roll your mouse cursor slowly over the list of e-mail addresses that appear in your Contacts list. Pop, pop, pop, up come little contact cards with descriptions of each individual contact, as shown in Figure 6-2. Unless either your contacts or you add more robust information, these listings appear rather plain. However, you can add more pertinent information, including pictures, which will help you remember what some of these people actually look like. (See the "Adding or Updating Contacts" section for details.)

**Figure 6-2:**
Pop-ups
display
more
detailed
contact
information
than what
appears
in the
Contacts
list.

With any luck, your friends and colleagues will update their own contact information. If they do, all the new information automatically appears in your Contacts list, so you don't need to worry about it. If they don't, you need to enter their details by hand. But remember, even if a contact entry is incomplete, you can still find just a name and an e-mail address valuable. In fact, you don't need to complete all the information for every contact in your list, unless you have a lot of time on your hands. Just enter the information that you think you'll need for each contact and keep it at that. If you find, over time, that you need more complete information, you can add to the record later.

# Using Quick Contacts in Gmail

The Quick Contacts list, just as the name implies, is designed to save you time and add convenience to your Gmail and Chat applications. You can also view your Contacts list by clicking the triangle beside a contact name, as shown in Figure 6-3. Clicking this triangle opens an abbreviated list called the Quick Contacts list.

**Figure 6-3:**
Open your Quick Contacts list by clicking the arrow.

Click to open the Quick Contacts list.

Contacts
▶ ● Cal Redwood
Search, add, or invite

## Knowing when your contacts are online

A green dot appears to the left of Cal Redwood's name in Figure 6-4. (Okay, in this black-and-white book, the dot looks gray — but trust us, it's green on-screen.) A green dot means that person is online — a useful bit of information if you want to have a real-time conversation with that person by using Gmail Chat or Google Talk. This can be a very handy productivity tool, as you can find out in Chapter 7.

If you don't want someone to see your green dot, you can block certain contacts so they don't interrupt you while you're working, playing, or attending a meeting. To block visitors, set your status by clicking the down arrow next to the words Set Status Here. See the following section for details.

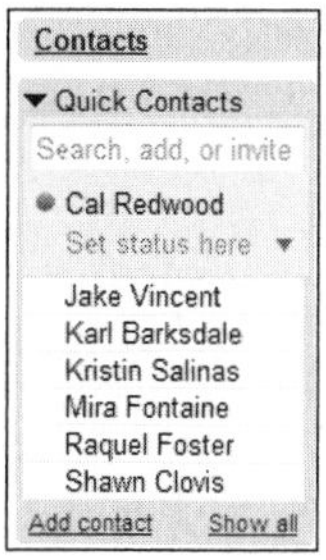

Contacts

▼ Quick Contacts

Search, add, or invite

● Cal Redwood
Set status here ▼

Jake Vincent
Karl Barksdale
Kristin Salinas
Mira Fontaine
Raquel Foster
Shawn Clovis

Add contact    Show all

**Figure 6-4:**
A green dot
means that
contact is
online.

# Prioritizing Quick Contacts

The Quick Contacts list displays your most frequently contacted people based on your past e-mail and chatting habits. The automatically generated list may not always reflect your wishes, so you can make changes and prioritize your contacts to your liking. By adjusting your list, you can tell at a glance whether your contact is online and available for a quick chat. Also, those contacts that you e-mail most often appear on the list, so you can simply click a name to launch a new Gmail message preaddressed to that person.

You may have other contacts that you need to banish to the background so they don't take up valuable space in the visible portion of your Quick Contacts list. Not that you consider them second-class contacts; you simply don't need to contact them frequently or in any great haste.

To customize your Quick Contacts list, display all your contacts by clicking the Show All link at the bottom of the Quick Contacts list (refer to Figure 6-4).

After you display all your contacts, decide which contacts you want to show up in your Quick Contacts list by selecting an option in the Show in Quick Contacts column (see Figure 6-5). Place only those contacts that you must contact frequently or need to reach immediately in your Quick Contacts list. You have four options:

- ✔ **Always:** Selecting Always shows this contact in your Quick Contacts list, well, always.

- ✔ **Auto:** Selecting Auto means that Gmail decides whether a contact is high frequency and should appear in your Quick Contacts list.

- ✔ **Never:** Selecting Never keeps this contact out of your Quick Contacts list.

- ✔ **Block:** Selecting Block prevents this person from contacting you via Chat. (However, this person can still e-mail you.)

**Figure 6-5:**
Prioritize
who
appears in
your Quick
Contacts
list.

## Unearthing lost contacts

Even if you select Never or Block for a contact (see the preceding section for more on the Quick Contacts list options), you can still get to that person's contact information whenever you need it by using the search tool in the Quick Contacts list. As Figure 6-6 shows, after you enter only a few letters in the search text box, a list of contact names appears in a list.

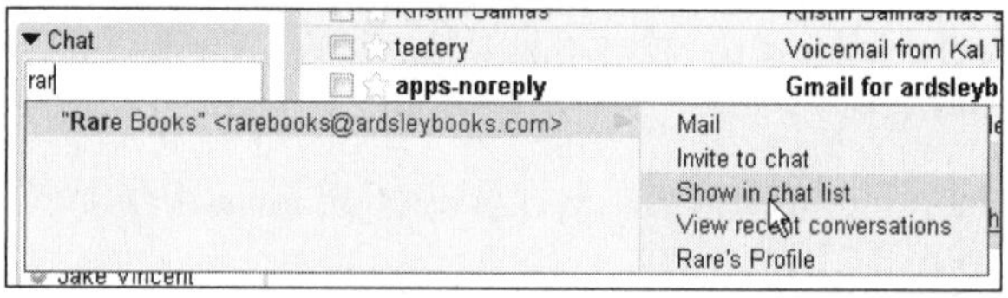

**Figure 6-6:**
Use the
contact
search
feature to
find the
contact
you're
looking for.

After you find the contact that you're looking for, the Quick Contacts search box displays several options for that contact. Click the option that you need:

🖊 **Mail:** E-mail that contact.

🖊 **Invite to Chat:** Invite the contact to a quick chat, plan lunch, share gossip, and maybe even get some work done.

✔ **Show in Quick Contacts:** Restore this person to your Quick Contacts list if you have deleted them for some reason.

✔ **View Recent Conversations:** Look up what you and your contact said while chatting.

✔ **<Name>'s Profile:** Open the contact's profile. You can view his or her statistics, or add your own data to his or her contact information. (Your changes only appear in your copy of another's profile.)

# Adding or Updating Contacts

In the detailed edit contact window, you can change your contacts' information. You can add info, alter details, or even change someone's picture. You can also add e-mail, phone, and address information at any time, so you can reach out to anyone and remind them to pick you up for that preposterous office party in the offing. You have three ways to begin updating or altering the information for any existing contact:

✔ Roll over any contact in your Quick Contacts list. When the contact card appears, click the "More" down arrow at the top of the contact card followed by the Contact Details. Then, click the Edit Contact Information link.

✔ Display all your contacts by choosing Contacts in the left panel, and then roll over any contact in your Contacts list and click Contact Details. Then, click the Edit Contact Information link.

✔ Search for a contact in the search box in the Quick Contacts list. When you find it, select <Name>'s Profile, click Contact Information, and finally, click the Edit Contact Information link from the card that appears.

To add a new contact from scratch, follow these steps:

1. **Open your Contacts list by clicking the Contacts or Show All link.**

2. **Click the Create Contact link.**

## Entering basic contact information

When you create a new contact, the following basic fields appear in the Add Contact window (shown in Figure 6-7):

✔ **Name:** Enter the contact's first name followed by last name in this text box.

✔ **Email:** Enter your contact's primary e-mail address in this text box.

✔ **Notes:** Place any pertinent notes that you want to remember about this contact in this text box.

✔ **Picture:** Choose whether you want to use your own picture (select the My Pick radio button) or use a picture that the contact added (select the Their Pick radio button). If you select the My Pick radio button, click the Upload Picture link below the My Pick picture box to use your own picture.

✔ **More Information:** Click this link if you want to add more fields of information.

✔ **Save:** Click the Save button after you finish entering all the necessary data.

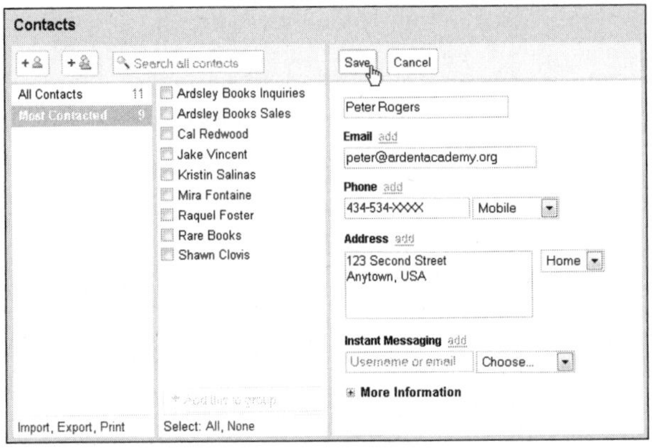

**Figure 6-7:**
Add contact
information
in the Add
Contact
window.

# Adding more information about a contact

You may need to add more fields than the basic ones provided in the Add Contact window, particularly if you're entering information for business contacts. You can easily add additional information by clicking the More Information link (refer to Figure 6-7). Two new sections appear, a Personal and a Work section. In these sections, you can add additional e-mail addresses and phone numbers, as well as complete address information.

Simply click inside a text box and enter the appropriate information. You can select the type of information that you want to enter by clicking the arrow to the right of the field name and selecting from the list that appears (see Figure 6-8).

You may not always have the data fields that you need for a unique contact, such as fields for a second mobile phone or for a pager. Gmail lets you add fields by clicking the Add Another Field link, which appears in each section on the right side of the window (see Figure 6-8). From there, you choose among the standard types of fields: E-mail, IM, Phone, Mobile, Pager, Fax, Company, Title, or Other. And, if you want to change the name or purpose of a field, click in the field box and type whatever name you want.

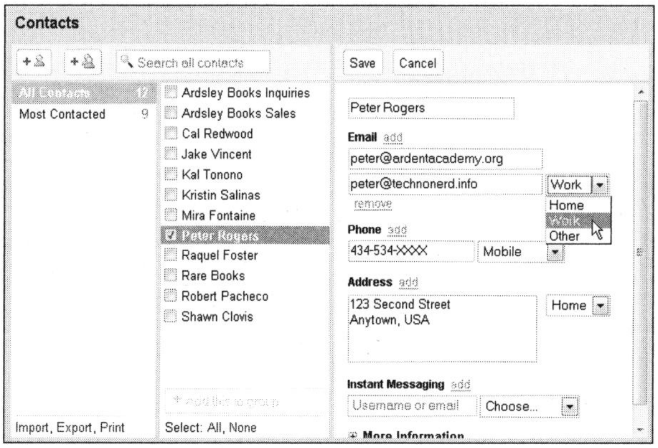

**Figure 6-8:**
Add extra blank fields by clicking the Add link.

## Adding a picture

You can add your picture into your personal contact information, and that picture is automatically shared with others throughout your network of contacts. So make sure you add a flattering photo.

You can use any image stored on your computer as your contact image. The only limitation is that the image must be in one of the following commonly-used file formats:

- **JPG or JPEG (Joint Photographic Experts Group):** A popular online graphics format using compression to reduce the size of images.

- **BMP (bitmap):** A graphics file format proprietary to Microsoft Corporation.

- **GIF (Graphic Interchange Format):** This highly compact, low-resolution format was originally designed by CompuServe for online use.

- **PNG (Portable Network Graphics):** This compressed image format is similar to JPEG in many ways, approved by the World Wide Web Consortium as a high-resolution alternative to the GIF format.

After you identify the picture that you want to use, click the name of your target contact. ***Remember:*** You can add your personal picture, as well, by choosing your name from the Contacts list.

Follow these steps to add a picture to a contact:

1. **Click Contacts from the side panel.**

2. **Scroll over the contact that you want to change and choose Edit Contact Information as explained in the previous section.**

3. **Select the My Pick radio button to the right of Picture.**

4. **Click the Upload Picture link.**

   The Upload a Picture window appears, as shown in Figure 6-9.

5. **Click the Browse button.**

   The Choose File dialog box appears.

6. **In the Choose File dialog box, browse to the picture file that you want to insert and click Open.**

   The dialog box closes.

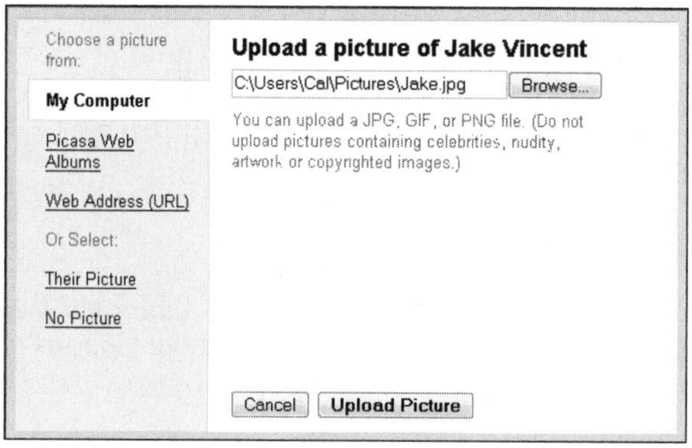

**Figure 6-9:**
Browse to
your file and
click the
Upload
Picture
button.

7. **Click the Upload Picture button in the Upload a Picture window.**

8. **(Optional) Crop the image.**

   To keep anyone from getting a big head, Gmail asks you to crop the image down to size. It displays the image in the Crop This Picture dialog box. To crop your image, follow these steps:

   a. *Drag the selection box into a flattering position.*

   b. *Drag the corners of the selection box to expand or reduce the selection box, as needed.*

   c. *When you're satisfied, click the Apply Changes button, as shown in Figure 6-10.*

**Figure 6-10:**
Crop the picture down to size.

The Edit Contact window reappears, and the picture you just uploaded and cropped now appears in the My Pick picture box. After a little adjustment, you can have nearly anyone, even your cross-eyed accountant friend down the hall, looking like a million bucks. The cropping doesn't change the original file, so if you make a mistake cropping the image, you can always go back and try, try again.

9. **In the Edit Contact window, click Save.**

   After you save a picture for a contact, the Suggest This Picture to <Name> dialog box appears, enabling you to share the picture that you choose with that contact.

10. **(Optional) If you have a flattering picture that you want to send to your boss or another colleague, enter a short note in the text box to the right of the picture in the Suggest This Picture to <Name> dialog box, and then click the Yes, Suggest This Picture button. (See Figure 6-11.)**

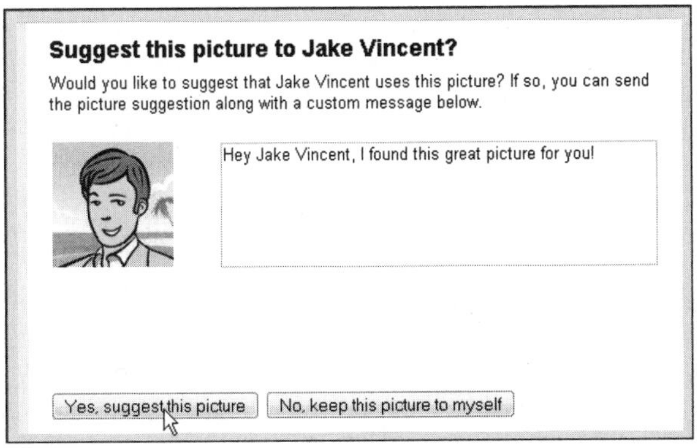

**Suggest this picture to Jake Vincent?**

Would you like to suggest that Jake Vincent uses this picture? If so, you can send the picture suggestion along with a custom message below.

Hey Jake Vincent, I found this great picture for you!

**Figure 6-11:**
Suggest a picture to a contact.

Yes, suggest this picture      No, keep this picture to myself

If you click the No, Keep This Picture to Myself button instead, Gmail doesn't send the contact the picture that you use for him or her in your personal Contacts list. (We suggest you resist the temptation to add a picture of a donkey to your boss's contact information, however, in case she happens to look over your shoulder one day.)

# Sorting Contacts into Groups

Groups make it a snap to contact large numbers of people at the same time. But you must invest the time to create your groups in order to save time later. Gmail assigns a single e-mail address (the group's address) that contains multiple e-mail addresses including each member of the group. When you enter a group name in the To field, Gmail enters all the e-mail addresses for the entire group's membership in a flash.

If you belong to a heads-up organization, an administrator may have already created some of the key groups within your organization for you. Your company might create groups consisting of all employees, employees in a specific department, all senior managers, and so on. Gmail allows you to create an unlimited number of your own groups, too. Groups aren't limited to business, of course — you can create a group of your friends, your immediate family members, or people who share your hobbies.

## Creating groupies

The best way to figure out how groups work is to create a group of your own. To create a group, follow these steps:

1. **Open your Contacts list and click the Groups tab.**

   If you haven't yet added a group, you see the screen shown in Figure 6-12.

2. **Click the New Group icon.**

3. **In the Create Group window that appears, click in the Group Name text box and enter a name that describes the group.**

4. **In the Add Contacts text box, enter however many e-mail addresses you want in the group. (See Figure 6-13.)**

   Fortunately, you can easily add addresses that are already in your Contacts list because Gmail automatically starts listing known addresses when you begin entering just a few letters in the Add Contacts text box.

5. **Click the Create Group button to save the group information.**

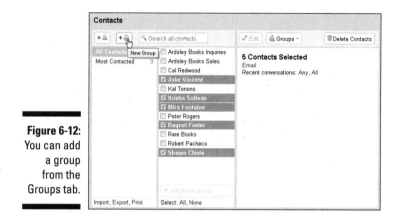

**Figure 6-12:**
You can add
a group
from the
Groups tab.

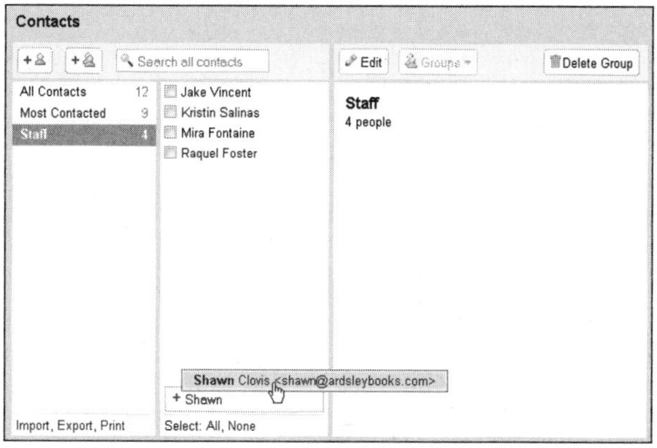

**Figure 6-13:**
Invent a
group name
and add
contacts to
the group.

# Viewing and editing an existing group

If you have a contact that you want to add or remove from a group, you can always edit the contacts in the group. You can also rename the group. To view or edit an existing group, follow these steps:

1. **Click Contacts and then click the Groups tab.**

2. **Double-click on any group that you've created from the list.**

**3. Make any changes that you want, including the following:**

- *Rename:* Click the Rename link to change the name of your group.

- *Add Contact to:* Type e-mail addresses into the Add Contacts text box, then click the Add Contacts button to add members to the group (see Figure 6-14).

- *Delete a Group:* Place a check mark next to the group's name and click the Delete Group button.

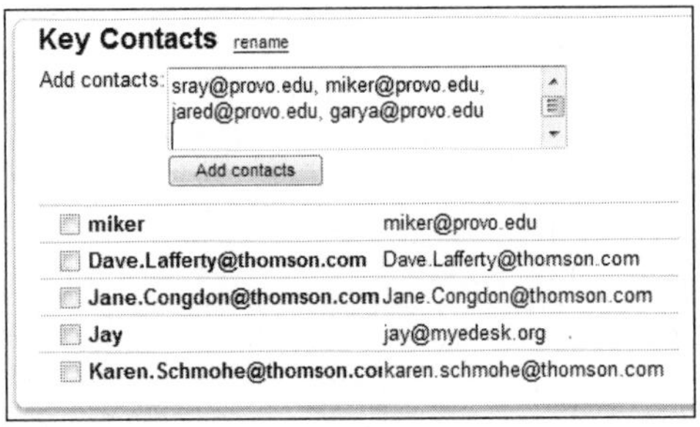

**Figure 6-14:**
Manage your group from the Groups tab.

# E-mailing a group

First, e-mail your groups and let them know what you're up to. Groups become part of your e-mail list database. You just have to start entering the first few letters in the To text box, and your group's name appears (as shown in Figure 6-15). Select the name of the group from the list of contacts that appears, and all the members' e-mail addresses suddenly appear in the To text box.

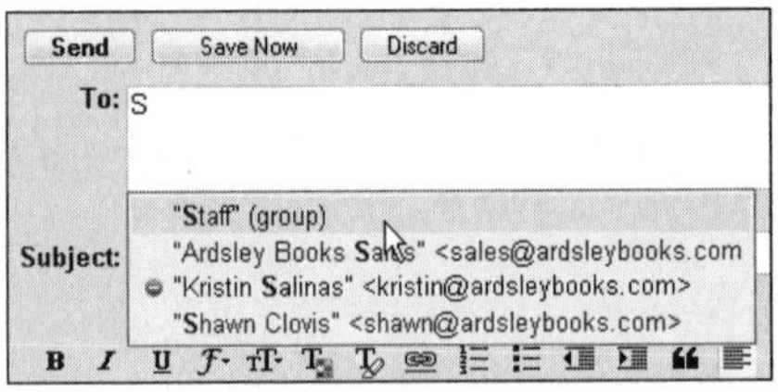

**Figure 6-15:**
E-mail a group address just like any e-mail address.

# Chapter 7

# Chatting with Gmail Chat and Google Talk

*I*f e-mail has a downside, it's that sometimes it just isn't instantaneous enough. Sure, it travels over the Internet at lightning speed, but you still have to wait for the other person to open his or her e-mail and read your very important message.

That's why instant messaging and short messaging service (SMS; text messaging to you mobile phone users) were invented — you want the recipient to get the message and reply to it a second after you press the Send button. Google takes care of your instant-messaging and SMS needs with Gmail Chat and Google Talk.

In this chapter, we cover how to use Gmail Chat and Google Talk to have a real-time conversation with one or more of your contacts. We also cover how you can use Google Talk to have a voice conversation.

Team Edition users, the first part of this chapter talks about Gmail Chat, which you won't have access to, so skip ahead to the "Upgrading to Google Talk" section, later in this chapter.

## Understanding Gmail Chat and Google Talk

Often, e-mail simply isn't fast enough when you need to have a conversation. Google has two options to help you out when you need to make contact right now:

✔ **Gmail Chat:** A basic instant-messaging program that's built right into Gmail.

Use Gmail Chat if you're already in Gmail and need to have just a simple instant-message conversation.

✔ **Google Talk:** A more robust instant-messaging program that you can use as a gadget on your Start Page or download and use as a standalone program. With Google Talk, you can type messages to a contact so you can chat in real time, just like in Chat. You can also use a microphone and speakers (or a headset) to have a voice conversation with a contact or to leave a voice message.

Use Google Talk when you want to use the telephony services to have a voice conversation.

# Using Gmail Chat

When you're ready to start chatting, you first need to figure out who's online and available. You can see who's ready to chat pretty simply; sign into Gmail (if you haven't already) and look for a green dot to the left of a contact's name in your Chat list. If you see the green dot, the contact's online and ready to chat.

## Inviting someone to chat in Gmail Chat

After you identify whether the person you want to instant message is online, starting up a chat in Gmail Chat is simple. Follow these steps:

1. **Sign into Gmail (if you haven't already).**

2. **In the Chat list on the left side of the screen, roll over the contact that you want to chat with and click the Chat button on the contact card that appears. (See Figure 7-1.)**

   If you want to chat with someone who isn't in your Chat list, click in the Chat search box, start to type the contact's name, select his or her name from the list of contacts that appears, and then select Invite to Chat from the options list that appears, as shown in Figure 7-2. This will let your contact know you want to talk. (At this point, you can also add the person to your Chat list by selecting Show in Chat List from the options list.)

   The Chat Invitations window appears.

3. **In the Chat Invitations window, enter the e-mail address(es) of the contact(s) with whom you want to chat, and then click the Send Invites button, as shown in Figure 7-3. Others that you can chat with will also appear so you can make a group invitation.**

**Figure 7-1:**
Click the
Chat button
to invite
someone
to chat.

**Figure 7-2:**
Search
for your
buddies and
invite them
to a chat.

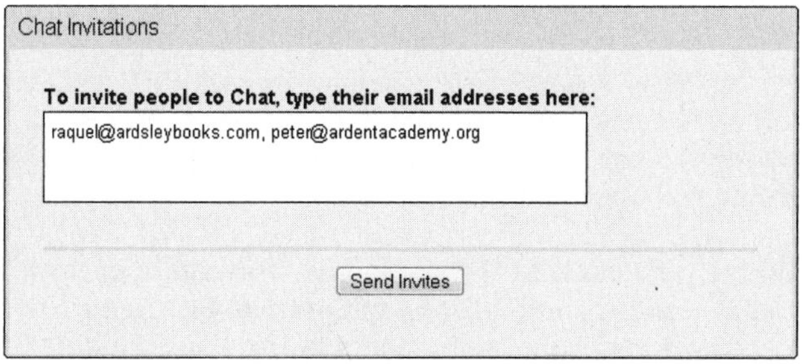

**Figure 7-3:**
Choose
multiple
individuals
in the Chat
Invitations
window.

After you send an invitation, a message appears in your invitee's Gmail window, asking if he or she wants to chat with you. (See Figure 7-4.) Don't be offended if he or she declines. Your contact may just be busy.

Also, if others want to chat with you, you receive similar invitations to the one shown in Figure 7-4. You need to accept their invitations if you also want to chat.

**Figure 7-4:**
Click Yes if
you want to
chat with
someone.

## Chatting away in Gmail Chat

After you set up everything for your chat and your contact has responded, start chatting! (See Figure 7-5.) Click in the text box at the bottom of the chat window, type a message, and press Enter to send the message.

You can use speech recognition software while chatting instead of typing. If you're using speech recognition software, say "Press Enter" to send the message.

**Figure 7-5:**
Chat away!

> **Kristin Salinas**
> **me:** Hello
> **Kristin:** How are you?
> **me:** Fine. Sold any books today?
> **Kristin:** I just got off the phone with a client. She's very interested in our first editions.
>
> Excellent!
>
> Options ▸       Pop-out ↗  ☺

Clicking the Pop-Out option separates your entry window from your conversation, which allows you to see more of your conversation. Also, to help you know what your partner in chat is doing, a message indicating that the person is typing will appear.

You can hold multiple chats at the same time. You can open several contacts in separate chat windows and talk to each of them independently. You can also have a chat with multiple participants in the same window (if you invite more than one person to a chat or are invited to a chat with multiple participants). You can have a lot of fun in a chat with multiple participants, but it can prove hectic. If the chat gets a little busy, or if someone is chatting way off topic, click the arrow to the right of Options and select Block <Name> to block someone from your chat, as shown in Figure 7-6. Ah, the power you feel blocking people right and left!

**Figure 7-6:**
Use your options to block undesirable elements.

> **karlbarksdale**
> **me:** Well, get with it!
>    Hey, don't tell me what to do!
> Sent at 4:51 PM on Sunday
> **me:** What, you going to block me?
>
> karlbarksdale is offline. Messages you send will be delivered when karlbarksdale comes online.
> **Press Enter to send your message.**
>
> Block karlbarksdale
> Options ▴       Pop-out ↗

## Keeping track of chats

If you need to keep a record of a chat you had in Gmail Chat or Google Talk for any reason, Gmail makes it easy by sending you an e-mail message containing the entire chat text, as shown in the following figure. And, because you can store and archive all your e-mail, you can always get to the chat record any time you want.

**Chat with mira@ardentbook.com**  Inbox

☆ ◎ "mira@ardentbook.com"    show details 4:41 pm (26 minutes ago)  ↩ Reply ▾

4:41 PM    **me**: How are you?
4:42 PM    **mira**: Fine:
           **me**: Sold any books today?
           **mira**: No.

↩ Reply  → Forward  ◎ mira is not available to chat

You can search for old chats as easily as you can search all your mail messages (which we explain how to do in Chapter 4). Simply enter any part of the chat that you can remember in the search window (a few key words will do), and options start appearing. You can also search for chats by contact name or by date.

# Changing your status for Chat

If you're signed into Gmail, you normally show up as online and available to chat to other people. To change your status (say, if you're busy and don't want your status to appear as online), follow these steps:

1. **To customize your personal chat settings, in the Chat section, click the down arrow to the right of Set Status Here and choose one of the following options from the list that appears:**

   • *Available:* Let people know you're available and willing to chat.

   • *Custom Message (for availability):* Write a customized message that people see when they check your availability.

   • *Busy:* Let people know you're busy and can't chat right now.

   • *Custom Message (for busyness):* Write a customized message that everyone sees when you're busy.

   • *Sign Out of Chat:* Close chat down temporarily.

2. **(Optional) To create a custom message, select the Custom Message option (shown in Figure 7-7), click in the empty text box that appears, and type a short message to your chat buddies. Clear this message later by clicking Set Status and selecting the custom message.**

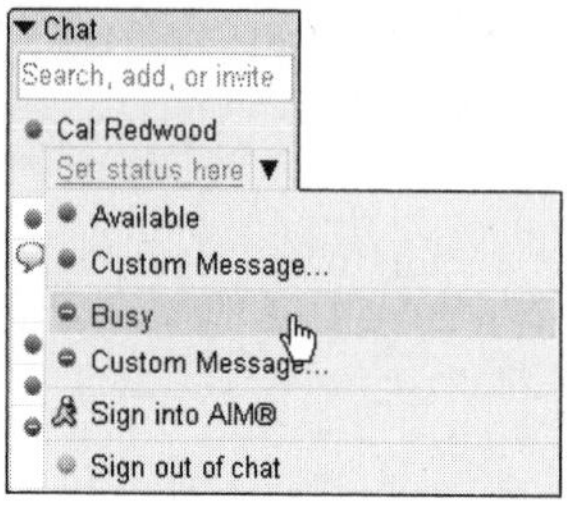

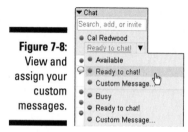

**Figure 7-7:**
Set your
chat status
and create
custom
messages.

Your custom message appears in your list of options, as shown in Figure 7-8. You can create several custom messages and apply them whenever you wish.

**Figure 7-8:**
View and
assign your
custom
messages.

# Upgrading to Google Talk

If you need a more powerful instant-message application than Gmail Chat, Google Talk is your answer. Google Talk is a gadget that you can add to your Start Page, as shown in Figure 7-9. (See Chapter 3 if you need help adding this gadget.)

If you're running Windows, you can add functionality to your Google Talk gadget, such as voice calls and file transfers, by downloading the Google Talk client. Go to www.google.com/talk and click the Download Google Talk button. Run the setup program and then log in, using your full e-mail address and password.

## Inviting a contact to chat in Google Talk

After you have Google Talk working, either from a gadget or from the client itself, you need to sign in. (Albeit, if you are already signed into Gmail or Google Apps, you will be recognized.) Your existing Gmail contacts automatically appear. To begin chatting, select users just like you do in Gmail

Chat (see the earlier section, "Inviting someone to chat in Gmail Chat.") It's a snap to invite new friends or accept invitations.

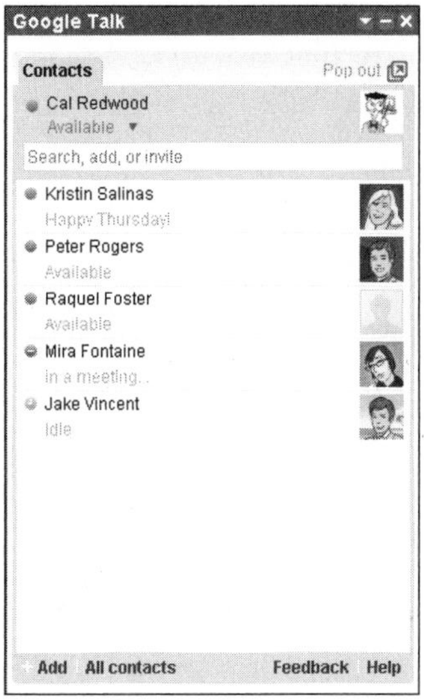

**Figure 7-9:**
Add Google
Talk as a
gadget to
your Start
Page.

To invite a contact to chat, follow these unbelievably easy steps:

1. **Click on their name in the list.**

2. **Start typing or click Call to have a phone call.**

   Honestly, isn't a simple call more personal than a bunch of text?

Use the search box (you know, the box with the spy glass in it) to find people to talk with by entering in part of their names or e-mail addresses. After you locate chat buddies, you can add them to your friends list and invite them to chat.

## Chatting with a contact in Google Talk

Google Talk works a lot like the Chat application in Gmail, described earlier in this chapter. In fact, it's almost 100 percent the same when it comes to chatting.

Just like in Chat, you simply click in the text box at the bottom of the screen (shown in Figure 7-10), type your message, and press Enter to send the message. Your message appears in the window above the text box, and so do replies from your contact.

You can insert an emoticon into your message by typing any of the common symbols, such as ;), which Google Talk replaces with a winking smiley in your message when you press Enter. You can also click the smiley to the right of the text box and select a face from the menu that appears.

**Figure 7-10:**
Talk with a contact by using the Google Talk gadget.

While you're using Google Talk, click the Email button in the upper-left corner to quickly switch to Gmail. Also, if you don't want to chat from within your gadget, you can click the Pop Out button in the top-right corner, which opens a separate window that you can use to talk. You may find the Pop Out feature very helpful if you're using other applications and don't want to leave your Start Page in the foreground of your desktop.

You can keep chats private by not creating an e-mail record of the messages in your Gmail. (See the sidebar "Keeping track of chats," in this chapter, for more information about storing and searching chats.) Have a chat on the sly by clicking the down arrow in the upper-right corner of the chat window and selecting Go Off the Record from the list that appears (shown in Figure 7-11).

Don't get the idea that someone can really block anything totally — appropriateness online matters. If you (or the person you're chatting with) feel the need to record an inappropriate message, you (or your contact) still can, even if one or the other person selected Go Off the Record. For example, as a last resort, you can snag a screen capture by pressing the Print Screen (Prt Scn) key, opening up a graphics program, and pasting the screen capture. Private isn't ever truly private in the online world.

## Chatting with a group

After you establish your list of contacts, you can chat with any or all of them as a group. Whether you are using Google Talk or Gmail Chat, setting up groups is a breeze. Group chat is a great way to get input from other people because you only have to respond once to a group rather than replying to many different people individually in several different windows. Remember how conference calling made meeting over the phone a whole lot easier? Group chat is kind of like that.

**Figure 7-11:**
Block a participant or go off the record.

After you have started a basic chat with a contact, click the Group Chat button in Google Talk (see Figure 7-12) or select Group Chat from the Options menu in Gmail Chat to add additional people to your conversation. In the text box that appears at the top of the chat window, enter the e-mail addresses of other users and press the Enter key. Right away, they will be able to begin chatting along with you (assuming they're online, of course).

To talk to someone privately outside of the group chat, click on that user's name in the Chat list and a separate tab (Talk) or chat window (Gmail Chat) will appear.

## Making a call

If you and a contact are both online, you can use Google Talk to make voice calls.

**Figure 7-12:**
Invite
multiple
contacts to
participate
in a group
chat.

Both you and your contact must have the Google Talk client installed on your computers for this function to work. For best results, use a high-quality headset microphone and double-check to make sure the sound levels are set properly before you begin.

To start a call, pick the name of the person you want to call. When their card appears, click the Call button or phone icon to the right of your contact's name, shown in Figure 7-13. You can then start a talkin' . . . it's that easy.

**Figure 7-13:**
Make a call
by using the
Google Talk
client.

When you're having a voice conversation in Google Talk, the talk window features the following options and indicators:

- **End Call:** Clicking this button terminates the current voice call.

- **Send Files:** Click this button to locate a document or photo on your
  computer that you want to send to your contact. (See Figure 7-14.) You
  can also drag a file from your computer desktop into your chat window
  to send it immediately.

- **Send Voicemail:** Click the down arrow to the right of the Send Files
  button and select Send Voicemail from the list that appears when you
  want to send someone a voice mail. If a contact doesn't answer when
  you try to call, you have the opportunity to leave a voice mail then, too.
  Check out Figure 7-15.

  Voice mail options are the same as the options you have for regular
  voice calls. You can send voice mail to any of your contacts, even if they
  don't use Google Talk or Gmail. Voice mail messages appear alongside
  regular messages in Gmail, and you can either play them directly from
  Gmail or download them as MP3 files, as you can see in Figure 7-16.

- **Mute:** Click this button to turn your microphone off temporarily.

- **Sound indicators:** Shows with a volume indicator whether your Talk
  software is receiving input from a microphone.

**Figure 7-14:**
Share
pictures
and files in
Google Talk.

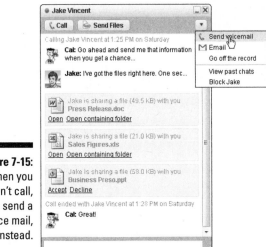

**Figure 7-15:**
When you
can't call,
send a
voice mail,
instead.

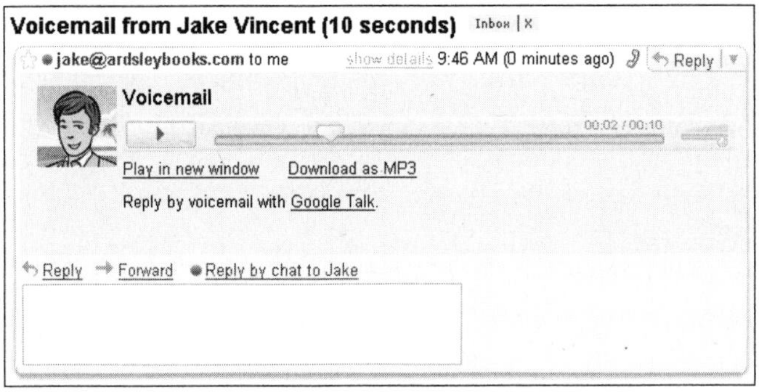

**Figure 7-16:**
Listen to
your voice
mails in
Gmail.

If you want to adjust your audio settings, click the Settings link in the upper-right corner of the Google Talk client window, then choose Audio from the options on the left. You may also have to adjust your volume settings in your operating system's control panel.

✔ **Internet connection strength:** Like bars on your mobile phone, these bars indicate your Internet connection's speed. The more bars, the better.

# Chapter 8

# Filling Your Calendar

. . . . . . . . . . . . . . . . . . . . . . . . . . . . . . . . . . . . . . . . . . . . .

. . . . . . . . . . . . . . . . . . . . . . . . . . . . . . . . . . . . . . . . . . . . .

*I*f you're like us, you never seem to have enough time. In spite of all the technological advances in the last few decades (or even just the last few years), every time you become more efficient, you quickly find something else to throw in that slot of saved time. Google Calendar can help you keep on time for all your daily events, whether you have to go watch a Little League game, hit a proposal out of the park at an important meeting, or pencil in some time for a power nap.

Google Calendar is an extremely useful calendar because it's online. (See Figure 8-1.) Instead of having to restrict it to a desktop computer or PDA, you can access Calendar from virtually any device with an Internet connection, just like the other Google Apps. With a few taps or clicks, you can view your agenda on your iPhone, schedule a meeting on your PC, and share a calendar with a colleague from an Internet café in Mumbai. In addition to having Google Calendar readily available from any Web-enabled computer, you can also easily use and share it.

This chapter takes you through logging into your Google Calendar, adding and changing events, setting event reminders, searching for events, and working with multiple calendars. (Chapter 9 covers how to share your calendar, access your appointments from a mobile phone, and sync up your events with Outlook and other calendaring software.)

**Figure 8-1:**
Use Google
Calendar to
keep on top
of your day.

Do you love shortcuts? Google Calendar uses some handy keyboard shortcuts that let you move around your calendar even faster. In this chapter,
we let you know the keyboard shortcuts to save you time — for example,
the Create Event shortcut is C. In this example, pressing the C key on your
keyboard allows you to create a new event and saves you a mouse click. You
can also find more keyboard shortcuts for all the Google Apps on the Cheat
Sheet at the beginning of this book.

# Starting Calendar

Like with the other Google Apps that we describe in this book, you can set up
Calendar for the first time in a snap. You should already have a username and
password. Check with your administrator if you don't.

Before you begin using Google Calendar for the first time, you may need
to authenticate your Google Apps account, if you haven't already. Flip to
Chapter 3 to review how to authenticate your account.

The first time you log into Google Calendar, you're asked to set a time zone. Establishing what time zone you're in can help if you need to coordinate schedules with colleagues in different time zones. (You can change the time zone later by clicking the Settings link at the top of your calendar screen.)

You can access Google Calendar in two ways:

- **Open Google Calendar from the Start Page:** Open your browser and navigate to your Start Page. On your Start Page, look for the Calendar gadget, shown in Figure 8-2. (You can use this gadget to quickly view your upcoming appointments.) Click the Google Calendar link in the title bar of the gadget to open your calendar.

- **Go directly to Google Calendar:** If you want to log into your Google Calendar directly, you can access it by typing **calendar** and the domain name of your organization in the address bar of your Web browser; for example, `http://calendar.ardsleybooks.com`. (Team Edition users should go to `http://calendar.google.com/a/yourdomain.com`.) This address takes you to your Google Calendar login page, as shown in Figure 8-3. Enter your username and password in the appropriate text boxes, then click the Sign In button to open your calendar.

You need to log in with your username and password every time you begin a new session of Calendar.

**Figure 8-2:**
Log into
Google
Calendar
from your
Start Page.

| Google Calendar | ▾ – ✕ |
| --- | --- |

| « | October 2007 | » |
| --- | --- | --- |

| S | M | T | W | T | F | S |
| --- | --- | --- | --- | --- | --- | --- |
| 23 | 24 | 25 | 26 | 27 | 28 | 29 |
| 30 | 1 | 2 | 3 | 4 | 5 | 6 |
| 7 | 8 | 9 | 10 | 11 | 12 | 13 |
| 14 | 15 | 16 | 17 | 18 | 19 | 20 |
| 21 | 22 | 23 | 24 | 25 | 26 | 27 |
| 28 | 29 | 30 | 31 | 1 | 2 | 3 |
| 4 | 5 | 6 | 7 | 8 | 9 | 10 |

Create Event  Hide Agenda

Today                                    Sat 10/13
              No events on October 13
Next Week                                Mon 10/15
12:00pm  Author meeting
                                         Wed 10/17
9:00am  Editor review
                                         Thu 10/18
6:30pm  Book launch party
In 2 weeks                               Mon 10/22
12:00pm  Author meeting

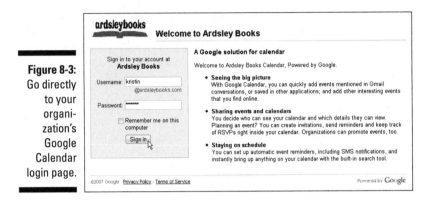

**Figure 8-3:** Go directly to your organization's Google Calendar login page.

# Creating and Changing Events

The most important Google Calendar procedure to know is how to add and change events. A blank calendar, after all, isn't very useful. Because users routinely need to add and change events, Google makes it incredibly simple to make those adjustments.

The following sections get you up and running in no time so that you can add and change events to your heart's delight. First, we show you five different ways to add events, then we go over how to change and delete them.

## Five ways to create events

You have multiple ways to add events easily to your calendar:

- ✔ **Quick Add:** Click the Quick Add link or press Q, and then simply click in the text box that appears and type your event details, as shown in the top of Figure 8-4. For example, you can enter something like **Brunch with Cal 11am Wednesday**. Google Calendar can figure out what you're saying, and it adds an event based on what you type into the Quick Add text box. It even creates recurring events if you enter an event like **Carpool with John 6:30am every Tuesday and Thursday**.

- ✔ **Highlight a time:** Using your mouse, click and drag to highlight a block of time. A white speech bubble will appear, similar to the one shown in Figure 8-4. Click in the What text box and type your event, then click the Create Event button.

If you want to add more event details, such as notes, locations, recurring options, or to add guests, click the Edit Event Details link rather than the Create Event button. This will take you to the Event Details screen, shown in Figure 8-5.

✔ **Create Event:** Click the Create Event link or press C to specify additional event details. On the Event Details screen that appears, you can specify What, When, Where, a Description, as shown in Figure 8-5.

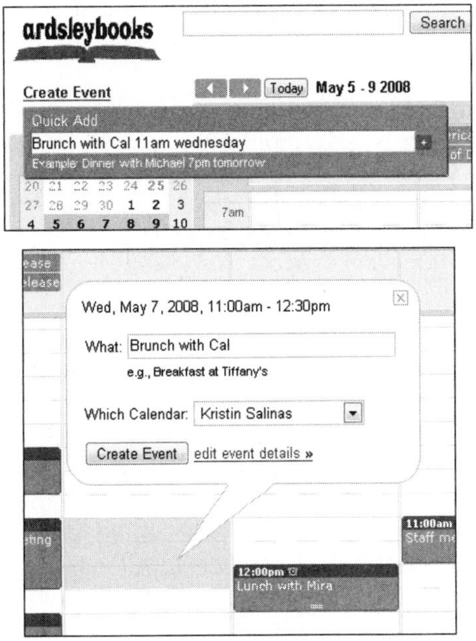

**Figure 8-4:**
Use Quick
Add (top) or
click a time
(bottom) to
enter an
event.

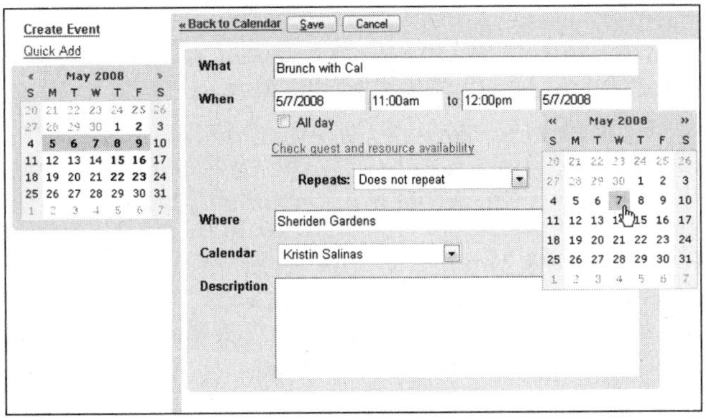

**Figure 8-5:**
Specify the
particulars
of an event.

Here are some hints for entering event details:

- *What:* Enter a brief description of the event in the What text box. Is it a meeting? A softball game? A trip to the stylist?

- *When:* Click in the When or To text box to make a pop-up calendar appear. This calendar helps you pinpoint the day on which an event begins or ends. When you click in the time text boxes, a drop-down list that features the time of day in half-hour increments appears. Select the day from the calendar and the time from the drop-down list, or type them in the appropriate text boxes. Selecting the All Day check box makes the event appear at the top of that particular day on your daily or weekly calendar.

- *Repeats:* Choose from this drop-down list whether you want your event to repeat daily, weekly, monthly, yearly, and more. Depending on what option you select, more options appear so that you can choose for how long you want the event to repeat. For example, if you choose Weekly from the Repeats drop-down list, the options to choose whether the event repeats every week and for how many weeks the event will repeat appears.

- *Where:* Enter a description of where the event takes place. If you enter a street address, the next time you look at your event, a Map link appears in the event speech bubble or in the Event Details screen. Clicking that link loads the address in Google Maps, which appears in a new window.

- *Calendar:* By default, events that you enter go to your main calendar (the one that is titled with your name). When you add multiple calendars, a Calendar drop-down list will appear and you can choose to add the event to a different calendar by choosing that calendar from the list.

- *Description:* Add details, such as directions or what you need to bring, or write a reminder to yourself.

When you finish entering the event's details, click the Save button to save the event and place it in your calendar.

✔ **Receive an invitation:** We discuss invitations in detail in Chapter 9, but here's a heads-up: If another Google Calendar user invites you to a meeting, that meeting appears automatically on your calendar with a question mark in the corner. Click the event to see the event bubble, as shown in Figure 8-6. You can tell the event host whether you can attend or not by clicking the Yes, No, or Maybe links. The event host receives your response automatically when you click one of these links. Declined events appear faded out in your calendar.

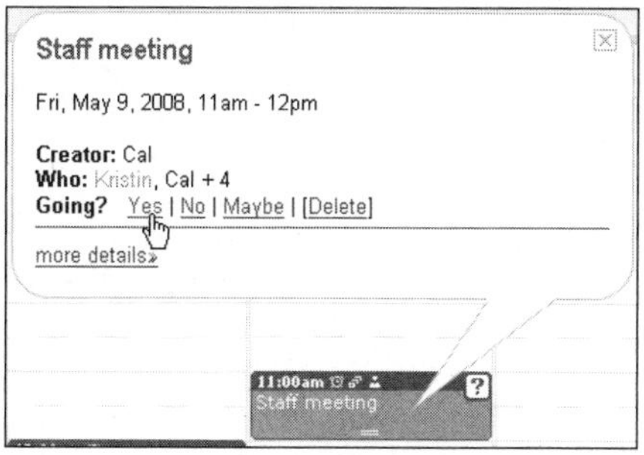

**Figure 8-6:**
Accept or
decline an
invitation on
your
calendar.

✔ **Add an event in Gmail:** You don't have to be in Calendar to add events. If someone sends you an e-mail with some dates and times, Gmail asks you whether you want to add the events discussed in the e-mail to your calendar, as shown in Figure 8-7. To add the events to your calendar from Gmail, click the Add to Calendar link that appears to the right of your e-mail message. A new Event Details window appears. Check the event details to see if they are correct and make any changes you want, and click Save Changes.

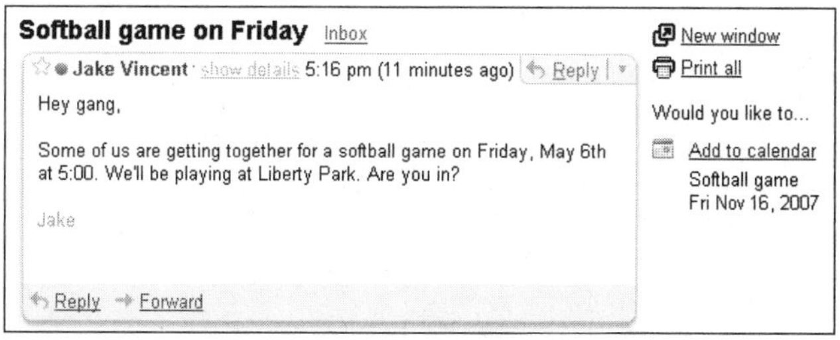

**Figure 8-7:**
Add an
event to
your
calendar
from Gmail.

## Moving your events around

An old saying goes that the only constant in life is change. Fortunately, making changes is easy in Google Calendar. When your meeting gets rescheduled and you need to move that event to a different time, you can change the event in your calendar in these ways:

✔ **To change the time of an event:** Simply click the shaded area of the event and drag it to the new time slot.

✔ **To extend or shorten an event:** Click and drag the double white lines along the bottom edge down to extend the event or up to shorten it.

✔ **To make more specific changes to an event:** Simply click the event and click the Edit Event Details link in the speech bubble that appears. Check out the previous section for additional info about the Event Details screen that appears.

If you change an event that you didn't create (such as a lunch your supervisor invited you to), the event doesn't change in the host's calendar. Make sure you call or e-mail your host so he or she can change the event in his or her calendar, too.

## Deleting events

To delete an event, simply click an event, then click the Delete link in the speech bubble that appears. Also, if you double-click an event, the Event Details screen appears, and you can click the Delete button at the top of that screen to delete that appointment.

# Setting Up Calendar Notifications

When you have events in your calendar, you can set Google Calendar to send you a reminder before an event. After all, what's the use of having an online calendar if you have to keep looking at it to see what's coming up in your day? Depending on how you set notifications, Google Calendar either shows you a pop-up reminder, sends a text message to your mobile phone, or sends you a friendly e-mail.

In the following sections, we cover how to set up universal event reminders for all your calendar events, then show you how to create custom reminders for only specific, very important events.

To see pop-up reminders, you must have a browser window open and Google Calendar loaded. To receive text messages, you must register your mobile phone (which we tell you how to do in the "Registering your mobile phone to receive notifications" section, later in this chapter).

## Creating universal event reminders

By default, your primary calendar displays a pop-up window ten minutes prior to every event you create. You may like this feature, or you may not. Whatever your preference, changing this setting is as easy as pie. Just follow these steps:

1. **To change your notifications, click the arrow to the right of a calendar from the list on the left side of the screen (your main calendar appears with your name as the title), and then select Notifications from the drop-down list that appears, as shown at the top of Figure 8-8.**

   The Notifications tab appears, as shown at the bottom of Figure 8-8.

2. **In the Event Reminders section of the Notifications tab, select Pop-Up, Email, or SMS (text message) from the By Default, Remind Me Via drop-down list; then select how soon before each event you want to receive the reminder from the Before Each Event drop-down list.**

   If SMS doesn't appear in the By Default, Remind Me Via drop-down list and you want to receive reminders on your mobile phone, follow the steps in the following section to register your mobile phone with Google Calendar, then return to these steps.

3. **Click the Add Another Reminder link to add up to five total notifications.**

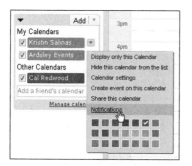

**Figure 8-8:**
Set default reminders and configure your mobile phone.

4. **In the Choose How You Would Like to Be Notified section, select the check boxes in the Email or SMS column (depending on which method you prefer).**

   For example, select the check box in the Email column to the right of New Invitations to receive an e-mail notification when someone sends you an invitation to an event.

5. **To disable a notification, click the Remove link to the right of the reminder.**

6. **When you're happy with your settings, click the Save button to return to your calendar.**

## Registering your mobile phone to receive notifications

Before your mobile phone can receive notifications from and communicate with your calendar, you must first register your phone with Google Calendar by following these steps:

1. **From the Notifications screen, click the Set Up Your Mobile Phone to Receive Notifications link.**

   Alternatively, from your main calendar, click the Settings link at the top of the page, and then click the Mobile Setup tab. The Mobile Setup tab appears, as shown in Figure 8-9.

2. **Choose your country from the Country drop-down list.**

3. **Click in the Phone Number text box and enter your mobile phone number.**

   It doesn't matter what format you use. 555-555-1212 will work the same as (555) 555-1212 or 5555551212.

**Figure 8-9:** Register your phone to enable SMS scheduling.

4. **Select your carrier from the Carrier drop-down list.**

If your carrier doesn't appear in the Carrier drop-down list, click the What Carriers Are Supported? link. If you are trying to connect from outside of the United States and the Carrier drop-down list doesn't appear, click the See Help Center for Supported Providers link. A list appears in a new window with all the supported carriers worldwide. If your provider appears on the Help Center page and is supported, return to your calendar notification settings, leave the Carrier field blank, and continue to Step 5.

5. **Click the Send Verification Code button.**

A text message appears on your phone within a few minutes.

6. **Click in the Verification Code text box and type the code that you received in your phone's text message, and then click the Finish Setup button.**

Although SMS notifications are free from Google, your mobile carrier may charge you for each text message that you send or receive. Be sure to check your phone's plan before you use SMS reminders extensively.

## Adding reminders to individual events

You can easily set reminders for individual events. Follow these steps to make sure you don't miss that important meeting or softball game:

1. **Click an event that you want to add a reminder to, and then click the Edit Event Details or More Details link at the bottom of the speech bubble that appears.**

You're taken to the Event Details screen.

2. **In the Options pane on the right of the Event Details screen, click the Add a Reminder link to add up to five different notifications, as shown in Figure 8-10.**

3. **Use the drop-down lists to select what type of notification you want and when.**

For example, to receive an e-mail reminder an hour before the event, select Email from the left drop-down list and 1 Hour from the right drop-down list.

4. **Click the Remove link to disable a notification.**

The event reminder disappears right away, and you'll have to rely on your own memory.

5. **Click the Save button to save your changes and return to your calendar.**

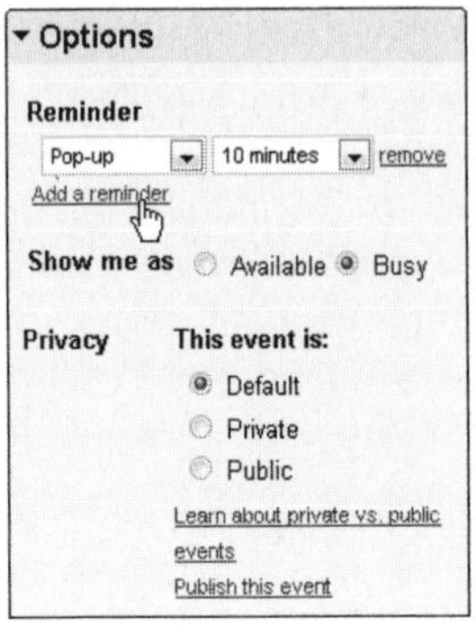

**Figure 8-10:**
Add a
reminder in
the Options
pane.

# Changing Your Calendar Views

Google Calendar lets you change the way you view your schedule — just click the blue tabs in the top-right corner of your screen. Here are the basic calendar views:

✓ **Day:** Click the Day tab or press D to view your appointments for a given day, starting with the first upcoming event.

✓ **Week:** Click the Week tab or press W to see a full week's worth of events. All-day events appear along the top of the calendar.

You can customize your week view to start on a day other than Sunday or to hide weekends. Click the Settings link in the top-left corner of the screen, then click the arrows to the right of Week Starts On and Show Weekends, and select the options that you want from the drop-down lists that appear. Then scroll to the bottom of the Settings screen and click Save to return to your calendar.

✓ **Month:** Click the Month tab or press M to see your month at a glance.

✓ **Next 4 Days:** Click the Next 4 Days tab or press X to see this custom view. To change the time period, click the Settings link at the top of the screen and locate the Custom View section (it's halfway down the Settings screen). Select your favorite custom time frame from the drop-down list in the Custom View section, such as Next 2 Days to Next 4 Weeks.

✓ **Agenda:** Click the Agenda tab or press A to see your agenda. The agenda is handy because it lists all the Calendar items in a condensed, easy-to-read format. When you click any event, it expands to show you the details.

You don't have to be limited to the options in the preceding list. You can view any number of days, from one day to seven weeks, by highlighting the days on the mini-calendar on the left of any of the calendar screens.

After you find a view that you like, use the arrows at the top left to move forward and backward in increments of that time period. You can also press N to move forward and P to move backward. To return to the current day, click the Today button or press T.

# Printing Your Calendar

You can use Google Calendar's powerful print feature to print a copy of any calendar view or save your calendar to a PDF that you can send to others. Simply select your preferred calendar view (see the preceding section for details), and then click the Print link to the left of the tabs. The Calendar Print Preview window appears, as shown in Figure 8-11.

In the Calendar Print Preview window, you can adjust the size of the font by selecting from the Font Size drop-down list, choose which direction you want it to print by selecting from the Orientation drop-down list, and print the calendar in black and white (which is best for laser printers) by selecting the Black & White check box. (To print in color, make sure the Black & White check box is deselected.) Click the Print button to complete printing. Click the Save As button to download a PDF version to your desktop.

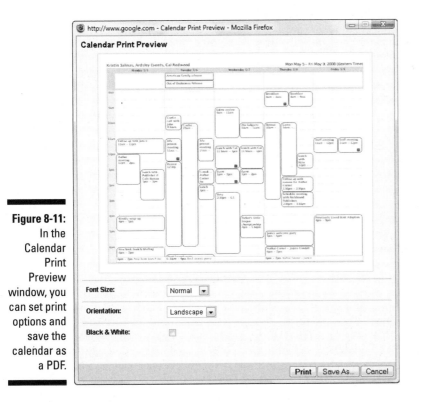

**Figure 8-11:**
In the Calendar Print Preview window, you can set print options and save the calendar as a PDF.

To print a blank calendar, return to your calendar screen and deselect the check box beside each of your calendars in the Calendars list on the left of the screen, and then click the Print link. When you finish, select the calendars' check boxes again to make your events reappear.

# Using Multiple Calendars

In the sections earlier in this chapter, we cover how to create events, how to add notifications, how to change your calendar view, and how to print your calendar. All these tools are pretty exciting, but in case you were worried, you have even more that you can explore in Google Calendar.

In the following sections, we show you how to create multiple calendars (for example, one for work, one for your bowling league, and one for your weekend adventures). We also cover how you can add public calendars, such as sports schedules, daily closing stock prices, and holidays. Put all your cares on Google Calendar so you can spend less time remembering appointments and more time doing the stuff you love.

## Adding calendars

First things first — check out the Add menu in the Calendars list to the left of your main calendar by clicking the arrow to the right of Add. You can see it in action in Figure 8-12. Using the options in this menu, you can create calendars, add public calendars, and more. Here's what each option in the Add menu does:

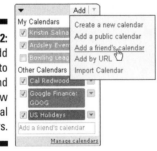

**Figure 8-12:** Use the Add menu to create and show additional calendars.

✔ **Create a New Calendar:** Select this option to create a separate calendar for your bowling league, child's soccer schedule, or other events that you don't want to appear on your main calendar.

✔ **Add a Public Calendar:** Select this option to explore calendars that others have made, including holidays, your alma mater's football game schedule, or stock quotes, and have them appear in your calendar next to your other events. When you select this option, you will see a screen that lets you browse the most popular public calendars. You can also use the Search text box at the top of the Calendar gallery screen to search for any of hundreds of others. To add a public calendar, simply click the Add to Calendar button. (The Calendar gallery is similar to the gadget directory that we discuss in Chapter 3.)

To follow stocks, enter the ticker symbol of your favorite company in the Search text box at the top of the Calendar gallery screen and click the Search Public Calendars button. Look for the Google Finance calendar for the company you want and click the Add to Calendar button. Each day's closing price appears at the top of each day on your calendar.

✔ **Add a Friend's Calendar:** Co-workers who use Google Calendar have shared calendars by default. To show a friend's or colleague's calendar alongside your calendar, first select this option and then enter your contact's e-mail address in the text box on the screen that appears. Finally, click the Add button to the right of the text box and your contact's shared calendar appears automatically so you can see what that contact is up to. If he or she doesn't have Google Calendar, you can invite him or her to create a calendar.

However, not all calendars may be available. We discuss how to make your calendar private in Chapter 9.

✔ **Add by URL:** When you come across a Web site that has a calendar feed that you want to add to your Google Calendar, copy the URL, and then return to your calendar. Click the Add menu in the Calendars list on the left-hand side of the screen, select Add by URL, and in the screen that appears, paste the URL into the Public Calendar Address text box. Don't forget to click the Add button when you're done.

✔ **Import Calendar:** Use this tool to add events from another calendar program, such as Outlook or iCal. See Chapter 9 for instructions on how to import and export events.

## Changing colors and settings

Whether you have only a few or a whole plethora of calendars, you can easily manage them from the Calendars list. To hide calendar events tied to a specific calendar, deselect the check box beside each calendar name. Select the check box again when you want to show that calendar. You may find hiding calendars particularly handy if your calendar is bursting with events.

In addition to selecting or deselecting the calendars' check boxes, clicking the down arrow to the right of a calendar gives you some more options, including specifying colors for that calendar (refer to the top of Figure 8-8):

- ✔ **Display Only This Calendar:** Instead of checking and unchecking boxes every time you want to see the events related to a specific calendar, select this option to see only the events on that calendar on your main calendar screen. Other calendars and events disappear from your main calendar screen until you select the calendars' check boxes again.

- ✔ **Hide This Calendar from the List:** Selecting this option makes the calendar disappear from the list. Click the Manage Calendars link at the bottom of the Calendars list for options to reveal, hide, and delete your calendars.

- ✔ **Calendar Settings:** Select this option to open the Calendar Details screen. You can change the calendar name and description, and see the calendar address. In the Calendar Details tab, you can also access the tool that you can use to embed your calendar on a Web page, which we cover in Chapter 9.

- ✔ **Create Event on This Calendar:** Selecting this option does the same thing as clicking the Create Event link at the top of the main Calendar screen, except it automatically assigns the event to the specific calendar. (When you have multiple calendars and click the Create Event link, you can specify on which calendar you want to create your event by choosing from the Calendar drop-down list on the Create Event screen.)

- ✔ **Share This Calendar:** Select this option to show the Calendar Details screen, where you can choose how much information you want to share for each calendar. We cover calendar sharing in depth in Chapter 9.

- ✔ **Notifications:** New calendars don't have notifications by default, but you can change those settings by selecting Notifications and choosing your options on the Calendar Details screen. (See the section "Setting Up Calendar Notifications," earlier in this chapter, for details.)

- ✔ **Color:** Clicking a color box changes all the events associated with that calendar to the selected color. In addition to being visually appealing, choosing different colors for different calendars can help you tell at a glance what's going on when and if you have any schedule conflicts.

Feel free to adjust these settings until you find a calendar that makes you smile. For more control over these settings, click the Manage Calendars link at the bottom of the Calendars list.

Be careful not to click the trash can icon in the Calendars screen (click the Manage Calendars link to go to the Calendars screen) unless you're certain that you want to delete a calendar. (See Figure 8-13.) You can add public calendars again, but if you delete one of your main calendars without sharing it with someone first, you have no way to get it back.

**Figure 8-13:**
Clicking
the trash
can icon
permanently
deletes a
calendar.

**Calendar Settings**

General  **Calendars**  Mobile Setup

**My Calendars**

| CALENDAR | SHARING | | | |
|---|---|---|---|---|
| ⊞ Kristin Salinas | Shared: Edit settings | Notifications | | 🗑 |
| ⊞ Ardsley Events | Shared: Edit settings | Notifications | Hide | 🗑 |
| ⊞ Bowling League | Share this calendar | Notifications | Hide | 🗑 |

Create new calendar

# Searching Your Calendar

Search is one of our favorite features of Google Calendar. Sometimes, you
may forget an event. You may even forget on which calendar the event is
located. No problem. Just click in the Search text box at the top of your
Calendar screen or press / (the backslash key); type a few words about the
event, such as **lunch**; and click the Search My Calendars button. A list of all
the lunches you have on your calendars appears, as shown in Figure 8-14.
Type in even more information, and you can find more specific events. Click
the Search My Calendars button to see results across all your calendars.

Your search results appear in a new tab along the top, so you can switch
between your normal calendar views and compare results. In your search
results, click the date to the left of an event to see that day's agenda. Click
the event time or name to see and edit the event's details.

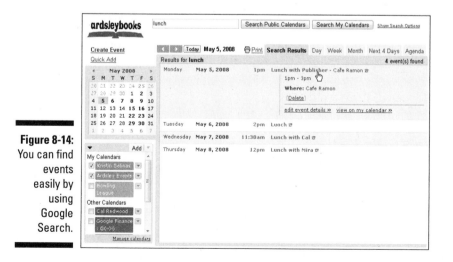

**Figure 8-14:**
You can find
events
easily by
using
Google
Search.

You can also use the Search text box to find public calendars at any time, as discussed in the section "Adding calendars," earlier in this chapter.

You can usually use the Search text box at the top of your Calendar screen to find the event that you can't remember. Suppose, however, that you want to see only meetings with your colleague Janice in a certain time period, and you can't remember any of the meeting specifics. Google has the answer. The Show Search Options link appears (in tiny type) to the right of the Search text box. Click that link to reveal more specific search text boxes, as shown in Figure 8-15. You can add details, such as a date range, that narrow the search results. Click the Search button, and your results appear.

When you finish with the advanced search, click the Cancel button or the Hide Search Options link in the top-right corner to hide the search options and return to the basic calendar screen.

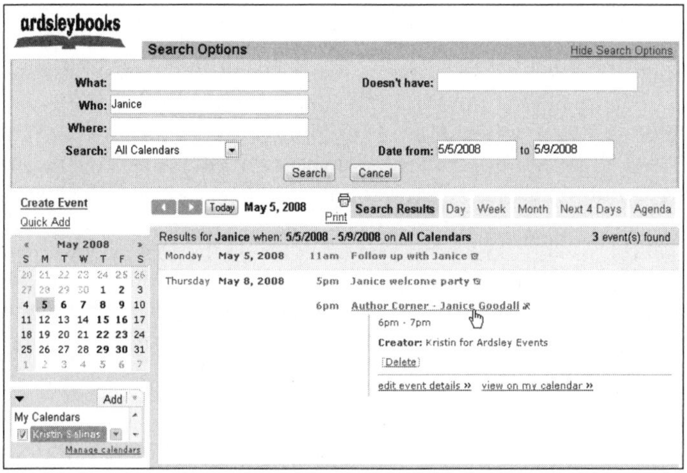

**Figure 8-15:** Narrow your calendar search with specific event details.

# Chapter 9

# Sharing Your Calendar with Others

*A*lthough it can't add an extra hour to every day, Google Calendar can be a huge time-saver for organizations, schools, businesses, and families. You can send out meeting and event invitations, and track people's responses, even if they use other calendaring programs. You can also share your calendar with people you know simply by sending them an e-mail, and you can create a public calendar to which anyone can subscribe. So, if your organization is going to have a fundraiser, you can easily publicize it by displaying it on your internal or external Web site.

An online calendar does you no good if you can't coordinate schedules or take your valuable information with you on the go. So, those brilliant Google engineers pulled together all the powerful collaborating tools to make your calendar work for you and your colleagues and play well with the other Google Apps.

Now, families can keep track of those family reunions, and parents can coordinate their kids' schedules from home or work. Salespeople can track leads and follow up with their customers. Schools can let teachers book time in the library, share a mobile computer lab, or work with parents to help their students. And don't forget about college students — they can follow a class schedule and book time with their study group by using the campus-wide Google Calendar.

This chapter shows you how to invite people to events, coordinate team meetings when everyone has a different schedule, reserve a conference room or equipment, publish your calendar to a Web site, and then take all your information with you — either on your laptop (with Outlook or iCal) or your Internet-enabled mobile device.

# Working with Invitations

How about a picnic or a party? You can easily send out invitations to any kind of event, whether it's a business meeting or poker night. Anyone can receive your invitations, even if they don't use Google Calendar or don't have a Google account.

## Creating invitations

Sending event invitations is a breeze; just follow these steps:

1. **To invite guests to a new event, click the Create Event link on the main Calendar screen; to invite guests to an event that already exists on your calendar, click the event to reveal its speech bubble and then click the Edit Event Details link.**

   On the Event Details screen, look for the pane titled Guests, as shown on the left side of Figure 9-1.

2. **In the text box in the Guests pane, enter the e-mail addresses of people that you want to invite to your event. Separate each address with a comma.**

   You can also click the Choose from Contacts link to select guests from your Contacts list, as shown on the right side of Figure 9-1.

3. **Select the check boxes in the Guests Can section if you want to allow guests to invite others and see the guest list.**

**Figure 9-1:** Enter other users' e-mail addresses to add them to an event as guests.

4. **When you finish adding your guests, click the Save button at the top of the Event Details screen.**

   The Send Update dialog box appears, giving you the option to send an e-mail to invite your guests.

5. **Click the Send button to send the invitation or the Don't Send button to save your event without notifying your guests.**

   Each of your guests promptly receives an e-mail message that asks him or her whether he or she plans to attend. Those guests who use Google Calendar see the event appear automatically on their calendars with a question mark in the event's top-right corner. Guests who use Outlook can respond directly from the e-mail, and the event appears automatically on their Outlook calendar, as well.

## *Responding to invitations*

You (or your guests) can respond to invitations in one of two ways. First, you can click a link in the e-mail that you receive, as shown in Figure 9-2. Simply click the Yes, No, or Maybe link, and the host's event is updated to indicate your response.

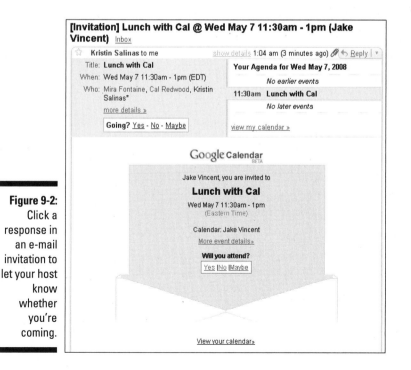

**Figure 9-2:**
Click a
response in
an e-mail
invitation to
let your host
know
whether
you're
coming.

Alternatively, you can respond directly from Google Calendar by clicking an event that shows a question mark in the top-right corner, and then in the event bubble that appears, clicking Yes, No, or Maybe, as shown in Figure 9-3. If you click Yes, the question mark disappears. If you click No, the event becomes faded out and the question mark disappears. If you click Maybe, the question mark remains, but your host will know that you're considering attending. You can always change your response later by clicking the event again.

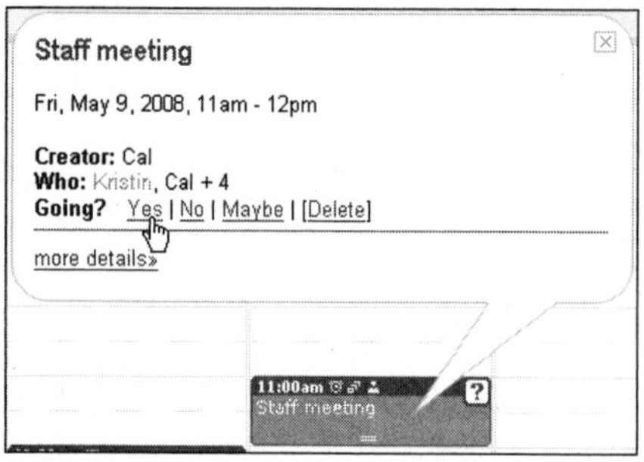

**Figure 9-3:** Click an event and indicate whether you plan to attend.

**Checking guest status and e-mailing guests**

When your event draws near, you may want to see how many people are planning to attend. You can check the status of your guests' responses by double-clicking the event, as shown in Figure 9-4.

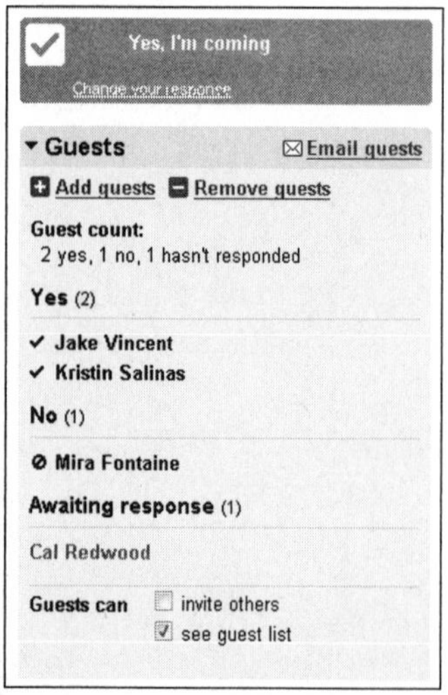

**Figure 9-4:** View who plans to attend in the event's details.

If you decide to change event details later in the Event Details screen, click Save and a dialog box appears, asking if you want to notify the guests about the change. To get in touch with your guests at any time, click the Email Guests link in the Guests pane to send a quick message. An e-mail window appears, similar to Figure 9-5. Don't forget to select the Send a Copy to Myself check box if you want to receive a copy of the message, as well.

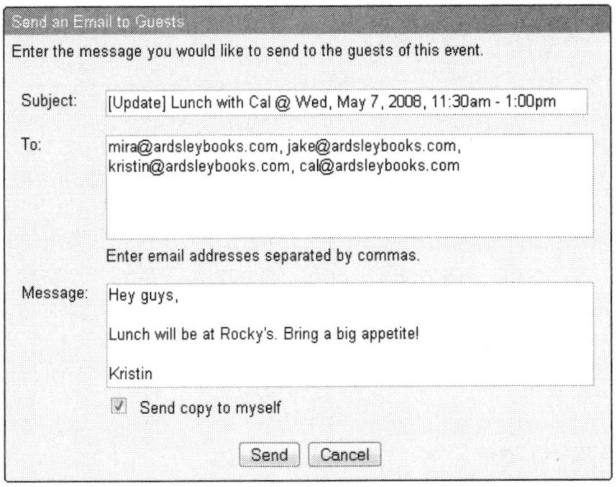

**Figure 9-5:**
E-mail your guests if you want to give them updates or reminders.

> **Send an Email to Guests**
> Enter the message you would like to send to the guests of this event.
>
> Subject: [Update] Lunch with Cal @ Wed, May 7, 2008, 11:30am - 1:00pm
>
> To: mira@ardsleybooks.com, jake@ardsleybooks.com, kristin@ardsleybooks.com, cal@ardsleybooks.com
>
> Enter email addresses separated by commas.
>
> Message: Hey guys,
> Lunch will be at Rocky's. Bring a big appetite!
> Kristin
>
> ☑ Send copy to myself
>
> [Send] [Cancel]

## Sending invitations directly from Gmail

Gmail likes to help you play the part of super awesome scheduler, too. Click the Add Event Info link, just below the subject line in the Compose Message window, to expand the event info area, allowing you to enter details for an event, as shown in Figure 9-6.

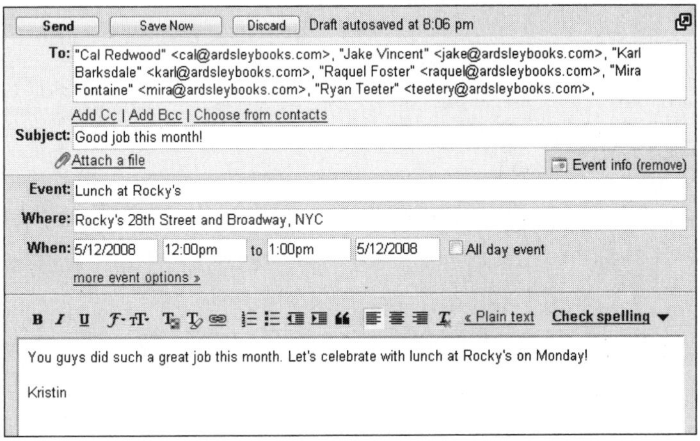

**Figure 9-6:**
Add event details while you're sending an e-mail.

> [Send] [Save Now] [Discard] Draft autosaved at 8:06 pm
>
> To: "Cal Redwood" <cal@ardsleybooks.com>, "Jake Vincent" <jake@ardsleybooks.com>, "Karl Barksdale" <karl@ardsleybooks.com>, "Raquel Foster" <raquel@ardsleybooks.com>, "Mira Fontaine" <mira@ardsleybooks.com>, "Ryan Teeter" <teetery@ardsleybooks.com>,
> Add Cc | Add Bcc | Choose from contacts
> Subject: Good job this month!
> 📎 Attach a file                    ☐ Event info (remove)
> Event: Lunch at Rocky's
> Where: Rocky's 28th Street and Broadway, NYC
> When: 5/12/2008  12:00pm  to 1:00pm  5/12/2008  ☐ All day event
> more event options »
>
> B *I* U *ℱ·𝕋·* T₂ T₂ ∞ ≣ ≣ ⫷ ⫸ 66 ≣ ≣ ≣ *I*  < Plain text   Check spelling ▾
>
> You guys did such a great job this month. Let's celebrate with lunch at Rocky's on Monday!
> Kristin

Enter your event details (see Chapter 8 for more on how to get the event details right), type your message, and click the Send button. The event is automatically added to your calendar, as well as your guests' calendars. Everyone can respond in the customary fashion. (See the "Responding to invitations" section, earlier in this chapter.)

# Making Your Calendar Available to Others

You can share your calendar with your friends, your soccer team, your family, and your colleagues. When you share with others, you can see each other's calendars side by side. By default, your main calendar can be accessed by other Google Apps users in your organization (or Internet domain), but no one outside of it. In the following sections, we go over how to adjust your sharing settings and make your calendar private, if you want.

## Sharing options

For each calendar that you manage, you can select how you want to share your events with others. To change these settings, click the down arrow beside a calendar in the Calendars list and select Share This Calendar from the drop-down list that appears. The Events Details screen appears with the Share This Calendar tab active, similar to Figure 9-7.

Depending on what your administrator chooses, you may or may not be able to share details from your main calendar with people outside your organization. Be sure to click the Save button after you make any changes.

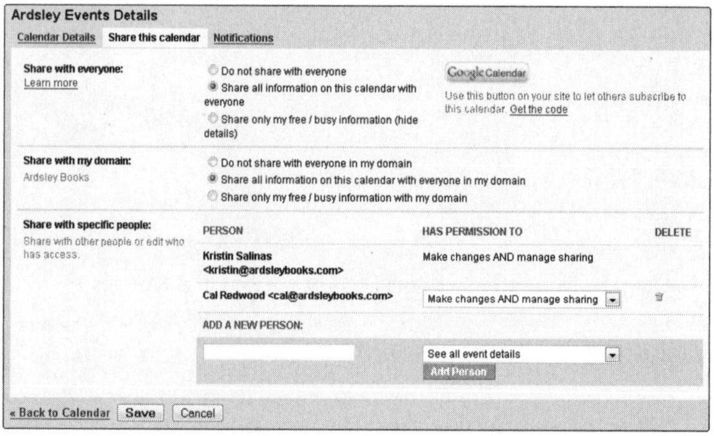

**Figure 9-7:** Choose how much information you want to share.

The Share This Calendar tab has the following areas:

✔ **Share with Everyone:** Choose how much event information you want to make publicly available. If you choose any option except the Do Not Share with Everyone radio button, anyone can search your publicly available calendar.

✔ **Share with My Domain:** Choose how much information you want your co-workers or colleagues to see.

✔ **Share with Specific People:** Allow individuals to view and/or manage events on your calendar. We cover these options in depth in the following section.

For the first two sections in the preceding list, you have the following options, which you can change at any time:

✔ **Do Not Share with Everyone:** If you select this radio button, no one other than individuals to whom you specifically give permission can access your calendar. This is the most private setting.

✔ **Share All My Information on This Calendar with Everyone:** Select this radio button if you want your co-workers or anyone, in general, to see your event details. Although we don't recommend using this setting to share your main calendar outside of your domain, you must select this radio button for calendars that you want to post on a Web site.

✔ **Share Only My Free/Busy Information (Hide Details):** Select this radio button to allow others to see when you have openings in your schedule but not allow them to see event specifics. They see only blocks labeled Busy in time periods in which you have scheduled events, as Figure 9-8 shows.

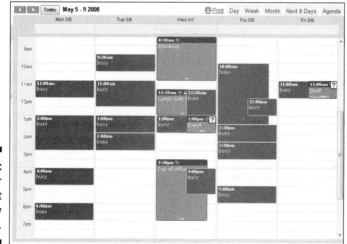

**Figure 9-8:**
Share your
time without
giving away
any details.

## Sharing with specific people

Not only can you let others see your calendar events, but you can give your friends and co-workers permission to make changes and add events, as well as invite others to join in.

Follow these steps to give a specific person permission to make changes on your calendar:

1. **In the Calendars list, select Share This Calendar from the appropriate calendar's drop-down list.**

   The Share This Calendar tab appears (refer to Figure 9-7).

2. **In the Add a New Person text box, enter the e-mail address of the person with whom you want to share your calendar.**

   If the e-mail address that you're adding is one of your contacts, the name appears automatically below the text box while you type.

3. **From the drop-down list in the Add a New Person section, choose what permissions you want to give that person. You can choose one of the following options:**

   - *Make Changes AND Manage Sharing:* Your friend or colleague can add, delete, and change events and also allow or deny other people access to make changes to your calendar.

   - *Make Changes to Events:* Your friend or co-worker can add and delete events or make changes to event details on your calendar.

   - *See All Event Details:* Other users can see all your event details on your calendar, but can't make any changes.

   - *See Free/Busy Information (No Details):* Other people can see when your events are scheduled, but can't view event details. Events will only say Busy (refer to Figure 9-8).

4. **Click the Add Person button.**

   Google Calendar sends an e-mail to that user to let him or her know that you've shared a calendar, and it also automatically adds your calendar to his or her Google Calendar.

5. **Repeat these steps for any other people with whom you want to share your calendar.**

## Scheduling Resources

The Google Apps Calendar lets you easily find the best time and place for everyone to meet. When you share calendars across your organization, you can view other people's schedules and immediately find the time slot that works well for everyone. Coordinating schedules has never been so simple. If you're using Premier Edition or Education Edition, you can schedule rooms, equipment, and other resources so the end-of-year party can go off without a hitch. (Sorry, non-Google Apps Google Calendar users, you don't get to work with other people's schedules, so go ahead and skip over this section.)

## Coordinating other people's schedules

When you need to schedule a meeting and you're not sure what time is optimal for everyone, follow these steps:

1. **Click the Create Event link.**

   You see the Event Details screen, where you can add the specifics of your meeting or party.

2. **Click the Check Guest and Resource Availability link.**

   The Find a Time window, similar to Figure 9-9, appears.

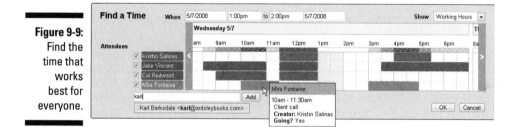

**Figure 9-9:**
Find the
time that
works
best for
everyone.

3. **Add a person to the list of attendees by clicking in the text box below the timeline, entering the name or e-mail address of the person that you want to attend, and then clicking the Add button.**

   Every time you click the Add button, each person's schedule appears in the timeline, showing blocks of time in which they already have events. If your organization is using Google Apps Premier Edition or Education Edition, you also see a Room Finder section below the timeline. The following section explains more about using the Room Finder.

   Now you can find a time that's free for everyone; to move forward or backward a time period, click the blue arrow bars to the right or left of the timeline, or click and drag the gray bar along the top of the timeline left or right.

4. **Highlight a block of time on the timeline that works best for everyone, and then click the OK button in the lower-right corner of the Find a Time window.**

Your event details are updated to include the attendees that you create in Step 3 and the time that you select in Step 4.

The thin bar directly below the hours in the schedule shows how heavily people are scheduled. Each busy person at a particular time makes the bar darker. If you can't find a free time slot (which appears white in the bar), look for light gray striped areas, which have only one or two busy people at that time. Hover your mouse cursor over a busy guest's scheduled block to see the details of that particular event, if they're being shared. Then check with that person about the possibility of changing a conflicting appointment.

5. **Back on the Event Details screen, enter your additional event details, such as a description and reminders, and click Save.**

    Just like when you add guests (see the "Creating invitations" section, earlier in this chapter), a dialog box appears that asks whether you want to send invitations to your attendees.

6. **Click the Send button to send the invitations or the Don't Send button to leave your attendees in the dark (the event will still appear on their calendar).**

## Using the Room Finder (Premier Edition and Education Edition only)

With Google Apps Premier Edition and Education Edition, you can schedule rooms and equipment, such as lecture halls, projectors, or company vehicles, in addition to coordinating schedules and times (see the previous section).

When you click the Check Guest and Resource Availability link in the Event Details screen, the Find a Time window opens, and the Room Finder section appears below the timeline, as shown in Figure 9-10. Use the Filter Room list box to quickly find the room or object that you're looking for. If it's available during the time that you select (we explain how to set an event's time in the preceding section), a green box appears to the left of the room name. If it's not available, a red X appears to the left of it, instead. Just like when you add attendees, select a room from the list and click the Add Room button to show the room's schedule. Locate a room or object that works well for you and your guests, as well as a time during which the room or object is available, and then click OK. When you save your event, the time that you specify for the event is blocked out on the room's or object's calendar so that others can't double-book it.

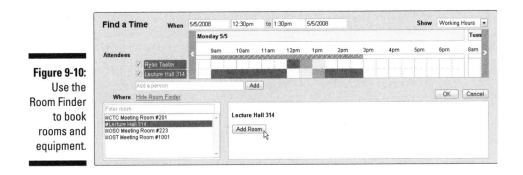

**Figure 9-10:**
Use the
Room Finder
to book
rooms and
equipment.

# Embedding Calendar on Your Web Site or Blog

While we've been surfing the Internet over the years, we've come across many organizations (particularly schools) that attempt to share calendars on their Web sites. Often, the tools that they use are so complicated (and frustrating) that the calendars falls into disrepair, and no one ever updates or visits them again. Is there something Google Calendar can do about it? Absolutely!

Google Calendar is easy to use and share in general. You can place your calendar on a Web site just as simply. And the best part is that after you put your calendar on a Web site, Google automatically updates it every time you add a new event, so you don't have to think twice about whether it'll work.

These steps show how to place your code by using Google Page Creator (check out `http://pages.google.com` or if you're a Google Apps administrator, see Chapter 15), but the steps work for just about any HTML editor:

1. **Create a new calendar by clicking the Add button in the Calendars list and selecting Create a New Calendar.**

   You see the Calendar Details screen.

   You probably don't want to share your personal calendar (and your administrator may restrict sharing outside of your domain), so creating a new calendar will be useful. If you already have an additional calendar you want to share, select Share This Calendar from that calendar's drop-down list to go to the Calendar Details screen.

2. **Enter a name for your calendar, and then select the Share All Information on This Calendar with Everyone radio button in the Share with Everyone section.**

As soon as you select the radio button, a dialog box appears, asking whether you're sure that you want to share your calendar with everyone. If you click Yes, the events on your specific calendar will be available to the public and anyone will be able to search for your events.

3. **To make your calendar available to publish on the Web, click the Yes button in the Are Your Sure? dialog box, and then click the Save button at the bottom of the screen.**

   You may see another dialog box asking you once again if you are really, really sure that you want your calendar shared with everyone on the Internet. Click the Yes button once again if this box appears.

4. **Configure your Web page calendar by clicking the arrow to the right of your calendar's name in the Calendars list and clicking the Calendar Settings link in the drop-down list that appears.**

   Scroll down to the Embed This Calendar tool, as shown in Figure 9-11. If you want a simple, full-screen monthly calendar, just select the HTML code that appears in the text box and copy it, then skip to Step 6.

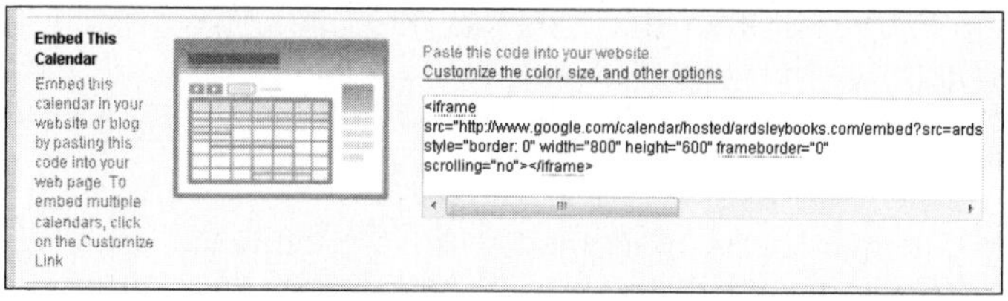

**Figure 9-11:** Copy the code to embed a monthly calendar.

5. **(Optional) Customize your calendar by clicking the Customize the Color, Size, and Other Options link.**

   Okay, now's the time to let your creative juices flow. A new window like the one in Figure 9-12 opens. The calendar on the right in the figure is a preview of the calendar as it will appear on your site. Select any of the options on the left and then click the Update HTML button to see your changes. When you're satisfied with a calendar and are ready to show it on your site, select the final HTML code that appears in the text box at the top of the window and copy it.

6. **Open your HTML editor and paste the HTML code you copied in Step 4 or Step 5. To use Google Page Creator to paste the code into your Web site and publish the page, follow these steps:**

   *a. In Google Page Creator, open the page on which you want to place the calendar by clicking the page title on the Site Manager screen.*

b. *Click inside the section of the page where you want to place your calendar, and then click the Edit HTML link in the bottom-right corner of the screen.*

A window appears on your screen, similar to Figure 9-13, that enables you to paste your code.

c. *Paste the code into the large text box and click the Update button to return to your page and continue editing.*

While you're editing the HTML, you can click the Preview tab in the top-right corner of the screen to make sure your calendar appears how you want it.

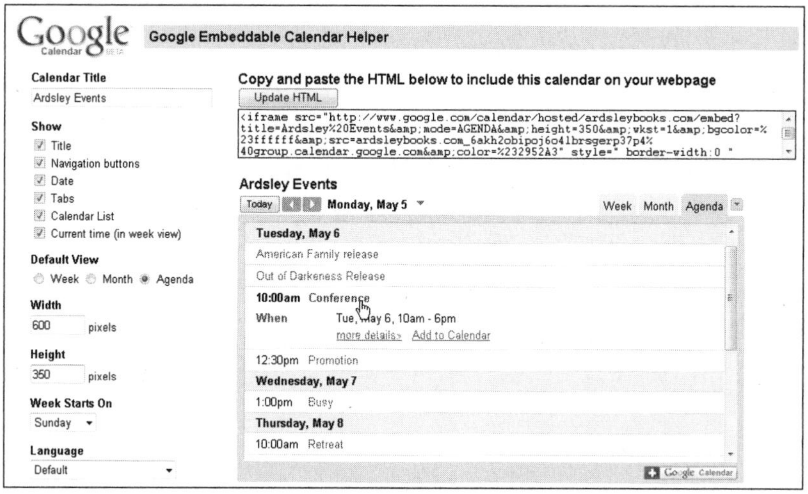

**Figure 9-12:** The options on the left enable you to customize your calendar.

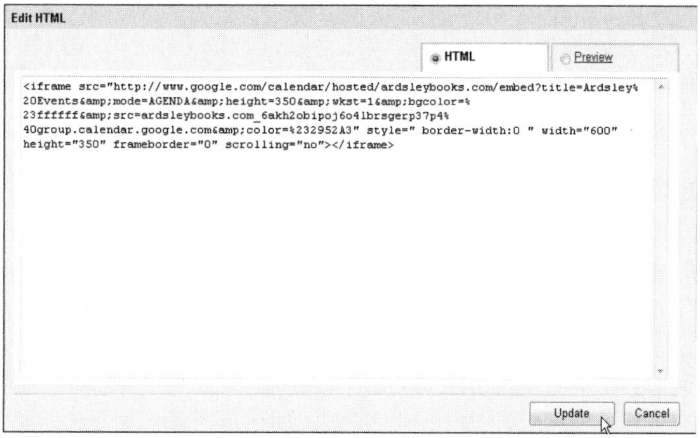

**Figure 9-13:** Paste the code into the text box on the HTML tab.

     *d. Make sure the calendar appears on your page how you want it, and then click the Publish button.*

        Your changes will be saved, and now anyone who visits your page will see your amazing calendar and be able to keep up with your public events.

     *e. Click the View Live or Preview link to the right of the Publish button to open your site in a new browser window and marvel at the beauty that you created.*

    Figure 9-14 shows what our calendar looks like after we embed it into a Web page.

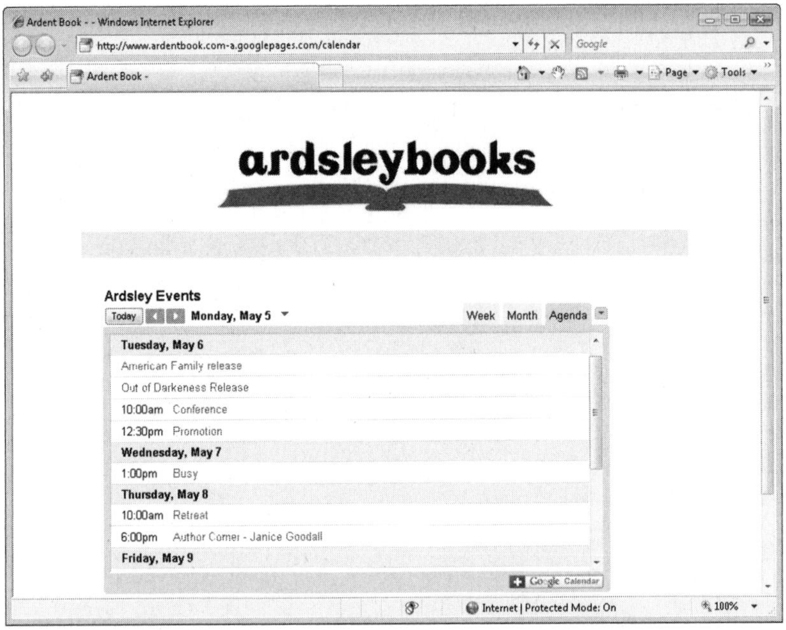

**Figure 9-14:**
A Google calendar, embedded into a Web page.

# Importing and Exporting Events

The following sections guide you through moving your calendar from Outlook to Google Calendar (and back . . . kind of).

We know that you might be using one of a bunch of other calendar programs, too, but we can't cover them all. If you want more specific instructions for importing or exporting to Google Calendar from another type of calendar program, click the Help link in the top-right corner of your Google Calendar window, then click the Import & Export topic link to see several help articles with the directions you need.

# Migrating events from Outlook to Google Calendar

Moving your events from Outlook to Google is a little tricky because you have to click through several options when exporting from Outlook, but if you follow the steps in the following sections, you shouldn't have any problems. To make things easier, we've broken the process into two parts. In the following section, you export your events from Outlook; in the section "Importing your events into Google Calendar," later in this chapter, you upload them to Google Calendar.

## Exporting your events from Outlook

Before you export your appointments, decide which ones are important. Do you want to include events from the past? How far in the future do you want to go? If you have more than a year's worth of events, Google recommends breaking your calendar into multiple, one-year segments to avoid technical errors in Outlook.

Outlook's export function doesn't export recurring events. Instead, it creates individual items for each of your recurring events that falls within the time frame you choose.

To export appointments from your Outlook calendar, follow these steps:

1. **Start Outlook and choose File⇨Import and Export.**

   The Import and Export Wizard window appears, as shown in Figure 9-15.

2. **Select Export to a File from the list, and then click Next.**

3. **Click Comma Separated Values (Windows), and then click Next.**

   You see a list of all your Outlook folders, including e-mail, notes, to-do lists, and calendars.

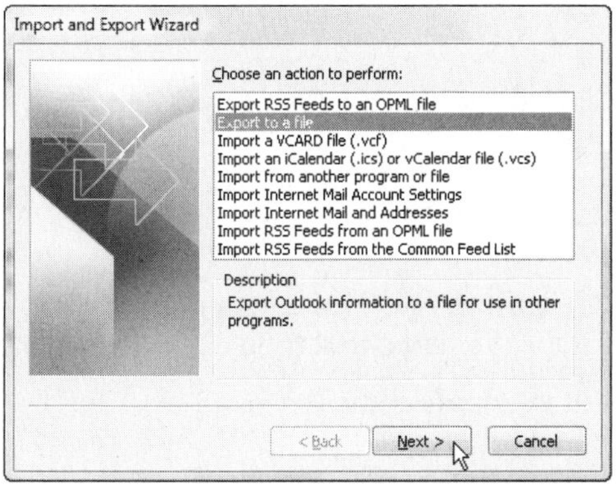

**Figure 9-15:** Export your Outlook calendar to a file.

4. **Select the calendar that you want to export from the list, and then click Next.**

   If you only have one calendar, click the Calendar folder. You're asked where you want to save your exported calendar.

5. **Click the Browse button and select where on your computer you want to save the exported file, and enter a name for the file in the File Name text box.**

   Select a place on your computer that you can easily find later (such as the desktop) and enter a name that you can remember for later, too.

6. **Click OK in the Browse window to return to the wizard, and then click Next.**

   The next screen in the wizard lets you select the appointments you want. There is usually only one option in the list and it is already checked.

7. **Click Finish.**

   A new window appears, asking you to specify a date range for appointments to be exported.

8. **In the Set Date Range window, type in the starting and ending dates for the range of events that you want to export, and then click OK.**

   Outlook takes a moment and exports all your events, and you return to the main Outlook screen.

9. **Repeat these steps for each year that you want to export.**

### Importing your events into Google Calendar

Now for the easy part. Time to get those events online!

To import your Outlook calendar into Google Calendar, follow these steps:

1. **Open Google Calendar.**

   If you want to import your events to a new calendar rather than any of your existing ones, use the Add menu in the Calendars list to create a new calendar.

2. **From the Add menu in the Calendars list, select Import Calendar.**

   A screen that looks like Figure 9-16 appears.

3. **Click the Browse button and locate the file you just exported (see the preceding section), and then click Open.**

4. **From the Choose Calendar drop-down list, select the calendar to which you want to import events, and then click the Import button.**

5. **Click OK to return to your calendar.**

   Your imported events now appear alongside any events you create online (see Chapter 8 for more about adding events).

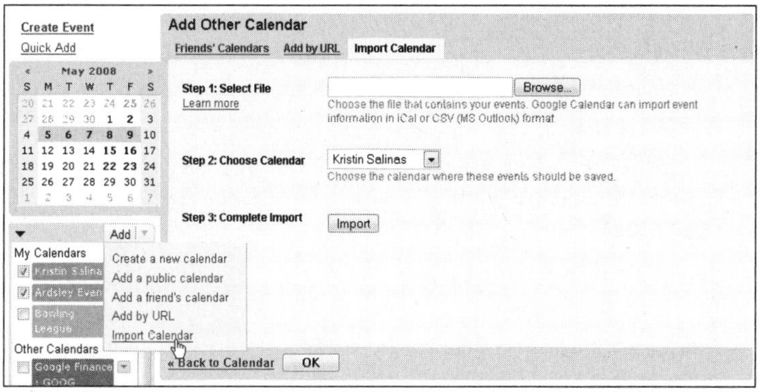

**Figure 9-16:**
Import a
calendar
into Google
Calendar.

6. **Repeat these steps for any other calendar files that you exported from Outlook.**

# Subscribing to Google Calendar in Outlook

Google Calendar is an amazingly powerful online calendar. But, sometimes, you may want to have your events available when you're not connected to the Internet. In this section, we show you a little trick to take your calendar with you in Outlook 2007 or later (or iCal or Thunderbird, for that matter).

Subscribing to an online calendar is more convenient than simply download-ing and importing your events. When you subscribe to Google Calendar, it automatically updates and syncs your calendar whenever you change or add events online, so you have to worry about updating it in only one place.

Even if you subscribe to Google Calendar in Outlook, you must still add and change events directly in Google Calendar. Any events that you add in Outlook don't appear on your online calendar.

Okay, so the method we give you in this section isn't the most intuitive, but it works very well. Keep sharp in Steps 2 and 3. Follow these steps for a quick and easy way to subscribe to your Google Calendar in Outlook 2007 or later:

1. **In Google Calendar, go to your Calendars list and select Calendar Settings from the appropriate calendar's drop-down list.**

2. **Scroll down to the Private Address section and click the green ICAL button, shown in Figure 9-17.**

   A gray box with a long Web address appears.

   *Don't click the address!*

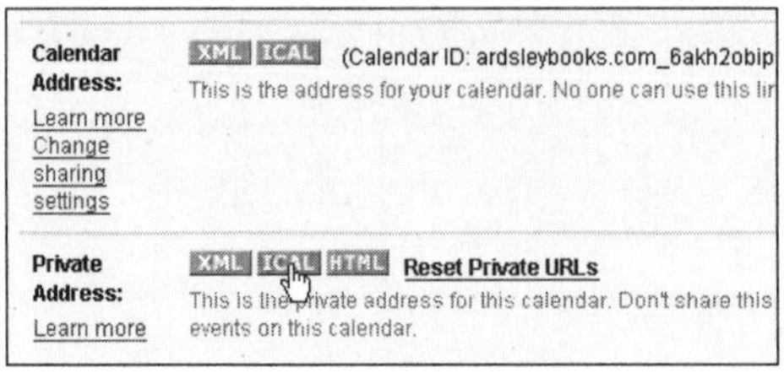

Figure 9-17:
Click the
ICAL button
to reveal the
calendar's
subscription
address.

| Calendar Address: | XML ICAL (Calendar ID: ardsleybooks.com_6akh2obip |
| --- | --- |
| Learn more Change sharing settings | This is the address for your calendar. No one can use this lir |
| Private Address: | XML ICAL HTML Reset Private URLs |
| Learn more | This is the private address for this calendar. Don't share this events on this calendar. |

If you don't see the Private Address section, your administrator may have restricted the sharing settings for your domain. These restrictions only affect your primary calendar, however. Because you can't subscribe to your primary calendar in this case, you may want to try this method with one of your other calendars.

If your calendar's private address is ever compromised (for example, if you share the address with your significant other and your relationship sadly fizzles out), click the Reset Private URLs link to create a new subscription address. Subscriptions to the old address in Outlook will no longer update with your new events, which means you'll have to re-subscribe to your calendar in Outlook if this does happen.

3. **Right-click the private address link and select Copy Link Location or Copy Shortcut from the contextual menu that appears.**

4. **Click in your browser's address bar and paste the address by pressing Ctrl+V or by right-clicking in the address bar and selecting Paste from the menu that appears.**

5. **Highlight the letters https at the beginning of the address and type** webcal, **as shown in Figure 9-18.**

   This changes the link from a normal Web address to a calendar subscription address that Outlook will recognize when you open it.

Figure 9-18:
Create a
subscription
link.

| Bookmarks Tools Help |
| --- |
| webcal ://www.google.com/ |

6. **Press Enter or click Go.**

   A security box may appear, asking whether you want to use Outlook. Depending on your browser, click the Allow button or the Launch Application button to open your calendar link in Outlook.

Outlook opens, and a dialog box appears, asking whether you want to add the calendar and subscribe to updates, as shown in Figure 9-19.

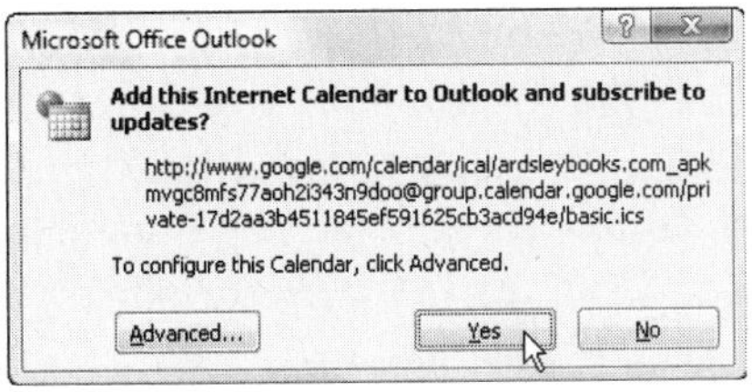

**Figure 9-19:**
Click the Yes
button to
subscribe to
Google
Calendar.

> **Microsoft Office Outlook**
>
> **Add this Internet Calendar to Outlook and subscribe to updates?**
>
> http://www.google.com/calendar/ical/ardsleybooks.com_apk
> mvgc8mfs77aoh2l343n9doo@group.calendar.google.com/pri
> vate-17d2aa3b4511845ef591625cb3acd94e/basic.ics
>
> To configure this Calendar, click Advanced.
>
> [Advanced...]   [Yes]   [No]

7. **Click the Yes button to add the calendar.**

   You can now see events in Outlook that you created in Google Calendar, even when you're not connected to the Internet. When you create new events in Google Calendar, they will automatically appear in Outlook when you connect to the Internet again.

8. **Repeat these steps for any other Google Calendars to which you want to subscribe in Outlook.**

## Exporting your events to a file

For that rare occasion when you want to save your events to your computer or use events with another program, Google Calendar lets you export your events into XML, iCal, or HTML files.

To export events in one of these file formats, follow these steps:

1. **In the Calendars list, click the down arrow to the right of the calendar you want to export and select Calendar Settings.**

   The Calendar Details screen appears.

2. **Scroll down to the bottom of the screen and click the brightly colored box for the format you want to export to:**

   - *XML:* Select this format if you want to access your calendar from a feed reader, such as Google Reader (http://reader.google.com) or FeedBurner (http://www.feedburner.com). Copy the link and paste it into your reader to begin seeing event updates. You can also save the XML file to your computer for use in other more technical programs.

   - *ICAL:* This is the best format to use for a simple export because it can be opened easily in other calendar programs. Copy this link to subscribe to your calendar in Outlook (see the previous section for instructions).

- *HTML:* Copy this link to open a read-only version of your calendar. Add it to your bookmarks when you want to quickly view your events without having to log into Google Calendar. Click the Configuration Tool link to customize your calendar (see the "Embedding Calendar on Your Web Site or Blog" section, earlier in this chapter).

3. **To save the file to your computer, right-click the private address link and choose Save File As from the contextual menu that appears.**

4. **In the dialog box that appears, browse to a folder on your computer, such as the desktop, and click the Save button.**

5. **When you're finished exporting your calendar, click OK to return to your Calendar Details screen, and then click Cancel to return to your calendar.**

# Using Calendar on Your Mobile Device

If you don't have a cellphone, go to your nearest cellphone store and buy one. They really are cool. Plus, once you have one you can access Google Calendar events from it or virtually any mobile device. Woohoo!

The following list describes the two ways that you can access your calendar on a mobile device (we cover both in more detail in the following sections):

- ✔ **Google Calendar for Mobile:** This method allows you to access a feature-rich version of your calendar on an iPhone, BlackBerry, or other XHTML-capable phone.

- ✔ **Short Messaging Service (SMS):** That's a fancy name for text messaging. Send a text message to Google, and it messages you back with your schedule details. This method is perfect for when you're on the run and need to know where you're heading next.

As always, text messaging and mobile phone data plans generally aren't free. Please check with your mobile provider first to see whether you have access and can afford it. Don't blame us if your next cellphone bill rivals your rent or mortgage payment.

## Using Google Calendar for Mobile

To access Google Calendar for Mobile, open your mobile Web browser and enter your direct calendar address (it's probably similar to the address you use to access your normal Google Calendar; for example, `http://calendar.ardleybooks.com`). A login screen may appear, asking you to enter your username and password. After your calendar loads, a simplified version of it appears in Agenda mode, similar to the image on the right of Figure 9-20.

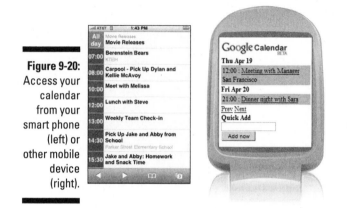

**Figure 9-20:** Access your calendar from your smart phone (left) or other mobile device (right).

To navigate your calendar, select any of the links on the screen. Clicking an event reveals its details. Click in the Quick Add text box and enter event information, then click Add Now to add a new event.

You can enter Quick Add events as a phrase, such as **Tennis lessons every Thursday at 9am**.

# Scheduling with SMS

Text messaging is a quick, easy way to find out what's coming up on your schedule — especially when you're away from your computer. You need to register your phone with your calendar first, though. Flip back to Chapter 8, which explains how to set up calendar notifications on your mobile phone.

After you set up your phone with Google Calendar, you can simply send a text message by using one of the commands in the following bullet list to GVENT (48368), and you receive a text message giving you the event information you request.

Although you can use the GVENT service for free, your mobile carrier may charge for each text message that you send and receive. Check your plan before using GVENT extensively.

---

## More resources for Google Calendar

If you want to know more about Google Calendar than we cover in this book, we're happy to point you to some great resources:

✔ **Google Calendar Help Center:** Go to `www.google.com/support/a/users` to find answers to frequently asked questions, find out how to communicate with other calendar programs, or troubleshoot an issue. You can also get to the Help Center

by clicking the Help link at the top of your calendar page.

✔ **What's new with Google Calendar:** Google Calendar is always changing, so find out what new bells and whistles those amazing engineers are adding by going to `www.google.com/googlecalendar/new.html`.

Tell them Ryan and Karl sent you!

---

Send any one of these commands in a text message to GVENT and wait for a response:

✔ **NEXT:** Receive the upcoming event for the day.

✔ **DAY:** Receive an agenda of today's events.

✔ **NDAY:** Receive an agenda of tomorrow's events.

✔ **"Meeting tomorrow at 2pm":** Send event details to create a new event on your calendar via Quick Add.

✔ **HELP:** Receive a list of these commands.

✔ **STOP:** Remove your phone number from Google Calendar to stop notifications and other calendar messages. You have to re-register your phone to use GVENT again.

# Part III

# Getting to Work: Documents, Spreadsheets, and Presentations

The 5th Wave          By Rich Tennant

"I wrote my entire cookbook in Docs. The other programs I saw just didn't look fresh."

## In this part . . .

*E*ver heard of *singledocumindedness?* We didn't think so. It's a word that we made up to describe how Google Docs changes the way you think about collaboration and document storage. Beyond explaining how you can take advantage of this new concept, this part takes you through the Google Docs Home and shows you how to create and share amazing documents, spreadsheets, and presentations. Old-fashioned desktop software is optional.

# Chapter 10

# Finding Your Way around the Google Docs Home

*In This Chapter*

▶ Looking at the pluses of Google Docs

▶ Getting started with Google Docs

▶ Putting the Docs Home to work

*T*his part of the book gives you a good start with Google's online word processing, spreadsheet, and presentation apps, collectively called Google Docs. This chapter shows you how Google Docs are organized inside the Google Docs Home. The Docs Home provides a trouble-free way to organize your word processing, spreadsheet, and presentation files.

## Advantages of Google Docs and the Docs Home

Google Docs is an online office productivity software suite that includes three powerful tools:

✔ **Documents:** An online word processing software app, similar to Microsoft Word or WordPerfect. It's called Documents, or Docs for short. (Word processing documents are explored in detail in Chapter 11.)

✔ **Spreadsheets:** An online spreadsheet app, similar to Microsoft Excel, Quattro Pro, or Lotus. (Spreadsheets are explained in detail in Chapter 12.)

✔ **Presentations:** A presentations app, similar to Microsoft PowerPoint. (Presentations are discussed in detail in Chapter 13.)

The starting point for all your Google productivity apps is called the Docs Home. This is document central, a powerful management tool that keeps everything you create organized and at the ready. You can manage all your documents, spreadsheets, and presentations from a single Docs Home, as shown in Figure 10-1.

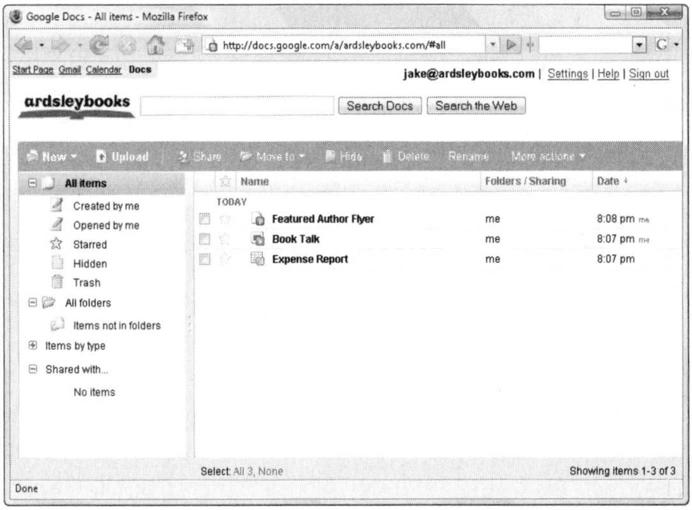

**Figure 10-1:**
All three online apps are managed from the Docs Home.

An obvious advantage of Google Docs is that you have access to your documents online anytime you need them from any computer in the world, as long as it's connected to the Web.

If you've ever lost a document before, you'll quickly come to appreciate another advantage of Google Docs — Google's famous search abilities. The old, offline way of handling documents is to save them in folders. The problem is, you can very easily forget what folder you saved a document in when you need that document three months later.

The Docs Home deploys Google's sophisticated search tools to find any document on any topic in your personal Docs library quickly, no matter how many documents or folders you've generated or how fuzzy your memory of where you placed that document.

The fact that multiple users can also have access to the same documents simultaneously makes sharing and collaboration much easier than anyone ever thought possible before Google Docs. Google Docs also has at least five additional advantages:

✔ Never misplaces a document

✔ Singledocumindedness for sharing, collaboration, and version control

✔ Multifolder support for the singledocuminded

✔ Platform independence

✔ Singledocumindedness in mail and IM attachments

## Singledocumindedness for sharing, collaboration, and version control

Okay, we made up the word *singledocumindedness,* but we couldn't think of a real word that seemed to fit. The point is, you don't need to keep multiple versions of any document ever again — not for yourself, not for your collaborators, not for anyone else in the world with whom you want to share your document. This new single-document approach enhances collaboration and sharing.

When it comes to sharing, you need only one copy, regardless of the number of collaborators, because your Docs Home catalogs and maintains changes within a single master document. Google Docs allows you to peek back in time to see what changes have been made at any point during the creation of that document — from start to finish.

You can always revert your document to a time before certain changes were made or determine who among your contributors made what changes. With the click of a button, you can compare versions of a document or turn the clock back to a time before certain changes found their way into your precious prose. (See Figure 10-2.) Thanks to Google Docs, version control has never been so simple. We go into more detail on this powerful reviewing feature for each individual Google App in Chapters 11 through 13.

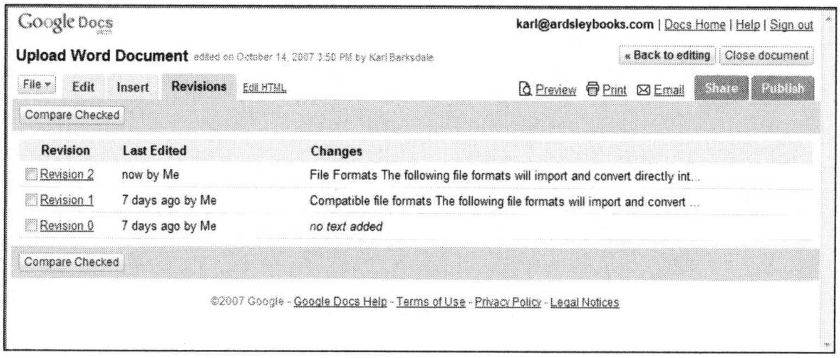

**Figure 10-2:**
Sharing and version control are easy with a single-document approach.

## Multifolder support for single documents

You can label a single file so that it appears in any number of folders without generating digital replicas — you don't save copies of the same document in multiple folders or on multiple drives. Instead, you can attach any number of folder names to a file as labels, so the document appears, like magic, in any folder you assign. See Figure 10-3 — the Practice 1, Practice 2, and Practice 3 documents appear in both the Practice Docs and the Urgent Docs folders. (It's a little bit like Dumbledore appearing on Harry and Ron's Chocolate Frog playing cards whenever they want to see him.)

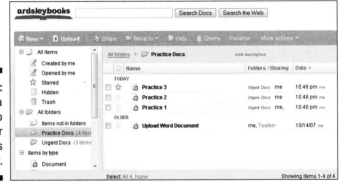

**Figure 10-3:**
Assign a
single file to
any number
of folders
you want.

Do you even need to make backups anymore? Yes, of course. But backing up isn't the headache or major concern it used to be. When you save your Google documents online in Google Data Center, Google says that it creates backups just about as fast as you make changes to your document. However, it's still just a bunch of computers out there, so back up the critical documents on your hard drive at a minimum; you know, all the legal stuff or that report you can't do without, but don't lose any sleep over the rest of your files.

## Platform independence

The Docs Home and all its apps don't care whether you're a Mac user, a Linux user, a Windows XP user, a Windows Vista user, or any other kind of user. You just need a Web browser, such as Internet Explorer, Firefox, or Safari, running on any platform.

Regardless of the platform, the concept of singledocumindedness applies. A Mac user can edit a document alongside a Windows Vista user in real time without conflicts, catcalls, or crashes. Oh, that the rest of the computing world could be so compatible.

One of the big advantages of Google Docs is that they run from any reasonably updated (within the last year or so) Web browser. But you may need to activate open source scripts on your browser from time to time. Some well-known browsers balk at the idea of running scripts. To enable scripts, follow the instructions that appear in the notification area of your browser, which is usually just below the address bar. You may need to change your browser's security settings for scripts to run properly. If you get tired of all the annoying reminders, you may want to try updating or even switching browsers. Taking a few minutes to download a free, updated Web browser may be worth the effort.

## Singledocumindedness for mail or IM attachments

Using and sharing single copies of documents in Google Docs also applies to e-mail and IM attachments. In the past, attaching a document to a message generated another copy of the document. Under the singledocumindedness theory, Google sends a Web address that links to a single original document, as shown in Figure 10-4, allowing others to view and collaborate on the same version of a shared online document from their personal Docs Homes.

Of course, if you want to rename a file and maintain a separate copy independently, Doc guidelines do allow that. (We think the official statement on this issue reads something like, "Sure, why not.")

The only downside to Google Docs is that you must be able to get online to access your documents. If you know ahead of time that you'll need to work offline, you can export your document from the Docs Home to your hard drive in a file format that your desktop software can understand. We show you how to overcome the online obstacle in Chapters 11 through 13.

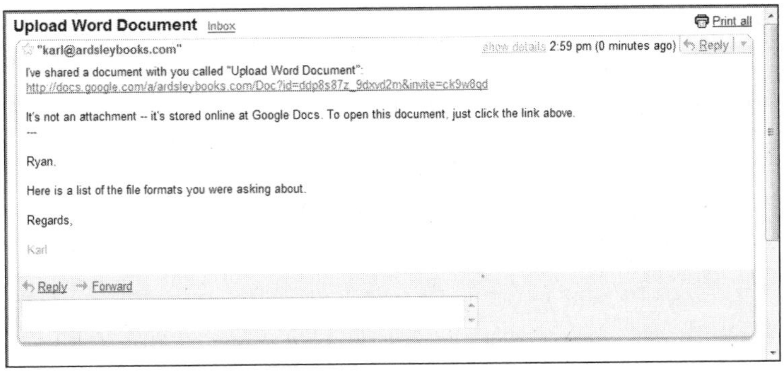

**Figure 10-4:**
Don't send a
file when
a Web
address
will do.

> **Upload Word Document**  Inbox                                    Print all
>
> ☆ "karl@ardsleybooks.com"                       show details 2:59 pm (0 minutes ago)  Reply ▼
>
> I've shared a document with you called "Upload Word Document":
> http://docs.google.com/a/ardsleybooks.com/Doc?id=ddp8s87z_9dxvd2m&invite=ck9w8qd
>
> It's not an attachment -- it's stored online at Google Docs. To open this document, just click the link above.
> ---
> Ryan.
>
> Here is a list of the file formats you were asking about.
>
> Regards,
>
> Karl
>
> ↰ Reply  → Forward

# Launching Your Docs Home

You can launch your Docs Home in two ways:

- ✔ Using a Start Page gadget
- ✔ Entering a Web address

## Adding a Google Docs gadget

You can run Google Docs conveniently from a gadget on your Start Page. (See Chapter 3 for directions on adding a gadget to your Start Page.)

After you add your gadget, you can access all three kinds of apps directly from the Google Docs link, which takes you to Docs Home. (See Figure 10-5.) You don't need to add separate gadgets for documents, spreadsheets, and presentations because your Docs Home launches and manages all three.

**Figure 10-5:**
Go to your
Google
Docs Home
with a
single click.

You can set up the Google Docs gadget in the same way in your iGoogle interface, even if your organization doesn't have Google Apps.

## Launching Docs from a Web address

You can start your Google Docs directly from the Web by simply clicking in the address bar and entering **docs** followed by your partnered domain name for Google Apps, as in http://docs.*yourdomain*.com. For example, http://docs.ardsleybooks.com. Team Edition users, go to http://docs.google.com/a/*yourdomain*.com.

You can go to your personal Google Docs Home by going to http://docs.google.com.

Like always, you need to sign in so that the system knows it's really you. You can typically gain access to your files by using the same e-mail address and password that you use for your Gmail account.

# Working and Collaborating in Google Docs

The Google Docs Home is the hub where you can access all your documents, spreadsheets, and presentations with ease. You can create new documents; display, hide, sort, or delete documents; import and export documents; organize your documents by folders or labels; and so on. The following sections describe how to do these tasks and more.

## Creating and naming new documents

When you first come to your lonely, blank, empty Docs Home, a heartfelt little message appears that gives you three tempting options:

- ✔ Create a new document from scratch.
- ✔ Upload an existing document.
- ✔ Learn more!

In this section, we focus on the first one — creating a document from scratch. To create a new word processing doc, follow these steps:

1. **In the Google Docs Home, click the New button and select Document from the drop-down list that appears, as shown in Figure 10-6.**

2. **Click in the word processing window and start typing!**

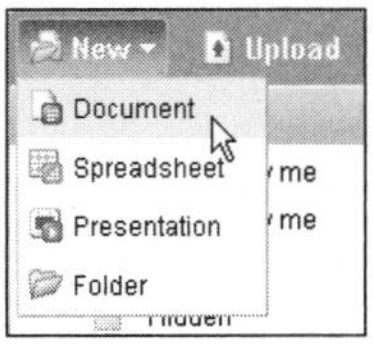

**Figure 10-6:**
Create
a new
document.

Whatever you type in the first line of your document becomes your default file name. Docs will name the file automatically within a few seconds. The title appears in the header at the top of the document, as shown in Figure 10-7. (If you don't enter anything, the document will be named Untitled by default.)

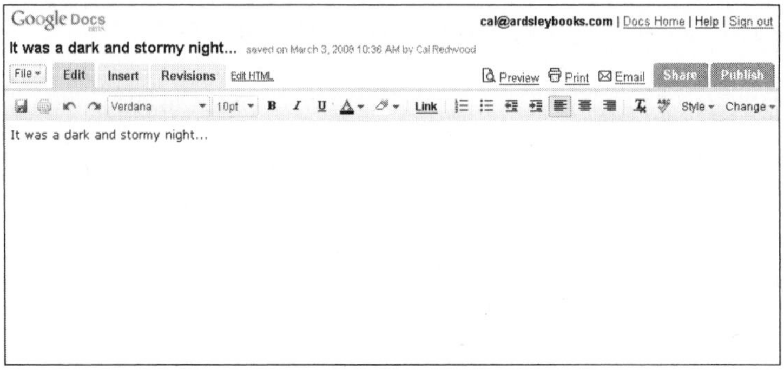

**Figure 10-7:**
The first few words you enter become the default file name.

The word Saving appears in a red box in the top-right corner of the Document window as Docs automatically saves the file. If you can't wait for the automatic saving to kick in, click one of the following buttons in the upper-right corner of the screen:

- ✔ **Save:** Click the Save button to quickly save your doc.
- ✔ **Save & Close:** Click the Save & Close button to save your doc and return to your Docs Home.
- ✔ **Discard Changes:** Click the Discard Changes button to quit the document without saving any changes that you made.

If you decide you don't like the default file name, you can always change it later. (We walk you through renaming in Chapter 11.)

## Viewing, sorting, hiding, or trashing your documents

When you create documents, they show up in the document list, with the most recent documents appearing at the top. If you want to sort the documents in another way, click the appropriate option (Name, Folders/Sharing, Date) on the column heading above the document list (refer to Figure 10-3):

- ✔ **Name:** Click Name to sort the files alphabetically (A–Z). Click Name again to reverse the order (Z–A).
- ✔ **Folders /Sharing:** After you start creating folders and sharing with collaborators, you can sort alphabetically by folder names by clicking this column heading.
- ✔ **Date:** Click Date to sort from the oldest to the newest document. Click Date again to sort from the newest to the oldest doc.

### Uncovering the Docs Home organization pane

The organization pane on the left side of your Docs Home holds a long list of valuable display options. Perhaps the list is too long for your liking. To roll up the options, click the minus sign (–) to the left of each major heading: All Items, All Folders, Items by Type, and Shared With (shown on the left in Figure10-8). To roll them out again, click the plus sign (+) to the left of each heading to reveal the options (shown on the right in Figure10-8).

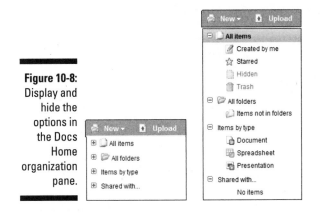

**Figure 10-8:** Display and hide the options in the Docs Home organization pane.

### Star struck

One of the most popular ways to sort files is with a star. (Yes, it's a gold star. Go to the head of the class.) To mark a document with a star, click the Star icon to the left of the document name, as shown in Figure 10-9.

You can star documents for any reason. They may be important, you may need to give them urgent attention, or you may want to jog your memory that you need to work on a particular doc. To display starred documents, click the Starred item in the Docs organization pane, as shown in Figure 10-9.

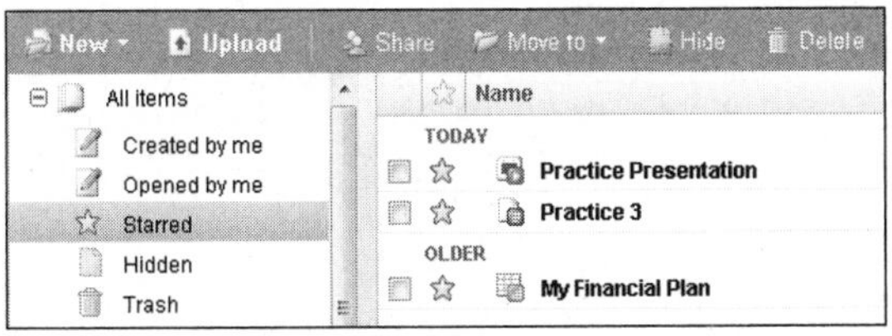

**Figure 10-9:** Star and display key documents.

### Hide stuff

The Docs Home allows users to hide documents from view. You may want to hide a document, for example, when it's in a very rough state and you're not yet ready for others to see and edit it.

To hide a doc, place a check mark to the left of each file name and click the Hide button. The documents are hidden, as shown in Figure 10-10. Choose the Hidden item in the Docs organization pane to display all the hidden documents again.

**Figure 10-10:**
Display your
hidden
documents.

### Show your stuff

If you look through Chapters 11, 12, and 13, you can find out much more about collaborating and sharing documents. If you actively share files with others, and others start sharing with you, document names proliferate throughout your Docs Home list. If you want to see only your own stuff and exclude documents created by others, click the aptly named Created by Me item in the organization pane.

Click All Items in the Docs organization pane if you've displayed just your own documents, starred documents, or hidden documents and now need to see your complete list.

### Empty the trash, or not

If you need to delete a document, select the document's check box and click the Delete button. Clicking this button sends the document to the Trash; but the document isn't lost forever, it still exists. Click the Trash icon in the Docs organization pane, select the item's check box, and delete it permanently by clicking Empty Trash. (You can also trash multiple documents at a time by selecting a group of them before clicking the Empty Trash button.)

If you change your mind and want to restore a file, go to the Trash, select the check box for the document that you want to recover, and click the Undelete button, shown in Figure 10-11. You really don't need to delete any items from the Trash — or, for that matter, to trash any documents in the first place — because Google gives you plenty of space in which to save your documents. However, if you find it helps to clear out a few documents now and again, no one will try to stop you!

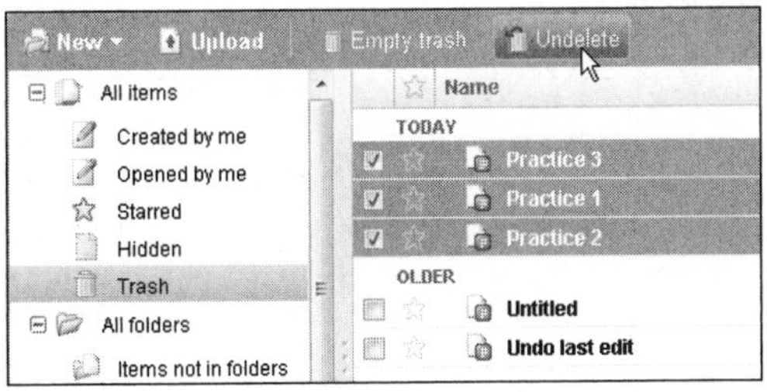

**Figure 10-11:**
Carefully
empty your
trash.

# Uploading or importing your existing documents

You can upload word processing documents, presentations, and spreadsheets that you've already created with many different programs to Google Docs.

Follow these steps to upload a document to the Docs Home:

1. **Sign into the Docs Home.**

   Refer to the section "Launching Your Docs Home," earlier in this chapter, for details.

2. **Click the Upload button.**

   The Upload a File screen appears, as shown in Figure 10-12.

   You can upload the following file types (see the left side of the Upload a File screen):

   - *Text and word processing documents:* .doc, .docx, .rtf, .txt, .sxw

   - *Presentations:* .ppt, .pptx

   - *Spreadsheets:* .csv, .xls, .xlsx, .ods

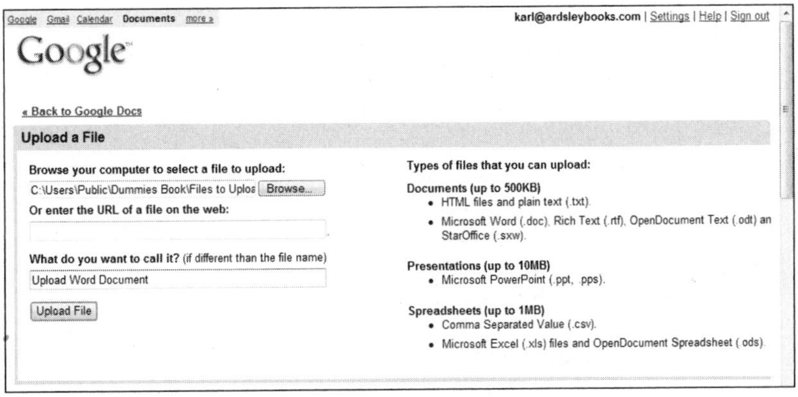

**Figure 10-12:**
Upload a file
from your
computer to
Google
Docs.

3. **Click the Browse button; in the Choose File dialog box that appears, select the file that you want to upload to Google Docs and click the Open button.**

   Alternatively, you can enter the file path to the file (if you know it) in the Browse Your Computer to Select a File to Upload text box, or you can enter a Web address in the Or Enter the URL of a File on the Web text box.

4. **(Optional) Enter a new name for the file in the What Do You Want to Call It text box.**

   If you don't name the file, it retains its current file name.

5. **Click the Upload File button.**

   The file that you upload opens as a Google doc. For example, in Figure 10-13, we uploaded a Word document. You can view and make any changes to your document in Google Docs.

6. **If you make any changes to your file, click the Save & Close button; otherwise, click the Docs Home link to return to the Docs Home.**

   The documents show up in your Docs Home, where you can keep them safe, sound, readable, and ready for editing.

You can also copy and paste from an existing document to a new Google document, instead of uploading a file. If you want to remove all the formatting from an existing document first, copy and paste the text into Notepad or another text editor, and then copy and past the text from the text editor into a Google doc.

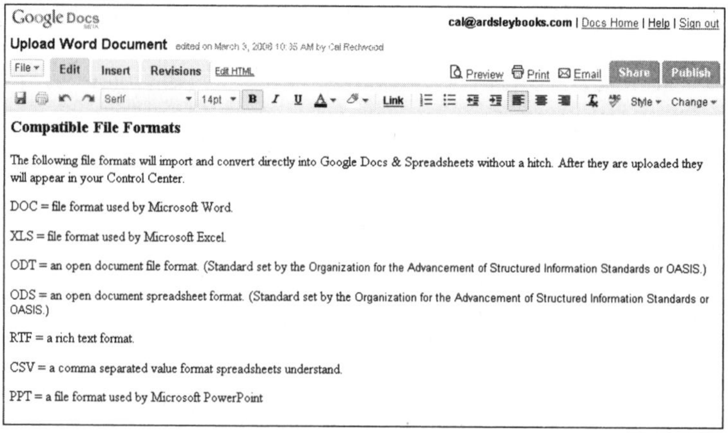

**Figure 10-13:**
The file you
upload
appears as
a Google
document.

Google Docs                                    cal@ardsleybooks.com | Docs Home | Help | Sign out

**Upload Word Document** edited on March 3, 2008 10:35 AM by Cal Redwood

File ▾   Edit   Insert   Revisions   Edit HTML              Preview  Print  Email   Share   Publish

**Compatible File Formats**

The following file formats will import and convert directly into Google Docs & Spreadsheets without a hitch. After they are uploaded they will appear in your Control Center.

DOC = file format used by Microsoft Word.

XLS = file format used by Microsoft Excel.

ODT = an open document file format. (Standard set by the Organization for the Advancement of Structured Information Standards or OASIS.)

ODS = an open document spreadsheet format. (Standard set by the Organization for the Advancement of Structured Information Standards or OASIS.)

RTF = a rich text format.

CSV = a comma separated value format spreadsheets understand.

PPT = a file format used by Microsoft PowerPoint

## Organizing your files by folders or labels

Folders provide a way to organize your files by many categories. In the single-document approach, you don't physically move or copy a file into a new folder — rather, you attach a folder name or a label to the document itself. You can attach as many labels to a file as you want.

This approach works like the files on an iPod or other digital media player. For example, the love song "Michelle," by the Beatles, has multiple labels, such as Beatles, 1960s, Love Songs, M, and My Playlist. Looking for any one of these different labels, you can quickly find and play the one copy of the file. (Singledocumindedness in action yet again.)

To create folders and/or labels while assigning documents to those folders, sign into Google Docs and then follow these steps:

1. **Click New and select Folder from the menu that appears.**

2. **Click in the New Folder text box and type a name for the folder. Press Enter.**

3. **Click All Items, and then select the check box of any documents that you want to label with your selected folder name.**

4. **Click Move To, select the folder name from the menu that appears, and click the Move to Folder button. (Click Cancel if you change your mind.)**

5. **To display only the files assigned to a folder:**

   • Click the folder name in the organization pane. (You may need to expand the All Folders item to see your folders.)

   • Click All Items in the organization pane and look under the Folders/Sharing column heading to see the folder(s) assigned to a document.

## Searching your documents

Google makes searching your document library ridiculously easy. You can search for any of your documents by entering either a name or typing keywords based on document content. Simply enter a few keywords in the text box and click the Search Docs button. Google Search tries to help you as much as it can. For example, in Figure 10-14, just entering the first few letters of a word in the Search text box found several files containing that word.

Search results appear in a special list, as shown in Figure 10-14. Remember, this list searches for documents only in your Docs Home.

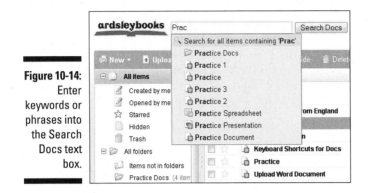

**Figure 10-14:**
Enter
keywords or
phrases into
the Search
Docs text
box.

# Converting and exporting files into other file formats

Google Docs may not give you all the options and settings that a high-end word processing, desktop publishing, spreadsheet, or presentation program can. You may need to download and convert a lot of documents, representing a lot of work on your part, into a file format that such a high-end application can handle.

You can make these conversions directly from Docs Home. Start by selecting the document you want to convert, and then clicking the More Actions button. From the menu that appears, select the file format that you need. (See Figure 10-15.)

A dialog box appears, asking whether you want to open or save the file. Click the Save button. In the Save As dialog box that appears, browse to where you want to save the file and click the Save button.

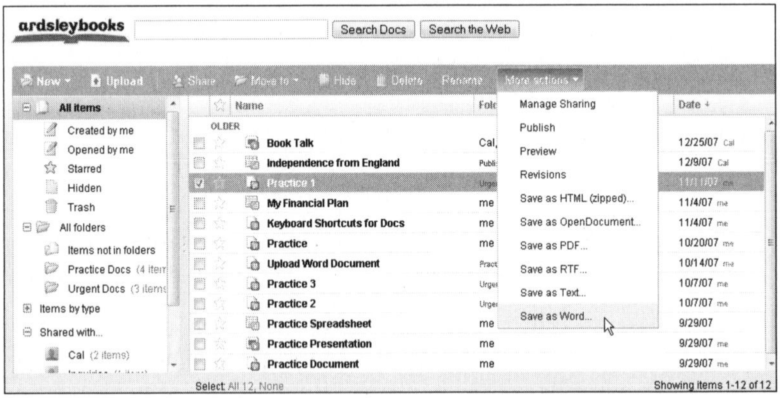

**Figure 10-15:**
To convert
a file,
choose the
document
and its
target file
format.

## Changing your language settings

Some users may need to change the language settings for Google Docs. You can change the language settings by clicking the Settings link and making the necessary changes in the Settings window. (See Figure 10-16.) For example, select a different language from the Language drop-down list. Click the Save button at the bottom of the screen to save your changes.

To change settings back to their original defaults, click the Settings link again. If you set the language to something other than English, you need to know the words for the options in that language. For example, *Settings* in Spanish is *Configuración*.

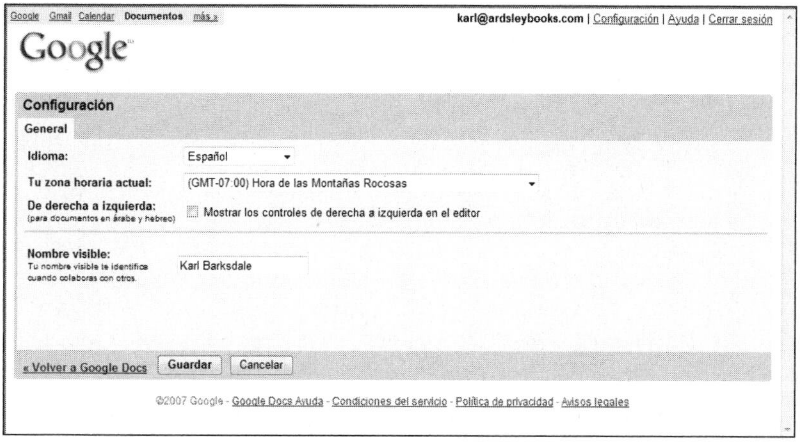

**Figure 10-16:**
Change
language
and
document
settings.

### Using Help and signing out of Google Docs

If you don't understand something (we can't describe every obscure detail in this book), click the Help link to find out more.

When you're done for the day, click the Sign Out link and take the rest of the day off.

You're probably wondering, "Do I really need to sign out?" Not really, but it's still a good idea. Just closing your browser may close your document before the automatic backup has kicked in. You may lose some last-second changes to a document if you don't click the Save & Close button or sign out first. Even if you do exit quickly without signing out, though, you shouldn't lose much work because Google makes frequent automatic saves for you.

# Chapter 11

# Word Processing with Google Docs

*T*his chapter tells you all about Docs, Google's online word-processing application. If you're thinking, "This app looks easy," you're absolutely correct — you can't find anything easier to use than the Docs part of Google Docs.

In this chapter, we show you the easy-to-use editing and formatting features of Docs. And finally, we show you how to print and publish the documents that you create in Docs. We save the best for last when we delve into the true power of Docs — its sharing and collaboration features. When it comes to real-time collaboration, Google has raised the bar. You can finally team up on a document in real time with ease.

## Getting Familiar with the Docs Screen

When you're ready to start writing and creating a new word-processing document in Docs, you start from the Google Docs Home. (See Chapter 10 for the skinny on Docs Home.) Log into Google Docs (go to `http://docs.`*`yourdomain.com`* or `http://docs.google.com`; Team Edition users go to `http://docs.google.com/a/`*`yourdomain.com`*). From the Docs Home, you can easily create a new word-processing document by clicking the New button and then selecting Document from the menu that appears. The word-processing interface opens to a new, blank document, as shown in Figure 11-1.

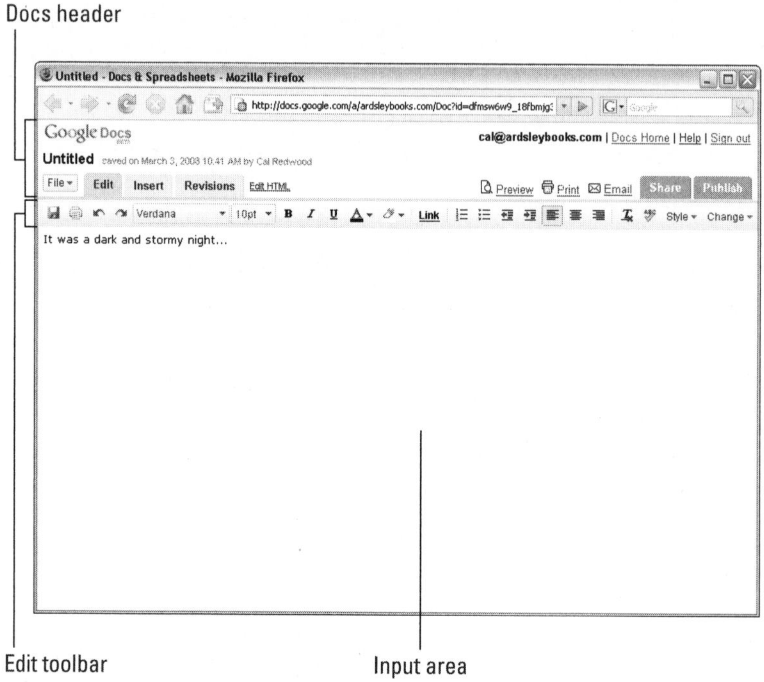

Docs header

**Figure 11-1:**
Find your
way around
the Doc
interface.

Edit toolbar                                           Input area

The Docs interface has the following parts:

- **The header section:** The *header section* is the upper section of the Docs interface (refer to Figure 11-1). Think of the header section as a control center for your document. You go to the header to save, print, edit, format, share, and publish your documents.

- **The File menu:** The Google Docs File menu enables you to create, save, print, rename, copy, delete, and close your document; export the document into various formats; get a word count; find and replace words or phrases in the document; and change settings.

- **Name of the document:** Documents are named automatically, based on whatever you enter in the first line of your text. This automatic naming feature can leave you with a file name that you don't want. Additionally, if you don't enter any text for a bit of time, you may get stuck with Untitled as the document's name. (Refer to Figure 11-1.) To rename a document, choose File⇨Rename and enter the name of your choice.

Depending on your browser settings, the first time you try to rename a document, your browser may prompt you to allow scripts. Follow the onscreen instructions and then try renaming the document again. You should be able to rename the document after allowing scripts.

✔ **Tabs and toolbar:** Each tab opens a different toolbar that displays different word-processing features and options. The tabs include

- *Edit:* Write and format your text.

- *Insert:* Insert tables, pictures, and Internet links.

- *Revisions:* Go back to a previous version of any document and track changes.

- *Share:* Share and collaborate on a document with other collaborators. All that's needed is an e-mail address for each collaborator.

- *Publish:* Publish your document online.

✔ **Input area:** You can find the input area below the tabs and toolbar. In this area, you type text, insert pictures, and so on.

✔ **Check Spelling:** The Check Spelling link appears at the bottom-right corner of the Google Docs interface. To check your spelling, simply click the Check Spelling link. All possible spelling errors are highlighted. Ignore any words or acronyms that you know are spelled correctly and just click any suspect words, such as the word *understandible* in Figure 11-2. When you click a highlighted word, a list of alternative spellings appears, and you can select the correct spelling from that list.

If Docs highlights a word as a spelling error that you know is spelled correctly (names often show up as spelling errors because they're not in the Docs spelling dictionary), you can add that word to the dictionary. Click the highlighted word and, from the list that appears, select Add to Dictionary. You can also use the option to recheck a document, just in case you feel you missed something. When you finish spell checking, click Done. (The Done link replaces the Check Spelling link after the spell check has been completed.)

**Figure 11-2:**
Pick the correct spelling.

---

## Don't print or save a Doc from the browser menu

When you create a new document or open up an existing document in Google Docs, all the customary browser buttons and tools appear above the Docs interface. Ignore all that. Especially ignore the browser's Print button and File menu (or the Page and Tools menus, depending on your browser). They won't do you any good for word processing. Focus on the Docs tools (refer to Figure 11-1). Instead of using the browser's commands to print or save a document, use the links and buttons in the Docs header. Click the Save button on the Edit toolbar to save your work; to print your work, click the Print button on the Edit toolbar or the Print link just above the toolbar.

---

# Editing a Document in Docs

If you've used any word-processing program before, you should find Docs extremely familiar and easy to use. The following sections take you through the basics of editing a document using Docs. (See Chapter 10 for details on creating a new document or loading an existing document.)

## Formatting and editing text in the Edit tab

When you're working on a document, you type the text in the input area. You probably need to apply some formatting to your text at some point, such as italics, bold, a bulleted list, and so on.

You can apply formatting when you're creating a document in one of the following ways:

- Select the text that you want to format, and then click the appropriate button on the Edit toolbar.
- Click the appropriate button on the Edit toolbar, and then type the text. The new text you type has the formatting applied.

You can also press a keyboard shortcut, instead of clicking a button on the Edit toolbar. See Tables 11-1 and 11-2 for common keyboard shortcuts.

Google certainly hopes that most of the buttons on the Edit tab look very familiar to you. Table 11-1 describes editing commands and shortcuts. You can access many of the commands from the Edit toolbar, as well as by using keyboard shortcuts.

| Table 11-1 | | Editing Commands and Shortcuts | |
|---|---|---|---|
| **Button** | **Command** | **Keyboard Shortcut** | **What It Does** |
| | Undo Last Edit | Ctrl+Z | Undoes the last change you made |
| | Redo Last Edit | Ctrl+Y | Undoes the last undo |
| | Cut | Ctrl+X | Cuts text (or graphics) and saves it to the Clipboard |
| | Copy | Ctrl+C | Copies text or graphics to the Clipboard |
| | Paste | Ctrl+V | Pastes copied or cut text from the Clipboard into the document |
| **B** | Bold | Ctrl+B | Applies bold formatting |
| *I* | Italic | Ctrl+I | Applies italic formatting |
| U | Underline | Ctrl+U | Underlines words |
| Verdana ▼ | Font | | Changes the style of the font |
| 18pt ▼ | Size | | Increases the font size |
| A ▼ | Text Color | | Changes the color of your text |
| ✎ ▼ | Highlight Color | | Adds a color behind just like a highlighter pen. |
| Link | Link | Ctrl+K | Creates a hyperlink in your document so that readers can click it to view a Web page or another resource |

*(continued)*

**Table 11-1** *(continued)*

| Button | Command | Keyboard Shortcut | What It Does |
|--------|---------|-------------------|--------------|
| 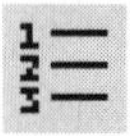 | Numbered List | | Creates a numbered list |
| 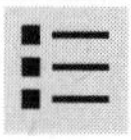 | Bulleted List | Ctrl+Shift+L | Creates a bulleted list |
|  | Indent Less | | Moves paragraphs or lists half an inch to the left |
|  | Indent More | | Moves paragraphs or lists half an inch to the right |
|  | Align Left | Ctrl+L | Aligns text to the left margin of a document |
|  | Align Center | Ctrl+E | Aligns text to the center of a document |
|  | Align Right | Ctrl+R | Aligns text to the right margin of a document |
|  | Remove Formatting | Ctrl+space | Strips any formatting, such as bold, underline, or font changes, from selected text |
|  | Check Spelling | | Scans the document and highlights all words that are spelled incorrectly |
|  Style ▼ | Style | | Applies a style to your text |
|  Change ▼ | Change | | Provides different options, depending on context, to change a table, list, or image |

### Cutting, copying, and pasting

When you need to move text (or an image, table, and so on), just cut or copy it, and then paste it where it needs to go. Select the items that you want to cut or copy (you can select almost anything — text, images, tables, and so on), and then click the Cut or Copy button (or press Ctrl+X or Ctrl+C, respectively).

To paste a cut or copied item, place your cursor where you want the item to appear and click the Paste button (or press Ctrl+V).

With some operating systems, when you cut, copy, and paste, you need to allow access to the system Clipboard. (The Clipboard is a holding place that saves your cut or copied text and graphics in memory until you're ready to paste them.) If you see a dialog box like the one shown in Figure 11-3 when you're attempting to cut (or copy) and paste, just click the Allow Access button and paste away.

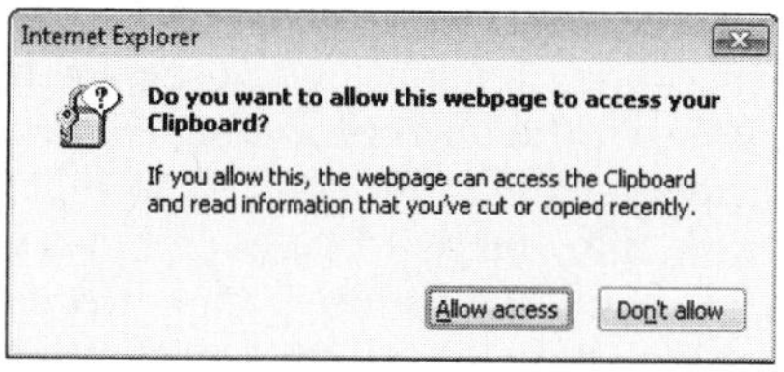

**Figure 11-3:**
Allow
system
access to
your
Clipboard.

> Internet Explorer
>
> **Do you want to allow this webpage to access your Clipboard?**
>
> If you allow this, the webpage can access the Clipboard and read information that you've cut or copied recently.
>
> [Allow access]   [Don't allow]

### Changing the font type, size, text color, or highlight color

To change the font, click the Font drop-down list and select a different font. (See Figure 11-4.)

To change the font size, click the Size drop-down list and select a different font size.

A typical Google document starts out with a Verdana 10pt font as its default. Verdana is an easy-to-read font, and 10pt is large enough for most readers; but you may not like these defaults. Change fonts and their sizes any time you want. You can

- ✔ Choose your new font and size before you start entering text.
- ✔ Select the text that you want to change in your document, and then apply your font and size choices.

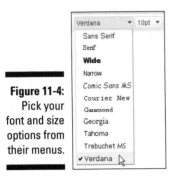

**Figure 11-4:**
Pick your
font and size
options from
their menus.

To change the color of the text, click the Text Color button. Select a color from the color palette that appears, as shown in Figure 11-5.

To add or change the highlight color, click the Highlight Color button and select the color that you want from the palette that appears.

If you plan to print a document in color, or you know it will be viewed on-screen, you can use colored text and highlighting to grab attention or to accent your message. Just be sure that the text color contrasts with the background color (the color of the paper, highlight, or screen) so that it's easy to read — you can easily read dark blue, deep red, or even burnt orange text on a light background or when it is printed on white paper. If your text is red, don't use the same red for your highlight color. (How well can you decipher invisible secret codes?)

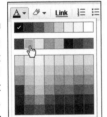

**Figure 11-5:**
Pick text
and
highlight
colors.

## Adding a link

Because the documents you create with Google Docs are online, you can easily link documents together or add a link to a Web page.

To create a hyperlink in a document, follow these steps:

1. **Select the text that you want to turn into a link and click the Insert tab followed by the Link button.**

   The Change Link window appears, as shown in Figure 11-6.

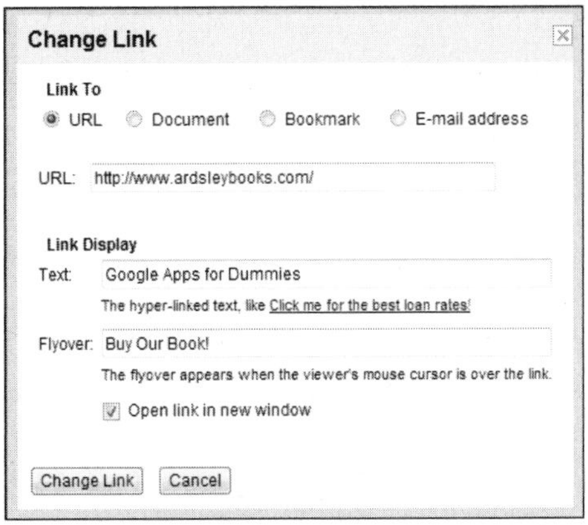

**Change Link**                                    [X]

**Link To**

◉ URL    ○ Document    ○ Bookmark    ○ E-mail address

URL:    http://www.ardsleybooks.com/

**Link Display**

Text:    Google Apps for Dummies

The hyper-linked text, like Click me for the best loan rates!

Flyover:    Buy Our Book!

The flyover appears when the viewer's mouse cursor is over the link.

☑ Open link in new window

[ Change Link ]   [ Cancel ]

**Figure 11-6:**
Create a
hyperlink to
a Web page,
an e-mail
address, or
another
document.

2. **Select a radio button to choose what you want to link to; when you select a radio button, the text box below the radio buttons changes so that you can type or select the appropriate item.**

   • *URL:* Link to a Web page. Enter the URL in the text box that appears.

   In the example in Figure 11-6, the Web address (URL) www. ardsleybooks.com has been entered. (Google Docs automatically adds the http:// for you.)

   • *Document:* Link to another document that you created in Docs. Select the document from the drop-down list that appears.

   • *Bookmark:* Link to a bookmark that you made inside your document. (See the section "Sticking a bookmark in your document," later in this chapter, for the steps to create a bookmark.) Select a bookmark from the drop-down list that appears.

   • *E-mail Address:* Link to an e-mail address. Type an e-mail address in the text box that appears.

3. **(Optional) Enter or change the text that's hyperlinked in the Text text box.**

4. **(Optional) In the Flyover text box, enter any text that you want to pop up when someone hovers the mouse cursor over the link.**

5. **(Optional) Select the Open Link in New Window check box if you want a new Web browser window to open when the user clicks the link.**

   If you don't select this check box, when a user clicks the link, the linked page replaces your existing document. Many users choose to pop open a separate window so that they can quickly flip back and forth between the original document and the linked page.

### Applying styles

Styles allow you to apply consistent and professional-looking formats. To apply a style, select a style from the Style drop-down list. You can apply the following styles:

- ✔ **Normal Paragraph:** Use this style for regular, run-of-the-mill paragraphs. You can also apply the Normal Paragraph style to remove formatting if, for example, you make a mistake or change your mind about how you want your text to look.

- ✔ **Header 1 (Huge):** Use this style for a title or section heading.

- ✔ **Header 2 (Big):** Apply this style to side headings and subheadings.

- ✔ **Header 3 (Standard):** Apply this style to side headings and subheadings.

- ✔ **Justify Text:** Use this style to align text equally to the left and right margins.

- ✔ **Strikeout:** Apply this style to put a line through (or *strike out*) words.

- ✔ **Superscript:** Apply this style to raise text above the line. This style is often used for footnote references and for exponents in mathematics, such as $2^3 = 8$.

- ✔ **Subscript:** Use this style to lower the text below the line. This style is used for chemical notations, such as $H_2O$.

## Using more keyboard shortcuts

Earlier in this chapter, Table 11-1 shows keyboard shortcuts for the common editing and formatting commands found on the Edit toolbar. But those keyboard shortcuts aren't the only ones you may want to use when you're editing a document. If you're hooked on keyboard shortcuts, Google Docs doesn't disappoint. Table 11-2 lists additional keyboard shortcuts that you can use when creating and editing a document in Google Docs.

| Table 11-2 | Keyboard Shortcuts for Docs | |
|---|---|---|
| *Keyboard Shortcut* | *Command* | *Use It To* |
| Ctrl+A | Select All | Select all text in a document. |
| Ctrl+F | Find | Find the text that you enter. |
| Ctrl+H | Replace | Find and replace the text that you enter. |
| Ctrl+J | Full Justify | Justify both the right and left margins. |

| Keyboard Shortcut | Command | Use It To |
|---|---|---|
| Ctrl+M | Insert Comment | Add a comment to the text. |
| Ctrl+P | Print | Print the document. |
| Ctrl+S | Save | Save the document. |
| Ctrl+Shift+Space | Non-breaking Space | Insert a non-breaking space. |
| Tab | | Insert a tab or move to the following cell in a table. |
| Shift+Tab | | Move to the preceding cell in a table. |
| Ctrl+1 | Header 1 | Apply the Header 1 (Huge) style. |
| Ctrl+2 | Header 2 | Apply the Header 2 (Big) style. |
| Ctrl+3 | Header 3 | Apply the Header 3 (Standard) style. |

# Inserting objects by using the Insert tab

When you click the Insert tab, all the fun stuff that allows you to insert images, links, comments, tables, bookmarks, separators, and special characters appears. We hit most of these useful objects in the following sections.

### Inserting an image

Adding images couldn't be easier. Just remember that you must upload images before you can insert and view them as explained in these steps.

1. **Position your cursor where you want an image to appear in the document.**

2. **Click the Insert tab, and then click the Image button.**

   The Insert Image dialog box appears, as shown in Figure 11-7.

3. **Select either the From This Computer radio button or the From the Web (URL) radio button.**

4. **Depending on which radio button you select in Step 3, the steps change a bit:**

   a. *If you select the From This Computer radio button,* click the Browse button. In the File Upload dialog box that appears, browse to your file, select it, and click the Open button which will place the path to the file in the browse box. Back in the Insert Image dialog box, click the Insert Image button.

b. *If you select the From the Web (URL) radio button,* type or paste the URL into the Enter Image Web Address text box. A preview of the image appears in the dialog box. Click the Insert Image button.

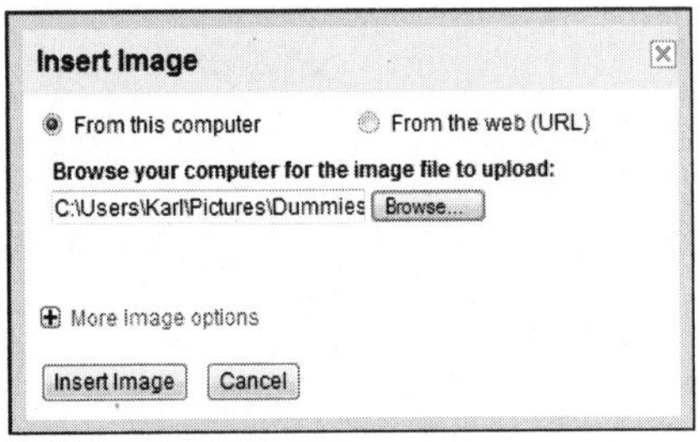

**Figure 11-7:**
Insert an image by uploading it first.

> **Insert Image** [X]
>
> ⦿ From this computer    ○ From the web (URL)
>
> **Browse your computer for the image file to upload:**
>
> C:\Users\Karl\Pictures\Dummies [Browse...]
>
> ⊞ More Image options
>
> [Insert Image] [Cancel]

### Giving shady comments

Comments are a valuable tool for tracking edits or discussing issues in a document, especially when you're working in a team to craft document content. To add a comment, follow these steps:

1. **Place your cursor where you want a comment to appear, and then click the Comment link in the Insert tab.**

   A box with your name, the date, and the time appears.

2. **Start typing in the comment box.**

3. **When you're done typing the comment, simply click elsewhere in the document.**

   Your comment appears as shaded text, as shown in Figure 11-8. All comments are marked with the name of the contributor/author, along with the date and time that he or she inserted the comment into the document.

4. **To edit your comment or change the color, click your comment.**

   A menu appears, giving you the options Close This Menu, Delete Comment, or Insert Comment Text into Document. You can select a color to change the color box around your comment — you can choose from Yellow, Orange, Pink, Green, Blue, and Purple.

   To edit your comment, simply ignore the menu and start typing.

**Figure 11-8:**
Add comments to Docs.

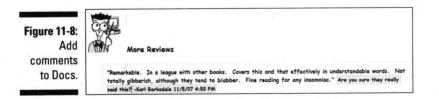

> **More Reviews**
>
> "Remarkable. In a league with other books. Covers this and that effectively in understandable words. Not totally gibberish, although they tend to blabber. Fine reading for any insomniac." Are you sure they really said this? -Karl Barksdale 11/5/07 4:53 PM

## Building a table

Tables are extremely valuable organizing tools for word-processing documents. Due to the popularity of tables, Google had to make sure that this feature works properly online — and it works pretty well.

Follow these steps to create a table:

1. **Click the Table button on the Insert tab.**

   The Insert Table dialog box opens, as shown in Figure 11-9.

2. **Enter how many cells you want in your table in the Rows and Columns text boxes.**

   Tables are calculated into columns and rows. In Figure 11-9, a 3 x 6 table (with three rows and six columns, for a total of 18 cells) is being created.

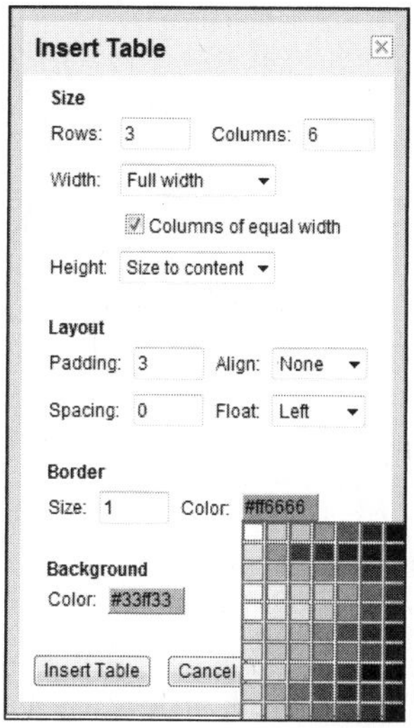

**Figure 11-9:** Specify the size and look of your table in advance.

3. **Select the options that you want from the Width and Height drop-down lists.**

   Width refers to the size of cells horizontally. Height refers to the size of cells vertically. You can choose from four possible options for each variable, which appear in their respective drop-down lists:

   • *Full Width/Full Height:* Use all the width and height available between the margins of a page.

   • *Size to Content:* Adjust the width and height of a table's cells to the size of the words or graphics within each cell.

- *Pixels:* Define the width and height of the cell to a specific number of pixels.

- *Percent:* Adjust cell width and height based on a percentage of the available space found between margins.

4. **(Optional) If you want to create a table with columns that are all the same width, select the Columns of Equal Width check box.**

5. **Adjust the padding and the spacing around the text inside cells by entering the number of pixels in the Padding and Spacing text boxes.**

   Increasing the spacing adds space between cells. Increasing the padding puts extra space around words inside the cells.

6. **From the Align drop-down list, select a cell alignment (Left, Center, Right, or leave it at None); if you add a value into the Spacing text box, you can select Left, Right, or None from the Float drop-down list, which creates spacing around your text.**

7. **To add a border, enter a number in the Size text box — the larger the number, the wider the border. To change the color of the border, click the Color box and select a color from the palette that appears.**

8. **To change the background color in the cells, click the Color box below Background and select a color from the palette that appears.**

9. **After you make your selections, click the Insert Table button.**

   Your table appears in your document.

After you create your table, you can still make changes using the Edit tab. For example, in Figure 11-10, columns 2 through 6 are centered. Color has been added in row 2, and graphics were inserted into row 3. Titles are bold, and the font has been changed from the default Verdana font.

You can really appreciate the power of tables only if you take the time to experiment with all the options available, so play around with each of the options that we explain in this section.

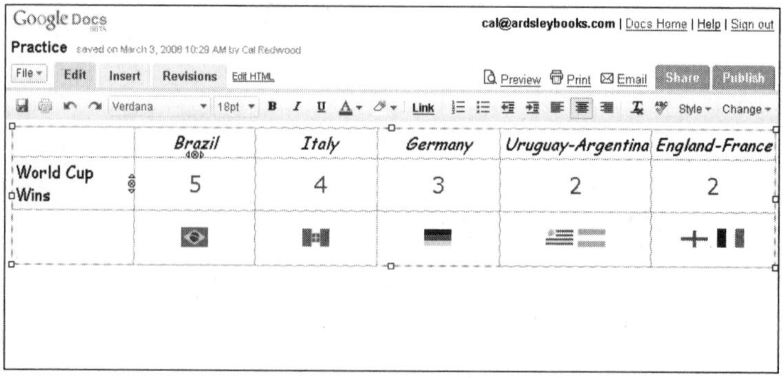

**Figure 11-10:**
A table
has been
created with
six columns
and three
rows.

| | Brazil | Italy | Germany | Uruguay-Argentina | England-France |
|---|---|---|---|---|---|
| World Cup Wins | 5 | 4 | 3 | 2 | 2 |
| | | | | | |

### Sticking a bookmark in your document

Bookmarks allow you to create links from one part of a document to another. You may find bookmarks especially useful in long documents, so you can avoid paging down endlessly until you find the passage that you're looking for.

To create a bookmark, follow these steps:

1. **Click the location where you want the bookmark to go.**

   This is the *destination point,* the spot where someone will land after he or she clicks your bookmark.

2. **Click the Insert tab, and then click the Bookmark button.**

   The Insert Bookmark dialog box appears, as shown in Figure 11-11.

3. **Click in the New Bookmark text box and type a name for your bookmark, and then click the Insert Bookmark button.**

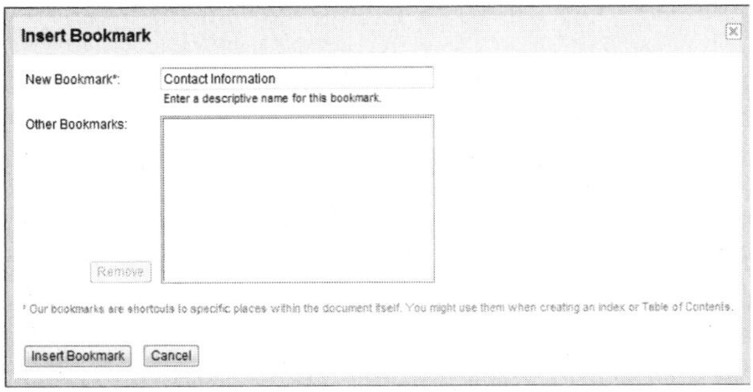

**Figure 11-11:**
Create your bookmark in the Insert Bookmark dialog box.

> Insert Bookmark
>
> New Bookmark*:    Contact Information
>            Enter a descriptive name for this bookmark.
>
> Other Bookmarks:
>
> Remove
>
> * Our bookmarks are shortcuts to specific places within the document itself. You might use them when creating an index or Table of Contents.
>
> Insert Bookmark   Cancel

You're only half done. The second half of the process requires you to create a link to your bookmark that readers can click to go to the bookmark. For example, you can create a table of contents at the top of a document that links to bookmarks for each chapter or section within the document. We describe how to create a link in the section "Adding a link," earlier in this chapter.

### Dividing paragraphs with a separator

Separators place lines that separate paragraphs of text. In Figure 11-12, a horizontal line has been inserted below a title.

**Figure 11-12:**
Insert a
separator.

| Image | Link | Comment | Table | Bookmark | Separator ▾ | Special character |
|-------|------|---------|-------|----------|-------------|-------------------|
| | | | | | Page break | |
| **Docs Keyboard Shortcuts** | | | | | Horizontal line | |

To insert a separator, click where you want the separator to appear. Then click Separator on the Insert tab and choose Horizontal Line from the menu that appears. (See Figure 11-12.)

You use the other option in the Separator menu, Page Break, to break text onto separate pages for printing. Use this option to control the amount of text on a single page, pushing the remaining text to the following page.

### Entering special characters

Now and again, you may need a character that doesn't appear on your keyboard. These characters can include anything from a copyright symbol (©), to a registered trademark (®), to an umlaut over an Albanian schwa (ë).

To insert a special character, click where you want to insert the character. Then, click the Special Character button on the Insert tab. The Insert Special Character dialog box appears, as shown in Figure 11-13, giving you hundreds of choices. If you don't see the character that you need, select the Asian Characters, Wingdings, or Advanced option.

The Advanced option enables you to pick a Unicode value for nearly any character in the world in every major language. If you need help with Unicode values, click the Help question mark in the Advanced dialog box, search for your language (even Bengali and Syriac), and find the numerical code for any special character that you may need.

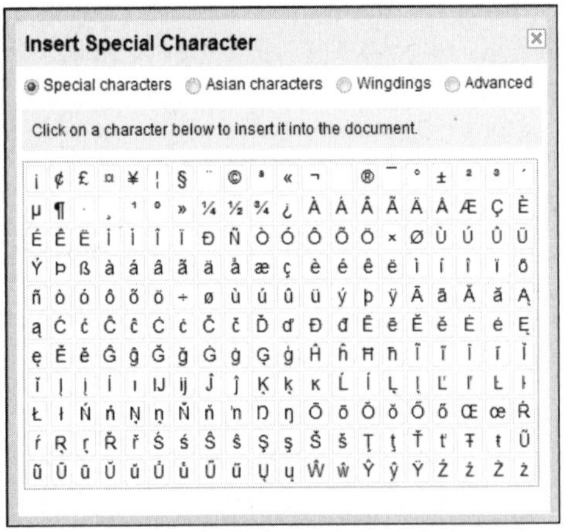

**Insert Special Character**

⦿ Special characters  ◯ Asian characters  ◯ Wingdings  ◯ Advanced

Click on a character below to insert it into the document.

**Figure 11-13:**
Pick your
favorite
symbols in
the Insert
Special
Character
dialog box.

# *Viewing or reverting to earlier document versions in the Revisions tab*

The revision system in Docs is so efficient that it eliminates the need to keep various versions of the same document. In Chapter 10, we refer to this as singledocumindedness — the idea that you only need one copy of a document as long as changes are tracked. Because of this feature, you don't need to save and keep track of multiple versions of any document ever again — not for yourself, not for your collaborators, not for anyone with whom you need to share a document.

On the Revisions tab, Google Docs catalogs and maintains changes within a single master document, as shown in Figure 11-14. You can peek back to see what changes users have made at any point during the creation of that document — from start to finish. You can also choose to go back in time and pick any previous version that you may need. To view any version of the document, just click a Revision # link in the far-right column.

**Figure 11-14:** You can more easily share and control document versions with a single-document approach.

| | Google Docs | | karl@ardsleybooks.com \| New features! \| Docs Home \| Help \| Sign out |
|---|---|---|---|
| **Practice 1** saved on November 1, 2007 9:17 PM by Karl Barksdale | | | « Back to editing    Close document |
| File ▾    Edit    Insert    **Revisions**    Edit HTML | | Preview  Print  Email    Share    Publish |

Compare Checked

| | Revision | Last Edited | Changes | |
|---|---|---|---|---|
| ☐ | Revision 80 | 49 seconds ago by Me | ☺Titles: More Google Apps for Dummies Even More Google Apps for Dummies Be... | |
| ☐ | Revision 79 | 3 minutes ago by Me | these other titles: More Google Apps for Dummies Even More Google Apps for D... | |
| ☐ | Revision 78 | 5 minutes ago by Me | *no text added* | |
| ☐ | Revision 77 | 7 minutes ago by Me | More Reviews "Remarkable. In a league with other books. Covers this and that eff... | |
| ☐ | Revision 76 | 8 minutes ago by Me | This may be the best thing ever written on Google Apps lately. Teeter and Barksd... | Revisions 70-76 |
| ☐ | Revision 70 | 15 minutes ago by Me | lately. Teeter and Barksdale go beyond their normal blathering to reveal the myst... | Revisions 64-70 |
| ☐ | Revision 64 | 5 days ago by Me | Remarkable. In a league with other books. Covers this and that effectively in unde... | Revisions 57-64 |
| ☐ | Revision 57 | 5 days ago by Me | These Other Titles: More Google Apps for Dummies Even More Google Apps for ... | Revisions 47-57 |
| ☐ | Revision 47 | 5 days ago by Me | This may be the best thing ever written on Google Apps this week. Teeter and Ba... | Revisions 7-47 |
| ☐ | Revision 7 | 5 days ago by Me | *no text added* | |
| ☐ | Revision 6 | 5 days ago by Me | *no text added* | |
| ☐ | Revision 5 | 5 days ago by Me | Google Apps for Dummies | Revisions 1-5 |
| ☐ | Revision 1 | 3 weeks ago by Me | Practice 1 | |
| ☐ | Revision 0 | 3 weeks ago by Me | *no text added* | |

Compare Checked

You can view a version before certain changes were made to determine who among your contributors made changes. You can also compare the changes made between different versions. To compare versions, select the check boxes to the left of the versions that you want to compare and click the Compare Checked button.

If you decide to revert back to an earlier version of a document, click the Revision # link in the far-right column to view that version. Then, click the Revert to This One button on the toolbar. A dialog box appears, asking whether you're sure that you want to revert to that version. If you click OK, your document reverts to that version, and you lose any changes made after that point.

# Printing, Publishing, and Converting to Other Formats

In the following sections, we explore printing, publishing, and converting documents into other file formats so that you can use them with other software applications that you may have on your computer.

## Previewing and printing

Printing a document in Google Docs is much like printing any other document from your computer. You have two ways to get to the Print Settings dialog box:

- ✔ Click the File button and select Print from the menu.
- ✔ Click the Print button on the Edit toolbar.
- ✔ Click the Print link in the header.

If you want to preview before you print, click the Preview link (it's to the left of the Print link). The window changes to show you a general idea of what the document will look like when you print it, as shown in Figure 11-15.

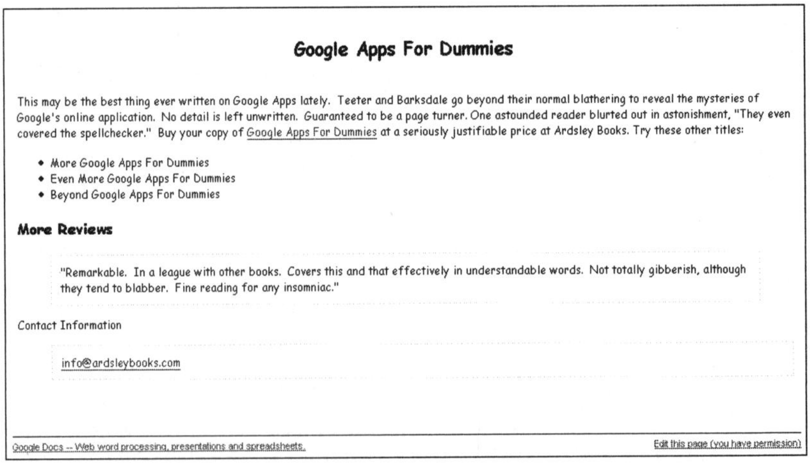

**Google Apps For Dummies**

This may be the best thing ever written on Google Apps lately. Teeter and Barksdale go beyond their normal blathering to reveal the mysteries of Google's online application. No detail is left unwritten. Guaranteed to be a page turner. One astounded reader blurted out in astonishment, "They even covered the spellchecker." Buy your copy of Google Apps For Dummies at a seriously justifiable price at Ardsley Books. Try these other titles:

- More Google Apps For Dummies
- Even More Google Apps For Dummies
- Beyond Google Apps For Dummies

**More Reviews**

"Remarkable. In a league with other books. Covers this and that effectively in understandable words. Not totally gibberish, although they tend to blabber. Fine reading for any insomniac."

Contact Information

info@ardsleybooks.com

Google Docs -- Web word processing, presentations and spreadsheets.                    Edit this page (you have permission)

**Figure 11-15:**
A document shown as a print preview.

# Publishing

The publishing feature allows you to post an online HTML version of your document or upload a copy to your company or personal blog. Click the Publish tab to explore the options (see Figure 11-16). When you are ready to publish, click the Publish button.

**Figure 11-16:**
Publish your document for online viewing.

## Creating a link to a published document

Your document is actually already published online. The Web address appears as soon as you hit the Publish button. You can select and copy the link, and then share it with anyone you want.

Google automatically e-mails the Web link to anyone that you list as a viewer on the Share tab. Copy and paste the link and IM or e-mail it to anyone you want. If you want others to be able to view the document, you can use the URL on the Publish tab to add a link in a Web page (your company's Web page or a personal Web page, for example) to the document. But, if you don't want to allow complete access to anyone, you can restrict access to just those users within your Google Apps domain area. And you can limit their access further by selecting the Viewers Must Sign In check box.

## Posting a document to a blog

To publish a document to a specific blog location, follow these steps:

1. **On the Publish tab, click the Post to Blog button.**

   The Blog Site Settings dialog box appears, as shown in Figure 11-17.

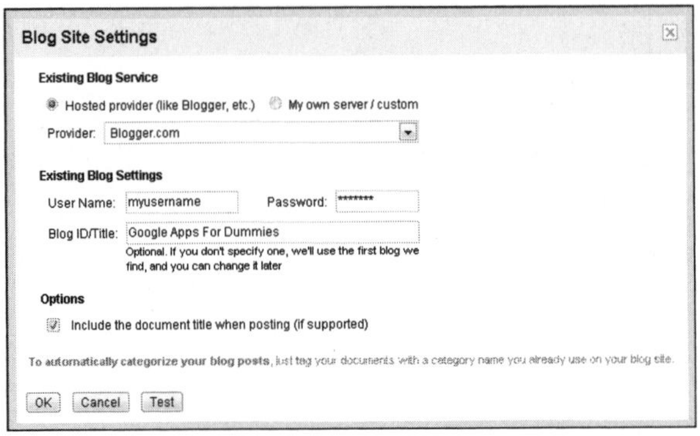

**Figure 11-17:**
Enter the
settings for
your blog.

2. **Select the Hosted Provider radio button if your blog is on a major blogging service, and then select the name of the service from the Provider drop-down list. If you host your own blog, select the My Own Server/Custom radio button.**

   If you select the My Own Server/Custom radio button, you can enter all the data necessary to upload directly to your personal, corporate, or organization Web site or the blog associated with it. Be sure to complete each field in the detailed sign-in options, as shown in Figure 11-18. If you don't know the information, ask your system administrator for advice.

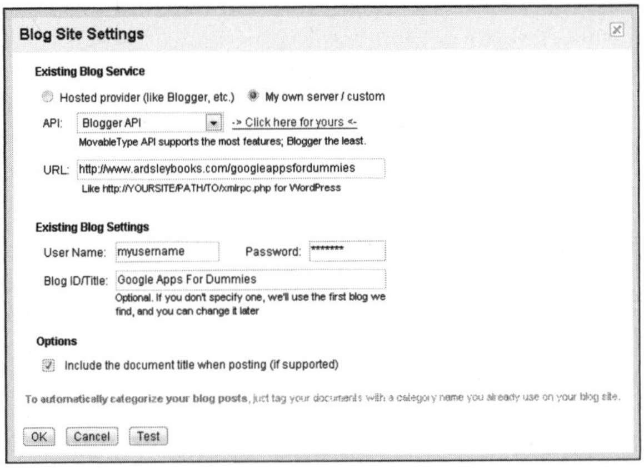

**Figure 11-18:**
Enter your
custom Web
server
or blog
address.

3. **Enter your username and password in the User Name and Password text boxes to sync with the site.**

4. **(Optional) Enter the name of your blog in the Blog ID/Title text box.**

**5. Click OK when you're ready to post the document to your blog.**

You can publish to a Web site or blog directly by clicking the Set Your Blog Site Settings link at the bottom of the Publish tab. After you enter the settings, as described in the preceding steps, you can simply click the Post to Blog button to post a document to your blog.

This feature works extremely well with Blogger, Google's free blogging software (check out www.blogger.com). You can also publish directly to a Start Page gadget, which you may find extremely valuable for team or company announcements. Of course, you need to know the various passwords and login names for whatever online site to which you're publishing.

## Editing a document's underlying HTML

If you're HTML-wise and an online publishing perfectionist, you can go right to the HTML code underlying your document before you publish and make any changes you want directly into the tags themselves, as shown in Figure 11-19. You can get to the code by clicking the Edit HTML link.

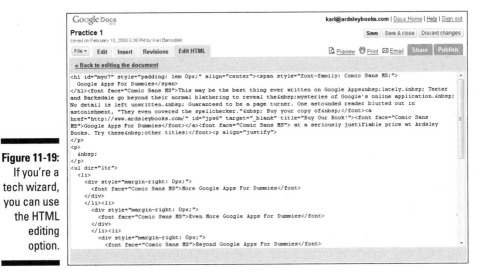

**Figure 11-19:** If you're a tech wizard, you can use the HTML editing option.

Most of us should forget we ever saw Figure 11-19 — so full of HTML tags — and go back to the relative safety of the normal Edit tab. By using that tab, you can live a life of HTML ignorance and word-processing simplicity and bliss.

## Exporting and converting documents into a variety of formats

The Google Docs File menu allows you to export documents into other file formats, such as Word, PDF, zipped HTML, RTF, OpenOffice, simple text, or a presentation. To convert your file from the Docs standard, select the format that you want from the File menu. Depending on which option you choose, the dialog box that appears provides you with different options. Pick a folder on your hard drive in which to dump the converted file and click the Save button.

# Sharing and Collaboration

This is a classic case of saving the very best feature for last.

The most amazing feature of Google Docs is the ability for people from anywhere in the world to work simultaneously on a document with very little fuss and bother. The only things users need to collaborate are an e-mail address, an Internet connection, and the knowledge that everyone can be writing at the same time on the same document without losing any changes or messing each other up.

## Collaborating on a document

If you haven't tried collaborating, you're in for a treat. Two or more people can be working from different computers in the same room or halfway around the world with equal ease. Multiple collaborators can enter data into the same document at the same time, or at different times of the day — when doesn't matter because Google Docs tracks all changes to maintain quality control.

Google Docs keeps track of the changes and shares an updated document every few seconds with everyone on the collaborating team — a good example of singledocumindedness in action. Your team is *not* working on separate documents that you reconcile later, but on the exact same document at exactly the same time. (See Figure 11-20.)

Don't worry if someone messes things up by adding something silly or deleting your perfect prose. You can always revert back to a previous version that Google saved several minutes, hours, days, or even months ago. (See the section "Viewing or reverting to earlier document versions in the Revisions tab," earlier in this chapter, for how to revert to a previous version.)

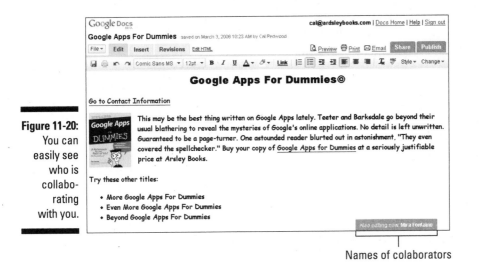

Names of colaborators

When you open a document window, who's actively collaborating on that document at any one time appears at the bottom of the screen. And, even if two or more collaborators are typing in the same paragraph at the same time, their changes appear and are refreshed every few seconds. Also, Google tracks changes that others make not just by name, but also by color, so you can quickly see who's been adding text, what he or she added, and where he or she added it.

## Setting up for sharing and inviting collaborators

By getting the sharing and collaboration feature to work efficiently, Google Docs made collaboration much more hassle free.

To start sharing, follow these steps:

1. **Click the Share tab in the upper-right corner of the Docs screen, as shown in Figure 11-21.**

2. **Select the As Collaborators radio button to allow the people that you invite to make changes to the document. Select the As Viewers radio button to restrict the people you invite so that they can read the Doc itself but can't make changes.**

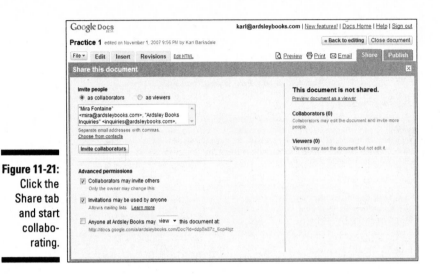

**Figure 11-21:**
Click the
Share tab
and start
collabo-
rating.

3. **Enter the e-mail addresses of the people with whom you want to share the document in the text box in the Invite People section.**

   This feature makes use of your Contacts list, so you can as easily invite collaborators as you can enter e-mail addresses into Gmail.

4. **(Optional) Select any or all of the check boxes in the Advanced Permissions section.**

   If you're feeling secretive, you may want to use some of the Advanced Permissions features. Give or deny your collaborators the right to invite other collaborators or viewers by selecting (to grant) or deselecting (to deny) the Collaborators May Invite Others check box. You can also allow or disallow collaborators the right to broadcast the page to mailing lists by selecting (to allow) or deselecting (to disallow) the Invitations May Be Used by Anyone check box. Normally, users select these first two default options; however, if you want to keep everything private, simply remove the check marks from these two options.

   Finally, you can choose to allow only users from within a company or organization to view the document by requiring them to log in. Technically, this is a publishing feature, but you can conveniently control the setting from the Share tab and from the Publish tab.

5. **Click the Invite Collaborators button.**

   An invitation screen appears, as shown in Figure 11-22. Treat this screen exactly like an e-mail message. Your collaborators and viewers automatically appear in the To box.

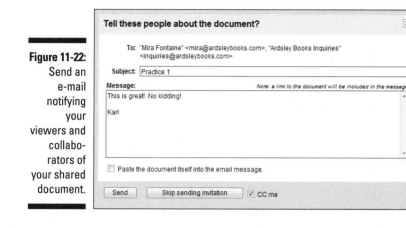

6. **Click in the Subject text box and type a subject, and click in the Message text box and type a message to your collaborators.**

7. **(Optional) Paste a copy of the document into the e-mail message by selecting the Paste the Document Itself into the Email Message check box.**

   You don't have to include the document with the message, but some viewers may find the easy access to the document convenient. However, if you have a long document, you probably shouldn't paste it into the message because it will be harder to read in a Gmail window. Just let the users click the link in the message, which takes them to the document.

8. **Click the Send button to send the invitation.**

If you click the Share tab after you share a document, a list of your collaborators and viewers appears in the right pane of the Share tab, as shown in Figure 11-23. If you need to send additional e-mail messages or updates of your document to a team, click the Email Collaborators link and a new e-mail form appears. Fill it out and send it. If you need to add or delete collaborators, click the check box next to their name.

The documents that you share appear in the Docs Home page for all your collaborators to open, view, and edit. They can then organize the documents in any way that suits them — by assigning labels or folders — just like they can for documents of their own creation. They can work with the document as if they had actually started it themselves, and they can access the list of all those collaborating on the document. (See Chapter 10 for more information on how to manage documents.)

**Figure 11-23:**
Continue to
update and
communi-
cate with
your
collabo-
rators by
using the
Share tab.

# Chapter 12

# Crunching Numbers with Google Spreadsheets

*S*preadsheets perform calculations and organize data. Sounds boring, but the more you know about them, the more valuable they become. And regardless of whether your needs are lightweight or heavy duty, Google Spreadsheets can help you make an impression and get the job done. For instance, Google Spreadsheets can help you if you need to

✔ Add a bundle of numbers or create a family budget

✔ "Number crunch" mountains of data with colleagues

✔ Create a few clever charts and graphs for an upcoming business proposal

✔ Create a spreadsheet with fiendishly complex formulas

✔ Make a spreadsheet available online to impress a client with your digital acumen

Google Spreadsheets is easy to use yet has heady capabilities. Most home or even business users don't need all the capabilities that are built into Google Spreadsheets. In this chapter, we start simple and give you what you need to use Google Spreadsheets. We cover entering, editing, and formatting basics, and then we go on to talk about creating charts and graphs, and using formulas and functions to crunch numbers. We show you how to share and collaborate on spreadsheets. And finally, we describe how to preview, print, and publish your spreadsheets.

# Starting Up a Spreadsheet

If you read Chapter 11, you're way ahead on the learning curve when it comes to using Google Spreadsheets. When you're ready to create a new spreadsheet, log into Google Docs Home (go to `http://docs.yourdomain.com` or `http://docs.google.com`). (See Chapter 10 for details about Docs Home.) You can easily create a new spreadsheet by clicking New from Docs Home and then selecting Spreadsheet from the menu that appears. Google Spreadsheets opens to a new, blank spreadsheet, as shown in Figure 12-1.

Header

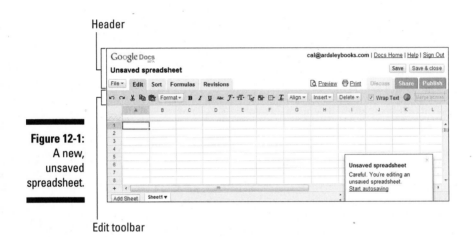

**Figure 12-1:**
A new,
unsaved
spreadsheet.

Edit toolbar

## Cells, rows, and columns

Like all spreadsheets, Google's online version is a grid. Each rectangle in the grid is called a *cell*. The cells are organized horizontally in *rows* and vertically in *columns:*

✔ **Rows:** Numbered 1, 2, 3, and so on.

✔ **Columns:** Lettered A, B, C, and so on. When the spreadsheet runs out of letters in the alphabet, it doubles up the letters and starts

using AA, AB, AC, and so on; then BA, BB, BC, and so on.

✔ **Cells:** Identified by the intersection of a row and column. This is called the *cell address.* For instance, cell D8 is located at the intersection of column D and row 8.

Google Spreadsheets provides a huge number of cells, rows, and columns — so many that you're unlikely to need them all.

## Start autosaving immediately

In contrast to other Google Apps, Google Spreadsheets wants to start autosaving immediately so that you don't lose any important data. A pop-up message appears in the lower-right corner of the screen just a few moments after you create a new spreadsheet. Click the Start Autosaving link (refer to Figure 12-1); a dialog box appears in which you can name your spreadsheet, as shown in Figure 12-2. If you decide later that you need to rename a file, you can do that from the Docs File menu.

**Figure 12-2:**
Name your
spreadsheet
immediately.

Google Docs -- Webpage Dialog

http://spreadsheets.google.com/cli?id=0

Rename spreadsheet as:

Independence from England

OK      Cancel

Internet | Protected Mode: On

*Note:* The sample spreadsheet that you see in the figures in this chapter organizes statistics about five former British Colonies and the order in which they received independence. Incidentally, we want to visit all these places — no offense to the Falkland Islands or the 50 other members of the Commonwealth.

## Getting familiar with the Google Spreadsheets header and Edit tab

The header for Google's spreadsheet and its Edit tab are nearly identical to the Docs word-processing interface explained in Chapter 11. (Refer to Figure 12-1.) Atop the spreadsheet, the familiar Docs Home, Help, and Sign Out links appear, as well as the Save and Save & Close buttons. Like with Docs, your login name, the file's name, and the date that the spreadsheet was last updated appear in the header. You can also find the familiar Print and Print Preview links in the header as well.

The big differences between the spreadsheet and word-processing interfaces appear in the tabs. Google Spreadsheets includes the Discuss and Formulas tabs, which don't appear in Docs. Even on the Edit tab, several buttons on the Edit toolbar differ from Docs. *Note:* The buttons for Bold, Italic, changing font size and color, and so on work similarly to those found on the Edit toolbar in Docs, so we won't bore you and repeat that information here — see Chapter 11 for details.

In the following list, we describe the buttons on the Edit toolbar that are specific to Google Spreadsheets (we also show you a few clever tricks in the process):

- **Format button:** Formats numbers by adding commas, currency symbols, and other possible number formats.

- **Align button:** Aligns values to the left, right, or center of the cell, column, or row.

- **Insert button:** Adds new rows or columns anywhere you need them in an existing spreadsheet.

- **Delete command:** Deletes columns, rows, or specific cells, along with the text and numerical values contained in those areas.

- **Wrap Text check box:** Wraps text within a cell when checked; keeps text on one line when unchecked.

- **Charting feature:** Creates charts and graphs.

- **Merge Across:** Merges cells together to accommodate larger titles or to improve the appearance of a spreadsheet.

Ignore all your Web browser buttons and menus, such as its File, Save, and Print options, when you want to save or print your spreadsheet. Save, export, and print your spreadsheet by using the buttons or links in the header section of Google Spreadsheets.

# Entering, Editing, and Other Spreadsheet Basics

After you create a new spreadsheet and name it, you're ready to start entering data and making it look good. The following sections go over these basic spreadsheet chores.

## Entering values

Any data entered into a cell is called a *value*. The most common values are

- **Numbers or numerical values:** Used for calculations. Numerical values include both numbers and a few symbols, such as +, −, the comma as a separator, and the percent sign (%).

- **Text values:** Letters or words.

- **Labels:** Text values that act like a heading to identify columns or rows of values.

You can only enter values into an active cell. Make a cell active by clicking it or by using the keyboard, as described in Table 12-1. Active cells are highlighted. In Figure 12-3, cell A2 is active. After you make a cell active, you can enter values directly into that slightly expanded cell.

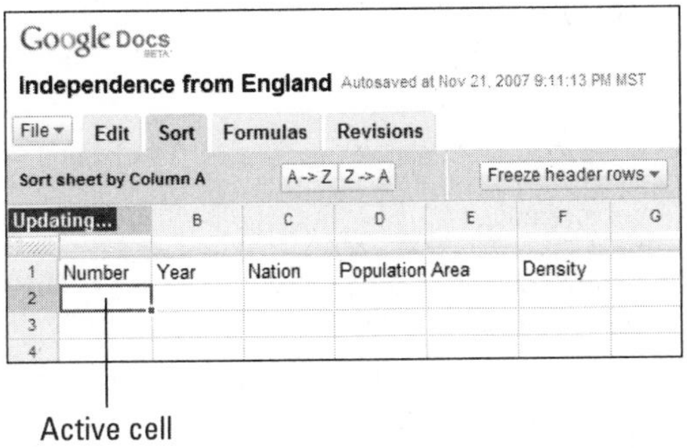

**Figure 12-3:** Enter values directly into an active cell.

Active cell

After you enter a value into the cell, you must activate another cell for the values to update in the spreadsheet. (You need to take this step in all spreadsheets.) For example, in Figure 12-3, we added six text labels and made cell A2 active. You can update values in a cell in several ways. Start by clicking in a cell and typing in the values, and then

✔ Press Enter, Tab, or any of the arrow keys.

✔ Click a different cell.

Table 12-1 lists the keystrokes that you can use to navigate around a spreadsheet, allowing you to move from cell to cell.

| Table 12-1 | | Keystrokes for Spreadsheet Navigation | |
|---|---|---|---|
| *Press* | *Action* | *Press* | *Action* |
| Tab | Move one cell to the right | Shift+Tab | Move one cell to the left |
| Enter or Return | Move down one cell | Shift+Enter or Shift+Return | Move up one cell |
| Left arrow | Move left one cell | Right arrow | Move right one cell |
| Up arrow | Move up one cell | Down arrow | Move down one cell |
| Ctrl+Home | Go to first cell | Ctrl+End | Go to last cell |

*(continued)*

### Table 12-1 *(continued)*

| Press | Action | Press | Action |
|---|---|---|---|
| Ctrl+down arrow | Go to bottom-most cell in the current column | Ctrl+up arrow | Go to top-most cell in the current column |
| Ctrl+left arrow | Go to left-most cell in the current row | Ctrl+right arrow | Go to right-most cell in the current row |
| F2 | Edit active cell | Esc | Cancel cell entry |
| Ctrl+spacebar | Select entire column | Shift+spacebar | Select entire row |
| Shift+Page Up/Down | Extend the selection up/down one screen | Shift+down, up, left, right arrow key | Manual select |
| Ctrl+D | Copy down (used with Shift+down arrow) | Ctrl+R | Copy right (used with Shift+right arrow) |
| Page Up | Move up one screen | Page Down | Move down one screen |
| Ctrl+Page Down | Move to following sheet | Ctrl+Page Up | Move to preceding sheet |

## Selecting multiple cells

You can select a single cell by clicking it or moving to it using the navigation keys described in Table 12-1. To select a range of cells, either

- ✔ **Use the mouse:** Click a cell and drag to highlight all the cells you want to select.
- ✔ **Use the keyboard:** Navigate to a cell, then hold down Shift as you use the arrow keys to highlight the cells you want to select.

You can select an entire row by clicking the row header, or select an entire column by clicking the column header. Alternatively, press Ctrl+Shift+right arrow to select a row or Ctrl+Shift+down arrow to select a column.

## Formatting multiple cells

You can put information in a spreadsheet as simply as clicking a cell and typing. Generally, text values are short — most often, just a few words in any given cell. Spreadsheets aren't the place for longwinded ramblings — save that for Google Docs or Blogger.

In Figure 12-4, we started a spreadsheet that compares a few former British Colonies in the order of their independence. To start the worksheet, we entered the words Number, Year (for the year of independence), Nation, Population, Area (for land area), and Density (for population density) into the first six columns in the first row.

You can format the six text values at the same time by selecting the six cells (or selecting the entire row by clicking the 1 at the beginning of the row). Then, start clicking the formatting buttons: Bold, Italic, Font style, and so on. In Figure 12-4, we selected cells A1 to F1 as a group. We made the labels bold and shaded, applied a different color, and increased the labels to an 18-point font size.

See Chapter 11 if you need some additional info on the Edit toolbar's basic formatting features. Also, the keyboard shortcuts for formatting that we give in Chapter 11 for Google Docs also work in Google Spreadsheets.

**Figure 12-4:** Format values in multiple cells by using the Edit toolbar.

# Changing the column width or row height

In Figure 12-4, the label Number is too long for the width of the column. The word is simply too big, so you can't see all of it. You can resolve this issue quickly — just adjust the width of the column. Hover your mouse pointer directly over the line between the column headers. A thick blue line with a double-sided arrow pointer appears over it — this line is called the *Column Width slider*. Click and drag the line to the left or right to resize the entire column, as needed. (Look at Figure 12-5 to see how the resized column A looks.)

The same technique works for resizing rows, too — hover the mouse pointer over the line between row headers, and then click and drag up or down to resize the height of a row.

# Entering sequences quickly with the Fill Handle

One of the important features in any spreadsheet is its ability to anticipate any patterns that you're creating and to increment the values automatically. For example, in Figure 12-5, we need to create a list of numbers from 1 to 5. When we enter 1 in Cell A2 and 2 in Cell A3, Spreadsheets recognizes a pattern and can fill in the rest of the numbers in the sequence.

**Figure 12-5:**
Select and drag the Fill Handle to automatically generate value patterns.

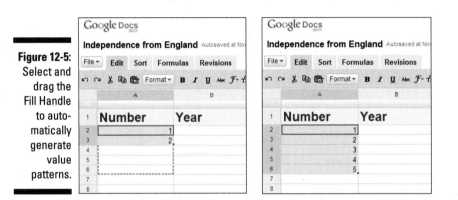

To use the Fill Handle to quickly complete a sequence, follow these steps:

1. **Enter the first few values in the sequence in their own cells.**

   For example, enter **5** in one cell and **10** in another cell if you want to make Spreadsheets count by fives. (***Note:*** The cells must be touching — either in the same row or the same column, such as cells B1 and B2, or cells A6 and B6.)

2. **Select the cells as described in the "Selecting multiple cells" section.**

   In the bottom-right corner of the selected cells (cell A3 in Figure 12-5), a little dark square appears. This square is the *Fill Handle.*

3. **Click the Fill Handle and drag it down (to fill in a sequence within a column) or right (to fill in a sequence within a row).**

   Google Spreadsheets fills in the pattern to all selected cells. For example, in Figure 12-5, it fills each selected cell with the numbers 1 through 5.

The same technique works for almost any sequence or pattern, such as

- ✔ Days of the week
- ✔ Months of the year
- ✔ Multiple years

✔ Formulas (which we discuss in the section "Formula Fixin'," later in this chapter)

✔ Other types of data in which a pattern is obvious

## Changing values and undoing mistakes

To change or edit an existing value in any cell, double-click the offending cell to make it active. Delete the error and make the desired change. Press Enter or move to a different cell to make Spreadsheets accept the new value.

If you make a mistake (and we all make mistakes), click the Undo button on the Edit toolbar or press Ctrl+Z. If you make a mistake with your undo, click the Redo button or press Ctrl+Y to undo the undo you just undid (phew!).

## Inserting new rows or columns

You need to plan out spreadsheets in advance; but you can't anticipate everything. Fortunately, you can insert rows and columns anywhere you need them. In the sample spreadsheet that we created, for example, we didn't plan a row for a title.

To add a row or column, follow these steps:

1. **To add a row, highlight the entire row by clicking the number at the beginning of the row; to add a column, highlight the entire column by clicking the letter at the top of the column.**

2. **Click the Insert button on the Edit toolbar and select the appropriate command from the menu.**

   - If you select a row in Step 1, select either Row Above or Row Below from the menu.

   - If you select a column in Step 1, select either Column Left or Column Right from the menu.

## Merging and aligning cells

When you enter text that's too long to appear in its entirety in a cell, you can adjust the column width. But, sometimes, you don't want a column to be that wide — for example, if you have a long title for a spreadsheet. In that case, use the Merge Across button to merge two or more cells together. (See Figure 12-6.)

To merge cells, follow these steps:

1. **Click in a cell and enter text.**
2. **Select the cells that you want to merge together.**
3. **Click the Merge Across button on the Edit tab.**

   Google Spreadsheets merges the cells together, and any text that you enter in the cell in Step 1 now spreads across the newly merged cell.

TIP

If you want to break a merged cell back into separate cells, select the merged cell and click the Break Apart button on the Edit toolbar.

You probably want to center align the text in a merged cell. To align text (or numbers), select the cell(s), row(s), or column(s) that you want to align, and then click the Align button on the Edit toolbar. Click the alignment that you want from the menu that appears, as shown in Figure 12-6.

For example, in Figure 12-6, we centered the numbers in column A, aligned Column B's text values to the right, and aligned the values in column C to the left.

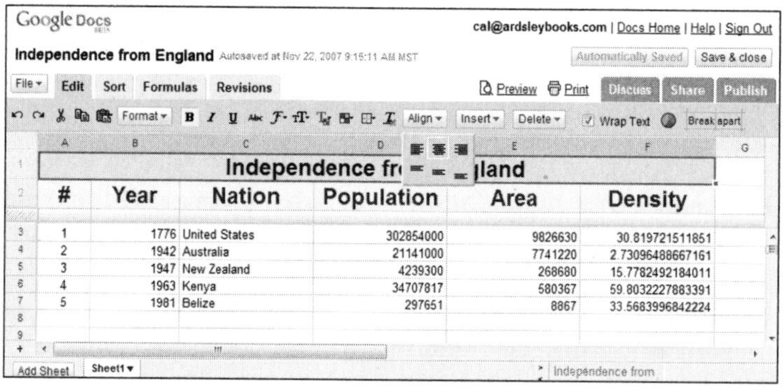
Google Docs
cal@ardsleybooks.com | Docs Home | Help | Sign Out
Independence from England
Save & close
File Edit Sort Formulas Revisions
Preview Print Discuss Share Publish
Format Align Insert Delete Wrap Text Break apart
Independence fr land
# Year Nation Population Area Density
1 1776 United States 302854000 9826630 30.819721511851
2 1942 Australia 21141000 7741220 2.73096488667161
3 1947 New Zealand 4239300 268680 15.7782492184011
4 1963 Kenya 34707817 580367 59.8032227883391
5 1981 Belize 297651 8867 33.5683996842224
Add Sheet Sheet1

**Figure 12-6:** Select entire rows or columns, then apply alignments or formats.

## Deleting rows and columns

You delete rows and columns much like you insert rows and columns — if you have an extra column or row that you don't want, simply select the entire row or column by clicking its number or letter, respectively, and then click the Delete button. From the menu that appears, select Delete Row or Delete Column.

# Formatting numbers

Number values can take a lot of different forms. You can change these forms, called *number formats,* by using the Format button. For example, Google Spread sheets can represent numbers as digits, in percents, in currency values, with decimals, and with or without commas. Even dates and times have their own unique formats. You can use the 24-hour clock or the 12-hour clock, or you can use the American month/day/year date format or the day/month/year date format used in most other countries. In our sample spreadsheet (of British Colonies), we need to change the number format in column F to round the decimal place so that the decimals don't run on forever. We also need to add comma separators to columns D and E so that users can more easily read the numbers. (Refer to Figure 12-6.)

To apply a number format, follow these steps:

1. **Select the columns, rows, or any cells that you want to change.**

2. **Click the Format button and select the number format that you need from the menu that appears, as shown in Figure 12-7.**

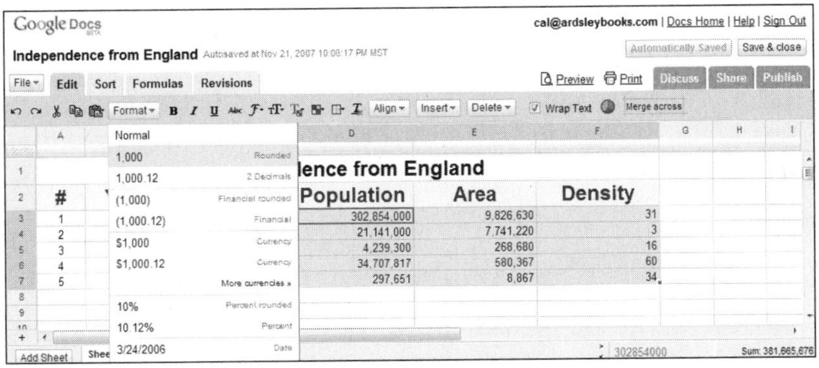

**Figure 12-7:** Select multiple columns and apply number formats.

# Freezing rows and columns

Sometimes, you may need to freeze certain cells at the top and left of the spreadsheet. *Freezing* locks cells in position so that when you scroll the spreadsheet, those rows remain at the top of the screen and those columns remain at the left, no matter how long or wide the spreadsheet gets. For example, if we expanded our sample spreadsheet to include 50 new rows for the current members of the British Commonwealth, we would need to freeze the top two rows. By freezing the labels in the topmost rows, you can scroll down to row 20, row 50, or row 5,000 and still read the labels at the top of each column.

You can freeze rows and columns in two ways:

✔ Click the Sort tab and click the Freeze Header Rows or Freeze Columns button. From the menu that appears, select how many rows or columns you want to freeze. In Figure 12-8, we selected Freeze 2 Rows from the menu.

✔ Click and drag the Freeze/Sort bar (seen above or below Row 1) down a couple of rows or left a few columns, as indicated in Figure 12-8.

To unfreeze rows or columns, click the Sort tab, click the Frozen Rows or Frozen Columns button, and select No Frozen Headers or No Frozen Columns, respectively, from the menu that appears. You can also drag the Freeze/Sort bar to the top or left of the spreadsheet.

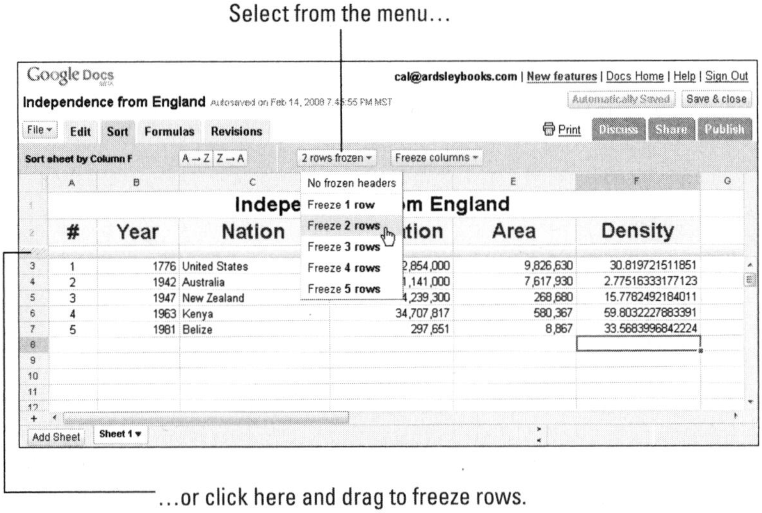

Select from the menu…

**Figure 12-8:** Freeze the labels at the top of the spreadsheet.

…or click here and drag to freeze rows.

# Sorting from A to Z and Z to A

Sorting text and numbers is one of the essential power-user features of Google Spreadsheets. You can sort in two ways:

✔ **A→Z:** Sort alphabetically from A to Z or numerically from one to infinity.

✔ **Z→A:** Sort alphabetically from Z to A or numerically from infinity to one.

Google Spreadsheets gives you two sorting options. You can sort by any column that you want by using either the Freeze/Sort bar or the Sort tab. For example, to sort data, you can

✔ Click the Freeze/Sort bar at the column you want to sort, and select A→Z.

✔ Highlight the column that you want to sort by, click the Sort tab, and click the A→Z button.

Either way you choose to do it, Spreadsheets sorts all the data in the adjacent rows to reflect your sort. (In Figure 12-9, the country with the lowest population density would move to the top of the list.)

If you want to reverse the sort order (for example, place the country with the greatest population density at the top), repeat the sort process, but this time, click Z→A.

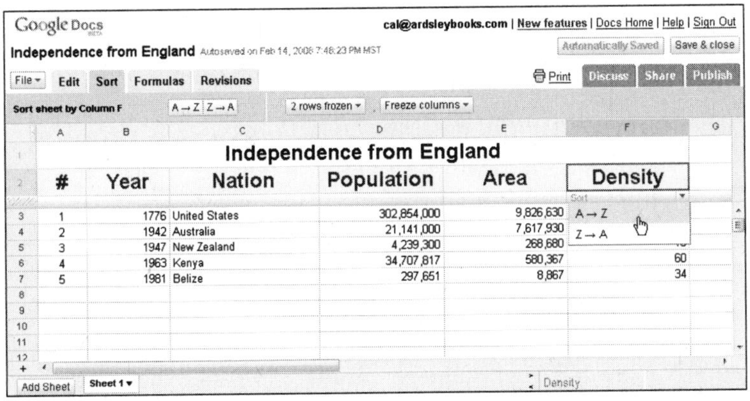

**Figure 12-9:** Sort your data from the Freeze/Sort bar or from the Sort tab.

# Using Charts, Graphs, and Diagrams

Many people are graphically impaired. Fortunately, you can easily create charts and graphs with Google Spreadsheets. To create a chart, simply select labels and the related numbers (called a *range*), and then click the Add Chart button on the Edit tab.

Google Spreadsheets lets you display information by using many different charting and graphing styles, including

✔ Column charts

✔ Bar charts

✔ Line graphs

✔ Pie charts

✔ Scatter diagrams

# Defining a range of data for your chart

Before you create a chart or graph, you must define your data range. When you're creating a chart, you need to select labels (either at the top of columns or the beginning of rows) and then choose data that corresponds with your labels. For example, in Figure 12-10, we chose three former British Colonies, their populations, and their land areas by selecting a range of cells from C5 to E7.

You define a range by clicking a beginning cell in the upper-left corner of the data set and extending down to the lower-right cell in the data set. Spreadsheets typically separate a range with a colon (:). For example, C5:E7 means "look at cells C5, E7, and everything in between."

**Figure 12-10:**
Select your
data range.

| | A | B | C | D | E | F |
|---|---|---|---|---|---|---|
| 1 | | | **Independence from England** | | | |
| 2 | **#** | **Year** | **Nation** | **Population** | **Area** | **Density** |
| 3 | 5 | 1981 | Belize | 297,651 | 8,867 | 34 |
| 4 | 3 | 1947 | New Zealand | 4,239,300 | 268,680 | 16 |
| 5 | 2 | 1942 | Australia | 21,141,000 | 7,617,930 | 3 |
| 6 | 4 | 1963 | Kenya | 34,707,817 | 580,367 | 60 |
| 7 | 1 | 1776 | United States | 302,854,000 | 9,826,630 | 31 |
| 8 | | | | | | |

# Creating a chart

After you decide what range you want, follow these steps to create a chart:

1. **Select the range by clicking and dragging over the desired cells.**

2. **Click the Add Chart button on the Edit tab. (It looks like a pie chart.)**

   The Create Chart dialog box appears, as shown in Figure 12-11.

3. **Select the charting options according to how you want your chart to look.**

   You can select different options in the following areas:

   - *What Type:* Click one of the icons in the What Type section — Columns, Bars, Lines, Pie, or Scatter. You can then refine your choice by clicking one of the Sub Type icons, which include variations on that chart type.

     You need to decide which type of chart can represent your data in the best possible way. For instance, you could compare the population of the United States with that of Australia and Kenya (see the data range in Figure 12-10) in a visually appealing pie chart. However, the selection of cells in Figure 12-10 includes Population and Area, so a pie chart may not represent the data properly; you might find a column or bar chart to be a better choice.

- *What Data:* The cell range that you select in Step 1 appears in the What Data text box. You can also choose how to group the data by selecting the Rows or Columns radio button. Select one of the check boxes (Use Row X as Labels or Use Column X as Labels) to tell Google Spreadsheets where to find the labels for the chart.

- *Labels:* Click in the Chart Title, Horizontal Axis, and Vertical Axis text boxes, and enter labels for those parts of the chart. Select where you want the legend to appear on your chart from the Legend drop-down list — you can choose No Legend, On Right, On Left, On Top, or On Bottom.

  If you set your spreadsheet up by adding either column or row labels to a range of numerical data, the labels automatically appear as a legend in the chart. (See Figure 12-11.)

  Depending on the chart type, you can add a title and place subtitles on the horizontal and vertical axes. You may find labeling the horizontal and vertical axes especially helpful when you create a column, bar, or line chart.

- *Preview:* Look at the Preview window to see how your changes affect the chart.

4. **Click the Save Chart button in the bottom-right corner of the Create Chart dialog box.**

   Your chart appears on top of your spreadsheet.

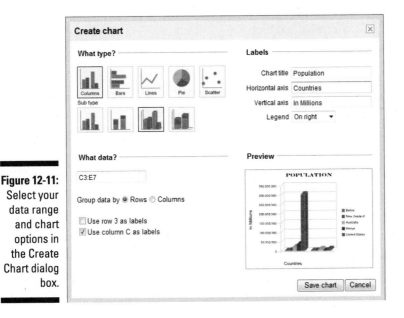

**Figure 12-11:** Select your data range and chart options in the Create Chart dialog box.

## *Managing charts*

After you have a chart in your spreadsheet, you're not finished! You can do more. Just click the chart to activate it, and then click the down arrow at the top of the chart window. (See Figure 12-12.) From the Chart menu that appears, you have the following options:

✔ **Edit Chart:** Change the look or data range of your chart.

✔ **Delete Chart:** Get rid of the chart and start over.

✔ **Save Image:** Save your chart as a graphic file to use in other documents.

✔ **Publish Chart:** Publish your chart online for others to view easily. (For more on publishing, see the "Printing and Publishing Spreadsheets" section, later in this chapter.)

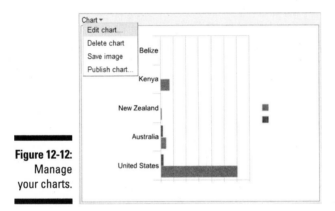

**Figure 12-12:**
Manage
your charts.

# *Formula Fixin'*

*Formulas* are mathematical expressions that solve numeric problems. Don't let this technical definition deter you from using formulas — Google has made them easy to use and understand. Formulas can use familiar operators, such as those seen in Table 12-2.

| Table 12-2 | Mathematical Operators | |
|---|---|---|
| *Operator* | *Meaning* | *Used To* |
| + | Addition or plus sign | Add two or more numbers together |
| – | Subtraction or negative sign | Subtract numbers or indicate a negative number |
| * | Multiplication sign | Multiply two or more numbers together |
| / | Division sign | Divide numbers or indicate a fraction |
| ^ | Exponential notation sign | Indicate that the number following the caret (^) is an exponent |
| ( ) | Parentheses | Group part of a formula to indicate that operation should be performed first |

You can write formulas that use these operators directly into any cell to perform simple mathematical calculations. To enter a formula into a cell, follow these steps:

1. **Select the cell and press =.**

   A formula starts with an = (equal) sign. The = sign is a trigger that tells the spreadsheet to start calculating.

2. **Type the formula.**

   You can use rather simple formulas, involving a single operator, or much more complicated formulas, involving multiple operators, multiple cell references, and the order of operations. (See the sidebar "The order of operations," in this chapter, for information on how operations must be sequenced and grouped.)

3. **Press Enter to enter the formula in the cell.**

   After you enter a formula, that formula disappears, and you can see only the answer to that formula.

To view or change the formula itself, you must double-click the cell again to make the formula reappear. You can now change the formula the same way you change any value.

Take a peek at some sample formulas in Table 12-3.

| Table 12-3 | Simple In-Cell Formulas |
|---|---|
| *In-Cell Formula* | *Answer Returned* |
| =2+3 | 5 |
| =2–3 | –1 |
| =2*3 | 6 |
| =2/3 | 0.666667 |
| =2^3 or =2*2*2 | 8 |
| =(2*3)–(2/3) | 5.333333 |

# Using cell references and selecting a range

Writing formulas with numerical values inside single cells is too manual and inflexible, and it doesn't take advantage of the power of spreadsheet functions and formulas. Spreadsheets are really good at performing calculations on numerical values in multiple cells at the same time. When performing this magical spreadsheet wizardry, use cell references (you remember the cell address like A1 or E5).

You can reference any cell that contains a value. In fact, any formula can reference any value in any cell. If the numerical values change, the formulas remain intact and automatically update their calculations.

When you have a bunch of numbers in a row or column, you can perform calculations on all of them by defining a cell range inside a formula. (See the section "Defining a range of data for your chart," earlier in this chapter, for an explanation of cell ranges. For example, C5:D7 means that all the numbers from cell C5 down to cell D7 are included as part of the range.) When you use a cell range in a formula, the beginning and ending cells are separated with a colon and are enclosed in parentheses (A1:F15).

To preselect a range, simply click the top-left cell and drag to the bottom-right cell. Using this method, you can add the entire range automatically to your formula.

# The order of operations

Calculations in spreadsheets are performed from left to right. All formulas are subject to the order of operations. The order of operations prioritizes which actions are performed first. Here's how the order of operations works:

1. Calculate anything inside parentheses.

   For instance, you convert (3*5)+(15/5) to (15)+(3) before adding the numbers together.

2. Calculate any exponents.

   For example, in 5*2^2, you first calculate 2^2 before multiplying.

3. Multiply and divide.

   In the example 3*4+6/3, first multiply and divide, and then add.

4. Add and subtract.

   Using the preceding example, add the results of the multiplication and division: 12+2.

You may remember the mnemonic phrase *Please Excuse My Dear Aunt Sally* from math class to help you recall the order of operations: Parentheses, Exponents, Multiply, Divide, Add, Subtract.

## *Built-in functions*

Functions define the type of operation that a spreadsheet will perform. Functions are built into Google Spreadsheets. You, as the spreadsheet user, can choose from hundreds of functions. A few of the more commonly used functions appear right on the Formulas tab, providing you one-click access. We explain these functions in Table 12-4.

| Table 12-4 | A Few Built-in Functions | |
|---|---|---|
| *Function* | *How It's Written into a Formula* | *What It Does* |
| Sum | =Sum(range) | Adds all the numbers in a range to find a sum total |
| Min | =Min(range) | Finds the lowest number in a range |
| Max | =Max(range) | Finds the highest number in a range |
| Count | =Count(range) | Counts how many cells contain numbers in the range |
| Average | =Average(range) | Averages all the numbers in a range |
| Product | =Product(range) | Finds the *product* (the results of multiplying) for a range of cells |

You can best see how these functions work inside formulas by looking at a few examples. We applied the Sum, Min, Max, Count, and Average functions in our sample colonial spreadsheet, shown in Figure 12-13. We used each function in a formula that has a range, and we applied them in the Population column. Each formula and each function uses the same range, (D3:D7); for example, =Sum (D3:D7) and =Average(D3:D7). In Figure 12-13, we added a label in column C for each function in column D to show how the functions calculate.

Follow these steps to use a function in a formula:

1. **Click the Formulas tab.**

2. **Click the cell in which you want the formula and function to reside.**

3. **Click the function link that you need in the upper-right corner of the Formulas tab and enter an open parenthesis.**

   We clicked the Average link in Figure 12-13.

4. **Click and drag over the range of numbers that you want to calculate.**

5. **Press Enter.**

   If you press Enter, you don't need to type a close parenthesis.

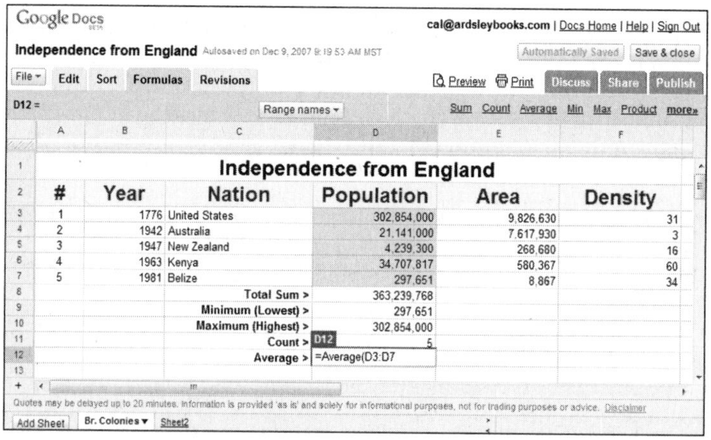

**Figure 12-13:**
You can apply basic functions to a range of data.

## Filling formulas

To apply the same functions and formulas from one column to another column (or columns), select the cells containing the formulas, drag the Fill Handle that appears in the corner of the cell across the columns you want to include, and release the mouse button. See Figure 12-14.

*Presto!* You've created multiple formulas. Also, the spreadsheet applies the incremental concept, explained in the "Entering sequences quickly with the Fill Handle" section, earlier in this chapter, to the range of cells listed in the formula. For example, instead of again applying the formulas to the same data range (D2:D7 in Figure 12-14), the cell references have been incremented when they move across the columns. For example, in Figure 12-14, the cell references were incremented to include (E2:E7) and (F2:F7). How's that for convenience?

If you don't want cells to automatically increment when you use the Fill Handle, add $ to cell references to fix their positions in your formulas. For example, using the cell reference ($D$2:$D$7) prevents the data from cells D2 to D7 from incrementing when they're copied.

**Figure 12-14:**
Use the
Fill Handle
to copy
formulas
and
functions.

| Google Docs | | | cal@ardsleybooks.com | Docs Home | Help | Sign Out |
| --- | --- | --- | --- | --- | --- |

**Independence from England** Autosaved on Dec 9, 2007 9:23:37 AM MST

File | Edit | Sort | Formulas | Revisions — Preview | Print | Discuss | Share | Publish

D8 = Sum(D3:D7) — Range names — Sum Count Average Min Max Product more»

| | A | B | C | D | E | F |
| --- | --- | --- | --- | --- | --- | --- |
| 2 | # | Year | Nation | Population | Area | Density |
| 3 | 1 | 1776 | United States | 302,854,000 | 9,826,630 | 31 |
| 4 | 2 | 1942 | Australia | 21,141,000 | 7,617,930 | 3 |
| 5 | 3 | 1947 | New Zealand | 4,239,300 | 268,680 | 16 |
| 6 | 4 | 1963 | Kenya | 34,707,817 | 580,367 | 60 |
| 7 | 5 | 1981 | Belize | 297,651 | 8,867 | 34 |
| 8 | | | Total Sum > | 363,239,768 | | |
| 9 | | | Minimum (Lowest) > | 297,651 | | |
| 10 | | | Maximum (Highest) > | 302,854,000 | | |
| 11 | | | Count > | 5 | | |
| 12 | | | Average > | 72,647,954 | | |
| 13 | | | | | | |
| 14 | | | | | | |
| 15 | | | | | | |

Quotes may be delayed up to 20 minutes. Information is provided 'as is' and solely for informational purposes, not for trading purposes or advice. Disclaimer

Add Sheet | Br. Colonies ▾ | Sheet2 — Sum(D3:D7) — Sum: 739039377.6

## Advanced and creative online functions

If you need to apply more advanced functions, click the More link in the top-right corner of the Formulas tab. The Insert a Function dialog box appears. This dialog box stores every possible function you should ever need; at least, Google hopes they've accounted for everything you might want to do! (See Figure 12-15.) The dialog box divides the functions into nine separate categories to make them easier to scour through: Math, Financial, Logical, Date, Lookup, Statistical, Text, Info, and Google. (In Figure 12-15, you can see the Math category on the left side and the Google category on the right side.)

Google has supplied some creative, beyond-the-normal spreadsheet functionality that allows you to integrate and update data directly from the Internet into a spreadsheet. For example, you can insert stock quotes into a spreadsheet (see the sidebar "Inserting a stock quote," in this chapter, for the steps).

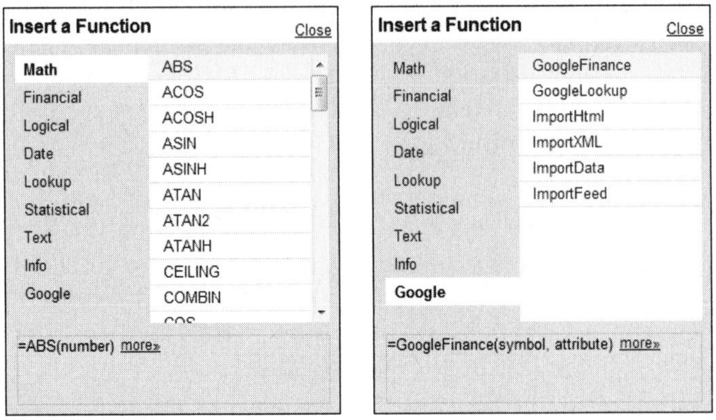

**Figure 12-15:**
Access
advanced
built-in
functions by
category in
the Insert a
Function
dialog box.

| Insert a Function | | Close |
|---|---|---|
| **Math** | ABS | |
| Financial | ACOS | |
| Logical | ACOSH | |
| Date | ASIN | |
| Lookup | ASINH | |
| Statistical | ATAN | |
| Text | ATAN2 | |
| Info | ATANH | |
| Google | CEILING | |
| | COMBIN | |
| | COS | |

=ABS(number) more»

| Insert a Function | | Close |
|---|---|---|
| Math | GoogleFinance | |
| Financial | GoogleLookup | |
| Logical | ImportHtml | |
| Date | ImportXML | |
| Lookup | ImportData | |
| Statistical | ImportFeed | |
| Text | | |
| Info | | |
| **Google** | | |

=GoogleFinance(symbol, attribute) more»

# Creating multiple sheets

Google Spreadsheets allows you to create multiple sheets in the same spreadsheet. (Microsoft Excel calls these sheets *worksheets*.) You may find using multiple sheets extremely helpful. Say you're working on the company budget; you can create a separate sheet for each department or each team.

You can use numbers from one sheet in formulas on another sheet, which means the sheets can interact with each other. For example, if you're calculating multiple expenses from three separate departments, the total expenses for multiple departments can appear on a summary balance sheet for each and every sheet in the spreadsheet.

To create a new sheet, simply click the Add Sheet button at the bottom of the Google Spreadsheets screen, as shown in Figure 12-16. To make sheets easier to find, you can give each sheet a unique name. You can even rearrange the order of the sheets, if you want.

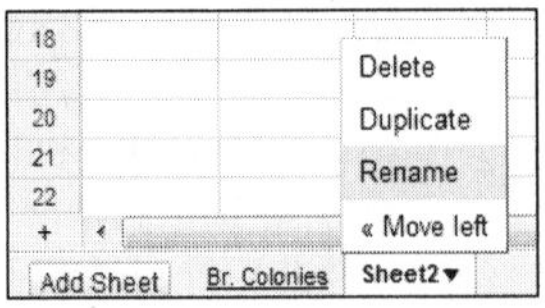

**Figure 12-16:**
Create
multiple
sheets.

| 18 | | |
|---|---|---|
| 19 | | Delete |
| 20 | | Duplicate |
| 21 | | Rename |
| 22 | | |
| + | ◄ | « Move left |

Add Sheet   Br. Colonies   Sheet2 ▼

## Inserting a stock quote

If you want the current, updated price of a stock displayed in a spreadsheet, click the More link on the Formulas tab, click the Google category in the Insert a Function dialog box that appears, and select the GoogleFinance stock ticker function (refer to the right side of Figure 12-15). After your spreadsheet inserts the formula, the stock price updates from GoogleFinance every few seconds. You have a lot of options to explore under the More link. By clicking it and exploring the Insert a Function dialog box, you can find out more about the variables and attributes that you need to make the function work properly.

The GoogleFinance function requires both a ticker symbol and an attribute. For example: = GoogleFinance("GOOG"; "price"). Quotation marks appear around the ticker symbol and the attribute, and a semicolon is placed between them. All these symbols and words, and the way they're organized, are called the *syntax* of the formula. You can easily find ticker symbols on the http://finance.google.com Web site. Here are a few examples:

✔ GOOG for Google

✔ MSFT for Microsoft

✔ APPL for Apple

Attributes include commonly required stock info, such as volume and price. Click the More link to the right of the function description at the bottom of the Insert a Function dialog box to view a Web page that describes all the attributes that function uses.

# *Sharing and Collaboration*

We explain sharing and collaboration in Google Docs in Chapter 11. We won't repeat the information that we present in that chapter — we just provide you with the nuances of how collaboration and sharing differ between apps. If you want a more in-depth understanding of sharing and collaboration than this chapter provides, check out Chapter 11.

When you share a spreadsheet, colleagues from anywhere can collaborate on that spreadsheet simultaneously. The concept of singledocumindedness applies to spreadsheets. Like with Docs, Spreadsheets tracks all spreadsheet changes to maintain quality and version control. Spreadsheets updates changes made by any number of collaborators every few seconds. Keeping a single version of a spreadsheet, while maintaining a record of all the changes made to it, is much more efficient than keeping multiple versions of the same sheet, especially when collaborating with a group of people on the same spreadsheet. And Google Spreadsheets always lets you know who's currently contributing to the spreadsheet by listing the names of collaborators at the bottom of the screen.

To share a spreadsheet, click the Share tab. Invite collaborators and viewers by entering their e-mail addresses in the Invite People text box, as shown in Figure 12-17. (While you type, Google displays matching names from your Contacts list. Click a name to select it from the list. It will be inserted automatically.)

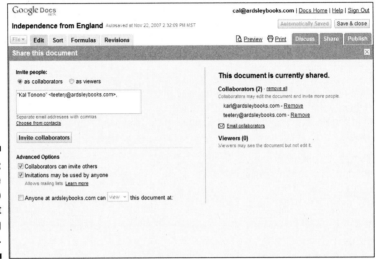

**Figure 12-17:**
Click the
Share tab
and start
entering
contributors.

You need to decide whether you want the people you invite to be collaborators or simply viewers. Collaborators can make changes; viewers can only read the spreadsheet.

Set permissions that can lock the spreadsheet down from the Advanced Options area of the Share tab. We explain these options in more detail in Chapter 11. Essentially, if you want to keep things private, add or remove check marks from any options that concern you.

When you're done choosing your security settings, click the Invite Collaborators button. An Invitation screen appears, showing the e-mail message that goes out to all your collaborators and viewers. This e-mail includes a Web link that the recipients can click to access the spreadsheet. (See Figure 12-18.)

Shared spreadsheets appear in the Docs Home page list, along with other documents, spreadsheets, and presentations. You can organize them all by folders and labels, as explained in Chapter 10. If you need to send additional e-mail updates concerning your spreadsheet to viewers and collaborators, click the Share tab and click the Email Collaborators link. (Refer to Figure 12-17.) If you need to add or delete collaborators, you can do that from the Share tab at any time.

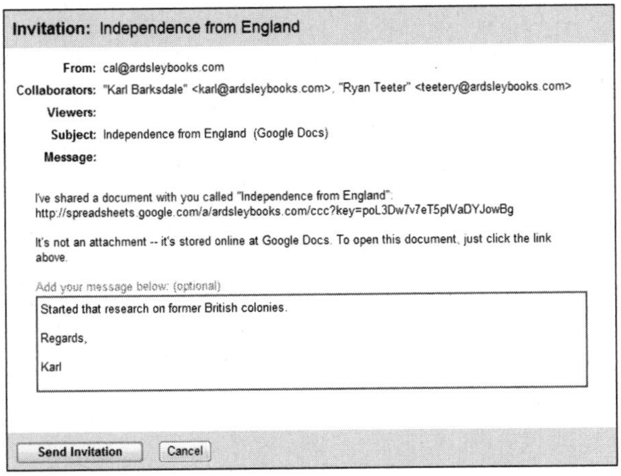

**Figure 12-18:**
Notify your
collabo-
rators
of your
spread-
sheet's
address.

---

## Discuss while you go

The Discuss tab offers another great feature for spreadsheet collaborators. If you're working with others, you can chat about the spreadsheet while you work on it, as shown in Figure 12-19. In fact, you can chat about almost anything you want. We bet that, after a few minutes, chatting about the spreadsheet becomes a low priority.

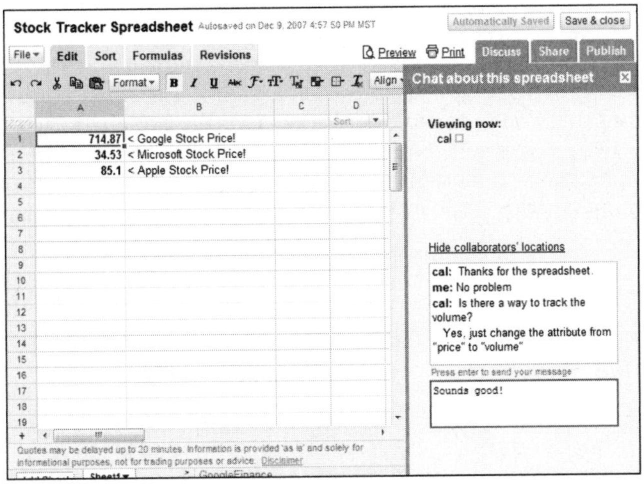

**Figure 12-19:**
Discuss the
spreadsheet
while you
work on it.

## *Version controls*

To view changes to a spreadsheet or to revert back to an earlier spreadsheet, click the Revisions tab, then click the Older or Newer button to view the various versions. (See Figure 12-20.) If you decide that you want to revert back to an earlier version, click the Revert to This One button. A dialog box appears, asking you to verify your decision.

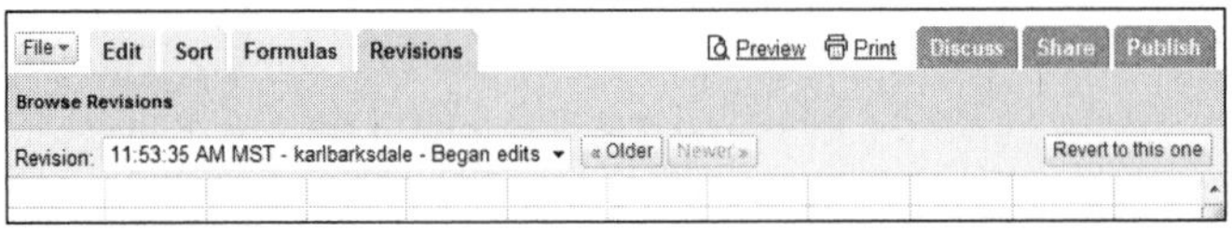

**Figure 12-20:**
View versions of your spreadsheet.

# *Converting and Exporting to Other File Formats*

You may need to convert a Google spreadsheet to a file format that desktop spreadsheet applications, such as Microsoft Excel or OpenOffice, use. You can make these conversions by clicking the File button and selecting Export from the menu that appears, as shown in Figure 12-21. Then choose the spreadsheet format that you need from the submenu. (We explain these formats in Table 12-5.) When you select any option, a dialog box appears that allows you to set options and parameters for exporting your spreadsheet. If you're even remotely familiar with these formats, the screens should be self-explanatory.

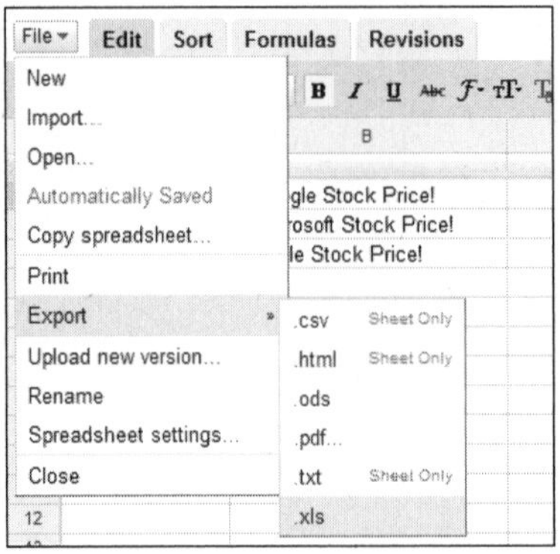

**Figure 12-21:**
The File menu presents your Export format options.

| Table 12-5 | Spreadsheet Conversions |
|---|---|
| *Format* | *Explanation of Format* |
| .html | A format that displays the data in a Web page format. |
| .csv | A comma-separated format in which you can transfer data to another spreadsheet application or to a database. |
| .txt | This text format simply preserves the data but loses all the formulas that you may have applied. |
| .ods | An open document format that applies to a universal set of applications. An ideal format for those using OpenOffice or another open source application. |
| .pdf | The portable document format that captures a picture of the data. Use this format if you want to lock the data down so that no one can make changes. |
| .xls | The Microsoft Excel spreadsheet format. |

# Printing and Publishing Spreadsheets

Like with Docs, you have two ways to print your spreadsheet:

- Click the File button and select Print from the menu that appears (refer to Figure 12-21).
- Click the Print link in the header.

If you want to preview before you print, click the Preview link. A document appears that gives you a general idea of what the spreadsheet will look like when you print it.

The publishing feature posts an online HTML version of your spreadsheet and uploads a copy to your Web site or blog. You may find this a nice advantage if you want to share the spreadsheet with audiences beyond those in your collaborators list. Access the publishing features by clicking the Publish tab and clicking the Publish Now button, as shown in Figure 12-22.

After you publish your spreadsheet, you can still make changes or upload fixes to the spreadsheet publication by clicking the Publish tab again. From the update screen that appears, you can republish changes to your document, stop publishing altogether, select just the parts that you want to share, or select the Automatically Re-Publish When Changes Are Made check box. (See Figure 12-23.)

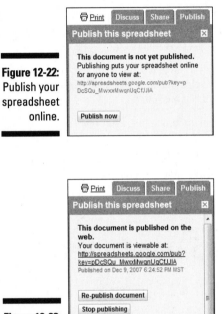

**Figure 12-22:**
Publish your
spreadsheet
online.

**Figure 12-23:**
Republish
changes
to your
spreadsheet
publication.

# Chapter 13

# Creating Amazing Google Presentations

*N*eed a quality presentation in a hurry and don't have the time (or the patience) for a complicated, ultra-sophisticated, über-difficult desktop presentation program? Then you'll like Google Presentations.

You may take advantage of the portability of Google Presentations more than Docs or Spreadsheets. You can access and run your presentations by logging into your Google Apps account from any computer (as long as it has an Internet connection) — which means you don't need to store gigabytes of presentations on your laptop or jump drive. You don't even need to bring your laptop or other devices to your next presentation. If you're traveling, you can slide through airport security unencumbered by a laptop (okay, you may take your iPod or Zune), and you can be confident that your presentation is safe on a Google server, ready for you to access anytime or anyplace you need it.

In this chapter, we cover all the basics that you need to know to create a presentation — adding and formatting text, inserting images and shapes, and so on. We then cover how to present your work, as well as how to share and collaborate. Finally, we cover publishing your presentation.

# Starting Up Presentations

Google Presentations is the third jewel in the crown of Google Docs, the online productivity suite. To create a new presentation, you start from Google Docs Home. (See Chapter 10 for details about Docs Home.) Log into Google Docs (go to `http://docs.yourdomain.com` or `http://docs.google.com`; Team Edition users, go to `http://docs.google.com/a/yourdomain.com`). Click New and select Presentation from the menu that appears. A new, blank presentation opens, as shown in Figure 13-1.

Header                                                                 Formatting toolbar

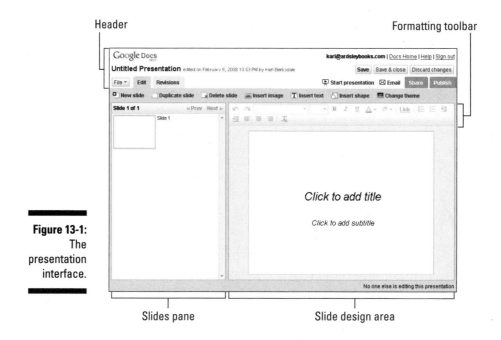

**Figure 13-1:**
The
presentation
interface.

Slides pane                                                            Slide design area

## Similarities in the header

Many features between the three Google Docs apps (Docs, Spreadsheets, and Presentations) are integrated or very similar. The header section contains links and tools similar to those in Docs and Spreadsheets (as we describe in Chapters 11 and 12): Docs Home, Help, and Sign Out links; the Save, Save & Close, and the Discard Changes buttons; your e-mail address; and the file name.

When you create your presentations, the File menu is essential. This menu allows you to do many tasks, such as importing, renaming, deleting, saving a presentation as an HTML file, starting your presentation, and saving. (We cover these tasks in the "Using the File Menu" section, later in this chapter.)

## Big differences below the header

Below the header in Presentations, the layout departs from the other apps. A Start Presentation link replaces the Preview link that appears in the other two apps. You use the Start Presentation link to view a presentation after you create it. The formatting tools are in a slightly different place than in the other apps, just above the slide design area on the right side of the screen — which makes them more accessible when you're working on a slide. The space where the Edit toolbar sits in Docs and Spreadsheets is filled with a few unique options:

- ✔ **New Slide:** Add a new slide to your presentation and choose from a variety of slide layouts for each new slide.

- ✔ **Duplicate Slide:** Select a slide and use this link to make an exact duplicate of the existing slide.

- ✔ **Delete Slide:** Remove a slide completely.

- ✔ **Insert Image:** Upload and insert an image into your presentation.

- ✔ **Insert Text:** Create separate text boxes.

- ✔ **Insert Shape:** Add a shape, such as a square, circle, speech bubble, starburst, or arrow, to your presentation.

- ✔ **Change Theme:** Choose a colorful theme to provide background style, design, color, and texture to your presentations.

Don't use the browser's File menu to save or print your presentation; it won't work! Instead, use the File button and the Save and Save & Close buttons in the Presentations header (refer to Figure 13-1) to save, print, or rename a file (and more).

# Adding Themes, Text, Shapes, and Images to Slides

When you start Presentations, it displays a new slide that has placeholder text. You probably don't want to give a presentation about "Click to add title," so we show you the basics of slide creation. In the following sections, you can find out how to change the *theme* (look) of slides, add and edit text, add a shape, and add images to your slides.

## Changing the placeholder text

If you're a beginner, let Presentations make the font size and style decisions for you until you get to know the app fairly well and feel your creative confidence coming on. Presentations can make your presentation look good without you having to think too much about its design, leaving you free to focus on your message.

As soon as you start a new presentation, Presentations creates a title slide — refer to Figure 13-1. Click the Click to Add Title placeholder text on your slide. A text box appears in its place; click in it and type a new title. Although it's optional, you can add a subtitle (such as your name) by clicking the Click to Add Subtitle placeholder text, clicking in the text box that appears, and typing a subtitle. After you change the placeholder text, the tiny preview slide in the slide pane on the left updates, as shown in Figure 13-2.

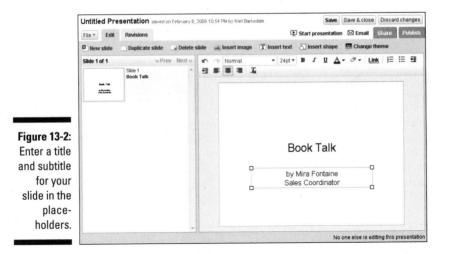

**Figure 13-2:**
Enter a title and subtitle for your slide in the place-holders.

## Changing themes

Themes bring together color schemes, templates, and font choices that are designed to work well together. Some artistic person somewhere created the themes so that the rest of us can just click and type, and still create a great-looking presentation.

Pick an attractive theme by clicking the Edit tab's Change Theme button (refer to Figure 13-2). The Choose Theme dialog box appears, as shown in Figure 13-3, giving you many premade themes to select from. Happily, Presentations offers some great options, so you can avoid any obnoxious color schemes. Remember to keep your audience in mind when choosing a theme for your presentation. For example, Pink n' Pretty is very, well, pretty — but you should probably avoid it unless you're Elle Woods (you know, from the *Legally Blonde* movies). For the sample presentation shown in the figures throughout this chapter, we used the Chalkboard theme; it's a stark choice, but it shows up well on the black-and-white pages of this book.

**Figure 13-3:** Pick a theme from the Choose Theme dialog box.

Some old-school presenters say that you should enter all your content into a blank presentation first, and then pick a theme and color scheme later. However, we prefer to pick a colorful theme right off the bat, and then start adding content. It's much more fun that way. Colors, stripes, images, fades, and textures get the creative juices flowing. After all, presentations are a visual medium, so why be boring at the start?

Another value of picking your theme early is that each one has a different layout. You may need to tweak your words and pictures a bit so that everything looks readable and balanced. Besides, if you suddenly decide that a particular theme isn't right, you can always change it midstream by clicking the Change Theme button again and picking a new theme entirely. You never need to be stuck with a boring theme.

## Inserting text boxes and formatting text

If you're using a theme, a few default text boxes appear in the slides. To create a text box that doesn't fit inside the normal template, follow these steps:

1. **Click the Insert Text button.**

   A new text box appears with the placeholder text Click to Add Content.

2. **Click in the text box and type away.**

   You can also paste text that you cut or copied from elsewhere.

   Much like in Docs, you can type, format, and edit text in the text box. When you finish typing, click outside the text box. (See Figure 13-4.)

3. **Move the text box or resize it as needed to accommodate the text you added (you may need to click the text box to select it):**

   • *Move:* Hover your cursor over the side of the text box; when the cursor changes into a cross with four arrows, click and drag to move the text box wherever you need it.

   • *Resize and reshape:* Click a corner handle and drag to reshape and resize any text box anyway you want. If you have text inside the text box, the text reflows to fit the new dimensions.

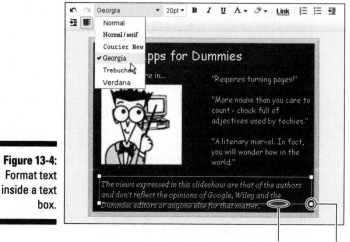

**Figure 13-4:** Format text inside a text box.

Drag a side to move the text box.     Drag a handle to resize the text box

Take a close look at the formatting tools at the top of the slide design area in Figure 13-4. We used the formatting buttons to change the text in the bottom text box to the Georgia font. We also added italics and changed the text color to yellow.

We cover all the formatting tools available in Presentations in detail in Chapter 11. They all work the same way in Presentations as they do in Docs or Spreadsheets (click the button and type, or select text and click a button to apply that format to the selected text). They also share the same keyboard shortcuts (if applicable).

Table 13-1 shows the keyboard shortcuts specific to Presentations. (For more keyboard shortcuts, see Chapter 11.)

| Table 13-1 | Keyboard Shortcuts for Google Presentations |
|---|---|
| *Keyboard Shortcut* | *What It Does* |
| Ctrl+A | Selects all text in a text box |
| Ctrl+Space | Removes formatting |
| Page Down | Moves to the bottom of a text box |
| Page Up | Moves to the top of a text box |
| Ctrl+Home | Goes to the top of a text box |
| Ctrl+End | Goes to the bottom of a text box |
| Ctrl+M | Inserts a new slide |
| Ctrl+S | Saves |
| Ctrl+P | Prints |
| Esc | Closes a live presentation |
| Ctrl+F5 | Starts a presentation |
| F11 | Displays your browser in full screen or returns to the browser window from full screen |

You can add a link in your presentation (see Chapter 11 for the steps to add a link). Putting a hypertext link into your presentation has advantages. If you need to access Web sites or online articles during your presentation, list them in your slides so that they're ready when you want them to appear. Also, you can put a link to your company or school Web page somewhere convenient (such as on the title slide) so that you can link to it quickly. In the example at the top of Figure 13-5, we entered the URL www.ardsleybooks.com.

On your presentation, you can click any hyperlinked text to edit or remove the hyperlink. (See the bottom of Figure 13-5.)

A few buttons that you can use in Docs and Spreadsheets don't appear in the Presentations formatting toolbar. You don't need options such as the Docs Style feature in Presentations because you determine the styles by selecting a theme, as described in the "Changing themes" section, earlier in this chapter.

The Cut, Copy, and Paste buttons don't appear in Presentations. However, you can still cut, copy, and paste text, shapes, and graphics by using the keyboard shortcuts Ctrl+X, Ctrl+C, and Ctrl+V (Windows) or ⌘+X, ⌘+C, and ⌘+V (Mac). You can also select your text and then right-click to bring these options up in a contextual menu, as shown in Figure 13-6.

**WARNING!**

With some browsers and operating systems, when you cut, copy, and paste, a warning dialog box appears, asking whether you want to allow the Web page to have access to the system Clipboard. Click the Allow Access button to allow temporary access, and then try your operation again.

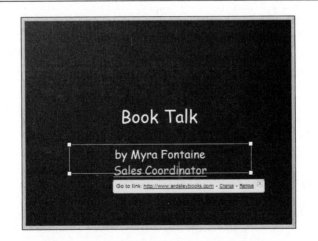

**Figure 13-5:** Create, change, or remove a hyperlink to a Web page or e-mail address.

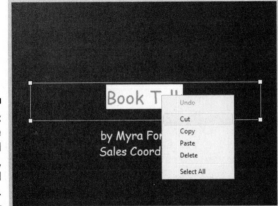

**Figure 13-6:** Use the contextual menu to cut, copy, and paste.

## Inserting shapes

You can add simple shapes to your presentation, such as squares, circles, speech bubbles, starbursts, and arrows. For example, you can add arrow shapes to create a simple flowchart.

Follow these steps to insert a shape:

1. **Click the Insert Shape button.**
2. **From the menu that appears, select the shape that you want to insert.**

   The shape appears in the middle of your slide.
3. **Move, resize, and recolor the shape, as needed:**
   - *Move:* Click and drag the shape to move it into position.
   - *Resize:* Click a corner handle (you may need to click the shape first to select it), and then drag to resize or reshape the image.
   - *Add color:* Click the Paint Bucket or Line Color button in the top-left corner (you may need to click the shape first to select it), and then pick a color square from the menu that appears, as shown in Figure 13-7.

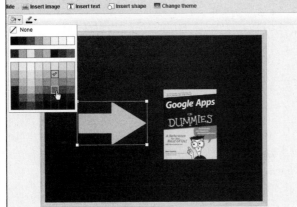

**Figure 13-7:**
Insert shapes and make them appear how you want them.

## Inserting images

A presentation can be boring if it's all text (even with a theme applied). You can add images to your slides to make your presentation more visually appealing to the audience. You can also insert images, such as charts or graphs, that you create in Google Spreadsheets.

To insert an image into a slide, follow these steps:

1. **Click the Insert Image button.**

   The Insert Image dialog box appears, as shown in Figure 13-8.

2. **Click the Browse button.**

3. **In the Choose File dialog box that appears, browse to your picture file, select it, and click the Open button to return to the Insert Image dialog box.**

   You can use only Web-compatible image files: `.jpg`, `.gif`, or `.png`. (Presentations can't load other types of image files, such as `.tif`.)

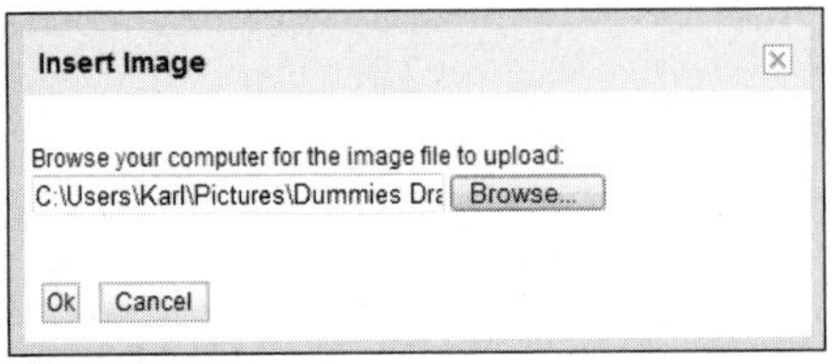

**Figure 13-8:**
Click
Browse to
find the
image that
you want to
insert into
your
present-
ation.

Insert Image

Browse your computer for the image file to upload:

C:\Users\Karl\Pictures\Dummies Dra    Browse...

Ok    Cancel

You can insert a chart or graph that you create in Google Spreadsheets. (See Chapter 12 for steps to create a chart.) In Spreadsheets, create your chart or open an existing chart. Click the chart to select it, and then click the Chart menu at the top of the chart. Select Save Image from the menu, and click the Save button in the dialog box that appears to save the file to your computer. Back in Presentations, follow Steps 1 through 3 in this list and select the chart's image file in the Choose File dialog box.

4. **Click OK in the Insert Image dialog box.**

   Presentations uploads and inserts a copy of the image file into your slide.

5. **Move and resize the image as needed.**

   The default placement of the image, dead center in your slide, is probably not the right spot. The image is probably too large, as well. To adjust your image

   • *Move:* Click and drag the image to move it into position.

   • *Resize:* Click a corner handle (you may need to click the image first to select it) and drag to resize or reshape the image. (See Figure 13-9.)

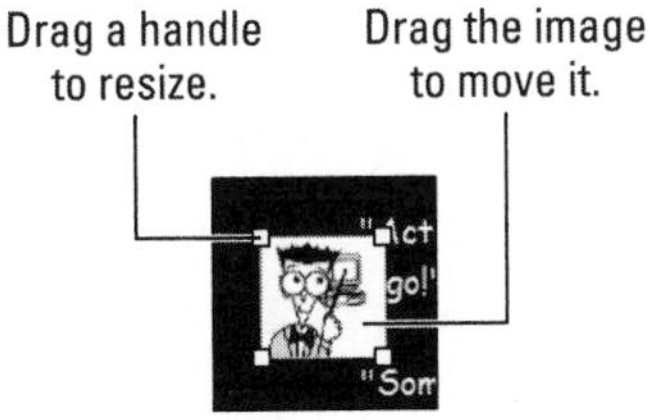

Drag a handle          Drag the image
  to resize.             to move it.

**Figure 13-9:**
Move and
resize your
picture.

If you right-click an image or a shape, a contextual menu appears that allows you to delete, cut, or copy the image. You can also choose to make the image look like it's in front of or behind text or another image by right-clicking and choosing Bring to Front or Send to Back, respectively. You can use this feature to make your presentation more visually appealing.

# Organizing Slides

Unless you're giving a ten-second presentation, you need to create more than one slide. And, when you have a presentation with several (maybe several dozen) slides, you may need to duplicate slides (to make the first and last slides identical, or to start a new slide based on a previous slide, for example), delete unneeded slides, and even change the order of slides. The following sections show you what you need to know to create new slides and keep them organized.

## Making a new slide

To build your presentation, you need to create new slides. After all, a one-slide presentation isn't very interesting — and it's really short!

To create a new slide, follow these steps:

1. **Click the New Slide button in the Edit tab.**

   The Choose a Slide Layout dialog box appears. In this dialog box, you choose among a variety of predefined slide layout options, as shown in Figure 13-10.

2. **Click the slide layout that you want.**

   The new slide appears in the slide design area. Unless you choose the Blank slide layout, placeholder text appears in the text boxes defined by the slide's layout.

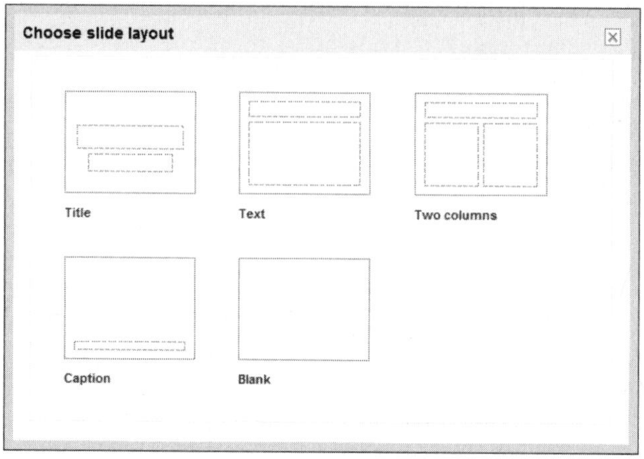

**Figure 13-10:**
Pick a slide
layout in the
Choose a
Slide Layout
dialog box.

For most slides within a presentation, either the Text or Two Columns layouts work well. But you can choose whichever one fits your content. In our example, we used the Two Columns layout. This template places two text boxes side by side, as illustrated by the dotted marquees (see Figure 13-10). In addition, another text box appears at the top that you can use for a title or caption. To enter a caption or a column of text, simply click any of the three text boxes and start typing. (See the section "Inserting text boxes and formatting text," earlier in this chapter, for details.)

## Duplicating, reordering, and deleting slides

The slide pane (sometimes called the slide navigator) is on the left side of the Presentations screen. This pane displays thumbnails listing the slide order and a caption for each slide, and you can keep your slides organized by deleting, duplicating, reordering, and so on in this pane.

Use the Prev and Next buttons and the scroll bar in the slide pane to navigate through the slide thumbnails. You can also use the Page Up and Page Down keys on your keyboard. You find this pane helpful when you have more than five slides and need to skip to a particular slide quickly.

There are two ways to rearrange your presentation in the slide pane. First, click and drag a slide to change its order, as shown on the left side of Figure 13-11. Second, if you right-click any slide in the slide pane, a contextual menu appears, as shown on the right side of Figure 13-11. This menu allows you to

   ✔ **Change the order of the slides:** Select Move Slide Up or Move Slide Down. (Remember, you can also click and drag a slide in the slide pane to change its order.)

✔ **Create a new slide:** Select New Slide. (See the preceding section for more information on creating a new slide.)

✔ **Duplicate an existing slide:** Select Duplicate Slide. When you duplicate a slide, you make an exact copy of a slide, including all the text, images, shapes, and layout of the existing slide. The duplicate slide appears below the original slide in the slide pane. (You can also click and drag a slide while holding the Ctrl key on your keyboard to create a duplicate wherever you like.)

✔ **Delete a slide:** Select Delete Slide. If you accidentally delete a slide, press Ctrl+Z (Windows) or ⌘+Z (Mac) or click the Undo link in the top center of the screen right away to restore your slide. You won't be able to retrieve it after you make any other edits.

✔ **Copy and paste an existing slide:** Select Copy Slide. Place the mouse cursor where you want the copied slide to appear in the slide pane, right-click, and select Paste Slide from the menu that appears. Your slide will appear immediately below the slide you clicked.

Of course, if you need to edit a slide, select it in the slide pane first to make it appear in the slide design area.

This simple idea can save you time: If you've worked hard on a slide and intend to use some of the same elements (caption, image, or text) in the following slide, click the Duplicate Slide button on the Edit toolbar or right-click and select Duplicate Slide from the contextual menu. Then, you can edit and change just a few elements, leaving the rest of the slide intact.

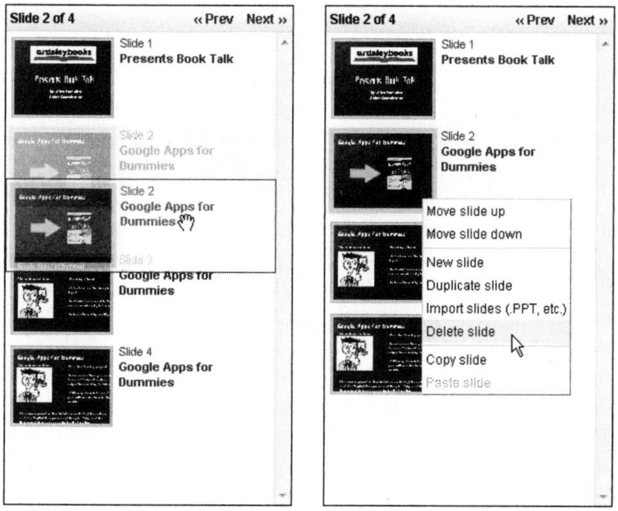

**Figure 13-11:**
Reorder and
delete slides
in the slide
navigator.

# Using the File Menu

One of the most important tools in Google Presentations likes to hang out inconspicuously in the top-left corner of the screen. Don't underestimate its power, though, as you create your presentations, you absolutely need to understand the Presentations File menu.

The File menu, shown in Figure 13-12, allows you to do many tasks, such as creating a new file; opening a file; uploading or importing a presentation; saving, renaming, and deleting a presentation; seeing a print preview; saving a file as HTML; and viewing a presentation.

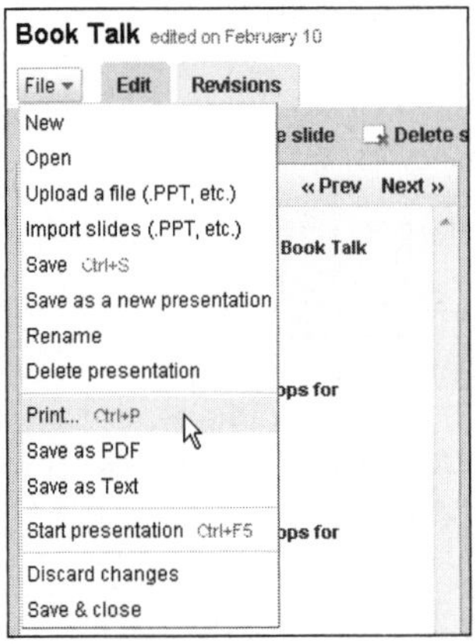

**Book Talk** edited on February 10

| File ▼ | Edit | Revisions |

New
Open                                                  e slide | Delete s
Upload a file (.PPT, etc.)                    « Prev  Next »
Import slides (.PPT, etc.)
Save  Ctrl+S                                       **Book Talk**
Save as a new presentation
Rename
Delete presentation                            bps for
Print...  Ctrl+P
Save as PDF
Save as Text
Start presentation  Ctrl+F5            bps for
Discard changes
Save & close

**Figure 13-12:**
Use the File
menu to
work with
your
presenta-
tion.

# Renaming a presentation

One of the key things that you can do from the File menu is rename your presentation. You may initially get stuck with a name like Untitled.

To rename a presentation, click the File button and choose Rename from the menu that appears. (You can also click the title itself to rename the presentation.) A dialog box pops up, and you can type a new presentation title in the textbox that appears.

A warning about scripted dialog boxes may appear in your browser when you try to rename a file — just click on the warning bar and choose Temporarily Allow Scripted Windows from the menu that appears. The browser then allows the dialog box to appear when you choose Rename from the File menu again, and you can rename your presentation by typing a new name in the text box that appears.

# Saving a PDF copy of your presentation

You can save a PDF copy of a presentation on your hard drive or jump drive in case you ever do need a backup. This is particularly handy if you will be presenting from a computer that doesn't have an Internet connection. To do this, click the File button and select Save As PDF from the menu. (Refer to Figure 13-12.) By choosing this command, you can save a small, compressed copy of your presentation.

If you have Adobe Reader installed (you can download it at www.adobe.com/reader), the PDF may appear directly in your browser window. Click the Save button on the Reader toolbar to show a dialog box that lets you choose where you would like to save your file. Otherwise, a dialog box appears directly in your browser, asking whether you want to open or save your file. Click the Save button, and browse to a location on your hard drive or a jump drive to save the File. After you save the file, you can open it later with Adobe Reader to view it.

To present your PDF presentation, open your PDF file in Adobe Reader, and then choose File⇨Full Screen Mode or press Ctrl+L (Windows) or ⌘+L (Mac). Use the arrow keys on your keyboard to move forward and backward.

# Printing the presentation

You can easily print a copy of your presentation. Click the File button and select Print from the menu that appears, or press Ctrl+P. Google Presentations then prepares the presentation for printing in the window that appears, as shown in Figure 13-13. Choose the number of slides you want to appear on each printed page by selecting from the Layout drop-down list. Click the Print button when you're ready to print a copy of your presentation. You can also click the Save As PDF button to save a PDF version.

# Uploading existing PowerPoint presentations

You may have a few PowerPoint presentations on your desktop computer that you want to convert into the Google Presentations format and save online. In fact, you may want to carefully preserve a copy of all your PowerPoint presentations on Google servers so that you don't lose all your hard work if a computer crashes. To upload a PowerPoint presentation, click the File button and select Upload a File (.PPT, etc.) from the menu that appears. The Upload a File screen appears, as shown in Figure 13-14.

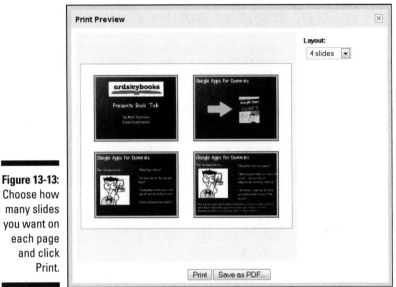

**Figure 13-13:**
Choose how
many slides
you want on
each page
and click
Print.

When the Upload a File screen appears, you can see the limitations on your PowerPoint uploads. For example, your uploaded presentation can't currently exceed 10MB. Click the Browse button to locate your PowerPoint presentation. (You can also convert other open source presentations.) If you want to rename the PowerPoint presentation, click in the What Do You Want to Call It text box and type a new name before you click the Upload File button.

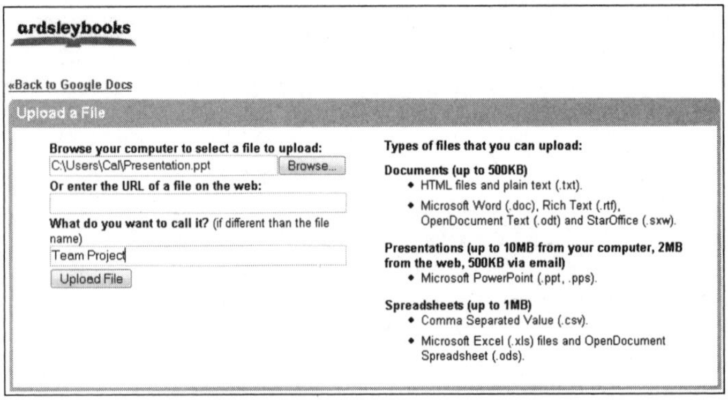

**Figure 13-14:**
Upload and
convert a
PowerPoint
presentation
into a
Google
Presenta-
tions file.

# Integrating other slides into a presentation

When you create a presentation, you may want to insert a slide, or series of slides, that you've already created for another presentation. You can integrate both PowerPoint and Google Presentations slides. To integrate individual slides from another file, click the File button and select Import Slides (.PPT, etc.) from the menu that appears. The Import Slides dialog box appears, as shown in Figure13-15. In this dialog box, just follow the steps — the first step asks you to choose the presentation from which you want to import slides.

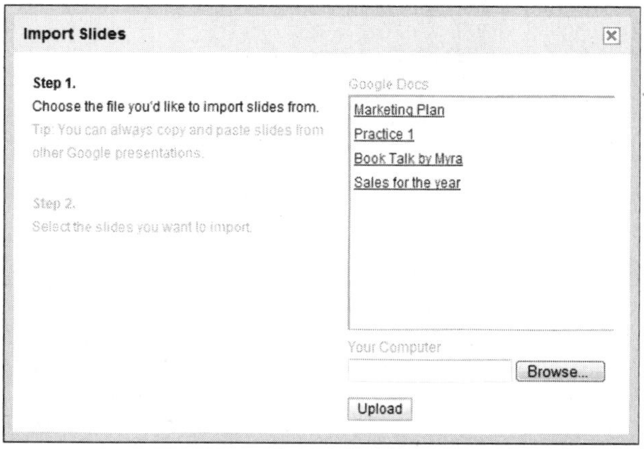

**Figure 13-15:**
Pick the document containing the slides that you need.

> **Import Slides**                                            ☒
>
> **Step 1.**                                    Google Docs
> Choose the file you'd like to import slides from.    Marketing Plan
> Tip: You can always copy and paste slides from      Practice 1
> other Google presentations.                 Book Talk by Myra
>                                              Sales for the year
> Step 2.
> Select the slides you want to import.
>
>                                              Your Computer
>                                                          [ Browse... ]
>                                              [ Upload ]

Thumbnails of the slides from the presentation that you choose appear in the Import Slides dialog box. You can then select the check box foreach slide that you want to integrate into your presentation, as shown in Figure 13-16. The slides that you select are copied into your existing presentation. As soon as you've selected all the slides you want, click the Import button, and the dialog box closes.

You may need to move the newly integrated slides up or down to place them in the order that you want, as we explain in the section "Duplicating, reordering, and deleting slides," earlier in this chapter. Alternatively, right-click any thumbnail in the slide pane and choose Move Slide Up or Move Slide Down.

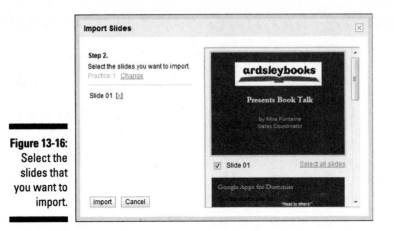

**Figure 13-16:**
Select the
slides that
you want to
import.

# *Viewing Revisions*

What if you make a mistake or add too many slides, and you need to retreat back to an earlier version of your presentation? Like with Docs and Spreadsheets, Presentations tracks every change that you, and those collaborating with you, make to your presentation in the Revisions tab, as shown in Figure 13-17.

You can always revert back to an earlier version by clicking a Revision # link on the left side of the Revisions tab. A preview of the older version appears in the Presentations window, and if you want to use that version, click the Revert to This Version button.

**Figure 13-17:**
Google
Presenta-
tions keeps
track of your
presentation
changes
and
revisions.

Google Docs

cal@ardsleybooks.com | Docs Home | Help | Sign out

**Book Talk** saved on December 15, 2007 3:19 PM by Cal Redwood    Save   Save & close   Discard changes

File    Edit    Revisions    Start presentation  ✉ Email   Share   Publish

| Revision | Last Edited | Changes | |
|---|---|---|---|
| Revision 40 | 1 second ago by Me | Modified 1 slide | |
| Revision 39 | 32 seconds ago by Me | Modified 1 slide | |
| Revision 38 | 62 seconds ago by Me | Modified 1 slide | |
| Revision 37 | 92 seconds ago by Me | Modified 1 slide | |
| Revision 36 | 2 minutes ago by Me | Added 2 slides, Deleted 2 slides | Revisions 31-36 |
| Revision 31 | 8 minutes ago by Me | No changes. | Revisions 29-31 |
| Revision 29 | 12 minutes ago by Karlbarksdale | Changed Title, Modified 1 slide | Revisions 24-29 |
| Revision 24 | 4 hours ago by Karlbarksdale | Added 2 slides, Modified 1 slide | Revisions 20-24 |
| Revision 20 | 4 hours ago by Karlbarksdale | Created. | Revisions 0-20 |

# Giving Your Presentation

Google Presentations gives you two great ways to present your presentation. First, you can display your presentation from any computer in the traditional way — by projecting it to an audience in a meeting room, classroom, or auditorium. This is a great way to present to a group of people that are gathered together in a room. Second, you can give your presentation on the Web and let other remote participants follow along on their computers and interact with you in a group chat. This is an excellent way to share your ideas with people in different locations or around the world.

## Projecting your presentation

To begin a large group presentation, first make sure you have an Internet-enabled computer that is hooked up to a projector. Then log into your Google Apps account, open your presentation, and click the Start Presentation link at the top of the screen or press Ctrl+F5 on your keyboard.

Your presentation loads in a new browser window at full-screen size. (However, you will probably still see the window border.) To hide the window and see your presentation full-screen, press F11. When you have finished viewing your presentation, press F11 again to restore your browser window. (Don't worry; if you forget about the F11 key, Google Presentations shows a temporary, transparent box at the top of your screen when you first start your presentation to remind you about it.)

You'll also notice the Audience panel that appears on the right side of the presentation. We talk more about the Audience panel in the "Discussing the presentation with your audience" section, later in this chapter. To hide that panel, simply click anywhere along the left edge of the panel (look for the little arrow), as shown in Figure 13-18.

To move from slide to slide, either forward or backward, click one of the arrows in the bottom-left corner of the presentation screen. These arrows appear in a transparent box, so you need to scroll over them to make them fully visible. You can also use your arrow keys, Page Up and Page Down, or the spacebar to advance slides.

If you use Internet Explorer, exit the full-screen mode by pressing either F11 or Esc. You can also move your mouse to the top-right corner of the screen, and the Close button appears. Click the Close button to end the presentation.

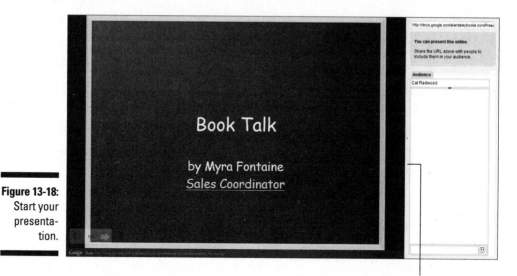

**Figure 13-18:**
Start your presentation.

Click here to minimize the discussion panel.

## Leading a Web presentation

One of the great advantages of Google Presentations is that you don't have to present your presentations face to face with your audience. Using Web presentations, you invite others to follow along with your presentation while you chat about it directly in your presentation, talk about it with Google Talk, or have a conference call on Skype (check out www.skype.com to find out more).

To start a Web presentation, you must first send each member of your audience a link to your presentation. After they have this link, they can view the presentation, print out slides, and participate in group chat. Here is the easiest way to create an audience:

1. **Log into Google Docs, open your presentation file, and click the Share tab in the top-right corner of the screen.**

   You see a screen similar to Figure 13-19.

2. **Click inside the text box below Invite People on the left side of the screen, and enter the e-mail addresses of the people you want to join your presentation.**

3. **(Optional) Click the Choose From Contacts link and select participants in the window that appears (selected contacts show a green check mark to the left of their names), and then click the Done button.**

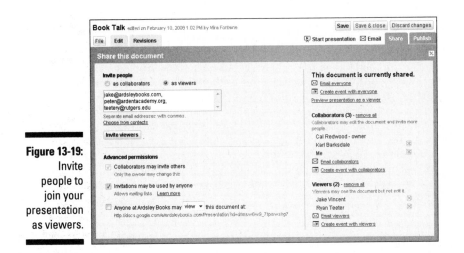

4. **Select the As Viewers radio button and click the Invite Viewers button.**

   Alternatively, to add co-presenters, repeat Steps 1 through 3, and in Step 4, select the As Collaborators radio button, and finally, click the Invite Collaborators button.

   The Email Presentation dialog box appears. If you enter e-mail addresses for participants that are outside of your domain, you see a dialog box asking you to confirm that you would like to invite them. Click OK to load the Email Presentation dialog box.

5. **Compose an e-mail message in the text boxes that appear (include a short message and details about your presentation), and then click the Send button to return to your Share screen.**

   Your message will be sent to your participants along with a link to view your presentation. In the message, you may want to include the specific date and time when you will discuss your presentation online. Also, participants must have a Google account or create one to be able to participate.

6. **(Optional) In the bottom-right corner of the Share screen, click the Create Event with Viewers link to create a Calendar event with your viewers.**

   In the new Event Details dialog box that appears, enter the date and time you would like to meet and click Save Changes. You may be warned about sending an invitation outside your domain (click OK) or asked if you want to send an e-mail invitation (click Send if you do). When you are finished creating your invitation, close the Event Details dialog box. *Note:* The event will include a link to your presentation as well.

7. **Click the Edit tab to return to your presentation. When you are ready to start your Web presentation, click the Start Presentation link at the top of the screen or press Ctrl+F5.**

When you start a Web presentation online, you're initially in control. Each member in your audience that has opened your presentation appears in a list in the Audience panel. You can deliver the presentation to your audience slide by slide, just like you would to an audience in an auditorium. When you click the Forward or Back button, your audience sees the slides that you want them to see in the order that you present them.

Audience members can choose to stop following you and to flip through slides at their own pace on their personal screens by clicking the left and right arrows on their screen. When this happens, they see a small slide in the top-right corner of their screen that reflects your current position. To start following you again, they should click the Follow the Presenter link, as shown in Figure 13-20.

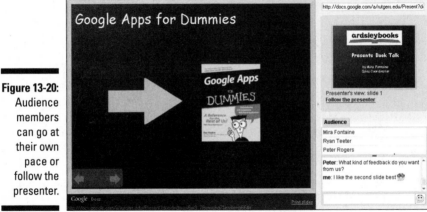

**Figure 13-20:** Audience members can go at their own pace or follow the presenter.

To add any latecomers to your presentation that were not invited previously, copy the presentation address that appears in a text box in the top-right corner of the Audience panel (refer to Figure 13-20) or as a link along the bottom of the screen, paste it into Google Talk or an e-mail message, and send that message to your contacts. These contacts must be users in your domain to join immediately; otherwise, you must add them as viewers (as described in the previous steps).

## Discussing the presentation with your audience

The Audience panel has similar features to Google Talk (see Chapter 7). You can discuss your presentation with your participants while you collectively view the presentation. This panel can serve another purpose: Your collaborators can chat about the presentation collectively and hammer out details as you all make changes. (Refer to Figure 13-20.)

When new people join your presentation, they appear in your Audience list. You can track the names of who's coming and going with a quick glance at your Audience panel.

Participants can also print hard copies of the slides in your presentation by clicking the Print Slides link in the bottom-right corner of the presentation. (See the "Printing the presentation" section, earlier in this chapter, for details.)

## Relinquishing control

You can hand the presentation off to a co-presenter by clicking the Stop Presenting link at the top of the Audience pane. Another presenter (whom you should have invited as a collaborator, as described in the "Leading a Web presentation" section, earlier in this chapter) can then take over the presentation by clicking the Take Control of Presentation button that appears in his or her Audience panel. (See Figure 13-21.)

If you're participating in a presentation and think that the current presenter is going too fast or too slow, you can always click back and forward through the presentation at your own pace.

**Figure 13-21:** Another presenter can take control of a presentation.

> http://docs.google.com/a/ardsleybooks.com/Pre-
>
> **This audience has no presenter.**
>
> Take control of presentation
>
> **Audience**
> Mira Fontaine
> Ryan Teeter
> Peter Rogers
>
> Peter entered group chat
> **me:** Good morning! 😊

# Sharing, Collaborating, and Publishing a Presentation

As with Documents and Spreadsheets, Google Presentations allows you to collaborate with other team members or contacts on your presentation without having to e-mail files back and forth and worry about having too many versions of the same presentation. (See Chapter 11 for more details on sharing and collaborating.) The collaboration feature is one of the reasons we like Google Docs so much.

In this section, we go over how to e-mail your presentation link to other users, set up collaborators, and finally, publish your presentation to a Web page so that anyone can view it.

## E-mail a presentation

You can easily share a presentation by e-mailing your audience a link to it. If you want to send the presentation to others, click the Email link in the header. A simple e-mail form appears, as shown in Figure 13-22. Click in the Subject text box and type a subject, and then click in the Message text box and type a message (we like to keep it short and sweet). Click Send. (You may want to Cc yourself by selecting the CC Me check box below the message.)

The e-mail message that your friend, family member, or colleague receives includes a link to the actual presentation itself. Remember that you're sharing only one copy of the presentation with however many people need it (single-documindedness). (See Figure 13-23.) After your contact receives the e-mail, he or she can view the entire presentation and even make changes if you give him or her collaborative rights, which we discuss in the following section. The presentation appears in his or her Docs Home list.

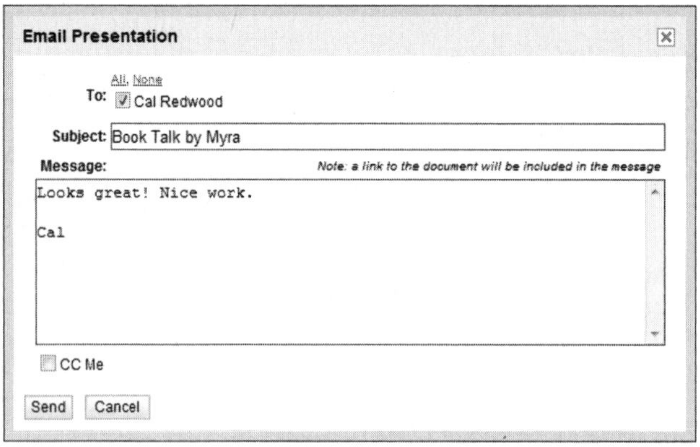

**Figure 13-22:**
Send your presentation to your audience via e-mail.

Email Presentation

To: ☑ Cal Redwood
All, None

Subject: Book Talk by Myra

Message: *Note: a link to the document will be included in the message*

Looks great! Nice work.

Cal

☐ CC Me

Send    Cancel

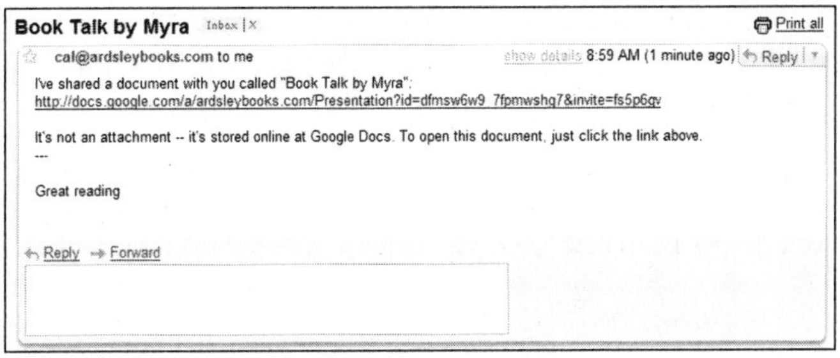

**Book Talk by Myra** Inbox | ×
🖨 Print all

☆ cal@ardsleybooks.com to me    show details 8:59 AM (1 minute ago) ↩ Reply | ▾

I've shared a document with you called "Book Talk by Myra":
http://docs.google.com/a/ardsleybooks.com/Presentation?id=dfmsw6w9_7fpmwshq7&invite=fs5p6qv

It's not an attachment -- it's stored online at Google Docs. To open this document, just click the link above.
---

Great reading

↩ Reply  ➡ Forward

**Figure 13-23:**
This e-mail includes a link to a presentation.

## Inviting collaborators and viewers

Beyond giving Web presentations, you can use Google Presentations to invite people as either collaborators or viewers. Collaborators can not only co-present with you, but also make changes to the presentation itself. And viewers don't have to participate in your presentation to flip through the slides on their own time.

Start inviting people by clicking the Share tab, as shown in Figure 13-24. Select the As Collaborators radio button to allow people that you invite to edit your presentation; select the As Viewers radio button to allow the people you invite to only view the presentation. Click in the Invite People text box and enter the e-mail addresses of the people that you want to invite.

TIP

You can further increase the security around your presentation by not selecting the Advanced Permissions check boxes, shown in Figure 13-24.

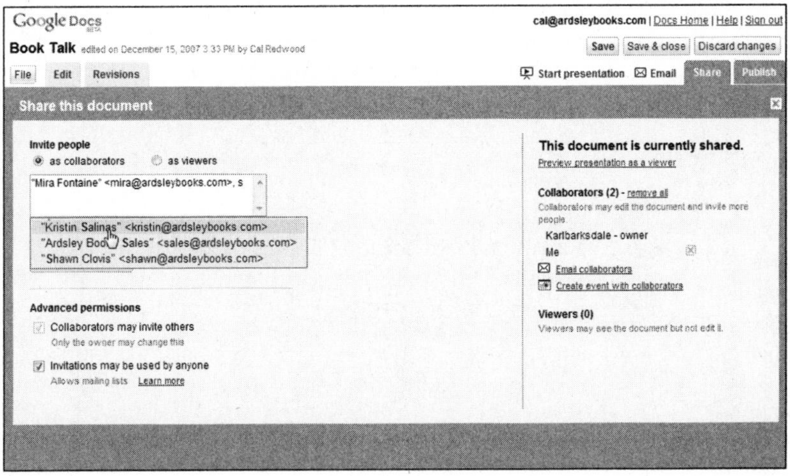

Google Docs
cal@ardsleybooks.com | Docs Home | Help | Sign out

**Book Talk** edited on December 15, 2007 3:33 PM by Cal Redwood
Save | Save & close | Discard changes

File | Edit | Revisions
🖳 Start presentation  ✉ Email  Share  Publish

**Share this document**                                                        ☒

**Invite people**
● as collaborators   ○ as viewers

"Mira Fontaine" <mira@ardsleybooks.com>, s

"Kristin Salinas" <kristin@ardsleybooks.com>
"Ardsley Book Sales" <sales@ardsleybooks.com>
"Shawn Clovis" <shawn@ardsleybooks.com>

**Advanced permissions**
☑ Collaborators may invite others
    Only the owner may change this
☑ Invitations may be used by anyone
    Allows mailing lists  Learn more

**This document is currently shared.**
Preview presentation as a viewer

**Collaborators (2)** - remove all
Collaborators may edit the document and invite more people
    Karlbarksdale - owner
    Me                                    ☒
✉ Email collaborators
📅 Create event with collaborators

**Viewers (0)**
Viewers may see the document but not edit it.

**Figure 13-24:**
Invite collaborators or viewers to contribute to your presentation.

When you finish specifying your security settings, click the Invite Collaborators (or Invite Viewers) button, and an e-mail invitation screen appears, letting you send an e-mail message to your collaborators or viewers. This e-mail provides its recipients with a link so that they can access the presentation.

If you need to send additional e-mail updates concerning your presentation, click the Share tab and click the Email Collaborators link. The Email Collaborators window appears, letting you write a message to your team. You can also create Calendar events using the Create Event with Collaborators link and filling in the details on the Events Details window that appears. If you need to add or delete collaborators, you can do that from the Share tab, as well, by clicking the X to the right of each contact's name.

## Publishing a presentation

The Google Presentations publishing feature may seem like a bit of an after-thought, considering all the sharing, e-mail notification, discussion, and col-laboration features explained in the preceding sections. However, because it's the only tab on the entire screen that we don't talk about in another section in this chapter, we give it a brief mention.

You can publish a presentation online with two or three simple clicks. Click the Publish tab, and then click the Publish Document button (shown in Figure 13-25).

After a few seconds, the URL (Web address) of the published presentation appears on the screen. You can copy the URL and send it to anyone who you would like to see your presentation. Additionally, the option to embed a mini player that will present your presentation on a Web page will appear. (See Figure 13-26.) Copy the code in the text box on the left and paste it into a Web page you have created to have your presentation appear (refer to Chapter 16 for instructions with Google Page Creator).

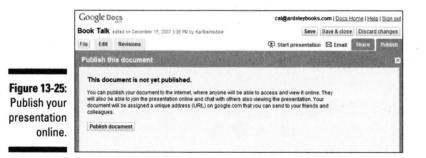

**Figure 13-25:** Publish your presentation online.

If you want to limit publication to just the members of your Google Apps domain, select the Viewers Must Sign In with a <*YourDomainName*> Account to View the Published Document check box.

If you decide that you want to stop publishing your presentation online, return to the Publish tab and click the Stop Publishing button, shown in Figure 13-26.

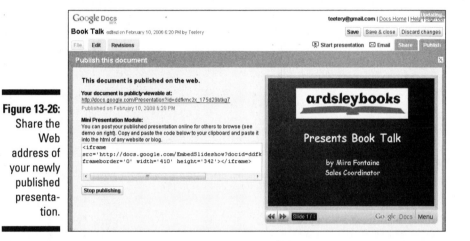

**Figure 13-26:**
Share the
Web
address of
your newly
published
presenta-
tion.

# Part IV

# Popping the Hood: Google Apps Administration

"I've used several spreadsheet programs, but this is the best one for designing quilt patterns."

## In this part . . .

*I*f you want to use Google Apps in your organization, you need to be familiar with a few more tools beyond the actual apps. So, for the administrator types, we put together the essentials for adding users, customizing your group or organization Start Page, creating a quick and easy Web site, and tweaking your Google Apps. You can do it all from the Dashboard, which we describe in the first chapter in this part.

# Chapter 14

# The Dashboard

## In This Chapter

▶ Getting familiar with the Dashboard

▶ Creating and managing user accounts

▶ Changing domain settings

*L*ike the rest of the apps, the Dashboard is designed to be simple to use and enables administrators to manage users and customize apps with a few clicks. (We're going to venture out on a limb on this one, but we bet you were just a little excited when you clicked that last Continue button during Google Apps setup and saw the Google Apps Dashboard for the first time.) Using the Dashboard, you can take control and share the Google power with everyone else in your organization.

Attention Team Edition users: One of the advantages of Team Edition is that there are no administrator controls to worry about. That being said, you can jump to the head of the class and skip to Part V for troubleshooting tips and other cool Google Apps. However, if you would like to create a simple Web page for your team, you might find the instructions for Google Page Creator (http://pages.google.com), located in Chapter 16, helpful. When your company or school finally makes the switch, all these tools, including the Dashboard, will be available for the administrators.

In this chapter, we point you to all the important options in the Dashboard, help you customize the look and feel of your apps, and get you on your way to empowering your users by sharing the Google Apps love and giving them administrator accounts, too.

# Exploring the Dashboard

Managing your Google Apps is straightforward and simple for administrators who use the Dashboard. The *Dashboard* is a control panel that gives you access to all your user settings, as well as apps settings and configuration options.

# Logging into the Dashboard

The Dashboard is powerful and incredibly simple, but if you can't remember how to get there, it's pretty useless. So, make sure you take a moment and memorize the following address (adding it to your bookmarks or favorites might not be a bad idea, either): `www.google.com/a/yourdomain.com`

You can find this address in the confirmation e-mail that you receive when you sign up for Google Apps. Of course, replace *yourdomain.com* with your actual domain name.

Now, open your browser and go to the preceding address. You know you're in the right place if your screen looks like Figure 14-1. After you get to this screen, log in by using your administrator account. (See Chapter 2 for instructions on setting up Google Apps and creating your administrator account.)

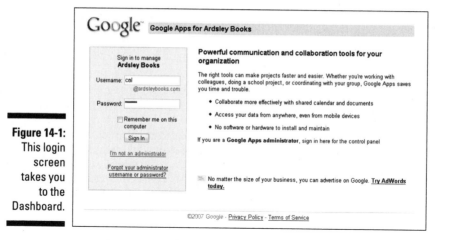

**Figure 14-1:**
This login
screen
takes you
to the
Dashboard.

# Getting familiar with the Dashboard

Google has a knack for making complex systems manageable and useable. The Dashboard is no exception. You can access all the tools that you need to manage your users and services from the Dashboard's main page, as shown in Figure 14-2.

The following list describes the key tools, which are conveniently grouped on the Dashboard:

✔ **Navigation bar:** Need to jump quickly to add new users or change domain settings? Just click the tabs on the blue Navigation bar at the top of the screen to jump right to the screen that you need.

✔ **Tips:** Each time you load the Dashboard, Google gives you a new tip to help you get the most out of Google Apps. Click the Learn More link to go to the corresponding page in the Help Center.

✔ **Account information:** The account information box shows your domain name and settings, and it gives you quick links to account and user settings. You can also see a graph of how active your users have been within the last 90 days.

✔ **Service settings:** Quickly see which Google Apps are active and adjust their settings in the Service Settings section of the Dashboard. We cover how to adjust settings in each of these apps in Chapters 15 through 17.

REMEMBER

For security reasons, the Dashboard automatically logs you out if you don't use it for a certain period of time. If you see the timeout screen, just log back in and continue where you left off.

Service settings

Account information

Tips

Navigation bar

**Figure 14-2:**
The Google
Apps
Dashboard
gives you all
the tools
that you
need to
manage
your
domain.

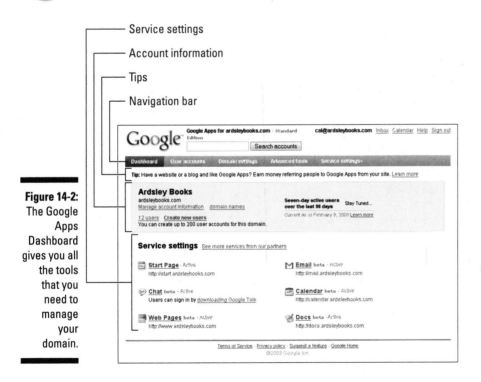

# Creating User Accounts

You're most likely not the only person running your company or group. For this reason, you need to know how to add and delete user accounts and adjust their account settings. In the following sections, we show you how to create individual accounts and upload a bunch of users at the same time by using a spreadsheet. We then show you how to update user account settings.

Unless users in your organization are getting to know Google Apps for the very first time, it's likely that many of your co-workers or fellow students and professors have already signed up for Google Apps Team Edition. If users already exist for your domain, they are transferred automatically to your user list when your organization signs up for Google Apps Standard Edition, Premier Edition, or Education Edition. For those users, you only have to migrate their e-mail from your old system to Gmail to complete the setup, as described in the section about migrating existing e-mail accounts in Chapter 17.

From the Dashboard, you can access user accounts by clicking the aptly named User Accounts button on the Navigation bar or by clicking the $X$ Users link (where $X$ is the number of current users in existence) in the account information area. The User Accounts screen opens, displaying your name and a list of users (if you have any set up), as shown in Figure 14-3.

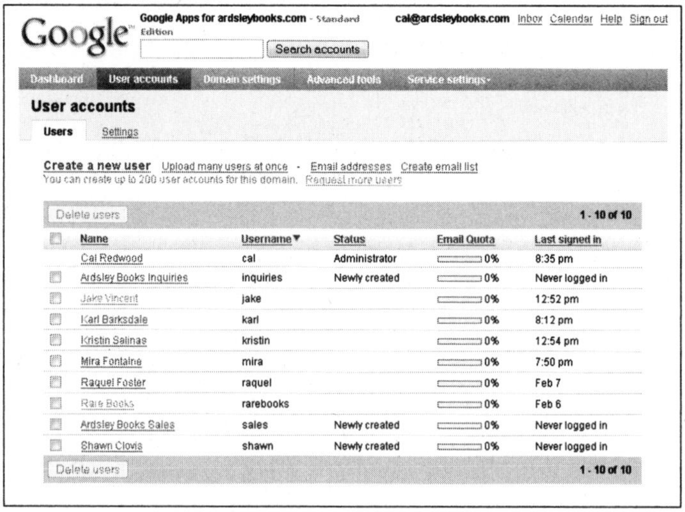

**Figure 14-3:**
The User Accounts screen lets you create users and change user settings.

# Creating new users, one at a time

Unless you're the only person in your organization who plans to use Google Apps, you need to create accounts for everyone else whom you want to have a Gmail address and access to Calendar, Docs, and Talk.

Follow these steps to create a new user account:

1. **If you haven't already, log into the Dashboard and click the User Accounts button on the Navigation bar.**

2. **Click the Create a New User link.**

   The Create a New User screen appears, as shown in Figure 14-4.

3. **Click in the First Name, Last Name, and Username text boxes and enter the user's first name, last name, and username, respectively.**

   When you create usernames for your employees, you should follow a set username format. For example, some organizations use their employees' first initial and last name, such as `credwood`. Another common format is to use the employee's full name with a period separating the first and last names, such as `cal.redwood`.

4. **(Optional) Google automatically assigns a temporary password for new users. To assign your own temporary password for the new user, click the Set Password link and type the password in the Password and Re-enter Password text boxes that appear in place of the link.**

   If you assign your own temporary password, make note of the password so that you can tell the user later.

**Figure 14-4:**
Enter a first name, last name, and username to create a new user.

Google Apps for ardsleybooks.com - Standard Edition

Search accounts

Dashboard | User accounts | Domain settings | Advanced tools

« Back to user list

**Create a new user**
Create multiple users

\* indicates a required field

First name \*    Last name \*
Jake           Vincent

Username \*
jake.vincent    @ ardsleybooks.com

Temporary password: E73329 Set password

Create new user    Cancel

Terms of Service - Privacy policy - Suggest a
©2008 Google Inc.

5. **Click the Create New User button.**

The new user information screen, displayed in Figure 14-5, shows the new user's information, including username and password, e-mail address, and the URL from which the user can log into his or her personal Start Page.

Click the Print Instructions link to print the new user's vital information, which makes a great letter to give to the user. If you need to access the user's information later, you can access the user information screen at any time by clicking a user's name in the User Accounts page.

**Figure 14-5:**
Print the new user information screen for each new user.

Google lets you create up to 200 accounts for your domain by default. If you need more, go to the User Accounts page (refer to Figure 14-3) and click the Request More Users link.

## Uploading many users at the same time

Creating individual user accounts can be fun for about the first ten users, but then it just gets tedious. If you have a whole slew of new user accounts that you need to create, you can save yourself a bunch of time and energy by creating many user accounts at the same time.

The first step to creating multiple users at the same time is to create a file that contains all your new users' basic information. Google Apps will only import a comma-separated values (CSV) file.

You can use any spreadsheet program (such as Google Spreadsheets or Excel) to create a CSV file by following these steps:

1. **Open your favorite spreadsheet program and create a new file.**

2. **In the first row, enter the following headers:** username, first name, last name, password.

   You must use these exact spellings with spaces in your headings — otherwise, Google doesn't recognize the information in your spreadsheet.

3. **In the following rows, fill in the users' information, as shown in Figure 14-6.**

**Figure 14-6:**
You can use a CSV file to create multiple users.

| | A | B | C | D |
|---|---|---|---|---|
| 1 | username | first name | last name | password |
| 2 | raquel | Raquel | Foster | 59h731 |
| 3 | mira | Mira | Fontaine | 6d8945 |
| 4 | jake | Jake | Vincent | 4r923m |
| 5 | shawn | Shawn | Clovis | sdf032 |
| 6 | kristin | Kristin | Salinas | s94d83 |
| 7 | inquiries | Ardent Book | Inquiries | 99k744 |
| 8 | sales | Ardent Book | Sales | s25sk7 |

4. **Save the file in the CSV format.**

   In Google Spreadsheets, follow these steps:

   *1. Choose File⇨Export⇨.csv.*

   *2. In your browser, choose File⇨Save As.*

   *3. Enter **users.csv** for the file name in the Save dialog box that appears, browse to your desktop, and click Save.*

   In Excel, follow these steps:

   *1. Choose File⇨Save As.*

   *2. Select CSV (Comma Delimited) from the Save As Type drop-down list.*

   *3. Enter **users.csv** for the file name in the Save dialog box that appears, browse to your desktop, and click Save.*

   We recommend that you save the file to your desktop so you can locate it easier in Step 8.

5. **Return to the Dashboard and go to the User Accounts screen.**

6. **Click the Upload Many Users at Once link.**

   Alternatively, you can click the Advanced Tools tab on the Navigation bar and click the User Accounts Bulk Update link.

7. **Select the check boxes to the left of the update options, as appropriate:**

   • *Create New Accounts:* This option is selected by default and automatically creates new user accounts for users that don't already have accounts.

   • *Update Existing Accounts:* If you select this check box and the spreadsheet you upload contains a user that already exists in Google Apps, that user's current information will be updated with the new details in the spreadsheet. (If the user's information in the spreadsheet is the same as an existing account, no changes will occur.)

   • *Require a Password Change:* If you select this option, Google requires users to create their own personal password the first time they log in. Selecting this option gives each user extra security.

8. **Click the Browse button, locate the `users.csv` file (it's on your desktop if you follow our advice in Step 4), and click Open.**

9. **Click the Upload and Continue button.**

   You now have a chance to preview the upload and make sure the first five users look okay. If the first five upload correctly, then chances are the rest will work correctly, too.

10. **If everything looks good, click the Confirm and Run Update button to finish importing all your users.**

   Google may take a few minutes to create accounts for all the users. It sends you an e-mail after it finishes.

# Adjusting User Account Settings

Inevitably, your organization changes and evolves. Employees come and go, get married and need to change their names, or forget their passwords.

You can accommodate these situations by adjusting the user's user account settings. You can change a user's name, reset his or her password, and delete the account of anyone who has moved on to less exciting things. We show you how to do all these user account updates and more in the following sections. Also, if you want to share your responsibility with others, we help you promote a user to administrator, as well.

## Viewing a user's account

When you need to make any changes to a user's account, you first need to view his or her current account settings. To view a user's account, follow these steps:

1. **Log into the Dashboard (if you haven't already) and click the User Accounts tab on the Navigation bar.**

2. **In the User Accounts screen that appears, click the name of the user whose details you want to change.**

   The user screen appears, similar to the screen shown in Figure 14-7.

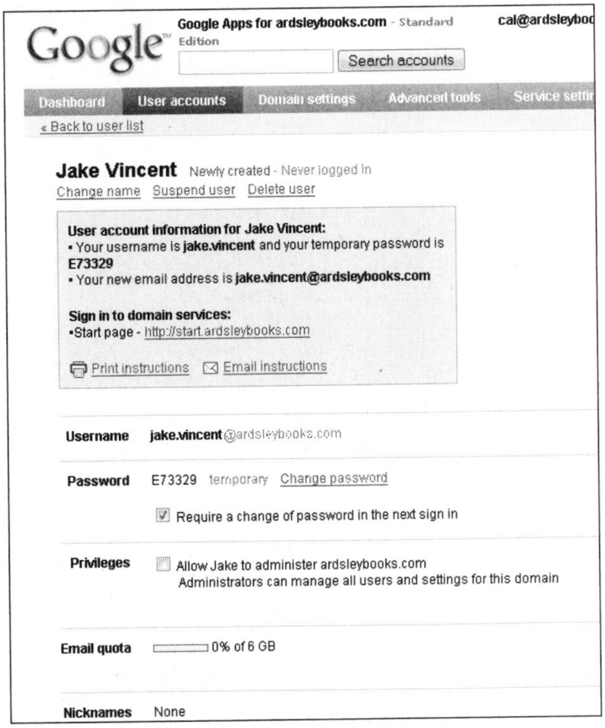

**Figure 14-7:**
View a
user's
account
settings.

## Changing a user's name

Sometimes, users decide they want to use a different name (such as using Tony rather than Anthony or changing a last name because of marriage or divorce). To change a user's name, follow these steps:

1. **Open that user's User Account page (see the preceding section for instructions).**

2. **Click the Change Name link that appears below the user's name.**

3. **In the text boxes that appear in place of the original name, enter the first and last names as you want them to appear for all users.**

4. **Click the Save Changes button at the bottom of the page to save the new name.**

   Google updates changes that you make to a User Account page in your company's shared address book, as well as in that user's Gmail account.

You can't change a person's username without creating a whole new account. But here's a neat trick: Click the Add a Nickname link and enter a new username in the text box that appears to create a new e-mail alias that automatically forwards messages to that user's main account. Now, any messages that are sent to either the original e-mail address or the e-mail alias will arrive in the same original user mailbox.

## Resetting a user's password

The user's current password is hidden by default, but you — as the administrator — can reset it to a default password.

If a user forgets his or her password, follow these steps to reset it:

1. **Open that user's User Account page (see the section "Viewing a user's account," earlier in this chapter, for instructions).**

2. **Click the Change Password link to reset the password to a default one.**

3. **(Optional) For added security, you can select the Require a Change of Password in the Next Sign In check box.**

   This setting forces the user to enter a new password when he or she logs in with the default password.

4. **Click the Save Changes button at the bottom of the screen to save the new password.**

## Suspending a user

Suspending a user disables his or her account without actually deleting it. The user can't log in or access any e-mail messages or files until you restore the account. (You can't access that user's e-mail or files until you restore the account, either.)

Because you can have unlimited users, suspending a user is a much safer way to disable someone's account than deleting it. Suspending a user also keeps his or her shared files intact so that you (or another administrator) can access them later, if necessary.

Follow these steps to suspend the user:

1. **Open the user's User Account page (see the section "Viewing a user's account," earlier in this chapter, for instructions).**

2. **Click the Suspend User link.**

   A peach-colored box appears below the username, asking whether you really want to suspend a user.

3. **Click the Suspend User button.**

   Another peach-colored box appears, indicating that the user has been suspended. The changes are saved automatically.

4. **Click the Back to User List link in the top-left corner of the screen to return to the User List screen.**

## Restoring a suspended user

If a user whose account you've suspended returns or you want to gain access to that account, you can restore that user's account. Follow these steps to restore access to a suspended account:

1. **Open that user's User Account page (see the section "Viewing a user's account," earlier in this chapter, for instructions).**

2. **Click the Restore User link.**

   A peach-colored box appears below the username, asking whether you really want to restore the user.

3. **Click the Restore User button that appears.**

   Changes are saved automatically and the user is instantly reactivated.

4. **Click the Back to User List link in the top-left corner of the screen to return to the User List screen.**

## Deleting a user

Deleting a user is permanent. When you delete a user, Google deletes all the user's files, including his or her e-mail messages, calendars, documents, spreadsheets, and presentations. Make sure that your other users save a copy of any shared files before you delete the user; otherwise, no one can access the deleted user's files, even if those files are shared. If no one else saves a copy, other users could lose access to these important files. Also, you must wait five days before you can create a new user with the same name as the person you're deleting. We still recommend suspending user accounts instead of deleting them (see the "Suspending a user" section, earlier in this chapter).

If, after reading the preceding warning, you still want to delete a user, follow these steps:

1. **Open that user's User Account page (see the section "Viewing a user's account," earlier in this chapter, for instructions).**

2. **Click the Delete User link.**

   A peach-colored box appears, asking whether you're sure that you want to delete a user and warning you that all the user's information will be lost.

3. **If you truly want to delete the user, click the Delete User button.**

   Like magic, that user's account, documents, folders, calendars, contacts, and e-mail messages will cease to exist and your changes will be saved automatically. Don't say we didn't warn you.

4. **Click the Back to User List link in the top-left corner of the screen to return to the User List screen.**

## Making a user an administrator

You can promote a user so that he or she has administrator privileges. Administrators, like you, have access to the Dashboard, user accounts, calendar resources (for Premier and Education Edition users), and Web page creation tools.

Administrators have access to user information and can change other user passwords, including yours! Make sure that you choose only trustworthy individuals to administer your domain.

To make a user an administrator, follow these steps:

1. **Open that user's User Account page (see the section "Viewing a user's account," earlier in this chapter, for instructions).**

2. **In the Privileges section, select the Allow *User* to Administer *YourDomain* check box (where *User* is the user's first name and *YourDomain* is your domain's name).**

   Administrators can log into the Dashboard and make changes to user accounts and services. Deselect the check box to remove a user's access.

3. **Click the Save Changes button to save the changes you made to the user's account.**

# Adjusting Domain Settings

Your company is unique. It has its own name, image, and domain. After you set up Google Apps and create users to go along with it, you can add your own special touch to your Google Apps, including a nice logo for your team, group, or company.

In the following sections, we show you how to customize the way your apps appear, including setting the color of your group's login screen and adding a custom logo to the Gmail, Calendar, and Docs screens.

## Changing general settings

First, adjust your domain's general settings. To go to the Domain Setting screen, log into the Dashboard (if you haven't already), and then click the Domain Settings tab on the Navigation bar. The Domain Settings screen appears, as shown in Figure 14-8.

You can change the following settings on the Domain Settings screen:

✔ **Organization Name:** Your organization name appears on every login screen that you and your users see. Your organization's name should already appear in this text box because Google asks you for it when you sign up. Still, if you want to change it, click in this text box and type the name that you want.

✔ **User Support:** When users forget their username or password, they can click the Forgot Your Username or Password link below the sign-in box for any of their apps and see the message that appears in this text box. Enter the e-mail address or telephone number of your favorite administrator guru in this box. Otherwise, users may come to you for help!

✔ **Language:** *Parlez-vous Français? Habla Español?* Your users can change their individual language settings, but if most of them speak a particular language, you can select a default language from the Language drop-down list (Google automatically assigns English) to make life easier for your users.

✔ **Time Zone:** Select a time zone that applies to where the majority of your users live from the Time Zone drop-down list. The time zone that you select becomes the default for Calendar. When users log into Calendar the first time, they will be presented with the option to change their own time zone.

✔ **Control Panel:** Google is always adding new features and tools to its apps. If you're not using the US English version, select the Current Version radio button to leave the control panel as it is. If you're using US English as your default language, you can select the Next Generation radio button to access all the new control panel features as soon as they're available.

By default, Google adds new features to Google Apps only after regular users have tested those features for some time. If your organization prefers to stay on the cutting edge, select the Turn On New Application Features to My Domain before They Are Rolled Out to All Google Apps Customers check box to access these features as soon as they're released. *Note:* Some of these features will still be in beta mode, and you don't receive support from Google if your users have issues with them.

REMEMBER

Don't forget to click the Save Changes button at the bottom of the page. Otherwise, you make all your changes in vain and they will be reverted to your last saved settings.

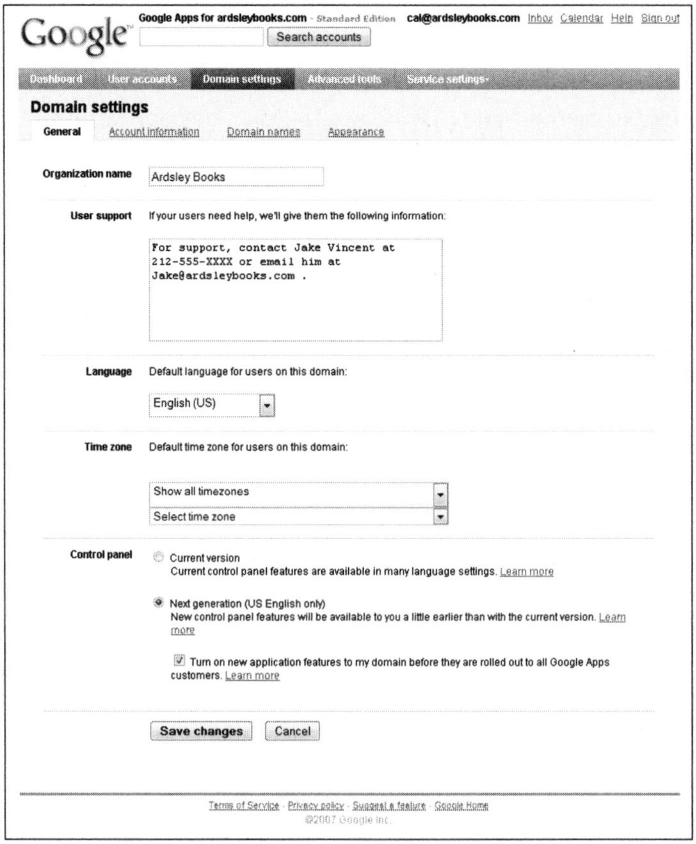

**Figure 14-8:**
Use the
Domain
Settings
screen to
personalize
your Google
Apps.

# Customizing your domain's appearance

You probably want to customize your domain's appearance right away. To change the appearance of your Google Apps screens, go to the Appearance tab by following these steps:

1. **Log into the Dashboard (if you haven't already).**

2. **Click the Domain Settings tab on the Navigation bar.**

3. **Click the Appearance link below the Domain Settings heading.**

   The Appearance tab, shown in Figure 14-9, appears.

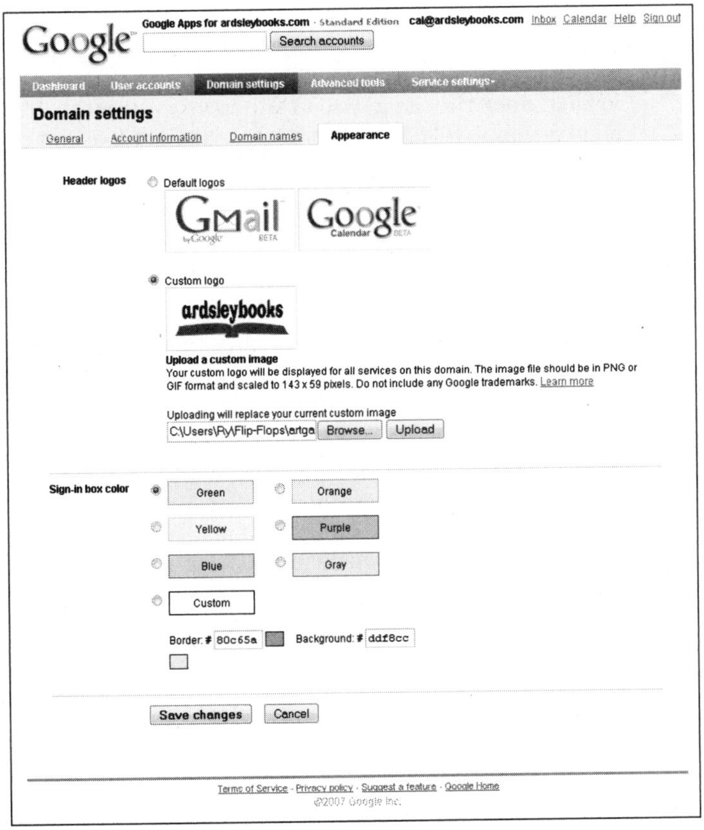

**Figure 14-9:** Add a personal touch by changing the header logo.

On the Appearance tab, you can set up your custom logo and change the color of your login box as follows:

✔ **Header Logos:** This is our favorite setting! In this section, you can choose to upload your organization's logo, and Google replaces the default logo in Gmail, Docs, and Calendar with your company's own logo. Follow these steps:

 1. *Select the Custom Logo radio button.*

 2. *Click the Browse button to the right of the Custom Image text box.*

 3. *In the dialog box that appears, locate the image file on your computer and click Open to return to the Appearance screen.*

 Google automatically scales your image to fit. Your logo looks best if you use an image editing program to resize your logo to 143 x 59 pixels before uploading it. You must save your logo in either PNG or GIF format before uploading it. If you have a graphic in another format, open the file in Paint (Windows) or Preview (Mac), choose File⇨Save As, select PNG or GIF for the file type, and click Save.

 4. *Click the Upload button in the Appearance tab to use your logo in place of the default Gmail and Google logos.*

 5. *Click the Save Changes button.*

 The next time your users log in, they see your logo in all its custom glory.

 You can always change your logo at a later time by returning to the Appearance tab in the Domain Settings screen. When you upload a new image, it replaces your existing one.

✔ **Sign-in Box Color:** You can select different options in this section of the Appearance tab to change the color of the sign-in box that your users see when they log into any of their Google Apps. Select the radio button beside one of the preset options to use that color or select the Custom radio button to enter your own custom colors. If you select the Custom radio button, click in the Border and Background text boxes and enter the hexadecimal values of the colors that you want to use for those features.

 To use the *hex value* (the combination of letters and numbers that represents a color) of the color that you want, find the color that you want at www.colorschemer.com/online.html, copy the value for your color, and paste it into the appropriate Custom text box on the Dashboard.

*Remember:* Click the Save Changes button when you finish making changes on the Appearance tab.

# Upgrading your account to Premier

What happens when your organization outgrows Google Apps Standard Edition? You move up to Premier! Check out Chapter 1 to see what Premier Edition offers over Standard Edition.

This section can help you make the jump to Premier and change other general account information. You probably don't need to change your basic account information, but just in case you do, you can make those changes on the Account Information tab.

To go to the Account Information tab and upgrade to Premier Edition of Google Apps, follow these steps:

1. **Log into the Dashboard (if you haven't already).**
2. **Click the Domain Settings tab on the Navigation bar.**
3. **Click the Account Information link below the Domain Settings heading.**

   The Account Information tab appears, as shown in Figure 14-10.

   Glance at the options available on this page:

   - *Account Type:* Displays your current Google Apps edition. If you are using Standard Edition, you can upgrade to Premier Edition by clicking the Upgrade to Google Apps Premier Edition link in this section.

   - *Admin Support:* Has links to the Google Help Center and discussion group. (Premier users have access to 24/7 telephone support.) When you contact e-mail or telephone support, you will need to provide the Customer PIN if you want any kind of help from Google.

   - *Contact Information:* Enter the e-mail address to which you want Google to send news when new features arrive or programs change in the Primary Email Address text box.

   - *Secondary Contact:* Enter an alternative e-mail address where Google can send news and notifications and your password, if you ever need to reset it.

   - *Email Notifications:* Select this check box to allow Google to contact you about new services or features.

   - *Feedback:* Selecting this check box lets you help Google become better by sharing your experiences.

**Figure 14-10:**
Adjust
account
information
and
upgrade
your
account in
the Account
Information
tab.

4. **If you're ready to move on up, click the Upgrade to Google Apps Premier Edition link in the Account Type area near the top of the page.**

A screen similar to Figure 14-11 appears.

Be sure that you want to make the jump. You pay $50 per user per year for Google Apps Premier Edition, after all. You also must have a minimum of ten accounts to upgrade.

5. **In the Quantity text box, enter the number of additional users your organization would like to use. If you are using currency other than US Dollars, select your currency from the Total drop-down list. Click the Recalculate Total button to update your subscription information.**

You can also select the check box below the subscription to have Google automatically renew your account every year and save you the hassle of remembering. (They send you an e-mail to remind you, of course.)

**Figure 14-11:**
Specify the
number of
accounts
that you
want to
upgrade to
Google
Apps
Premier
Edition.

**Welcome to Google Apps**

**Upgrade to Google Apps Premier Edition**

Payment is made by **credit card** via Google Checkout, currently available in English only. You may change the number of user accounts below. If you need an alternate payment method, contact us.

⚠ For a limited time, you can try Google Apps Premier Edition for 30 days. We'll authorize your credit card today, *but will not charge it* until the 30-day free trial period ends on March 10, 2008. You can cancel anytime until that date via the control panel. Learn more

ardsleybooks.com

| Product | Quantity | Total |
|---|---|---|
| Google Apps Premier Edition $50.00/user account/year | 11 active user accounts | $550.00 |
| | 39 additional user accounts | $1,950.00 |
| **Total** USD United States Dollars ▾ | **50 Premier user accounts** | **$2,500.00** Recalculate total |

☐ Automatically renew account every year. We will send you an email reminder.

6. **After you set your subscription information, click the I Accept. Proceed to Google Checkout button to complete the billing process, which is similar to the registration process outlined in Chapter 2.**

That was pretty painless, right?

## Managing your domain names

To manage your domain settings, follow these steps:

1. **Log into the Dashboard (if you haven't already).**

2. **Click the Domain Settings tab on the Navigation bar.**

3. **Click the Domain Names link.**

A screen similar to Figure 14-12 appears.

Your primary domain name appears on the Domain Names tab, as well as the date that you registered it with Google's registration partner. To adjust your domain settings, click the Advanced DNS Settings link. A page appears that contains your login information and gives you instructions of how to log in. If you registered with another company before signing up, a screen appears that offers general information on how to change your DNS settings with your registrar.

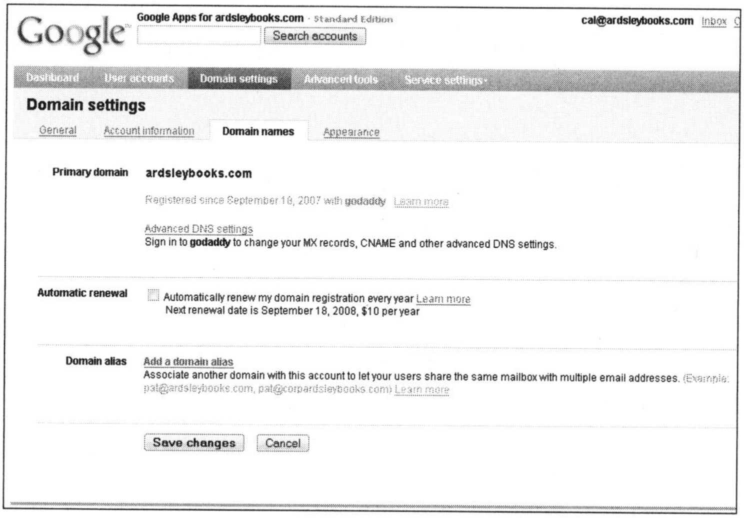

**Figure 14-12:** Manage your domain names from the Domain Names tab.

Here are a couple other helpful options available on this screen:

- ✔ **Automatic Renewal:** If you registered with a Google partner, you can choose to renew your domain name automatically by selecting the Automatic Renewal check box. When you select this check box, the charge for your domain name automatically shows up on the credit card bill for the card you used to register the domain originally.

- ✔ **Domain Alias:** Click the Add a Domain Alias link to go to the Add a Domain Alias screen, where you can add another domain to your e-mail accounts. You may find this option helpful if you want users to receive e-mail from more than one domain (such as `ardsleybooks.com` and `bookssite.net`) in the same account. Before you complete this setup, you must first register your additional domain with Google (see Chapter 2 to see how to register a new domain for Google Apps) or have access to the registrar login information for an existing domain. Enter a domain alias in the text box on this screen and click the Continue and Set Up Email Delivery button, and on the next screen, follow Google's instructions to set up the mail exchange (MX) records for your domain alias (see Chapter 17 for more details on adjusting MX records).

After you finish customizing Google Apps the way you want it in the Dashboard, you generally never need to adjust these settings again. But, if you ever read a Help file that tells you to change MX records, CNAME, or other DNS settings, you need to go to the Domain Name tab. We talk a bit more about MX, CNAME, DNS, and other cool acronyms in Chapter 17.

# Chapter 15

# Start Page Configuration and Administration

. . . . . . . . . . . . . . . . . . . . . . . . . . . . . . . . . . . . . . . . . .

## In This Chapter

▶ Creating the Start Page for your users

▶ Customizing content and adding default gadgets

▶ Making changes to a published Start Page

. . . . . . . . . . . . . . . . . . . . . . . . . . . . . . . . . . . . . . . . . .

*T*he Start Page has the potential to play an extremely important role for your team, business, organization, group, or family. It single-handedly unites all your Google Apps in one place and has the added bonus of allowing users to customize their own Start Pages by adding their favorite gadgets (such as news, weather, comic strips, and games).

This chapter shows you, the administrator or designated helper, how to customize the default Start Page template so that all users in your organization can see it. You can discover how to add style and flair to your organization's Start Page, as well as how to make it useful for your users.

If you're a user who flipped to this chapter hoping to find out how to customize your personal Start Page, turn to Chapter 3. Chapter 3 explains what gadgets are and how you can arrange them to help you locate information on your personal Start Page.

# Changing the Default Start Page Settings

When you first sign up for Google Apps, Google automatically creates a generic Start Page for you that looks similar to Figure 15-1. It may not look like anything really special at first, but we help you change that in this section.

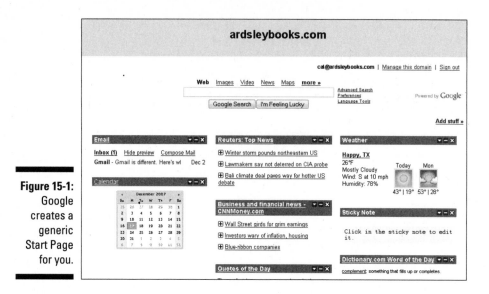

**Figure 15-1:**
Google creates a generic Start Page for you.

If you registered your domain name with Google, your Start Page is located at `http://start.yourdomain.com` as well as `http://www.yourdomain.com` until you create your own Web site (see Chapter 16 for information on how to set up a Web site with Google Page Creator). Otherwise, you get the address `http://partnerpage.google.com/yourdomain.com` until you customize the address on the Start Page administrator page.

To begin customizing your Start Page, first log into the Google Apps Dashboard (go to `www.google.com/a/yourdomain.com` in your browser). Then click Service Settings and select Start Page from the menu that appears, as shown in Figure 15-2.

From the Start Page Settings screen, you can do the following:

- ✔ **Customize Start Page:** Click this link to begin editing your Start Page. We take you through each step in the following section.

- ✔ **Change URL:** Click this link to choose to use the default Start Page address (`http://partnerpage.google.com/yourdomain.com`) or create your own custom address, such as `http://start.yourdomain.com` or `http://info.yourdomain.com`, as shown in Figure 15-3.

  If you did *not* register your domain with Google, you have to add a CNAME record with your domain registrar so that `start` or `info` points to `ghs.google.com`. Chapter 17 explains what this is and how to do it.

- ✔ **Disable Start Page:** If you decide that the Start Page just isn't for you or your group, click this link and confirm that you want to remove it. You can always add it back later by clicking the Add More Services link on the main Dashboard screen.

# Creating a Custom Start Page Template for Your Organization

On to the fun part — customizing your organization's Start Page. In the Start Page Settings screen, click the Customize Start Page link. (To get to the Start Page Settings screen, go to the Dashboard, click the Service Settings link, and select Start Page from the menu that appears.)

When you click the Customize Start Page link, the Get Started tab appears in the Start Page Editor, as shown in Figure 15-4. Personalizing your Start Page template is very straightforward — the Start Page Editor enables you to customize the Start Page by using five links along the top of the screen that take you to tabs: Layout, Colors, Header and Footer, Content, and Publish. We walk you through each of these tabs in the following sections. You can click any of the tabs at the top of the Start Page Editor or go through the tabs in order by clicking the Next link at the bottom of each tab.

**Figure 15-4:**
View your
Start Page
options on
the Get
Started tab.

On each of the tabs in the Start Page Editor, you also have the following options, located in the top-right corner of the screen:

- ✔ **Save:** Every so often, Google automatically saves any changes you've made. If that's not often enough for you, you can manually save changes at any time by clicking the Save button.

- ✔ **Publish:** When you're ready to make your changes permanent, click the Publish link. You also have the option to make your changes permanent on the Publish tab.

- ✔ **Preview:** To see what your Start Page looks like along the way and view any tweaks you've made, click the Preview link.

## Choosing a layout

To make basic changes to your Start Page template, begin by clicking the Layout tab at the top of the Start Page Editor screen. You have two options for the Start Page layout, as shown in Figure 15-5:

✔ **Fully Customizable:** Select this radio button to give your users complete control over what gadgets they can add, delete, and rearrange.

✔ **Locked Column:** Select this radio button to lock the left column but still allow users to change the other two columns. Use this layout if you have company or group links, a photo album that you want everyone to see, or a news feed that everyone should read.

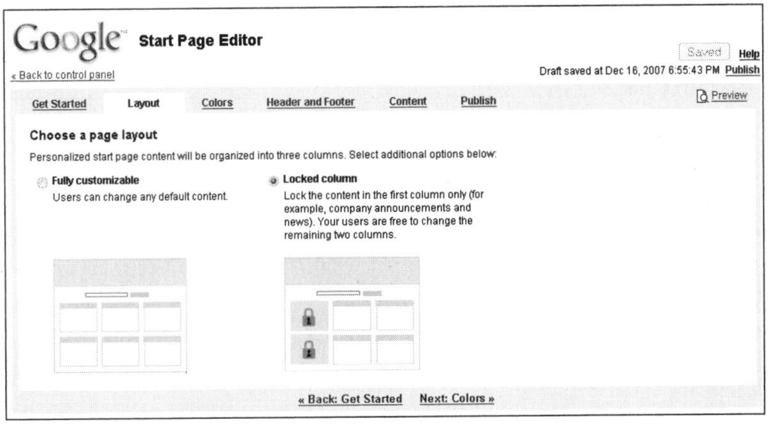

**Figure 15-5:**
Choose a
page layout.

# Customizing colors

After you make your layout choice, click the Next: Colors link at the bottom of the Layout tab or click the Colors tab. Your screen should now look similar to Figure 15-6. The Colors tab enables you to customize the colors for your organization's Start Page, including the colors of the background, gadgets, and links.

Follow these steps to create your masterpiece:

1. **Select a page element in the Choose a Page Element to Customize list box.**

   The names are pretty self-explanatory. The User Section and Locked Section choices control the look and feel of the gadgets on the Start Page. If you choose the Fully Customizable radio button on the Layout tab, you don't have to worry about the Locked Section elements.

2. **Click a color square.**

   When you click a color square, the Start Page preview at the bottom of the tab updates to show you how the element will look with that color. If you don't see the color you want, open www.colorschemer.com/online.html in a new window for more colors, and then copy the six-character color code (also called the *hex value*) and paste it into the Enter Color Code text box back on the Start Page Editor screen.

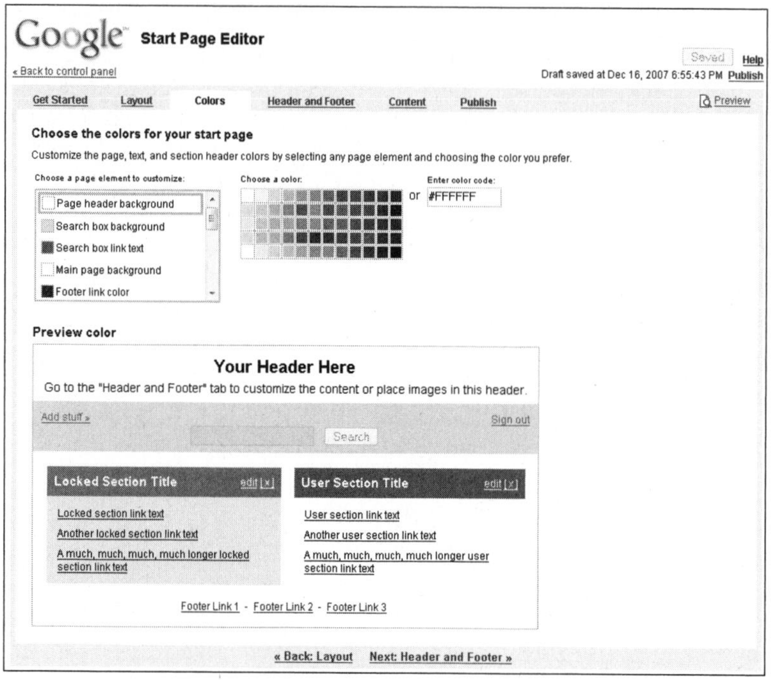

**Figure 15-6:**
Adjust the
colors for
your page
elements.

### 3. Rinse and repeat Steps 1 and 2.

Keep choosing colors for different elements until you have a color scheme that you like. The preview at the bottom of the tab shows your current color choices — to see what your Start Page template looks like full-screen, click the Preview link in the upper-right corner.

## Setting your header and footer

Click the Next: Header and Footer link at the bottom of the Colors tab or click the Header and Footer tab. Your screen now looks like Figure 15-7. The header and footer make up the top and bottom portions of the Start Page. The header generally contains a graphic, logo, or title for you business, organization, or group. The footer usually contains links to other Web sites or pages.

Using the toolbar, you can add text, images, and links to your header. These tools work just like Google Docs or any other word processor. If you know HTML, flex your coding muscles with the header by clicking the Edit HTML link to the right of the toolbar.

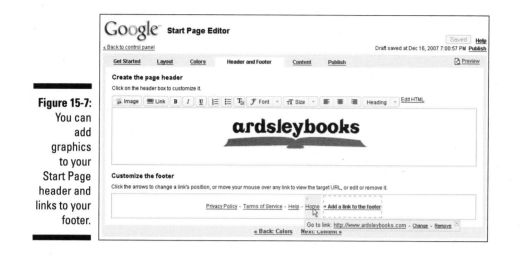

To add an image to the header, follow these steps:

1. **Click the Image button.**

   A screen like Figure 15-8 appears.

2. **To upload a file from your computer, click the Browse button; in the dialog box that appears, locate the image on your computer, and then click the Open button.**

   Alternatively, if the image is already on the Web, click the Web Address (URL) link and enter the address. If the address is correct, a preview of the image appears in the Add an Image window.

3. **Click the Add Image button.**

   The image appears in the preview of the header (refer to Figure 15-7).

**Figure 15-8:**
Upload an
image to
place in
your header.

Follow these steps to add a link to the header or footer:

1. **To add a link to the header, click the Link button on the toolbar. To add a link to the footer, click the Add a Link to the Footer link at the bottom of the tab.**

   The Edit Link screen appears, as shown in Figure 15-9.

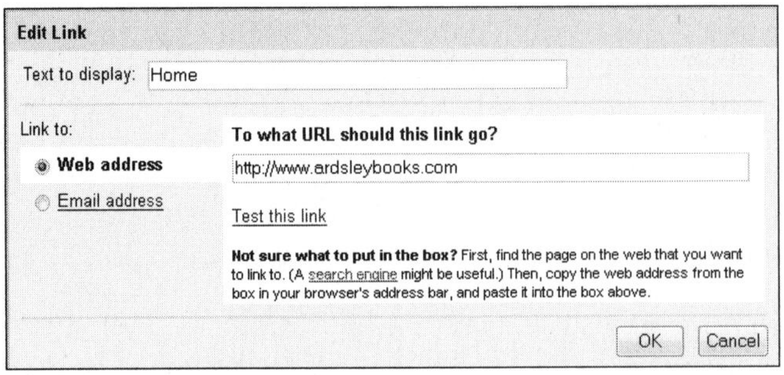

**Edit Link**

Text to display: Home

Link to:
- ● **Web address**
- ○ Email address

To what URL should this link go?

http://www.ardsleybooks.com

Test this link

**Not sure what to put in the box?** First, find the page on the web that you want to link to. (A search engine might be useful.) Then, copy the web address from the box in your browser's address bar, and paste it into the box above.

OK    Cancel

**Figure 15-9:**
Add a link to
the header
or footer.

2. **Enter the complete Web address of the page or file to which you want to link.**

   You can also link to an e-mail address (such as your support person) by clicking the Email Address link and entering the e-mail address.

3. **Click OK.**

To move a link in the footer to the left or right, select the link and click the < or > arrow above the link name. You can also edit or remove a link later by selecting the link and clicking the Change or Remove link (refer to Figure 15-7).

If your company already has a Web page template that you want to use as a header or backdrop, you can easily add it to the Start Page by using the `<iframe>` HTML tag. Grab your HTML editor or techie, and then enter the following code in the main body of the template:

```
<iframe src="http://start.yourdomain.com"> </iframe>
```

If you decide to use your own template, leave your Start Page header empty. After you save the Start Page, users who access the Start Page through the address where your template is located will see your Web page template, along with the layout and colors (and any custom gadget) you have chosen.

# *Customizing content*

When you're ready to select your default Start Page content, click Next: Content at the bottom of the Header and Footer tab or click the Content tab. Your screen should now look similar to Figure 15-10.

The Content tab enables you to choose the gadgets that your users see when they first see the Start Page.

After a user begins making changes to his or her Start Page, any edits you make to the default gadgets in the Start Page template have no effect on the user's personal Start Page. However, if you select the Locked Column radio button on the Layout tab (described in the "Choosing a layout" section, earlier in this chapter), users see any updates you make to the contents of the locked column.

## *Adding default gadgets*

To browse the Gadget Directory and add gadgets to the Start Page template, follow these steps:

1. **Click the Add Stuff link in the top-right corner of the content box on the Content tab.**

   Your screen should look similar to Figure 15-11. For descriptions of the gadget categories, see Chapter 3.

**Figure 15-10:** Set the default gadgets for your users.

2. **Find a gadget that you want and click the Add It Now button below the gadget to place that gadget on your Start Page.**

3. **Click the Back to Homepage link in the top-left corner of the tab to return to your Start Page and see the new addition.**

4. **Adjust the gadgets on your Start Page as follows:**

   • *Move a gadget:* Click a gadget's title bar and drag it to the location you prefer.

   • *Delete a gadget:* Click the small X in the gadget's title bar.

   • *Adjust gadget options:* Click the down-arrow button to the left of the small X in the gadget's title bar to edit its options.

### Creating custom gadgets

Custom gadgets let you add information that's specific to your organization, business, or group. Custom gadgets may include a list of links to company policies, partner Web sites, or photos. They can also include news feeds from blogs or online newspapers.

Follow these steps to create a custom gadget for your organization:

1. **On the Content tab, click the Add Stuff link in the top-right corner.**

   The Gadget Directory appears.

2. **Click the Create Custom Content link in the top-right corner of the Gadget Directory window.**

   The Update Custom Section screen appears, similar to Figure 15-12. This screen gives you the following options (for more information about an option, click the ? link at the end of that option's description):

   • *Static Text, Images, and Links:* If you select this radio button, you can use the Google Editor to add links, graphics, and text, just like you can for the header (as described in the "Setting your header and footer" section, earlier in this chapter).

   • *Frequently Updated Content Section:* Select this radio button to add an RSS feed from a blog or other site. To find the feed address, open the blog to which you want to link in your browser and click the feed icon (shown in the margin).

   Copy the address (it usually ends with .xml) and paste it into the Enter URL of the Atom or RSS Feed to Display text box, as shown in Figure 15-13.

   • *Google Gadget:* Select this radio button to create your own custom gadget. We don't go into how to actually create a custom gadget here, but if you create one or want to add one that someone else has created, enter or paste the address to it in the Enter URL of Section Code text box, as shown in Figure 15-14.

3. **Click the Create Section button to create your gadget.**

   Custom gadgets you create appear in the newly created Custom Sections list in the Gadget Directory, as shown in Figure 15-15.

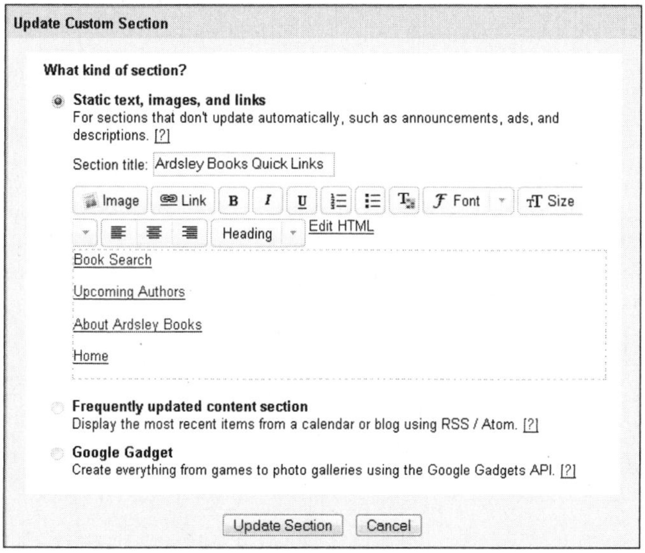

**Figure 15-12:**
Create a custom gadget for static text.

---

**Update Custom Section**

**What kind of section?**

◉ **Static text, images, and links**
For sections that don't update automatically, such as announcements, ads, and descriptions. [?]

Section title: Ardsley Books Quick Links

| 📷 Image | 🔗 Link | **B** | *I* | U̲ | ≣ | ≔ | T₂ | 𝓕 Font ▾ | ⊤T Size |

▾ | ≣ | ≣ | ≣ | Heading ▾ | Edit HTML

Book Search

Upcoming Authors

About Ardsley Books

Home

○ **Frequently updated content section**
Display the most recent items from a calendar or blog using RSS / Atom. [?]

○ **Google Gadget**
Create everything from games to photo galleries using the Google Gadgets API. [?]

Update Section    Cancel

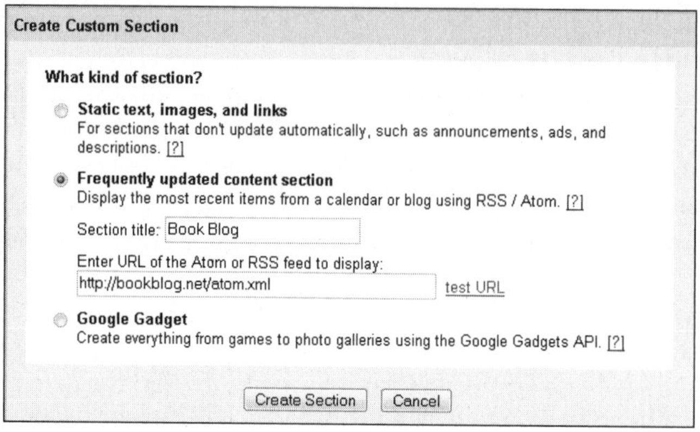

**Figure 15-13:**
Create a custom gadget for an RSS feed.

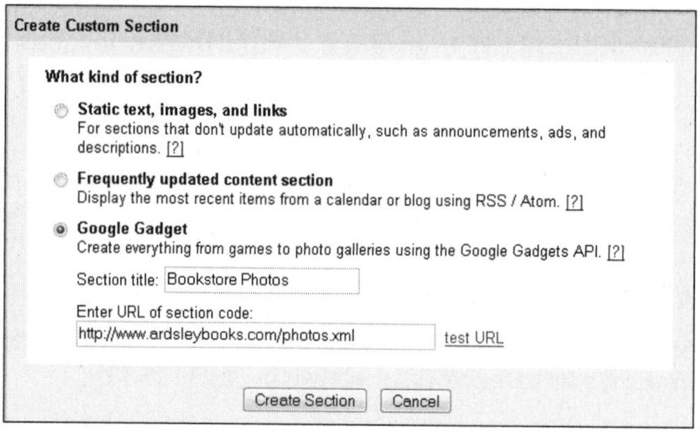

**Create Custom Section**

**What kind of section?**

○ **Static text, images, and links**
For sections that don't update automatically, such as announcements, ads, and descriptions. [?]

◉ **Frequently updated content section**
Display the most recent items from a calendar or blog using RSS / Atom. [?]

Section title: Book Blog

Enter URL of the Atom or RSS feed to display:
http://bookblog.net/atom.xml     test URL

○ **Google Gadget**
Create everything from games to photo galleries using the Google Gadgets API. [?]

[Create Section] [Cancel]

**Figure 15-14:**
Create a custom gadget for static text.

**Create Custom Section**

**What kind of section?**

○ **Static text, images, and links**
For sections that don't update automatically, such as announcements, ads, and descriptions. [?]

○ **Frequently updated content section**
Display the most recent items from a calendar or blog using RSS / Atom. [?]

◉ **Google Gadget**
Create everything from games to photo galleries using the Google Gadgets API. [?]

Section title: Bookstore Photos

Enter URL of section code:
http://www.ardsleybooks.com/photos.xml     test URL

[Create Section] [Cancel]

**Figure 15-15:**
Custom gadgets appear in their own section.

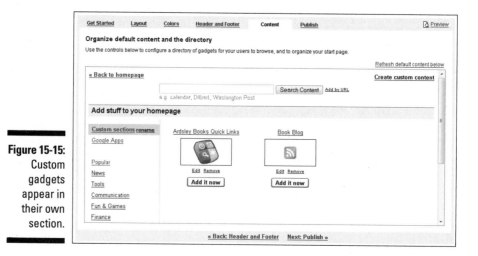

4. **Click the Add It Now button to add your custom gadget to your Start Page template.**

   You can always edit or remove custom gadgets later by returning to the directory and clicking the Edit or Remove link below the gadget. You can also rename your custom section by clicking the Rename link on the left.

5. **When you're finished, click the Back to Homepage link to return to your Start Page and preview your current gamut of Start Page gadgets.**

## Publishing your Start Page

After you have your Start Page template exactly how you want it — with the colors, images, and gadgets that you think your users will find useful and exciting — you're ready to publish your page. Click the Next: Publish link at the bottom of the Content tab or click the Publish tab. Your screen should now look similar to Figure 15-16.

**Figure 15-16:** Click Publish Updates to apply your changes to your users' Start Pages.

Before you click the Publish Updates button, make sure that you save all your changes (the button in the top-right corner should read Saved). If you haven't already, preview your new template before you publish it by clicking the Preview link in the upper-right corner one last time. A preview of your customized Start Page template appears, similar to Figure 15-17.

You can always go back to any of the tabs and make any adjustments that you think can make your page better.

If you're satisfied with what you see, return to the Publish tab and click the Publish Updates button. Now, your users can see what you see, and you can all rejoice!

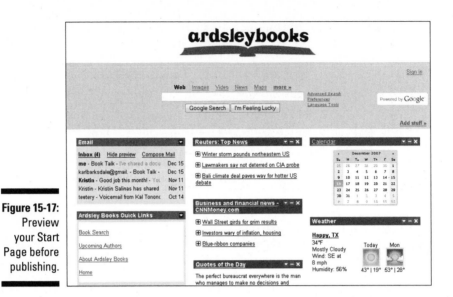

**Figure 15-17:**
Preview
your Start
Page before
publishing.

# Making Changes to the Start Page after Publishing

We don't expect your team, business, school, group, or family to stay the same year after year, so your Start Page shouldn't stay static, either. When the gadget technology improves and your organization evolves, you can return to the Dashboard and make changes to your Start Page and custom gadgets whenever you like.

Follow these steps to get back to the Start Page Editor as needed:

1. **Open your Web browser and log into your Dashboard.**

   The address is www.google.com/a/*yourdomain*.com.

2. **Click Service Settings on the Navigation bar and choose Start Page from the menu that appears (refer to Figure 15-2) or click the Start Page link in the Service Settings section on the main Dashboard screen.**

3. **Click the Customize Start Page link and click through the tabs, making any adjustments you see fit.**

   Refer to the sections earlier in this chapter for details on each tab.

4. **Click the Preview link to see your changes, and then click the Publish Updates button to save your updates.**

   New users who log into the Start Page will see your latest changes. Users who have already customized their Start Page will only see changes made to locked columns.

# Chapter 16

# Creating a Web Site for Your Organization

*T*o round out your Google Apps experience, Google provides an amazing tool that lets you create and edit a simple but professional-looking Web site right within your browser. The tool is called Google Page Creator, and we show you how to use it in this chapter.

If you're a Google Apps Team Edition user or normal Google user and want to create a personal Web page for personal or professional purposes, be sure to check out http://pages.google.com. On that page, you can create a free Google-hosted site by using the same tips and tricks that we discuss in this chapter. When we mention the Dashboard in this chapter, skip that step and log into Google Page Creator directly.

# Getting Started with Page Creator

You access Google Page Creator (or Google Web Pages, as it's sometimes called) from the Google Apps Dashboard. To begin editing your pages, log into your Dashboard (go to www.google.com/a/*yourdomain.com*), click Service Settings on the Navigation bar, and select Web Pages from the drop-down list that appears, as shown in Figure 16-1.

The Web Pages Setting screen that appears provides the following links for administering your Web site:

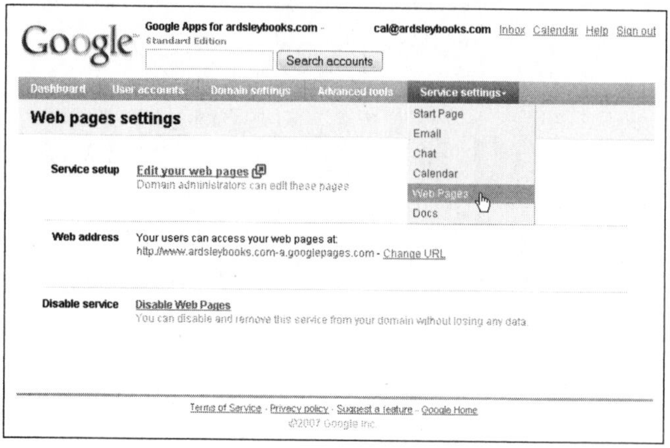

**Figure 16-1:**
Go to the
Web Pages
Settings
screen to
begin
editing your
pages.

> ✔ **Edit Your Web Pages.** Click this link to open Google Page Creator in a new window and begin creating or editing your pages.
>
> ✔ **Change URL.** The default Start Page address (`www.yourdomain.com-a.googlepages.com`) appears in the Web Address area, but you can create your own custom address, such as `www.yourdomain.com`, by clicking the Change URL link and you will be taken to a screen where you can enter your custom address.
>
> If you did *not* register your domain with Google, you have to add a CNAME record with your domain registrar so that `www` points to `ghs.google.com`. Chapter 17 covers how to add and change your CNAME records.
>
> ✔ **Disable Web Pages.** Click this link if you decide that you don't want to use Google Page Creator to create a Web site. You can always add Google Web Pages later by clicking the Add More Services link on the main Dashboard screen and then clicking the Add It Now button below the Web Pages option on the screen that appears.

On the Web Pages Settings screen, click the Edit Your Web Pages link to begin editing your pages. The very first time you load Page Creator, a brief overview of the service appears, as well as the Terms and Conditions. Select the I Have Read and Agree check box, and then click the I'm Ready to Create My Pages button.

## Site Manager

Google Page Creator consists of two parts: the Site Manager and the Page Editor. The Site Manager keeps track of all your pages and files, and it looks similar to Figure 16-2. The Page Editor lets you make changes to your pages and add content. We cover the Page Editor in the following section.

# Crash course in Web design

Normally, a section called "Crash course in Web design" would start out with an explanation of things called HTML tags. Fortunately for you, we can skip that because Google Page Creator takes all the technical mumbo jumbo out of the picture and gives mere mortals the ability to harness the power of the Internet with tools that are as easy to use as a word processor. To successfully create pages by using Google Page Creator, you only need to know how to type, copy and paste, and open a picture file on your computer — Google does the rest.

A word on Web site structure: You may want to draw a diagram of your Web site before you begin creating it. If you don't know how many pages to create, use the following list as a starting point. Many Web sites commonly consist of four main pages, diagrammed in the following figure. When you start creating your site, you make a new page for each of these topics. The following list gives you a brief description of what kind of information each of these pages generally displays:

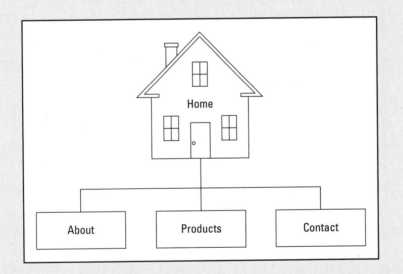

✔ **Home:** Your main welcome page. It should inform people of what to expect from your company, group, or organization.

✔ **About:** Tell your customers about your business, how it started, and why it should matter to them. Share your group's cause with the world, tell them who the cool people are, and explain what makes your organization special.

✔ **Products/Services/Projects:** Use this page to highlight your current offerings or tell when your next community project is. You

might want to embed a public calendar in this page, as well (see Chapter 9 to find out how to share your calendar).

✔ **Contact Info:** Let Web visitors know how to get ahold of the important people in your business or group.

The preceding structure may work as a good start for your site, but you ultimately decide whether you want more or fewer pages, depending on your organization and how much information you want to share. Don't be limited to the options in the preceding list.

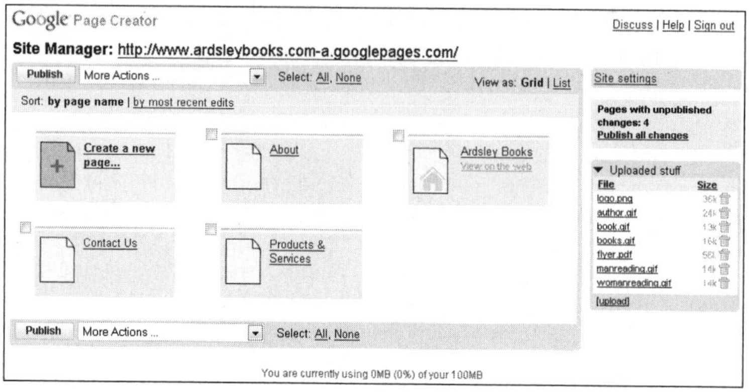

**Figure 16-2:**
The Site
Manager
shows you
all the
pages that
you've
created.

When you load Web Pages from the Google Apps Dashboard, the Site Manager appears. Here's what each of the tools on this page does:

✔ **Web site address:** This address appears at the top of the screen to the right of the Site Manager page title and shows you the address where people can visit your site. This address may appear different than the custom address (www.*yourdomain*.com) you create on the Web Pages Settings screen (see the previous section), but if you set up your custom address correctly, you can view your page at either address.

If you are a Google Apps Team Edition or other user, your Web site address will start with your username (http://*username*.googlepages.com). You can create up to two additional sites at different addresses by selecting Create Another Site from the Choose Another Site drop-down list in the top-right corner of the Site Manager screen. Follow the instructions on the next screen to choose an address, select a starting layout and look (more on that later in this chapter), and click the Create Site button.

✔ **Pages:** All the pages that you create appear in the middle of the Site Manager. Click a link to edit a page. Your primary (or home) page shows a little house in the page icon. (The *home page* is the first page that people see when they type in your main address.)

✔ **Create a New Page:** Click this link to create a new page.

✔ **View As:** Change the way you see your pages. Grid view shows a large icon for each page (refer to Figure 16-2). List view, shown in Figure 16-3, shows all your pages in (you guessed it!) a list. You may find List view especially helpful after you accumulate a large number of pages.

✔ **Site Settings:** Click this link on the right side of the screen to display the Settings screen and adjust your site name and other options. See the "Tweaking Your Site" section, later in this chapter, for more information.

✔ **Uploaded Stuff:** When you upload photos, documents, PDFs, and so on, they appear in the Uploaded Stuff list in the lower-right portion of the screen. In the Uploaded Stuff list, you can upload, view, and delete your Web site files.

**Figure 16-3:**
Click the List link to see your Web site's pages in a list.

Google Page Creator

Site Manager: http://www.ardsleybooks.com-a.googlepages.com/

Discuss | Help | Sign out

Publish | More Actions... | Select: All, None | View as: Grid | List | Site settings

+ Create a new page...

Pages with unpublished changes: 4
Publish all changes

| Page name ▲ / Status | Web Address (URL) | Last edited |
|---|---|---|
| ☐ About *unpublished* | www.ardsleybooks.com-a.googlepages.com/about | 0 minutes ago |
| ☐ Ardsley Books *in revision* | www.ardsleybooks.com-a.googlepages.com/home - Homepage | 12 minutes ago |
| ☐ Contact Us *unpublished* | www.ardsleybooks.com-a.googlepages.com/contactus | 19 minutes ago |
| ☐ Products & Services *unpublished* | www.ardsleybooks.com-a.googlepages.com/products&services | 19 minutes ago |

Publish | More Actions... | Select: All, None

▼ Uploaded stuff

| File | Size |
|---|---|
| logo.png | 36k |
| author.gif | 24k |
| book.gif | 13k |
| books.gif | 18k |
| flyer.pdf | 55k |
| manreading.gif | 14k |
| womanreading.gif | 14k |

[upload]

When you're editing a page and want to return to the Site Manager, click the Back to Site Manager link in the top-left corner of the screen.

# Page Editor

The main reason for using Page Creator is to get your information out on the Internet and share it with others. In the rest of this chapter, we show you how to use the Page Editor to change the way your pages look and how to add images, files, and gadgets to help you create a professional, compelling Web site.

When you open a page in the Page Editor (shown in Figure 16-4), it looks a lot like a document in Google Docs. The common formatting buttons and tools appear along the top of the window, and you can enter content in the middle of the window. Here's a list of the main tools and features in the Page Editor:

✔ **Publish:** When you have your page just right, click the Publish button to make it live. Changes that you make to each of your pages don't appear online until you click the Publish button.

✔ **Preview:** Click the Preview link to see how your page will appear to visitors.

✔ **Change Look:** Click this link to open the Templates screen, which allows you to view and select other styles for your Web page. Click the Preview link below a template to see a sample page in a new window. Click the Thumbnail image of the template you would like to use and your page will automatically be updated.

✔ **Change Layout:** Click this link to show the Layout screen, where you change how many columns appear on your page. Click a thumbnail to update your page.

✔ **Formatting toolbar:** The buttons on this toolbar work similarly to the buttons on the Editing toolbar in Google Docs. Use the buttons to change the look and feel of your page content by adding bold or italics, changing the font color and size, creating bulleted or numbered lists, and so on.

✔ **Editable area:** Editable areas appear in the middle of the page as text boxes with dashed borders. Enter text, graphics, gadgets, and so on into these areas.

✔ **Page address:** Each page has a unique address, which you can see at the bottom of the screen. Click this link to see the page as your visitors do.

✔ **Unpublish:** Click the Unpublish link to hide your page from other Internet visitors. Visitors that visit this page's address will see an error page until you click the Publish button again.

✔ **Add Gadget:** Click inside an editable area and then click this link to show the Gadget Directory. Click a gadget, enter the custom settings (if available) in the next screen, and then click OK to add the gadget to your page.

✔ **Edit HTML:** If you are savvy with HTML or want to play around with the code, click inside an editable area and then click this link to begin tweaking the code in the Edit HTML window. Click the Preview tab in the top-right corner of this window to see your changes before you click the Update button and make them official.

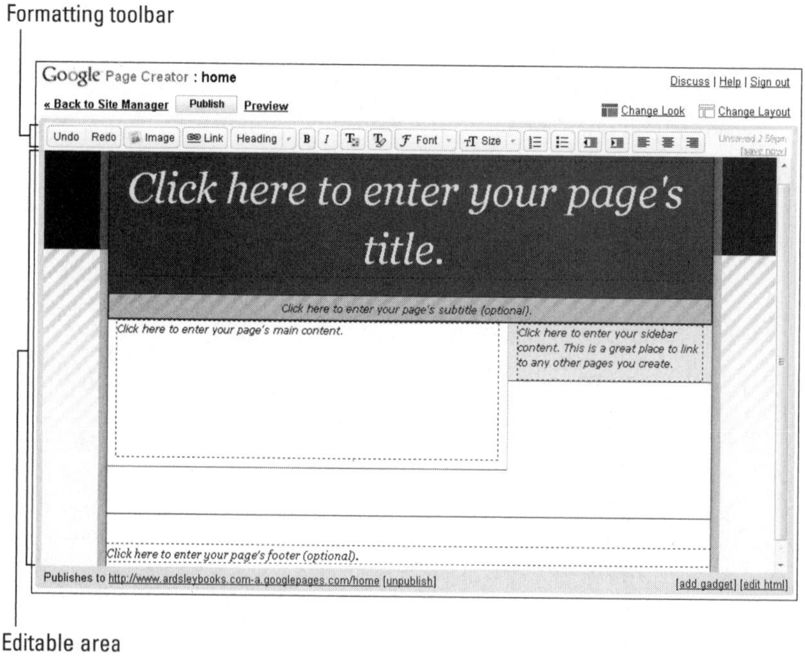

Formatting toolbar

**Figure 16-4:**
Add content to your Web page by using the Page Editor.

Editable area

Google automatically saves a draft of any changes that you make to your pages. When you're ready to share your changes with the world, click the Publish button.

# Editing Web Pages in Page Creator

When you open Page Creator for the first time, a home page is automatically created for you. The following sections describe how to add and edit all the basic Web page content — text, images, and links. We also show you how to add Google gadgets and, if you feel adventurous, how to edit the HTML code.

You don't have to be an HTML expert to create really nice looking Web pages in Google Page Creator. Think of it more as a word processor that happens to save your documents as Web pages. As we discuss in the following sections, you can enter text simply by typing it in or copying and pasting it from another document. Images can be dragged around to wherever you want them to appear. So be creative and fearless and enjoy creating your very own Web site in minutes.

## Adding text

Google gives you a basic page layout to work with that consists of five different editable areas. Just click in the editable area and type the appropriate information.

On a new page, each editable area will show text that begins with "Click here." When you click inside the area, the text will disappear and allow you to enter your desired information. The five areas you can edit are

- **Title:** Click in this area and type the title of your page. You generally want to keep the title short, such as "Contact Us" or "Ardsley Books."

- **Subtitle (optional):** Add a slogan or saying in this area. We also like to include links to other pages in this area.

- **Main content:** Your message goes in this area. Depending on what information you want on a particular page, you could enter contact information or a welcome paragraph. You can also add graphics, lists, addresses, and more to the main content area.

- **Sidebar:** Use the sidebar for a list of links, to highlight a featured item, to show off a nice photo, or for whatever you like.

If you don't see a sidebar, click the Change Layout link at the top of the Page Creator screen, and in the window that appears, choose a layout with a sidebar to add one.

> ✔ **Footer (optional):** Generally, some links to other information, such as copyright notices or legal pages, go in the footer.

After you add text to your page, you can format it just like you do in Google Docs. See Chapter 11 for details.

## Choosing a template

To give your site a unique and fun design, the gurus at Google have created some pretty nice *templates* (Web page designs) for you to choose from. To change the template for your page, click the Change Look link in the upper-right portion of the screen. The Choose Look screen appears, similar to Figure 16-5.

Click the Preview link below a style to see what the template looks like on a Web site. The sample Web site can also give you some great ideas about what information to put on your site if you're not sure what you want.

Your current template is highlighted in blue. To apply a different template to your current page, click the thumbnail of the style that you want. Google automatically saves your page with the new template and returns you to the Page Editor.

If you change your mind before you select a new style, click the Back to Page Editor link at the top to return to your page without changing your page's look. To revert to an old style, click the Change Look link and choose your old template. Your page is automatically updated.

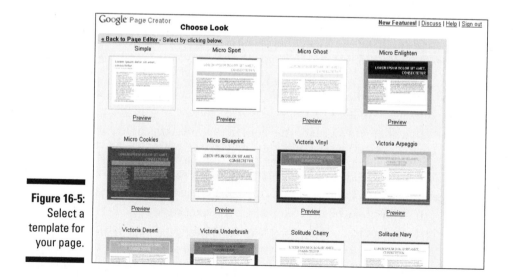

**Figure 16-5:** Select a template for your page.

If you decide to change your template after you create multiple pages, you have to open each page and select the new template for that page. New pages that you create match the template that you're currently using on your home page.

## Changing the layout

You don't have to be content with the default layout for your page content. You can choose from four layout styles, and you can find the layout that organizes your page just how you want it.

To change the page's layout, click the Change Layout link at the top-right of your Page Editor. A screen that looks like Figure 16-6 appears.

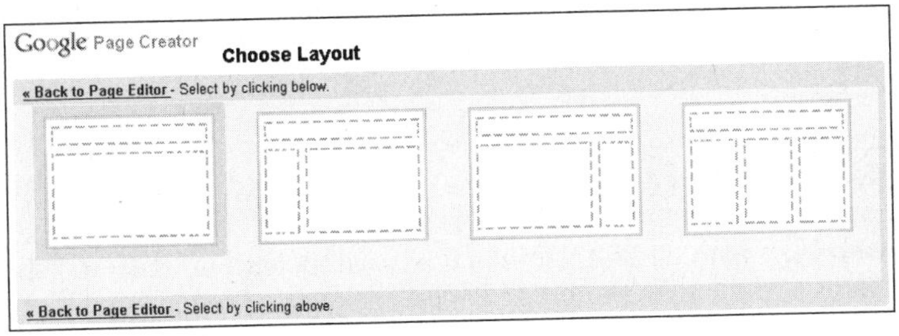

**Figure 16-6:**
Choose your
page layout.

Your current layout is highlighted in blue. Click the new layout that you want, and Google automatically updates your page. New pages that you create automatically match the layout that you currently apply to your home page.

## Using font styles

Besides using the usual Font, Size, and Color tools to make your text stand out, each template includes four font styles with preset colors and highlighting to match the theme, as shown in Figure 16-7. When you fill in your page, use these styles to give even more punch to your page:

- ✔ **Heading:** This biggest and boldest style helps you make clear distinctions between different sections on your page.

- ✔ **Subheading:** Use this style to break up a section so that viewers can more easily read it.

- ✔ **Minor Heading:** You can use minor headings to emphasize parts of your text.

- ✔ **Normal:** Use this style for normal text — it usually isn't anything special.

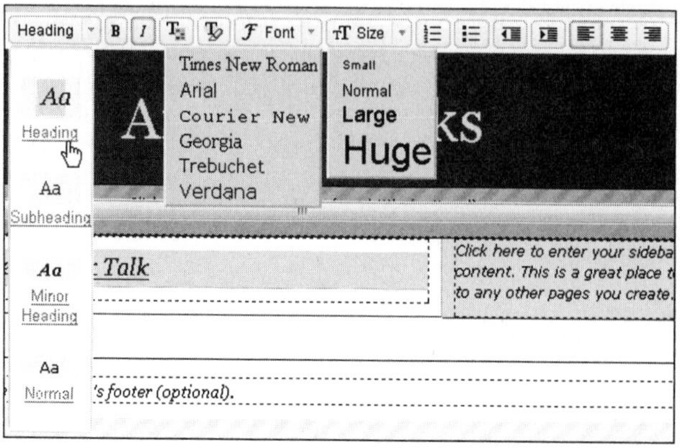

**Figure 16-7:**
Each
template
has unique
font styles,
found in the
Heading
menu.

*Note:* These font styles are different for each editable region on your page. Your sidebar uses different colors and borders than your main content section, for example.

## Inserting links

A Web page isn't all that useful if it's isolated, with no links to other pages. Luckily, adding links in Google Page Creator is a breeze.

To add a new link to your page, follow these steps:

1. **If you haven't already, log into Google Page Creator and open the page to which you want to add a link.**

2. **Highlight the text that you want to make into the link and click the Link button on the Formatting toolbar. (Refer to Figure 16-4.)**

   The Edit Link dialog box appears, as shown in Figure 16-8. You have four different options of places to link to. Select one of these radio buttons on the left to create a link:

   • *Your Pages:* A list of the pages that you've already created appears when you select this radio button. Simply highlight the page to which you want to link. If you want something other than the page name to appear, type what you want the link to say in the Text to Display text box at the top of the dialog box. When you're happy with your link, click OK to insert the link into your page.

   You can also create a new page directly from this dialog box by typing a name in the Create New Page text box at the bottom and then clicking the Add Page button.

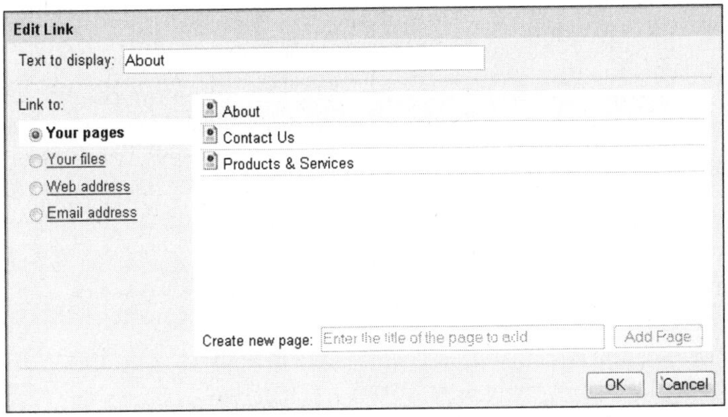

**Figure 16-8:**
Add a
hyperlink to
your page
by using the
Edit Link
dialog box.

- *Your Files:* A list of files that you've uploaded appears when you select this radio button. Select a file, enter or edit the text that you want to appear in the Text to Display text box at the top of the dialog box, and click OK. This option should look similar to Figure 16-9.

  To upload a file from your computer, click Browse, locate the file on your computer in the dialog box that appears, and click OK to return to the Edit Link dialog box. Your file will automatically begin uploading to Google Pages. Select your file and click OK when you're done to insert the link.

- *Web Address:* Select this radio button to create a link to the Web address of another page on the Internet. As shown in Figure 16-10, enter the address of the page to which you want to link, type or edit the link's text in the Text to Display text box at the top of the dialog box, and click OK.

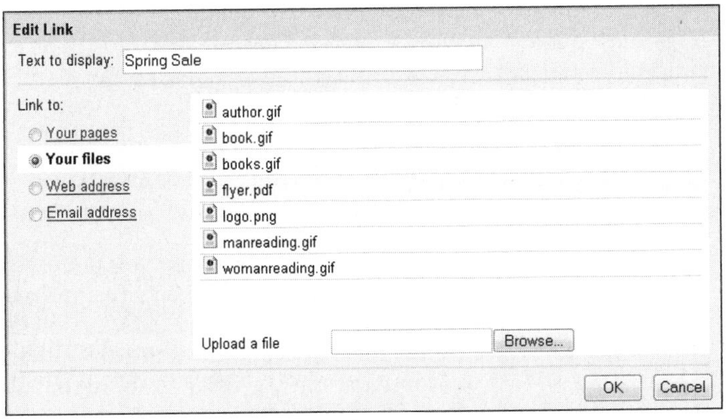

**Figure 16-9:**
Add a link to
a file that
you've
uploaded.

Click the Test This Link link to make sure that the address you entered opens the correct page.

If you don't know the Web address, open the page to which you want to link in another browser window. Then, highlight and copy the Web address in your browser's address bar. Return to the Page Editor and paste the address in the Edit Link window, then click OK to insert the link.

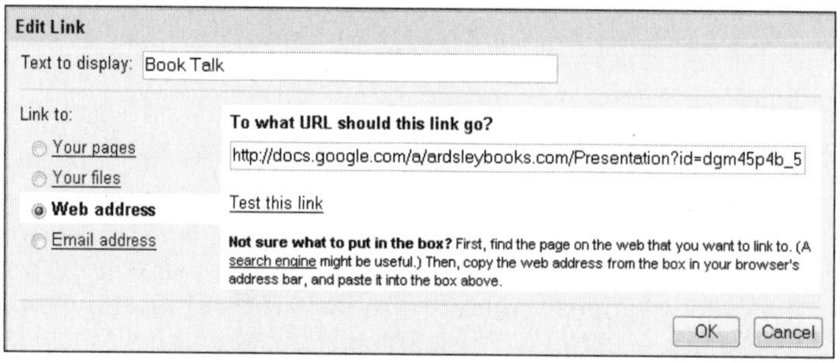

**Figure 16-10:**
Link to another page by entering that page's Web address.

> **Edit Link**
>
> Text to display: Book Talk
>
> Link to:
> - ○ Your pages
> - ○ Your files
> - ● Web address
> - ○ Email address
>
> **To what URL should this link go?**
>
> http://docs.google.com/a/ardsleybooks.com/Presentation?id=dgm45p4b_5
>
> Test this link
>
> **Not sure what to put in the box?** First, find the page on the web that you want to link to. (A search engine might be useful.) Then, copy the web address from the box in your browser's address bar, and paste it into the box above.
>
> [ OK ]  [ Cancel ]

- *Email Address:* Select this radio button to link to an e-mail address, as shown in Figure 16-11. When visitors click this link, they can send you an e-mail message. Enter the e-mail address to which you want to link in the To What Email Address Should This Link? text box. Enter or edit the link's text in the Text to Display text box at the top of the dialog box, and then click OK.

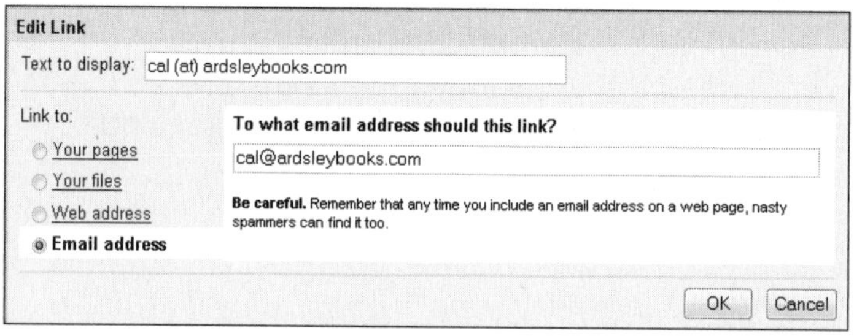

**Figure 16-11:**
Link to an e-mail address.

> **Edit Link**
>
> Text to display: cal (at) ardsleybooks.com
>
> Link to:
> - ○ Your pages
> - ○ Your files
> - ○ Web address
> - ● Email address
>
> **To what email address should this link?**
>
> cal@ardsleybooks.com
>
> **Be careful.** Remember that any time you include an email address on a web page, nasty spammers can find it too.
>
> [ OK ]  [ Cancel ]

A note on spam: Junk e-mailers love when you put a valid e-mail address on a Web page. They can easily add the address that appears on your Web page to their spam lists. To foil their evil plans for world annoyance, you should write any e-mail addresses as "*name* (at) *yourdomain*.com" or use a graphic that shows the e-mail address, instead of using text.

The link to another page or file appears on your page. Links appear underlined by default.

3. **To change or remove a link, click the linked text.**

   A blue toolbar appears, as shown in Figure 16-12. When you click the address in the blue bar, if the link points to a page that you created in Page Creator, a preview of that page opens. For your own pages, you also see an Edit Page link, which opens that page and lets you make changes to the page. Click the Change link to change the page or file it links to or how the link appears. Clicking the Remove link removes the link but leaves the text.

**Figure 16-12:**
Change a
link.

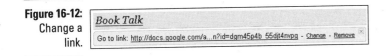

*Book Talk*

Go to link: http://docs.google.com/a...n?id=dgm45p4b_55djt4nvpg - Change - Remove

## *Inserting and editing images*

You can easily insert images into your Web page by using Google Page Creator. But the really neat thing about Google Page Creator is that it has powerful image editing tools that can help you get your graphics just right.

To add an image to your page in the Page Editor, click your mouse where you want to place the image, and then click the Image button.

The Add an Image dialog box appears, as shown in Figure 16-13. The Add an Image dialog box shows images that you've already uploaded. If you haven't uploaded any images before, the image area is empty.

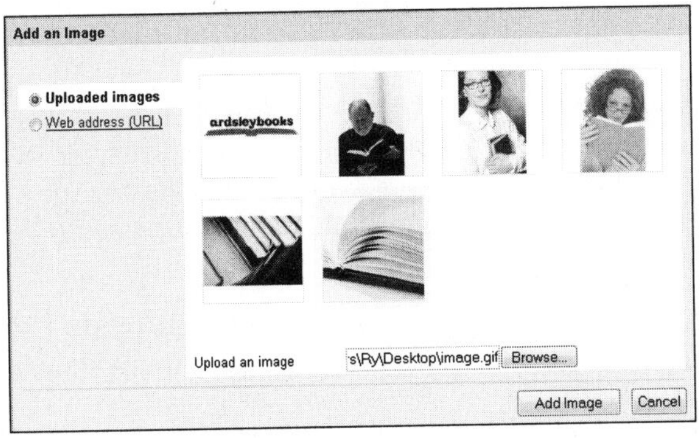

**Figure 16-13:**
Upload
images or
insert
images that
you've
uploaded
before.

Add an Image

○ **Uploaded images**
○ Web address (URL)

ardsleybooks

Upload an image    s:\Ry\Desktop\image.gif  Browse...

Add Image   Cancel

In the Add an Image dialog box, you have the following options:

- ✔ **Uploaded Images:** Select the Uploaded Images radio button to view the images that you've already uploaded or to upload a new image.

  To upload an image, click the Browse button. In the dialog box that appears, locate the image file on your computer. Click Open, and the image uploads automatically. (Be patient — larger images may take a few moments to upload.)

  Highlight the image that you want to insert and click the Add Image button. The dialog box closes and your image appears in your page.

- ✔ **Web Address (URL):** Select this radio button to add an image that's already on the Internet. (For example, you can add a photo that you have on a photo-hosting site.)

  Enter the address of the image that you want to use in the Image URL text box. If the address is correct, a preview of your image appears below the text box, as shown in Figure 16-14. Click the Add Image button to close the dialog box and insert the image into your page.

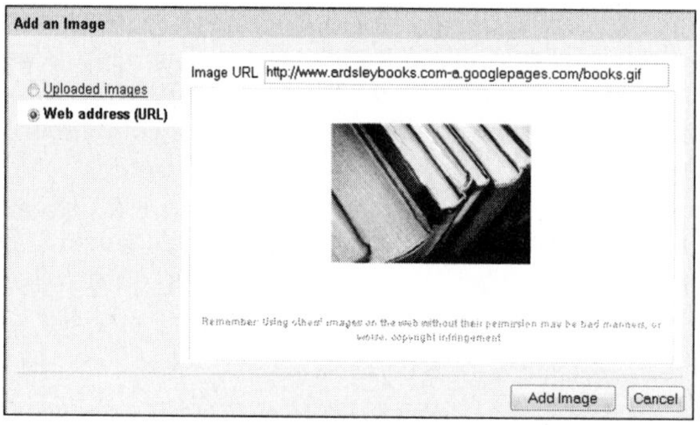

**Figure 16-14:**
Enter the address of an image that you want to insert from another Web page.

| Add an Image |
| --- |
| Image URL http://www.ardsleybooks.com-a.googlepages.com/books.gif |
| ○ Uploaded images |
| ◉ Web address (URL) |
| Remember: Using others' images on the web without their permission may be bad manners, or worse, copyright infringement. |
| Add Image   Cancel |

To find the address of a photo that you've seen on a Web site, first open that site in another window. Right-click the image (Control-click for Mac users) and choose Copy Shortcut (in Internet Explorer) or Copy Image Location (in Firefox). Then return to Page Editor and paste the address into the Image URL text box.

Some images may be subject to copyright. Make sure that you have permission to use any images that you get from Web sites you don't own.

You don't need fancy software to change the way your images look. Page Creator has the tools to do that right in your browser, as shown in Figure 16-15. After you place an image in your page, click and drag that image to the position you want. Drag the image left to make your text wrap around to the right side of the picture. Drag the image right to make your text flow along the left side of the picture. Drag the image to the center of your page to center it above or below your text.

**Figure 16-15:**
Edit your
image in the
Page Editor.

To access more advanced image editing tools, first click the image. In the light-blue bar that appears below the image, click the Edit Image link and the Edit Image window appears (see Figure 16-15). You can alternatively click the Remove link on this bar to delete the image from your page. Here's what each of the options on the Edit Image screen does:

- ✓ **Size:** Select another size from the Size drop-down list (Small, Medium, Large, Original Size, or Custom). For the custom size, type your desired pixel width and height in the text boxes that appear at the bottom of the screen.

- ✓ **Rotate:** Click these loops to turn your image 90 degrees counter-clockwise or clockwise.

- ✓ **Crop:** Click this button, and then adjust the handles surrounding your image to cut the image down to the right shape, as shown in Figure 16-16. Click the Crop To Selection button to crop the image or click Cancel Crop if you decide not to crop the image.

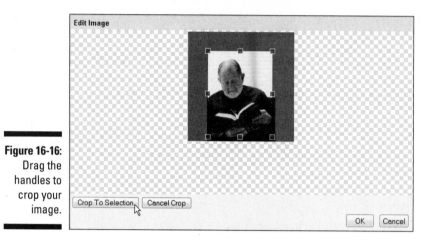

**Figure 16-16:**
Drag the handles to crop your image.

  ✔ **Effects:** Clicking the Effects drop-down list lets you choose other tools to enhance your image, create funky effects, and more. Check out these cool tools:

   • *Brightness:* Drag the slider left or right to make your image darker or lighter.

   • *Enhance:* Drag the slider right to enhance the image and produce more vivid colors.

   • *Grayscale:* Drag the slider right to reduce the colors in your image and turn it more black and white.

   • *Sharpen:* Drag the slider right to refine the picture and add more edge to it.

   • *Mash-Up:* Choose an image to use as a watermark, and then drag the slider left or right to make that watermark more or less transparent. See Figure 16-17.

   • *Reset:* Click this link to remove any effects that you've added. Select the effect from the list on the left of the slider bar and click the Reset link.

Play around — try some new and funky things with your images. Of course, some of these effects may not fit with your Web site's or business's image (no pun intended), so don't go overboard.

## *Putting gadgets on your page*

Don't forget all those nifty Google gadgets that we talk about for your Start Page in Chapters 3 and 15. You can add gadgets to your Web Pages, too. You may want to add a Google Maps gadget that shows your business location, a

News gadget to display a feed from your company blog, or a calendar gadget with a list of upcoming events.

To add a gadget, click the Add Gadget link in the bottom-right corner of the Page Editor screen. The Add a Gadget to Your Page dialog box appears, displaying the Gadget Directory, as shown in Figure 16-18.

After you locate a gadget that you want, click it. The Setup Your Gadget screen appears, and you can edit the gadget options. When the gadget looks just right, click OK to add it to your page. *Note:* The gadget may not load correctly until you preview or publish your page.

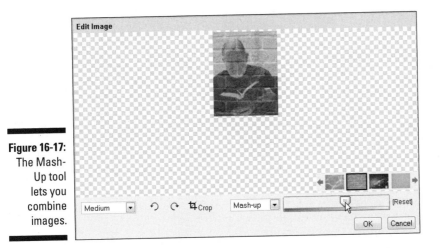

**Figure 16-17:**
The Mash-Up tool lets you combine images.

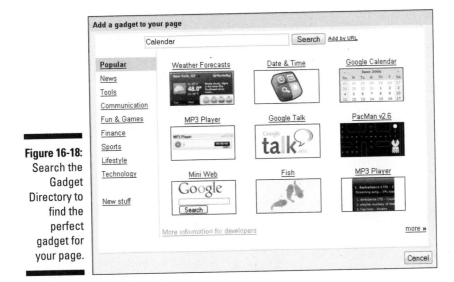

**Figure 16-18:**
Search the Gadget Directory to find the perfect gadget for your page.

To adjust a gadget that you've already added, click it and a blue preview box appears above the gadget. Click the Edit link in the top-left corner to open the Setup Your Gadget screen. You can always remove the gadget later by clicking the Remove Gadget link in the blue preview box.

## Making changes to the HTML code

If you're the adventuresome type or happen to have a little bit of HTML experience, and you want to tweak your page further, Google Page Creator doesn't leave you out in the dark. Click the Edit HTML link down in the bottom-right corner of the page to open the Edit HTML screen, where you can make changes to tags and other techie goodness. Figure 16-19 shows the Edit HTML screen.

From this screen, you can edit the code in the HTML tab, and then preview your changes by clicking the Preview tab. Click the Update button when you're done to return to the Page Editor and update your changes on the page.

Figure 16-19:
Make changes to the HTML code, if you dare....

```
Edit HTML

                                              ● HTML          ○ Preview

<h2>Welcome to Ardsley Books</h2>

<p class="separator" style="CLEAR: both; TEXT-ALIGN: center"></p>

<p class="separator" style="CLEAR: both; TEXT-ALIGN: center" hashCode="" closure=""></p>

<p class="" style="CLEAR: both; BORDER-RIGHT: medium none; BORDER-TOP: medium none; BORDER-
LEFT: medium none; BORDER-BOTTOM: medium none; TEXT-ALIGN: center" hashCode="" closure=""><a
style="BORDER-TOP-WIDTH: 0px; BORDER-LEFT-WIDTH: 0px; BORDER-BOTTOM-WIDTH: 0px; MARGIN-LEFT:
1em; MARGIN-RIGHT: 1em; BACKGROUND-COLOR: transparent; BORDER-RIGHT-WIDTH: 0px; TEXT-
DECORATION: none; cssFloat: " href="manreading.gif/manreading-
full;effect:sharpen,100;crop:0.18,0.12,0.82,0.95;blend:bricks,53.jpg" imageanchor="1"
hashCode="" closure=""><img style="BORDER-TOP-WIDTH: 0px; BORDER-LEFT-WIDTH: 0px; BORDER-
BOTTOM-WIDTH: 0px; BORDER-RIGHT-WIDTH: 0px; cssFloat: " tabindex="0"
src="manreading.gif/manreading-
medium;effect:sharpen,100;crop:0.18,0.12,0.82,0.95;blend:bricks,53.jpg" hashCode=""
closure="" GALLERYIMG="no"></a></p>

<p style="BORDER-RIGHT: medium none; BORDER-TOP: medium none; BORDER-LEFT: medium none;
BORDER-BOTTOM: medium none" hashCode="" closure="">We are one of the largest regional
booksellers in the greater bay area. We carry over 300,000 titles, including new books, used
books, rare books, audio books, music cds, music tapes, videos, dvds, records, calendars,
computer books, and vintage magazines</p>

                                                            Update    Cancel
```

The Edit HTML link lets you edit the code for only the selected region. For example, click inside the title area, and then click the Edit HTML link to make changes to the title text and graphics. As an added bonus, the `<style>` tag works beautifully if you want to have absolute power over how text, graphics, and the like appear.

# Publishing Your Web Pages

After you create your Web pages to your exact specifications — adding colors and links, optimizing your images, and finding the perfect gadgets — it's time to go live by publishing your pages.

You can publish your pages in two ways: individually or many at the same time. To publish an individual page, you can open each page individually and click the Publish button in the top-left corner of the screen. When you click this button, the Preview link changes to the View Live link.

At the bottom of the page, an orange bar appears that has two links: View It on the Web and Tell Your Friends. Click the Tell Your Friends link to open a new Gmail message announcing your new or updated site, as shown in Figure 16-20.

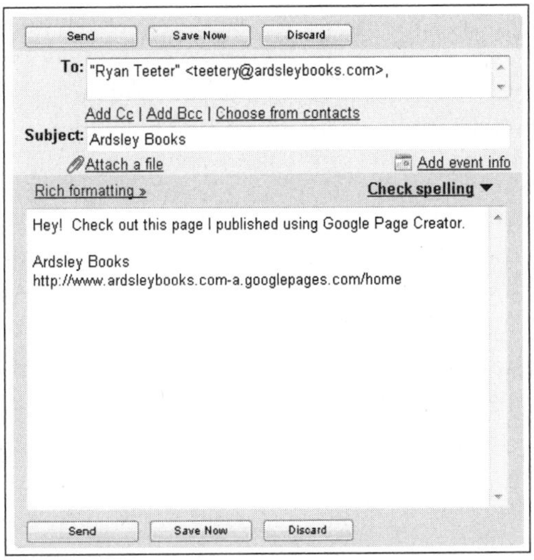

| Send | Save Now | Discard |

To: "Ryan Teeter" <teetery@ardsleybooks.com>,

Add Cc | Add Bcc | Choose from contacts

Subject: Ardsley Books

Attach a file                                    Add event info

Rich formatting »                          Check spelling ▼

Hey!  Check out this page I published using Google Page Creator.

Ardsley Books
http://www.ardsleybooks.com-a.googlepages.com/home

| Send | Save Now | Discard |

**Figure 16-20:**
Tell your friends about your updated page.

To unpublish a page, click the Unpublish link that appears at the bottom of each page.

To publish multiple pages at the same time, return to the Site Manager. Select the check box in the top-left corner of each page that you want to publish, and then click the Publish button. You can also unpublish multiple pages by selecting the pages and selecting Upublish from the More Actions drop-down list.

To view your live site, click the address at the top of the screen or open a new window and enter the custom address that you set up in Dashboard (see the "Getting Started with Page Creator" section, earlier in this chapter, to figure out your custom Web address).

Every site created with Google Page Creator is automatically optimized for viewing from a mobile browser on a mobile device.

# Tweaking Your Site

In this section, we help you make a few other adjustments from your Site Manager. Click the arrow to the right of More Actions to see a drop-down list of additional options for your pages.

Go through and clean up your Web site from time to time. An occasional cleaning keeps your information up to date and accurate. The tools in the More Actions drop-down list help you keep your site with the times.

Select the check boxes to the left of individual pages or click the Select: All link to choose all your pages. Then, select one of the following options from the More Actions drop-down list. In some cases, a dialog box will appear to let you confirm your choice. Otherwise, the tasks are performed automatically.

- ✔ **Tell Your Friends.** Select this option to compose an e-mail that tells your friends, customers, or group members about a particular page or group of pages.

- ✔ **Discard Unpublished Changes.** Choose this option to revert any pages back to the way they appeared the last time you published them.

- ✔ **Unpublish.** Choose this option to remove the selected pages from the Internet. Visitors get an error message when they try to load these pages.

- ✔ **Duplicate.** Select this option to create an exact copy of the selected page or pages.

- ✔ **Delete.** Choose this option to permanently remove pages from your site. Make sure that you really want to delete the page or pages before choosing this option because after you select this option, those pages permanently cease to exist.

Additionally, you can change some specific site settings to help optimize your site. Click the Site Settings link, and the Settings screen appears, as shown in Figure 16-21. You can then make the necessary changes to the settings:

✔ **Site Name:** Click in the Site Name text box and enter the name that you want to appear in the title of each of your pages. The name that you enter appears as a part of each page's title, such as "Ardsley Books — Home" or "Ardsley Books — Contact Us."

✔ **Site URL:** This section displays the address where people can access your site. The address that appears in this section may be different than the address you set in the Dashboard. See the beginning of this chapter to find out how to set up your custom URL.

✔ **Homepage:** Select the page that you want to make your default page from the Homepage drop-down list. This page loads first when someone visits your Web site.

✔ **Image Upload:** We recommend that you select the Optimize the Size of Uploaded Images check box to optimize your uploaded images. That's because this setting allows you to upload more photos to your site, and visitors can see your pages much more quickly.

✔ **Adult Content:** Although Google doesn't restrict adult content, it does ask you to select the The Content on My Pages May Be Unsuitable for Minors check box to help protect users who don't want to view adult material.

✔ **Hide This Site:** While you make changes, select the Make Pages in This Site Unavailable to the Public check box to make your site invisible to visitors (they will see an error page when they try to access the page directly). Published pages don't appear on the Internet until you unhide your Web site.

**Figure 16-21:**
Adjust your
site settings
in the
Settings
screen.

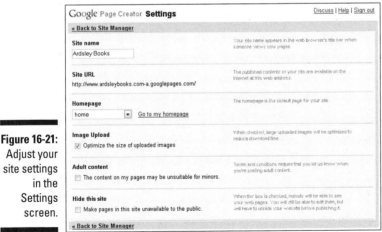

# Chapter 17

# Tweaking Your Apps

*Y*ou don't have to live with the default settings for your Google Apps if you don't want to. In this chapter, we show you the technical domain-altering tasks that you can use to tweak your apps to your heart's content and really nail down how you want them to behave.

This chapter starts by helping you get your custom addresses to work with your domain, and then it dives into how to change settings in Gmail and Talk. We finish up by showing you how to adjust your Calendar and Docs.

## Creating Custom Apps Addresses

If you registered your domain name with Google Apps, your apps already use the default custom addresses shown in Table 17-1. (We refer to these addresses throughout this book.)

If you sign up with Google Apps by using an existing domain, Google provides temporary alternative addresses because Google does not have access to change your domain's settings. To create custom addresses, you have to make changes to your domain's CNAME records with your registrar. You may find these temporary addresses really helpful if you want to make sure your Google Apps work smoothly before you make the complete transition.

| Table 17-1 | Default Custom Apps Addresses | |
|---|---|---|
| **App** | **Default Custom Address** | **Alternative Address** |
| Gmail | `http://mail.`<br>`yourdomain.com` | `http://mail.google.com/`<br>`a/yourdomain.com` |
| Calendar | `http://calendar.`<br>`yourdomain.com` | `www.google.com/calendar/`<br>`a/yourdomain.com` |
| Docs | `http://docs.`<br>`yourdomain.com` | `http://docs.google.com/`<br>`a/yourdomain.com` |
| Start Page | `http://start.`<br>`yourdomain.com` | `http://partnerpage.`<br>`google.com/yourdomain.`<br>`com` |
| Web pages | `www.yourdomain.com` | `www.yourdomain.com-a.`<br>`googlepages.com` |

To enable or create your own custom addresses, all at the same time, follow these steps:

1. **Log into your Dashboard.**

   The Web address for your Dashboard login page is `www.google.com/a/yourdomain.com`.

2. **Click the Service Settings button on the Navigation bar and, from the menu that appears, select the app that has the URL you want to change.**

   That app's Settings screen appears.

3. **In the Web Address section, click the Change URL link.**

   A screen similar to Figure 17-1 appears.

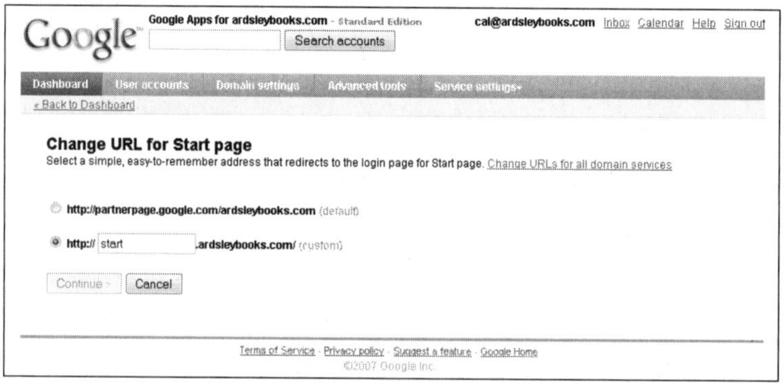

**Figure 17-1:** Create a custom URL for the Start Page or any other app.

**4. Select the radio button to the left of the custom address, click in the text box, and enter a custom address name.**

**5. (Optional) If you want to change the addresses for multiple apps at the same time, click the Change URLs for All Domain Services link.**

A new screen appears, listing all your apps' addresses with radio buttons that let you choose the default or custom address.

Unless you registered your domain directly with Google (see Chapter 2), changing the custom URL doesn't automatically make that address active and usable. You must add a CNAME record with your registrar to point the new address to Google's servers.

Depending on whom your organization registered its domain with, the next few steps could be a bit tricky. This process is similar to the CNAME domain name verification method described in Chapter 2.

To find specific instructions for different domain registrars, open `www.google.com/support/a` in your browser and search for *CNAME*. If you have trouble finding the DNS management page, contact your registrar's support center directly. They can show you exactly where you need to go.

**6. Open a new browser tab or window, log into your domain registrar's Web site, and open the DNS management page or control panel.**

This page should show a list of your CNAME entries, similar to the page in Figure 17-2.

**Figure 17-2:**
The DNS control panel for GoDaddy. com.

| Host | Points To | TTL | Actions |
|---|---|---|---|
| google8147eb996d7ec667.thecampanile.org | google.com | 1 Hour | |
| mail | ghs.google.com | 1 Hour | |
| www | @ | 1 Hour | |
| mobilemail | mobilemail-v01.prod.mesa1.secureserver.net | 1 Hour | |
| pda | mobilemail-v01.prod.mesa1.secureserver.net | 1 Hour | |
| email | email.secureserver.net | 1 Hour | |
| pop | pop.secureserver.net | 1 Hour | |
| smtp | smtp.secureserver.net | 1 Hour | |
| ftp | @ | 1 Hour | |
| webmail | webmail.secureserver.net | 1 Hour | |
| e | email.secureserver.net | 1 Hour | |

Total DNS Control Panel — Go Daddy.com — Version 2.11

CNAMES (Aliases) — Reset to Default Settings — Add New CNAME Record

MX (Mail Exchange) — Reset to Default Settings — Add New MX Record

7. **In the CNAME or Alias section (depending on your registrar), click the link or button that lets you add or create a new CNAME.**

   In Figure 17-2, it's the Add New CNAME Record button. A new screen appears, allowing you to enter your new CNAME values in various text boxes.

   *REMEMBER*

   Before you create a new CNAME entry, be sure to delete any existing entries that match the one you're trying to add. For example, if a CNAME for `mail` already exists, delete that CNAME before you add a new `mail` CNAME that points to Google's servers.

8. **Click in the Alias Name (or similar) text box and enter the custom name that you select in Step 4.**

9. **In the Value or Points To (or similar) text box, type** ghs.google.com.

10. **If the screen shows a TTL (or similar) text box or drop-down list, set TTL to the default value (usually 1 Hour) and click OK.**

    You are taken back to the main CNAME records screen, where you can make additional changes.

11. **Repeat Steps 6 through 10 for each custom domain that you change in Steps 1 through 5.**

# Enabling and Disabling Apps and Services

When you sign up for Google Apps, all the basic apps are active by default. On the Dashboard, these appear as Start Page, Chat, Web Pages, Email, Calendar, and Docs. If any of these services don't appear in the Dashboard, click the Add More Services link to the right of Service Settings, as shown in Figure 17-3.

**Figure 17-3:**
Click the
Add More
Services link
to enable
more apps.

In the Add More Services screen that appears, you can select which apps you want to add, as shown in Figure 17-4. Click the Add It Now button below a service to make that service active.

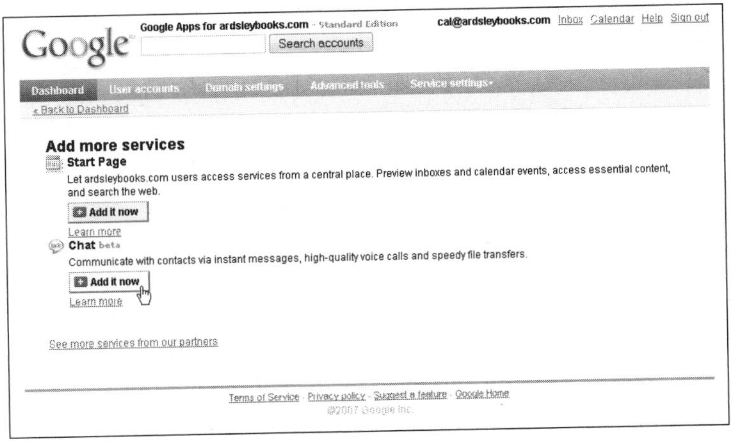

**Figure 17-4:** Choose an app and click the Add It Now button to make it active.

If you want to extend your Google Apps experience, click the See More Services from Our Partners link to find additional services, such as Google Apps setup, Gmail backup, or advanced Calendar tools. Unlike with the basic apps, you have to pay an additional monthly fee to use most of these add-on services.

# Tuning Gmail and Talk

Gmail is a very robust platform and provides you with a lot of control over your users and settings. Of course, to take advantage of the really cool tools, such as an e-mail gateway, you need to use Premier Edition or Education Edition.

## Standard Edition Gmail settings

For Google Apps Standard Edition, Gmail settings are pretty basic. You can access these settings by clicking the Email link on the Dashboard (see Figure 17-5). *Note:* If you're using Premier Edition or Education Edition, skip to the following section because your settings are completely different.

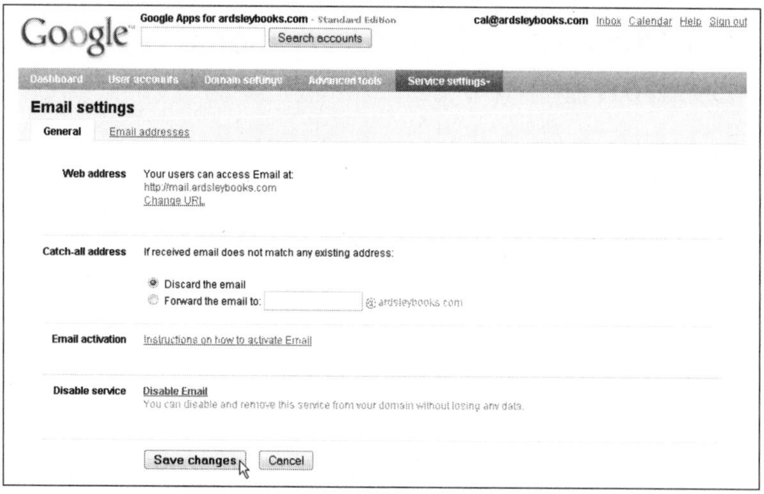

Google Apps for ardsleybooks.com - Standard Edition    cal@ardsleybooks.com  Inbox  Calendar  Help  Sign out

Search accounts

Dashboard    User accounts    Domain settings    Advanced tools    **Service settings**

**Email settings**

General    Email addresses

Web address    Your users can access Email at:
http://mail.ardsleybooks.com
Change URL.

Catch-all address    If received email does not match any existing address:
○ Discard the email
○ Forward the email to:  [          ] @ ardsleybooks.com

Email activation    Instructions on how to activate Email

Disable service    Disable Email
You can disable and remove this service from your domain without losing any data.

[ Save changes ]   [ Cancel ]

**Figure 17-5:**
Adjust your
Gmail
settings
from the
Dashboard.

Here's a description of what each setting does:

✔ **Web Address:** Click the Change URL link to create a custom address. See the "Creating Custom Apps Addresses" section, earlier in this chapter, for more information.

✔ **Catch-all Address:** Sometimes, messages sent to your domain have an incorrect username (either because that user doesn't exist or because the sender mistyped the username). A catch-all address can receive all these messages so that you or someone at your organization can review them and respond, as needed. Or you can choose to discard all messages sent to a non-existent or incorrect user, never giving those messages a second thought.

✔ **Email Activation:** Click the Instructions on How to Activate Email link to begin the activation process. We describe the process in the "Activating e-mail and configuring MX records" section, later in this chapter.

✔ **Disable Service:** If you decide that Gmail just isn't for you or your group, click the Disable Email link. A new screen appears asking if you are sure you want to disable e-mail. Click the Yes, Disable Email button to confirm that you want to remove Gmail. You can always add it back later by clicking the Add More Services link on the main Dashboard screen and clicking the Add It Now button below the Email service on the screen that appears.

REMEMBER

If you make any changes to your Gmail settings, be sure to click the Save Changes button at the bottom of the screen.

# Premier Edition and Education Edition Gmail settings

One of the key differences between Google Apps Standard Edition and both Premier Edition and Education Edition has to do with e-mail. Premier Edition and Education Edition allow you to add compliance and archiving, as well as enable certain e-mail types to always pass through the spam filter.

From the Dashboard, click Email. A screen similar to Figure 17-6 appears. The options available on this screen are described in the following list:

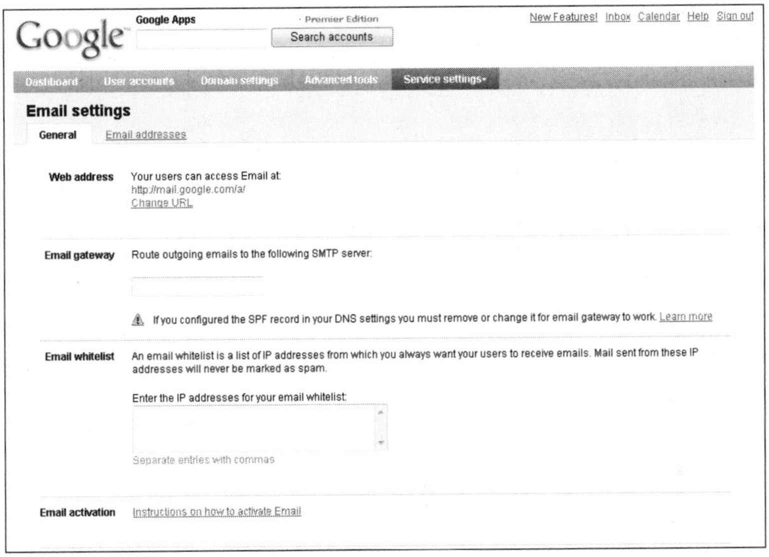

**Figure 17-6:** Premier Edition and Education Edition have e-mail settings beyond what Standard Edition offers.

- ✔ **Web Address:** Click the Change URL link to create a custom address. See the "Creating Custom Apps Addresses" section, earlier in this chapter, for more information.

- ✔ **Email Gateway:** This option allows you to route your outgoing e-mail to another server. You generally use this option for archiving, filtering, monitoring, and/or compliance. To find out how to set up this option, click the Learn More link or click the Help link in the top-right corner of the screen and search for *Email gateway* in the Help Center.

- ✔ **Email Whitelist:** If you know that your users will be receiving some important e-mails from another outside server, you can add that server's

IP address (such as 64.233.167.99) to the Email Whitelist text box so that Google never marks mail from that server as spam.

✔ **Email Activation:** Click this link to begin the activation process. We describe this process in the following section.

✔ **Email Routing:** This tool allows you to reroute messages to your server or to a catch-all address that you establish for messages sent to a user who doesn't exist. Click the Learn More link to see a description of how to adjust these settings and discover the different destinations and settings that you can choose.

✔ **Disable service:** Click the Disable Email button to turn Gmail off and disable the service. Simple as that.

## Activating e-mail and configuring MX records

You need to follow two steps to activate e-mail for your domain. First, create users in Google Apps. If you're switching from another service, make sure that you create user accounts to match the ones that already exist on your other service. If you're unsure how to create users, flip back to Chapter 14. The second step requires you to configure your MX records through your domain registrar.

You can still test Gmail before activating the service and switching your MX records. Users can access temporary e-mail messages by logging into your domain's custom Gmail Web address. Until you change the MX records, they can receive messages sent to a temporary Gmail address that looks like this: `user@yourdomain.com`.`test-google-a.com`.

When you're ready to change your MX record to point to Gmail, and allow users to begin receiving messages sent to their normal address (`user@yourdomain. com`) in Gmail, grab your registrar login information and complete the following steps:

1. **Log into your domain registrar's Web site, using the login name and password that you used to register the domain.**

2. **Open the page in which you can make changes to your MX records.**

   In most cases, you can make these changes in a section called DNS Management or Mail Server Configuration. If you don't see any section with this kind of name, call your registrar for help.

3. **Delete any MX records that already exist.**

   Deleting all records prevents any conflicts that might arise later.

4. **Create an MX record for each value that you see in Table 17-2.**

   Be sure to include the period (.) at the end of each server address. Depending on your registrar, you may have to enter different priority values (such as 1,3,3,5,5,5,5) instead of those that appear in the table below. Just make sure that the order stays the same.

5. **Set any TTL values to their maximum.**

| Table 17-2 | MX Record Values |
|---|---|
| *MX Server Address* | *Priority* |
| ASPMX.L.GOOGLE.COM. | 10 |
| ALT1.ASPMX.L.GOOGLE.COM. | 20 |
| ALT2.ASPMX.L.GOOGLE.COM. | 20 |
| ASPMX2.GOOGLEMAIL.COM. | 30 |
| ASPMX3.GOOGLEMAIL.COM. | 30 |
| ASPMX4.GOOGLEMAIL.COM. | 30 |
| ASPMX5.GOOGLEMAIL.COM. | 30 |

6. **Save any changes that you make.**

   Although most changes take effect fairly quickly, you may have to wait up to 24 hours for the settings to take effect and to begin receiving e-mail at your new address.

For more detailed, registrar-specific instructions, click the Email link on the Dashboard. The Email Settings screen appears. Click the Instructions on How to Activate Email link, and then click the Change MX Records link at the bottom of the screen. Select your registrar from the drop-down list. If your domain registrar doesn't appear in the list, select Any Hosting Company.

## Using Gmail tools

From the Dashboard, click the Email link in the Service Settings section to access additional tools for creating group mailing lists, exporting users to a spreadsheet file for analysis of quotas, adding first and last login times, and so on. Click the Email Addresses tab to see a list of all the addresses and lists associated with your domain. Click any address to view that user's account information or click any list to see who's in that list. Here are a couple other options that you can access from this page:

- ✔ **Create a New Email List.** Click this link to easily create group mailing lists, as shown in Figure 17-7. Click in the Choose a Name for the New Email List text box and enter a name for the list. Then, click in the Add a Recipient text box, type the username of a user whom you want to add to the list, and click the Add Recipient button. If you want to add a lot of users to your list, you can click the Add Everyone in My Domain button and then remove those users you don't want to add.

    To remove users from a list, first click the list address on the Email Addresses screen. Select the check box beside the user's name, as shown in Figure 17-8, and then click the Remove from This List button.

    When you add Google Apps users to a list, you have to type only their usernames, as shown in Figure 17-8. If you want to add users from outside your domain, type their full e-mail addresses. Also, you can click a user in the list to view that user's account information.

- ✔ **Download User List as CSV.** Click this link (located at the bottom of the screen) to save a spreadsheet filled with all your users' usernames, first and last names, quota (how much space the users' e-mail messages use), and first and last login dates. (Sorry, you don't get any passwords in this spreadsheet.) You may find this spreadsheet helpful when you want to analyze how your users take advantage of Google Apps.

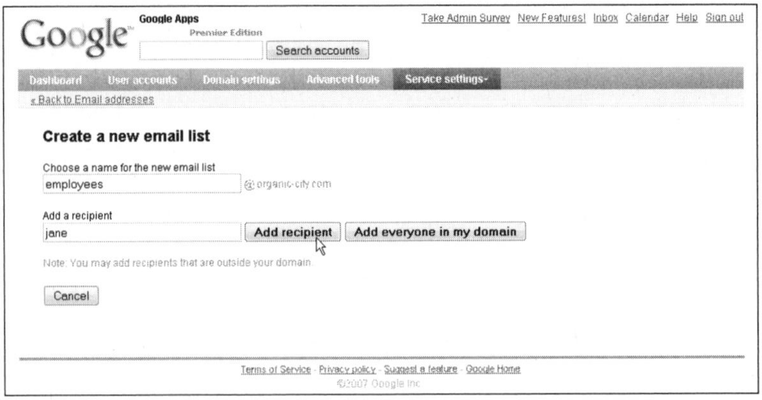

**Figure 17-7:**
Create
groups by
adding
users to an
e-mail list.

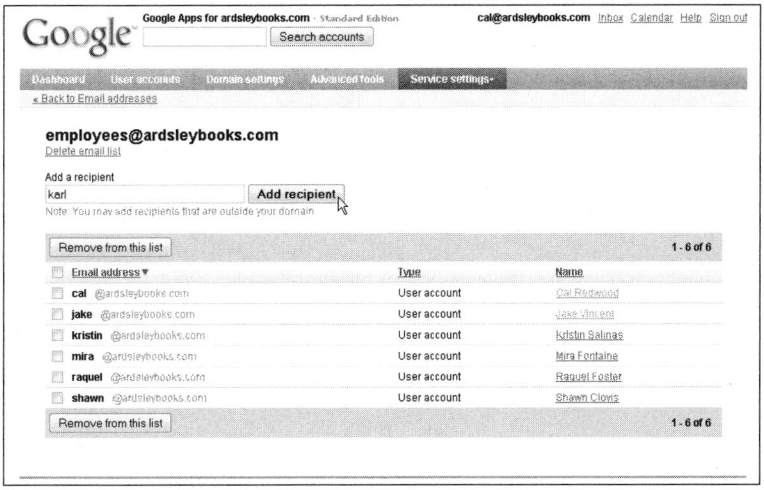

Figure 17-8:
You can add
or remove
users to
a list at
any time.

Google Apps for ardsleybooks.com · Standard Edition

cal@ardsleybooks.com  Inbox  Calendar  Help  Sign out

Google

Search accounts

Dashboard  User accounts  Domain settings  Advanced tools  **Service settings**

« Back to Email addresses

**employees@ardsleybooks.com**
Delete email list

Add a recipient

karl    [Add recipient]

Note: You may add recipients that are outside your domain

[Remove from this list]    1 - 6 of 6

| | Email address ▼ | Type | Name |
| --- | --- | --- | --- |
| ☐ | **cal** @ardsleybooks.com | User account | Cal Redwood |
| ☐ | **jake** @ardsleybooks.com | User account | Jake Vincent |
| ☐ | **kristin** @ardsleybooks.com | User account | Kristin Salinas |
| ☐ | **mira** @ardsleybooks.com | User account | Mira Fontaine |
| ☐ | **raquel** @ardsleybooks.com | User account | Raquel Foster |
| ☐ | **shawn** @ardsleybooks.com | User account | Shawn Clovis |

[Remove from this list]    1 - 6 of 6

## Migrating existing e-mail accounts

For users of Google Apps Premier Edition or Education Edition, Google provides tools to help move e-mail messages from your existing non-Google e-mail
system to Google Apps. For more in-depth information on how to move your
messages to Google Apps, click the Advanced Tools tab on the Navigation bar
in the Dashboard, and then click the Learn More link in the Email Migration
section.

You must first create Google Apps user accounts for everyone whose mail
you want to migrate. For larger organizations, such as schools, you can most
easily create a bunch of accounts by creating a CSV file that contains all your
users' information and uploading it. Chapter 14 covers the steps you need to
follow to create the CSV file and upload it.

To move your e-mail messages from your old server to Gmail, your old server
must allow IMAP access. Only a few e-mail server platforms are officially supported by Google. If your server doesn't appear in the migration list found by
clicking the Learn More link, you can still try to migrate your accounts, but
you must search the Help Center or Google Groups for answers if you run
into problems.

After you create the CSV file and upload it (as described in Chapter 14),
follow these steps to migrate your e-mail accounts:

1. **From the Dashboard, click the Advanced Tools tab on the Navigation bar, and then click the Set Up Mail (IMAP) Migration link in the Email Migration section.**

   A screen similar to Figure 17-9 appears.

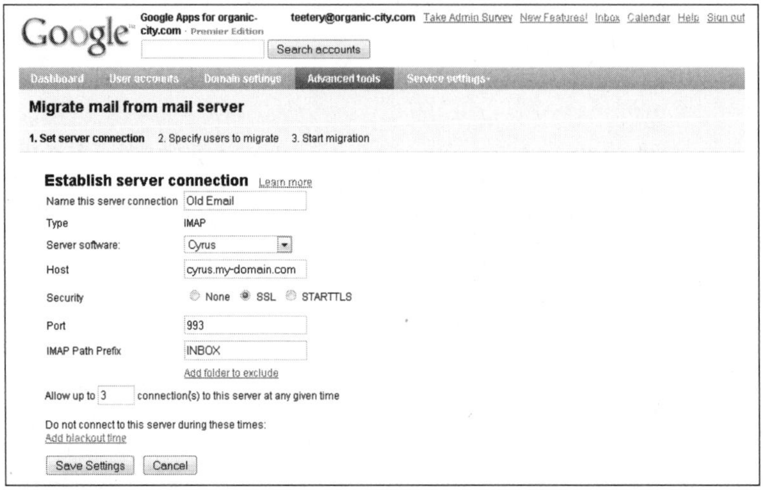

**Figure 17-9:**
Specify a
server from
which you
want to
migrate
e-mail.

2. **Select the Add New Server Connection radio button, and enter your server settings in the form that appears in the Establish Server Connection screen.**

3. **Click the Save Settings button, and then click the Continue button at the bottom of the screen.**

4. **On the Specify How Many Users screen that appears, select the Specify a Few User Accounts radio button to test individual users or select the Specify Many User Accounts Via File Upload radio button to upload a list of users; click the Continue button.**

   On the next screen, you need to provide a Google Apps username, an old (source) username, and an old (source) password for each user.

   If you select the Specify Many User Accounts Via File Upload option to upload a list of users, follow the instructions on the Bulk Upload Accounts screen that appears to upload a CSV file. The spreadsheet file should look similar to Figure 17-10.

5. **After you've selected your spreadsheet file, click the Upload and Test Connection button.**

   On the next screen, Google tests the first few users to make sure that their e-mail messages can transfer correctly.

**Figure 17-10:**
Upload a
CSV file to
migrate
many users
at the same
time.

|   | A | B | C |
|---|---|---|---|
| 1 | username | source username | source password |
| 2 | raquel | raquel | 59h731 |
| 3 | mira | mira | 6d8945 |
| 4 | jake | jake | 4r923m |
| 5 | shawn | shawn | sdf032 |
| 6 | kristin | kristin | s94d83 |

6. **If the Test Connection screen indicates a successful connection, and you're ready to begin the migration, click the Start Migration button. If the connection fails, adjust your spreadsheet or server settings on the previous screens and try again.**

A lot of data may be transferred from your old server to the new one. We recommend that you transfer batches of users at a time, rather than the whole tamale. Choose 10 to 50 users for each migration, and then verify that the transfer was successful for those users by having them log in and check their Gmail Inboxes.

## Adjusting Talk settings

You can adjust your Google Talk settings from the Dashboard. Log into Dashboard and click the Chat link to access the screen that looks like Figure 17-11. Here are the options that you can set:

**Figure 17-11:**
Change
your Talk
settings
from the
Dashboard.

**Chat settings**

| | |
|---|---|
| Download | To use Chat, users must download Google Talk (Windows only) |
| Sharing options | **Chatting outside this domain** (within the Google network)<br>Users can automatically chat with other Google Apps and Gmail users (Google network).<br><br>☑ Display users' chat status outside this domain<br>☐ Warn users when chatting outside this domain<br><br>**Outside the Google network**<br>Google makes it possible for your users to chat with people using other messaging services within a larger federated network. To let users chat outside the Google network, you will need to edit your Service (SRV) records in domain settings. Learn more |
| Disable service | Disable Chat<br>You can disable and remove this service from your domain without losing any data. |

Save changes    Cancel

✔ **Download:** Click the Download Google Talk link and click the Run or Save button in the download screen that appears to download and install the Google Talk client to your computer, or right-click the link and choose Copy Link Location from the menu that appears and paste it into an e-mail to other users who may want to download it.

✔ **Sharing Options:** Limit whether people outside your domain can see your users' chat status. If you select the Warn Users When Chatting Outside This Domain check box, a warning appears each time a user starts a new chat with people outside your domain. Click the Learn More link to go to the Help Center, where you can find instructions on how to set SRV records and allow your users to chat with other Gmail users.

✔ **Disable Service:** If Chat isn't part of your group's mission, or it's more a nuisance than a tool, turn it off by clicking the Disable Chat link and verifying that you really want to do that on the next screen. (Of course, if you change your mind about the usefulness of Chat, you can always add it later from the Dashboard.)

# Empowering Calendar

You can adjust some basic settings for Google Calendar from the Dashboard, too. These settings are fairly nuanced, but they deal primarily with sharing calendars outside of the domain. The Calendar app can, most importantly, display a tool for everyone to schedule resources, such as rooms and equipment. (This scheduling feature is only available for Premier Edition and Education Edition users.)

You may need to restrict Calendar sharing in several situations — for example, you might not want to let your top-secret meeting plans out of the bag.

Log into the Dashboard and click the Calendar link to go to the Calendar Settings screen, as shown in Figure 17-12. The following list describes the basic options that you can change:

✔ **Web Address:** Click the Change URL link and choose the default Google Apps address or create a custom address on the next screen. See the "Creating Custom Apps Addresses" section, earlier in this chapter, for more information.

✔ **Sharing Options:** The options in this section allow you to limit who can view your users' calendars and how much information users can share.

Unlike other apps, with Calendar, you set the highest amount of sharing with users outside of your domain. This way you can restrict outside users from seeing your group's personal meeting schedules. For users within your domain, you can also select the default sharing options, although users can always change their own settings if they choose. Select the Only Free/Busy Information (Hide Event Details) radio button to set the tightest security. Select the Share All Information, But Outsiders Cannot Change Calendar radio button for medium security. Finally, select the Share All Information, and Outsiders Can Change Calendars radio button for the least restrictions on Calendar security.

✔ **Disable Service:** If you decide that Calendar just isn't for you or your group, click the Disable Calendar link. On the next screen, click the Yes, Disable Calendar button to confirm that you want to remove access to Calendar for your users. (You can always add it back later by clicking the Add More Services link from the main Dashboard screen and clicking the Add Service button below the Calendar module on the screen that appears.)

If you have Premier Edition or Education Edition, Calendar enables users to not only fill their own calendars, but also use the Room Finder to book rooms, cars, and anything else that you (the administrator) let them.

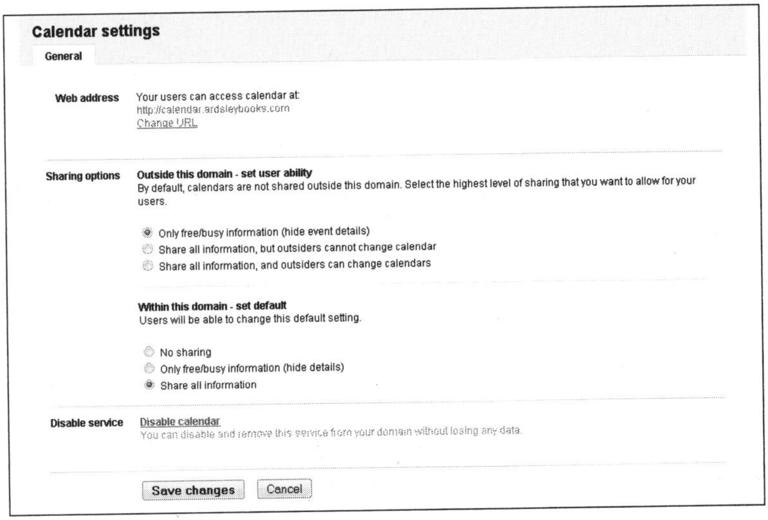

**Figure 17-12:**
Adjust
Calendar
settings
in the
Calendar
Settings
screen.

To create and edit Calendar resources, follow these steps:

1. **Log into the Dashboard and click the Calendar link to load the Service Settings screen.**

2. **Click the Resources tab near the top of the screen, as shown in Figure 17-13.**

3. **Click the Create a New Resource link at the top of the tab to begin adding a resource.**

4. **In the Create a New Resources screen that appears, click in the text boxes and enter a name, type, and description for the resource.**

5. **Click the Create Resource button.**

   Your new resource now appears automatically in your users' Room Finder the next time they want to use a room, vehicle, bike, or other available resource.

6. **After you create a resource, you can edit or delete it, as follows:**

   • *To edit a resource:* Click the name of the resource in the list (see Figure 17-13). On the Edit Resource screen that appears, click in any of the text boxes and enter the changes you want. When you are finished, click the Save Changes button at the bottom of the screen to return to the Calendar Settings screen.

   • *To delete a resource:* Select the check box for the resource in the list (see Figure 17-13) and click one of the Delete Resource(s) buttons that appear at the bottom and top of the list.

As an administrator, you can view and change resource calendars from your own Google Calendar. Simply log into your Calendar (click the Calendar link at the top of the screen if you want to zip to it quickly), click in the Other Calendars text box, type the name of the resource, and press Enter. The calendar (and all its scheduled events) will appear alongside your own events. You can then edit or change any resource events or add new ones, just like any other event (see Chapter 8 for details on adding and changing events).

All administrators can schedule blocks of time for resources, view and change your users' meetings (if necessary), or simply see when certain rooms or resources are being used, as shown in Figure 17-14.

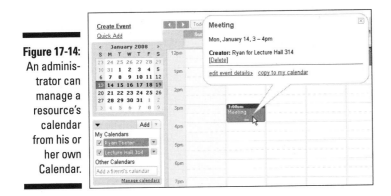

**Figure 17-14:**
An administrator can manage a resource's calendar from his or her own Calendar.

# Securing Docs

Like Chat, Docs has several simple options that you can adjust. From the Dashboard, click the Docs link to open the Docs Setting screen (as shown in Figure 17-15), where you can view and change the settings for Docs. Here's what each of the settings does:

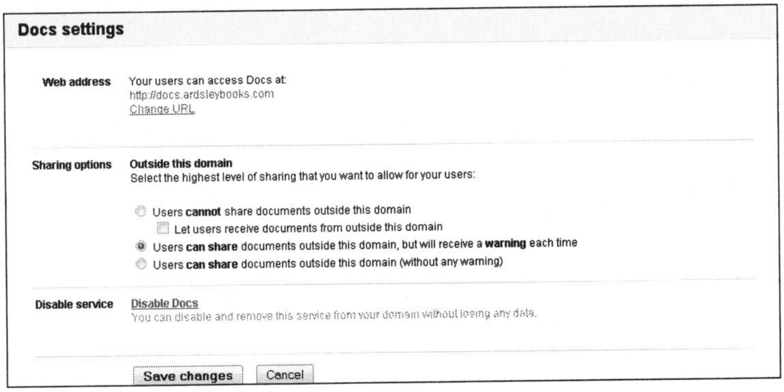

**Figure 17-15:**
Decide whether your users can share their documents.

✔ **Web Address:** Click the Change URL link to open the screen that allows you to create a custom address for Docs. (See the "Creating Custom Apps Addresses" section, earlier in this chapter, for details on how to change this address.)

✔ **Sharing Options:** The options in this area enable you to choose to whom your users can send document links for sharing. If your users generally work on sensitive information, you should probably select either the Users Cannot Share Documents Outside This Domain radio button or the Users Can Share Documents Outside This Domain, But Will Receive a Warning Each Time radio button. (When you select that option, at least they know what they're doing before they send a trade secret to a double agent.) If you want your users to be able to freely share documents (and you know it doesn't pose a security threat), select the Users Can Share Documents Outside This Domain (Without Any Warning) radio button.

✔ **Disable Service:** Click the Disable Docs link and click the Yes, Disable Docs button on the next screen to take access to Google Docs away from everyone. Think of this as a self-destruct button. (You can always give Docs back to your users later by clicking the Add More Services link from the main Dashboard screen and clicking the Add It Now button below the Docs service.)

# Part V
# The Part of Tens

The 5th Wave    By Rich Tennant

"This is amazing. You can stop looking for Derek. According to a Google search I did, he's hiding behind the dryer in the basement."

# In this part . . .

This wouldn't be a *For Dummies* book without a Part of Tens. We're not ones to argue with tradition, so we included ten great tips to help you get out of a variety of Google-related technical jams. And we show you where to go for help if you ever need it.

We end this part by giving you ten more Google Apps for your organization. Sadly, we could include only ten of our favorite other free apps (you can find more than thirty out there), but we picked the very best ones to list in this book. We show you how to find where they and their friends are hiding.

# Chapter 18

# Ten Solutions to Common Problems

*In This Chapter*

▶ Solving general Google Apps issues

▶ Making Gmail work

▶ Troubleshooting Chat and Talk

▶ Fixing a broken Calendar

▶ Helping Docs behave

**A**s ideal and wonderful as the Internet and Google Apps are, sometimes they don't work exactly right. After all, if everything worked perfectly all the time, no one would need brilliant Googlers, authors of *For Dummies* books, or techno-nerds.

In this chapter, we help you find solutions to some of the common headaches that you may encounter when you use Google Apps.

Before we delve into the nitty gritty, we want to point out some great places to find help with your Google Apps:

✔ **Help Center:** Google provides a Help Center full of solutions. To access the Help Center, click the Help link in the top-right corner of any Google Apps window.

✔ **Google Groups:** Other users just like you have come across all kinds of problems with Google Apps, and they can help you find answers to your own. Do a quick search by entering keywords in the Search text box in the top-right corner of the screen and click the Search This Group button to see whether someone else has already fixed a similar problem; or select a problem category and click the Post Your Question button to the right of the topic area, join the group on the screen that appears, enter your specific problem in the Message text box, and click the Post Message button to post your question. Other users usually post responses to your question with helpful suggestions in no time flat. For more technical solutions, *Googlers* (Google employees) are on the scene, too. Just look for the blue G badge to the right of the moderator's name right below a topic link.

✔ **Premier Support:** Organizations that have Google Apps Premier accounts receive extra help for big issues. Administrators can locate the Google telephone support number (and customer PIN) in the Dashboard. Log into the Dashboard, click the Domain Settings tab on the Navigation bar, and then click the Account Information link. On the Account Information tab that appears, you can find links to the Help Center and e-mail support, as well as the telephone support info.

# Oops! Errors in Google Apps

When you try to log into Google Apps, if Google displays an error message, don't panic. You get this kind of error message when Google is updating a server or making some other changes. You can't do anything directly to fix the problem, so here are our best suggestions for what you can do to get things working again:

✔ **Wait a few minutes, and then try again.** The error generally goes away within five to ten minutes. Take a quick coffee break, and you can probably get back to work when you return.

✔ **Notify your administrator if errors persist.** In the rare case that the error doesn't go away in a few minutes, tell your administrator or support team. They can look into it and call Google, if they need to.

# Can't Log Into Google Apps

We know it's frustrating to try to log in and get nowhere. It's happened to us, too. (We're not talking about not being able to log in because you forgot your password in this section, though that happens to everyone at some point.) If you can't log in, and you've checked with the powers that be to make sure you're using the correct username and password, give these suggestions a try:

✔ **Try a different browser.** For example, if you're using Firefox, try Internet Explorer or Safari.

✔ **Clear the browser cache.** Whenever you visit a Web page, a copy of the page is saved to your browser cache so that it loads faster the next time you visit. Sometimes, the cache file gets corrupted and causes your Google Apps to not function properly. Clearing the browser cache gives the App a chance to load again and usually fixes the problem.

Follow these steps to clear the browser cache in Internet Explorer 7:

1. *Choose Tools⇨Internet Options.*

   The Internet Options dialog box appears.

2. *Select the General tab and click the Delete button in the Browsing History section.*

3. *In the dialog box that appears, click the Delete Files button to clear your temporary Internet files.*

4. *For an extra measure of goodness (and to be sure that your cache is really cleared), close Internet Explorer completely and reopen it.*

Follow these steps to clear the browser cache in Firefox:

1. *Choose Tools⇨Clear Private Data.*

2. *Make sure that the Cache check box is selected, and then click the Clear Private Data Now button.*

3. *For an extra measure of goodness (and to be sure that your cache is really cleared), close Firefox completely and reopen it.*

Follow these steps to clear the browser cache in Safari:

1. *Choose Edit⇨Empty Cache.*

2. *In the dialog box that appears, click the Empty button.*

✔ **Configure third-party software.** Occasionally, some software on your computer conflicts with your Internet connection. Check your firewall or antivirus software (you may have to call that software's support people) and disable it, if necessary.

# POP/IMAP Doesn't Work Correctly for Gmail

The number-one issue for Google users deals with getting POP/IMAP access to work with Outlook. E-mail clients work differently and are more complicated than Web browsers. Here are five tips for getting your Outlook program back up and running with your Gmail account:

- ✔ **Enable POP/IMAP access in Gmail settings.** Click the Settings link at the top-right corner of the Gmail main screen. In the Settings page that appears, click the Forwarding and POP/IMAP link. Make sure that the Enable POP or Enable IMAP radio button is selected in the POP Download or IMAP Access section, respectively. Click the Save Changes button after you make any changes.

- ✔ **Check client configuration.** Generally, POP and IMAP don't work if you don't set the correct port and select the Use SSL check box. To check your client configuration in Outlook, follow these steps:

  1. *Choose Tools⇨Account Settings.*

     The Account Settings dialog box appears.

  2. *Highlight your e-mail account and click the Change button.*

     The Change E-Mail Account dialog box appears.

  3. *Click the More Settings button.*

  4. *In the Internet E-mail Settings dialog box, click the Advanced tab.*

     If you get errors when trying to send messages, make sure SMTP is set to 465 or 25.

- ✔ **Run the POP Troubleshooter Tool.** This tool works on Windows. It helps you pinpoint the exact problem and provides instructions to solve that problem. Go to `http://mail.google.com/support/bin/answer.py?answer=44769` and click the Download the Gmail POP Troubleshooter link. Run the tool and it tells you what the problem is.

- ✔ **Use IMAP, rather than POP, when you access your Gmail from more than one computer.** If you're using multiple computers, IMAP works better because it syncs your messages — POP only downloads them. When you use POP on multiple computers, the most recent messages download only to the last computer that accessed them.

## Can't Send Attachments in Gmail

When you try to send files to other people, Google may not allow the file type (see the section about opening attachments in Chapter 5), or your Web browser may be hanging on to some corrupted cache files. To fix issues with attachments, take the following suggestions to heart:

✔ **Don't send programs or .exe files.** To keep your files safe from viruses and other bad stuff on the Internet, Google automatically restricts programs and executable (.exe) files, even if they're hidden away in Zip files. You should have no trouble sending documents, photos, movies, or Zip files (as long as the Zip files don't contain programs or executable files, of course).

✔ **Clear the browser cache.** If the browser cache gets corrupted, the attachment function may not work properly in Gmail. See the "Can't Log Into Google Apps" section, earlier in this chapter, for instructions on how to clear the browser cache.

✔ **Try a different interface.** At the bottom of the Gmail Inbox screen, click the Basic HTML link to reload a simple version of your Inbox and try sending your attachment(s) again from the Compose Mail screen. This approach works especially well if you're using a nontraditional browser, such as Opera.

# Chat Disappears in Gmail

Chat usually doesn't work in Gmail if you're not using a supported Web browser (search the Help Center for *supported browsers*). Try accessing Gmail in Internet Explorer or Firefox to see whether Chat appears. If you still don't see Chat, scroll to the bottom of your Gmail page. Click the Standard link to the right of Gmail View at the bottom of the screen. Your fully featured Inbox will reload. If the Standard link is selected and Chat still doesn't appear, look for the Turn On Chat link at the bottom of the screen. Click that link to re-enable Chat. If none of these solutions work, click the Help link at the top-right corner of the Gmail page and search the Help Center that appears for more options.

# Voice Chat Doesn't Work

After you install Google Talk on your computer, voice communication may not work the first time you use it or if you change your audio equipment or settings. When audio is being sent and received, you should see the blue audio bars at the top of the call window moving up and down. If you or your buddy can't hear the other, try the following fixes:

✔ **Make sure your system sound settings are correct.** Use your system's control panel to check that your microphone and speakers are enabled, and that the volume is high enough. Also, check to make sure that you've attached your microphone properly.

✔ **Check your Google Talk sound settings.** Open Talk and click the Settings link in the top-right corner of the window. From the list on the left side of the Settings screen that appears, click Audio, then make sure that the correct microphone and speakers are selected on the right.

If neither solution works, click the Help link on the main Google Talk window and search the Google Help Center.

# Everything Looks Garbled in Calendar

Like Gmail, Calendar can run into issues from time to time. It may not load correctly, or you may find an event missing once in a while.

When Calendar doesn't load, partially loads, or shows strange characters, try the following solutions (one is bound to make Calendar work properly again):

✔ **Clear the browser cache.** You can clear the cache as a general fixer-upper. See the "Can't Log Into Google Apps" section, earlier in this chapter, if you don't know how to clear your browser cache.

✔ **Try using a secure connection.** Look at your Web address in your browser's address bar. Where it says `http://`, change it to `https://` (the *s* is for secure) and press Enter.

✔ **Contact your administrator.** Tell your administrator that Calendar isn't working. If the other solutions in this list don't work, other people in your organization are probably having the same problem. Your administrator can check the Internet connection or contact Google for some extra help.

If these fixes don't work, click the Help link in the top-right corner of the Calendar screen to open the Google Help Center.

# Events Don't Show Up in Calendar

Here's one of the worst feelings: You know that you have a meeting this morning with some very important people, and when you check Calendar, the meeting's not there! Aaaaaaaahhhhh! Before you panic, try these suggestions (they may help you find those previously existing events, after all):

✔ **Check the Calendars list.** Make sure your calendar is selected in your Calendars list on the left side of your main Calendar screen. Deselected calendars don't appear on the main calendar.

✔ **Check with the event creator.** If you received an invitation to an event that you can no longer find on your calendar, check with the creator of the event. He or she may have deleted or changed the event — or removed you from the guest list without notifying you.

# Documents, Spreadsheets, or Presentations Don't Appear in Docs Home

Google Docs are very near and dear to our hearts. So, when they don't work exactly right, it makes us a little sad. Whether documents, spreadsheets, or presentations disappear or don't load properly, we do our best to restore your Docs Home bliss in this section. (You can also consult the Google Help Center to find answers to more technical problems.)

When files don't appear in Docs Home, it's a similar issue to when events don't appear in Calendar (see the preceding section). Documents, spreadsheets, and presentations that you've created should appear in Docs Home just fine. If you don't see some files in Docs Home that you know should be there, try these fixes:

✔ **Click the Hidden and Trash labels in the list on the left of Docs Home.** If you hid or deleted the file, you should find it under one of these labels.

✔ **Search for the file.** If the file hasn't been permanently deleted, you should find it using the Google Docs Search box and searching for any words that you know appear in the document's, spreadsheet's, or presentation's name or within the file.

✔ **If someone else shared the file with you, check with that person to make sure that they didn't remove you from the Share list.** If they did, they can add your name to the list again to make the missing file reappear magically in the blink of an eye.

# *Documents Don't Load Properly*

This problem's a little tricky. Not because it's technical, but because Google Apps deals with different types of files. Documents, spreadsheets, and presentations that you create directly in Google Docs should have no problems. If they do, follow the steps in the "Everything Looks Garbled in Calendar" section, earlier in this chapter.

If, however, the files were created in Microsoft Office, OpenOffice, or another program, the conversion of certain elements in the file may fail and those elements may not appear correctly — especially if the file contains advanced formatting and graphics options, such as borders. If the file doesn't import correctly the first time, remove some of the special formatting and try to import the file again in Docs, Spreadsheets, or Presentations. Like with any conversion process, YMMV (your mileage may vary).

# Chapter 19

# Ten More Google Apps for Your Business, Group, or Organization

*W*e know that Google Apps is going to make your organization more effi-cient, streamlined, and hip. And just because you're using the four basic Google Apps (Gmail, Calendar, Talk, and Docs) doesn't mean you have to stop there. After all, you can find numerous other free Google Apps and services that can help make your life easier.

So, before we send you off to get your work done, we want to take a moment to tell you about some of our favorite Google products. We can't list them all in this chapter, and Google is adding new ones all the time. For a complete list, go to www.google.com/options — and if you're extra adventurous, see what's bubbling in Google Labs at www.google.com/labs.

In no particular order of importance, we present our favorite *other* Google Apps.

## 1-800-GOOG-411

This app has nothing to do with the Internet — at least, not directly. Google offers free phone directory assistance for local businesses. Call this number (1-800-GOOG-411), and Google not only lists the most relevant businesses that you are looking for, but sends you an SMS text message with the listing you want and connects you to the company you choose for free. You'll be amazed at how good the service is. Here are the key prompts and voice commands, in order:

- ✔ **What city and state?** Say the city and state about which you want to find information, such as "Duluth, Minnesota."

- ✔ **What business name or category?** Say the name of the business that you're looking for, such as "Dentist" or "John Smith."

- ✔ **Say, "Number X":** Listen to the list of results. When you hear the business that you want more information on, say the corresponding number. You don't have to wait until the list ends. Google connects you automatically, or you can say one of these commands:

  - *"Details":* Listen to the full address and phone number of the business. It repeats the information twice, so you can make sure your pen is working correctly.

  - *"Text message":* If you're using a mobile phone, say this command to receive a text message with the address and phone number of the business.

# Creating a Google account

To use most Google services, you need a Google account. A Google account is different than your Google Apps account, but you can use your Google Apps e-mail address to sign up for a Google account and add some of the additional features that we talk about in this chapter.

Sign up for a Google account by following these steps:

1. In your Web browser, go to `www.google.com/accounts`.

2. Click the **Create a New Account** link (it may also appear as **Create an Account Now**) on the right side of the screen.

   The Create an Account screen appears.

3. Enter your Google Apps e-mail address in the **Your Current Email Address** text box, then type your password in the **Choose a Password** and **Re-enter Password** text boxes.

4. Choose your country from the Location drop-down list.

5. Enter the characters that appear in the word verification image in the text box below.

6. When you're ready, click the **I Accept. Create My Account** button.

At this point, you need to verify your e-mail address. Log into your Google Apps Gmail account and open the message that has the subject line "Google Email Verification." Click the link inside this message to activate your Google account. Now, you can use the other apps listed in this chapter for your personal edu-tainment.

*Warning:* Your Google account is still separate from your Google *Apps* account. If you change your Google Apps password and want your Google account password to be the same, you have to return to `www.google.com/accounts` and change your Google account password, as well.

✔ **Say, "Go back":** Return to the previous prompt.

✔ **Say, "Start over":** Begin your search again with the city and state.

# AdWords

`http://adwords.google.com`

What better way can you get your message out there than to advertise on Google? With AdWords, you can quickly and easily set up an account and decide how much you want to pay for advertising. It's a cost-per-click service, so you decide how many times your ad appears and can be clicked. You're in control of how much you pay.

Visit `www.google.com/businesseducators` to download a free handbook and discover more about advertising with Google.

# AdSense

`http://adsense.google.com`

AdSense is Google's way of renting space on your Web site for advertisements. You have control over the advertisement categories that appear as well as the color scheme. Every time your visitors click a link, you make money. It's as simple as that!

Follow the tutorial on `http://adsense.google.com` to set up your account and begin making easy money.

# Google Notebook

`http://google.com/notebook`

We love this tool. Notebook lets you take notes in your Web browser and keep them online and accessible from anywhere. Copy snippets of Web pages (including tables and images), make to-do lists, and more. For added convenience, you can also download the Notebook browser plug-in and note things when you're surfing the Web without having to open another window.

# Google Finance

`http://finance.google.com`

Track your stock portfolio or follow your favorite companies from one convenient place. Google Finance brings information from multiple finance and news sites, and places them in one location. Sift through financial statements, check the historical stock prices, and watch the latest videos from the experts. As a bonus, you can add a Google Finance gadget to your Start Page and see how your stocks are doing while you peruse your Gmail Inbox.

# Google Product Search

`www.google.com/products`

Looking for a printer or vintage coffee maker? Google Product Search looks through a large selection of Internet stores so you don't have to. Sort your results by price, and you can find the best deal around. Adding Google Checkout (`http://checkout.google.com`) to your Google account saves time that you'd otherwise spend filling out forms, and you keep your credit card information safe. Product Search lets you sort your results by price or relevance, and other users like you have rated the stores, so you know what you're getting into.

# Google Reader

`www.google.com/reader`

Instead of taking a lot of time to visit all your favorite news sites and blogs, make them come to you. Google Reader helps you corral all your sources into one place, and it automatically updates your top stories. After you log in the first time, be sure to take the tour. Click the Add Subscription button on the left side of the screen and a text box will appear, allowing you to search for your favorite Web site feeds. Click the Subscribe button on the search results page and you will begin receiving messages and articles right away.

Think of Reader as an inbox for the Web. Rather than messages from other people, you get articles from other Web sites.

# Google Maps

http://maps.google.com

Google Maps is intuitive and fun. Find addresses, locate businesses, or get directions from place to place. Our favorite map views include

- ✔ **Street View:** Get down to street level and take a panoramic tour of major cities, as shown in Figure 19-1. Use the plus and minus buttons to zoom in close, and then drag the little yellow man onto an outlined street to see what passersby see on their way to work.

- ✔ **Traffic:** Google taps into several traffic monitoring sources to give you current traffic conditions. Green is good, red is bad. Google even takes into account bad traffic when giving you directions to your destination.

- ✔ **Map:** Quickly find your way around with the default map view. Search the map for local businesses, get directions from one place to another, print out your maps, or e-mail them to your friends.

- ✔ **Satellite:** See a bird's-eye view of your local shopping center or historic statue. When you click the Satellite button, you can also check the Show Labels box to see street names on the map.

- ✔ **Terrain:** See the world in topographical form, including all the nooks and crannies of the Grand Canyon or your ski resort.

**Figure 19-1:**
Use Google
Maps to find
your way
around your
town or
around the
world.

Don't forget to check out the My Maps tab to add your own points of interest, draw borders, and shade in areas.

# Google Pack

```
http://pack.google.com
```

Google Pack brings together all the free software that you need (and none that you don't) in one easy-to-use installer. These programs include Web tools, Internet security programs, and other productivity software. Pack even keeps your software up to date automatically. Here are our favorite Google Pack programs:

- ✔ **Google Earth:** Take Google Maps to the next level with a 3D atlas of the world. Zoom into famous landmarks, search for your house, see community photos of places, and globetrot without leaving your home.

- ✔ **Google Desktop:** Add Google Search to your computer desktop. Google Desktop helps you quickly find documents, images, and music on your computer as easily as you find pages on the Internet.

- ✔ **Picasa:** Organize and edit your photos with simple yet powerful tools. Picasa also has an online counterpart called Picasa Web Albums (`http://picasaweb.google.com`), which lets you post your photos into your own online gallery with one click.

- ✔ **StarOffice:** For documents that need a little more oomph than Google Docs provides, try this free alternative to Microsoft Office. It includes all the tools that you need to create documents, spreadsheets, presentations, drawings, and databases.

The Google Installer will notify you of program updates. Check back from time to time for more programs by returning to `http://pack.google.com`.

# Google Translate

```
http://translate.google.com
```

Get yourself out of a pinch by using Google Translate. With support for over 20 languages and the ability to translate entire Web sites in a single bound, Translate saves the day time and again. Go to `http://translate.google.com` and click one of the tabs along the top. Here's how they work:

- ✔ **Text and Web:** Enter a word, phrase, or paragraph in the Original Text text box at the top of the page or enter a Web address in the Translate a Web Page text box at the bottom of the page; use the drop-down list to select the language combination that you want to translate from/to; then click the Translate button. In a moment, a translation appears on the right side of the screen. Web pages load in their entirety in the same window.

Google Translate, like other automated translation services, can do a decent job of translating basic text. However, many times, you get a quite literal and not very accurate translation, which can be funny or just plain confusing. If you need to translate an important document, make sure you have a native speaker read through the translation before you send the document. (You don't want to inadvertently insult some-one with an inaccurate translation.)

✔ **Translated Search:** Google Translate can help you find a search term in Web pages that are written in a language other than English. See Figure 19-2 for an example.

✔ **Dictionary:** Use this language translation dictionary when you're stumped by a foreign word you have come across. Enter a word in the Enter Word text box, choose a language translation in the drop-down list to the right, and the foreign language equivalent appears.

✔ **Tools:** Add a Google Translate gadget to your Web page so that your visi-tors can translate your page in a flash. Simply choose your page's lan-guage and then copy the HTML code that appears in the box below Step 2 into your page. If you translate pages often, make life simple — add one of the translate buttons listed at the bottom of the screen to your browser's toolbar by clicking the link and dragging it to your browser's bookmarks or favorites bar. Then, when you visit a site, simply click the button to translate the page instantly.

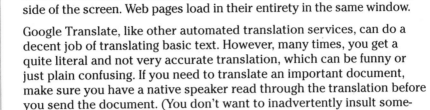

**Figure 19-2:**
Use
Translated
Search to
find pages
in different
languages.

# Index

• **E** •

## SINESS, CAREERS & PERSONAL FINANCE

0-7645-9847-3

0-7645-2431-3

**Also available:**
- Business Plans Kit For Dummies
  0-7645-9794-9
- Economics For Dummies
  0-7645-5726-2
- Grant Writing For Dummies
  0-7645-8416-2
- Home Buying For Dummies
  0-7645-5331-3
- Managing For Dummies
  0-7645-1771-6
- Marketing For Dummies
  0-7645-5600-2

- Personal Finance For Dummies
  0-7645-2590-5*
- Resumes For Dummies
  0-7645-5471-9
- Selling For Dummies
  0-7645-5363-1
- Six Sigma For Dummies
  0-7645-6798-5
- Small Business Kit For Dummies
  0-7645-5984-2
- Starting an eBay Business For Dummies
  0-7645-6924-4
- Your Dream Career For Dummies
  0-7645-9795-7

## ME & BUSINESS COMPUTER BASICS

0-470-05432-8

0-471-75421-8

**Also available:**
- Cleaning Windows Vista For Dummies
  0-471-78293-9
- Excel 2007 For Dummies
  0-470-03737-7
- Mac OS X Tiger For Dummies
  0-7645-7675-5
- MacBook For Dummies
  0-470-04859-X
- Macs For Dummies
  0-470-04849-2
- Office 2007 For Dummies
  0-470-00923-3

- Outlook 2007 For Dummies
  0-470-03830-6
- PCs For Dummies
  0-7645-8958-X
- Salesforce.com For Dummies
  0-470-04893-X
- Upgrading & Fixing Laptops For Dummies
  0-7645-8959-8
- Word 2007 For Dummies
  0-470-03658-3
- Quicken 2007 For Dummies
  0-470-04600-7

## OD, HOME, GARDEN, HOBBIES, MUSIC & PETS

0-7645-8404-9

0-7645-9904-6

**Also available:**
- Candy Making For Dummies
  0-7645-9734-5
- Card Games For Dummies
  0-7645-9910-0
- Crocheting For Dummies
  0-7645-4151-X
- Dog Training For Dummies
  0-7645-8418-9
- Healthy Carb Cookbook For Dummies
  0-7645-8476-6
- Home Maintenance For Dummies
  0-7645-5215-5

- Horses For Dummies
  0-7645-9797-3
- Jewelry Making & Beading For Dummies
  0-7645-2571-9
- Orchids For Dummies
  0-7645-6759-4
- Puppies For Dummies
  0-7645-5255-4
- Rock Guitar For Dummies
  0-7645-5356-9
- Sewing For Dummies
  0-7645-6847-7
- Singing For Dummies
  0-7645-2475-5

## NTERNET & DIGITAL MEDIA

0-470-04529-9

0-470-04894-8

**Also available:**
- Blogging For Dummies
  0-471-77084-1
- Digital Photography For Dummies
  0-7645-9802-3
- Digital Photography All-in-One Desk Reference For Dummies
  0-470-03743-1
- Digital SLR Cameras and Photography For Dummies
  0-7645-9803-1
- eBay Business All-in-One Desk Reference For Dummies
  0-7645-8438-3
- HDTV For Dummies
  0-470-09673-X

- Home Entertainment PCs For Dummies
  0-470-05523-5
- MySpace For Dummies
  0-470-09529-6
- Search Engine Optimization For Dummies
  0-471-97998-8
- Skype For Dummies
  0-470-04891-3
- The Internet For Dummies
  0-7645-8996-2
- Wiring Your Digital Home For Dummies
  0-471-91830-X

* Separate Canadian edition also available
* Separate U.K. edition also available

## SPORTS, FITNESS, PARENTING, RELIGION & SPIRITUALITY

0-471-76871-5          0-7645-7841-3

**Also available:**
- Catholicism For Dummies
  0-7645-5391-7
- Exercise Balls For Dummies
  0-7645-5623-1
- Fitness For Dummies
  0-7645-7851-0
- Football For Dummies
  0-7645-3936-1
- Judaism For Dummies
  0-7645-5299-6
- Potty Training For Dummies
  0-7645-5417-4
- Buddhism For Dummies
  0-7645-5359-3

- Pregnancy For Dummies
  0-7645-4483-7 †
- Ten Minute Tone-Ups For Dummies
  0-7645-7207-5
- NASCAR For Dummies
  0-7645-7681-X
- Religion For Dummies
  0-7645-5264-3
- Soccer For Dummies
  0-7645-5229-5
- Women in the Bible For Dummies
  0-7645-8475-8

## TRAVEL

0-7645-7749-2          0-7645-6945-7

**Also available:**
- Alaska For Dummies
  0-7645-7746-8
- Cruise Vacations For Dummies
  0-7645-6941-4
- England For Dummies
  0-7645-4276-1
- Europe For Dummies
  0-7645-7529-5
- Germany For Dummies
  0-7645-7823-5
- Hawaii For Dummies
  0-7645-7402-7

- Italy For Dummies
  0-7645-7386-1
- Las Vegas For Dummies
  0-7645-7382-9
- London For Dummies
  0-7645-4277-X
- Paris For Dummies
  0-7645-7630-5
- RV Vacations For Dummies
  0-7645-4442-X
- Walt Disney World & Orlando
  For Dummies
  0-7645-9660-8

## GRAPHICS, DESIGN & WEB DEVELOPMENT

0-7645-8815-X          0-7645-9571-7

**Also available:**
- 3D Game Animation For Dummies
  0-7645-8789-7
- AutoCAD 2006 For Dummies
  0-7645-8925-3
- Building a Web Site For Dummies
  0-7645-7144-3
- Creating Web Pages For Dummies
  0-470-08030-2
- Creating Web Pages All-in-One Desk
  Reference For Dummies
  0-7645-4345-8
- Dreamweaver 8 For Dummies
  0-7645-9649-7

- InDesign CS2 For Dummies
  0-7645-9572-5
- Macromedia Flash 8 For Dummies
  0-7645-9691-8
- Photoshop CS2 and Digital
  Photography For Dummies
  0-7645-9580-6
- Photoshop Elements 4 For Dummies
  0-471-77483-9
- Syndicating Web Sites with RSS Feeds
  For Dummies
  0-7645-8848-6
- Yahoo! SiteBuilder For Dummies
  0-7645-9800-7

## NETWORKING, SECURITY, PROGRAMMING & DATABASES

0-7645-7728-X          0-471-74940-0

**Also available:**
- Access 2007 For Dummies
  0-470-04612-0
- ASP.NET 2 For Dummies
  0-7645-7907-X
- C# 2005 For Dummies
  0-7645-9704-3
- Hacking For Dummies
  0-470-05235-X
- Hacking Wireless Networks
  For Dummies
  0-7645-9730-2
- Java For Dummies
  0-470-08716-1

- Microsoft SQL Server 2005 For Dummies
  0-7645-7755-7
- Networking All-in-One Desk Reference
  For Dummies
  0-7645-9939-9
- Preventing Identity Theft For Dummies
  0-7645-7336-5
- Telecom For Dummies
  0-471-77085-X
- Visual Studio 2005 All-in-One Desk
  Reference For Dummies
  0-7645-9775-2
- XML For Dummies
  0-7645-8845-1